Medical-Legal Aspects of Drugs

Compiled and Edited by
Marcelline Burns, Ph.D.

Contributors
Donald J. Bartell
Michael Corbett
Johan J. de Gier
Olaf H. Drummer
Anne D. ImObersteg
David S. Isenschmid
Wayne Jeffrey
Caroline T. J. Lamers
Barry K. Logan
Stephen J. McAndrew
Thomas E. Page
Trinka Poratta
Johannes G. Ramaekers
Wim J. Riedel
Laurent Rivier
David Sandler
Jeroen A. J. Schmitt

Lawyers & Judges
Publishing Company, Inc.

Lawyers & Judges Publishing Company, Inc.
P.O. Box 30040 • Tucson, AZ 85751-0040
(800) 209-7109 • FAX (800) 330-8795
e-mail: sales@lawyersandjudges.com

online
www.lawyersandjudges.com

ISBN 1-930056-19-2
Printed in the United States of America
10 9 8 7 6 5 4 3 2 1

Table of Contents

Introduction

Marcelline Burns

Drug use is at least as long-standing as recorded history. Many centuries ago humans, as well as some animal species, discovered medicinal and intoxicant properties of a variety of plants. Nowadays drug users' options have been vastly expanded by new discoveries of plant materials and by new compounds developed in both legal and illegal laboratories. Relieving, healing, and intoxicating are powerful properties. The use and abuse of drugs will continue.

Drugs are not a new phenomenon, but the problems associated with them take on new dimensions in the conditions of modern societies. Although it is possible that in early agrarian societies the available potions and intoxicants did not seriously impede users' activities, in today's more complex environments drug use can have significant social and individual costs. The problems, complicated by the widely varying contexts of use and by abundant, accessible substances, are no longer limited to a particular kind of urban setting or to stereotypical individuals. Understanding the drug problem of even a decade ago does not suffice today. Thus, to stay informed about the rapidly changing drug scene is challenging indeed.

This book addresses the challenge with accurate, cutting-edge information from acknowledged experts. Although overall objectives were defined during early planning of the book, the details of organizing the broad topic, drugs, and the identification of chapter authors charted new territory.

A first task focused on the reality of page limitation versus hundreds of different drugs. Even limiting the coverage to psychoactive drugs, which are the principal source of legal issues, it was clear that the organization would require stringent inclusion and exclusion criteria. Fortunately, the classification of drugs that is used by law enforcement's drug recognition expert (DRE) program provides a parsimonious approach, and it is that scheme that has directed the organization of this book. Chapter 1 describes the history and rationale of the DRE drug categorizations.

Psychoactive substances are numerous and diverse, and the body of knowledge for some of them is limited. The issue is further complicated, because the boundaries between drugs-as-medicines and drugs-as-intoxicants have become blurred. By definition, any use of illegal drugs is abuse, and when medicines are taken in incorrect amounts and for non-therapeutic purposes, that also is abuse. For example, heroin has no legal use and clearly is an abused drug. Xanax also is an abused drug, but it is an efficacious medicine. Phencyclidine is a dangerous drug of abuse that has no legitimate use, whereas its analogue, Ketamine, has desirable properties as an anesthetic, but it is for sale on the street drug market.

The state-of-the-science of drug effects on behavior and performance is uneven, at best. The dual facts of many drugs and limited resources explain that unevenness in part, but the restrictions that apply to drug studies are also relevant. A drug's potential for causing harm or leading to addiction constrains any scientific investigation that would require its administration to human subjects. For the more dangerous substances, the limits imposed by ethical issues are unlikely to be resolved. Even when drug use by a subset of the population creates hazards for the general public, scientists are not allowed by regulatory bodies, nor would they be willing, to place subjects at risk for study purposes. Consequently, there are large gaps in the scientific drug literature. To address issues for which there are scant scientific data, therefore, it is necessary to draw from a body of critical knowledge that has arisen outside the ranks of scientists.

For drugs that have been subjected to scientific study, this book is grounded in chapters written by internationally acknowledged experts. We benefit from their generous sharing of what they know about an esoteric subject matter. The benefit to us of their specific knowledge potentially extends beyond the words they have written. The information they provide about drugs that have been studied can also inform us to some degree about drugs within the same categories that have not been studied. In an oversimplified illustration, consider that although central nervous system (CNS) depressants differ one from the other, they also share characteristics such as the direction of the effects on the CNS. Within the category, benzodiazepines, individual drugs differ in duration and potency but share a mode of action.

A specimen, typically breath, blood, or urine, is obtained from a suspected offender near the time of an incident. If analysis of the specimen reveals the presence of a drug or drugs, that finding can become critical evidence in legal proceedings. The admissibility or weight of the evidence then frequently is argued. Was the analysis of a specimen conducted properly? Were the instruments and procedures reliable and appropriate? What statements can be made about the effects of a given level of a drug found in a specific specimen? Such highly technical questions are beyond common knowledge, and we are fortunate here to be instructed about these issues by the authors of Chapters 2–5.

Psychoactive medicines and recently developed illegal drugs now add to, but have not displaced, the illicit substances that have a long history of abuse. Despite the toll of addiction and the threat of legal sanction, illicit drug use continues decade after decade, typically with relatively modest changes in overall incidence and prevalence. Because the associated problems and scientific study extend across national borders, it is particularly appropriate that European investigators provide a scholarly review in Chapter 6 of the impairing effects of widely used illicit drugs.

The relief of serious medical conditions for millions of patients is attributable to the development of anxiolytics, antidepressants, and antihistamines. These effective medications for depression, insomnia, anxiety, chronic allergic rhinitis, and numerous other disorders are a great boon to medical practice. Unfortunately, there is also a cost in terms of safety, both when the drugs are used appropriately and when they are abused. The author of Chapter 7 capably brings us up-to-date with a review of the scientific data.

Problem identification, as in the case of the hazards associated with medicines, is a beginning from which some resolution possibly can emerge. Questions of how to minimize harm or contain risk are difficult, however, given that impairment arises from drugs that also improve the quality of life for patients. Who bears the responsibility and what is the best method for effectively warning patients of the risks of driving under the influence of psychoactive medicines? European nations acting separately, and under the auspices of the European Union, are actively addressing the problem. Since regulatory agencies worldwide must deal with questions about drug information for patients, the Chapter 11 review of approaches that have been implemented or are pending in Europe is timely and instructive.

Stimulant use surged during the 1970s and 1980s. Powder cocaine was the trendy drug of choice for a time. It could be found on the streets of ghettos and barrios and in affluent suburbia, among artists and athletes, among college kids, business executives, and gang members. Eventually its popularity faded somewhat, but crack cocaine appeared albeit with a somewhat narrower base of users. Crack in turn has been largely displaced by methamphetamine. Current prevalence of methamphetamine use may or may not have reached epidemic proportions. Epidemiological data are lacking, and it is not possible to know the extent of use with certainty, but available indices suggest that it is the current drug of choice. Just as the level of use is unknown, so also is the level of risk unknown. Laboratory research with stimulants is uniquely difficult. Unlike CNS depressants, which act uni-directionally, stimulants, exert bi-directional effects. In low to moderate amounts they arouse, alert, and speed. In higher amounts, they overstimulate and impair. Since large doses cannot be given to human subjects, it is difficult to study those impairing effects in a laboratory setting. An important study of methamphetamine and vehicle crashes, however, has been accomplished. Its author and his colleague are uniquely qualified, as can be seen in Chapter 8, to inform us about these substances.

As a long-standing drug of choice for youth, marijuana has generated a sizable literature covering several decades of study. The author of Chapter 9, mindful that the scientific literature already offers comprehensive reviews, focuses on recent studies to re-examine some persistent questions about marijuana effects.

Rave parties vividly illustrate the dilemma stemming from a lack of scientific data. Although thousands of young people attend all-night raves (and smaller but similar club-sponsored events), the venues usually are remote, and the activities escape observation and regulation. Raves, which have been described as places of unbridled "drugs and sex," have not attracted scientific study. Data are sparse. The author of Chapter 10, however, has access to the rave scene and is uniquely positioned to know about the drugs. Her chapter provides startling information about this emerging problem.

Police officers are the front line defense in society's efforts to deal with drug-related problems. They are on-scene in the aftermath of drug-related violent crimes, spousal abuse, sexual assaults and automobile crashes. Yet their views about drugs and drug polices seldom are solicited, and their voices rarely are heard in discussions of social policy. From the perspective of a college campus, a former police officer has written Chapter 13. It is a thought-provoking examination of drug policy from the viewpoint of law enforcement.

Drugs often have a lead role in the dramas that play out in courtrooms. In many civil and criminal trials, the outcomes hinge on allegations of drug influence. Competent legal representation requires an attorney to know about drug effects, or lacking that, to call upon credible expert witnesses. There is much unplowed legal ground, so to speak, in this area of law. Chapters 14 and 16 consider the issues from the perspective of a prosecutor, for whom criminal trials involving drugs are a daily responsibility. Whenever a trial involves allegations of drug influence, defense counsel confronts a body of knowledge that may be largely unfamiliar to him/her but that is critical to competent representation of the defendant. The author of Chapter 15 tackles this dilemma. Whatever an attorney's, or the court's, experience in this area of law, this is an informative chapter written from a defense attorney's point of view.

Drugs diminish workplace safety. Although the three-martini lunch seems to have faded as a routine event, some occupations continue to tolerate alcohol consumption in close proximity to the time and place of work. Increasingly, drugs other than alcohol create workplace hazards. Although the risks associated with drug use differ as a function of the work environment, job performance and safety inevitably are diminished by drug-related impairment. The problem has spawned regulations, urine drug testing, and employee assistance programs. The author of Chapter 12 provides us with a comprehensive review of the emerging landscape of drugs in the workplace.

These wide-ranging examinations of the medicolegal aspects of drugs have been written by a group of uniquely knowledgeable individuals. Their willingness to share their expertise about drugs merits our collective gratitude. I personally am indebted to all of them for their time and effort, and to Jene Moio-Johnson whose very capable assistance made my task do-able.

Chapter 1

The Classification of Drugs by Category

Thomas E. Page

Synopsis

The assignment of drugs to categories admittedly is somewhat arbitrary. Importantly, however, arbitrary is not the same as capricious or whimsical. Categorization is done for convenience, for understanding, for making sense of something. It seems to be a fact of the human condition, something that is intrinsic to mankind. We order and classify ourselves by where we live, our ages, our socioeconomic status, or our interests. To a large degree we learn by comparing the new and the novel with the old and the known. The purpose of classification is the ordering of differences and similarities. The drugs that are the focus of this book are ordered by their placement into categories with similar drugs. The issue then is the basis for this particular categorization.

1.1 Drug Categories and the Drug Recognition Expert (DRE)

A. Overview

The DRE program uses a scheme of seven categories of drugs. All of the substances in the seven categories have in common that they are abused substances. Only substances that have mind or mood altering properties are likely to be abused, which means further that the drugs in the seven categories are psychoactive. They act on the central nervous system (CNS). Alcohol, the number one drug of abuse in American society as well as in many others, is a CNS-active drug. Although it also has effects on other physiological systems, it is abused because of its effects on the CNS. It is unlikely that any drinker consumes alcohol primarily because it produces gait ataxia, a side effect that conceivably is not always unwelcome but that is not the raison d'etre for drinking.

An example of an abused substance from the world of so-called hard drugs is cocaine. Its CNS effects are both positively and negatively reinforcing. In addition, it acts peripherally as a topical anesthetic by hindering peripheral nerve transmission, a property useful in eye, nose, and other surgeries. Novocain™ (or procaine), another local or topical anesthetic, creates numbness and the thick-lipped feeling experienced by dental patients. Unlike cocaine, it lacks pleasurable CNS effects, and it is not abused. Even in the most drug-ravaged communities, people don't buy and sell Novocain on street corners and in alleyways in order to get numb. Crack cocaine houses were a huge problem during the 1980s and 1990s; Novocain houses were not.

Interestingly, cocaine users equate greater numbness with higher quality and rely on it to confirm that a substance is cocaine. The movie portrayal of a detective tasting a substance has some basis in the reality of illicit drug dealing. The small taste is expected to produce sufficient numbness to demonstrate that the substance actually is cocaine. Since more numbness means more profit, dealers have been known to increase their profits by cutting the more expensive drug, cocaine, with Novocain.

It is important to note the differences between drug abuse and drug misuse. A patient misuses a bactericidal such as amoxicillin by using it to treat a virus such as the common cold. The patient isn't using the drug to get high but simply is using it inappropriately. Certain drugs, however, have no medicinal value and can only be abused. These illegal substances are Schedule I drugs, as scheduled by the Drug Enforcement Administration. Heroin, which has no legitimate use in the United States, is a classic example of a substance that can only be abused.

Drugs of concern to a DRE are psychoactive drugs that have abuse potential. Abuse is not due to CNS effects in general, but to the specific CNS effects that are pleasurable. Through various physiological mechanisms, these drugs activate the body's reward pathways, generally associated with dopaminergic neurotransmitter systems.

The titles of the seven categories of drugs in the DRE categorization are the subject of discussion within the DRE community, as are the placement of specific substances. Some of the naming controversies involve cannabis, primarily marijuana in its various forms, and the narcotic analgesics, also referred to as opiates and opioids. Notwithstanding these ongoing discussions, police officers, prosecutors, and toxicologists accept the categories that are listed below in alphabetical order. Notice that although the CNS label is attached only to stimulants and depressants, all are CNS active.

cannabis
CNS depressants
CNS stimulants
hallucinogens
inhalants
narcotic analgesics
phencyclidine (PCP)

The DRE drug classification system provides structure for a discussion of drugs. Although the system is limited to abused substances, it encompasses legal and illegal drugs, natural and synthetic drugs, as well as non-pharmaceuticals (e.g., toluene). To borrow a phrase used by courts in rulings on the admissibility of DRE testimony, the system is "tried and true," having been used virtually without alteration since the DRE training curriculum was formalized. The course, which was developed with the assistance of the National Highway Traffic Safety Administration, has been used since 1988 to train officers throughout the United States and Canada.

B. Premise of DRE classification

The critical premise of the classification system is that drugs of abuse produce detectable, observable effects and can be logically grouped according to similar or shared patterns of effects. A key concept is pattern, because it acknowledges that drugs have multiple rather than single effects. An example of a single effect would be conjunctival injection (i.e., the bloodshot eyes that are commonly seen with marijuana use). Bloodshot eyes also occur with other substances such as alcohol and inhalants. With marijuana, however, that particular effect is accompanied by tachycardia (elevated heart rate) even though the user appears relaxed and non-physically stressed. These signs in combination then are key indicators that the person may have used marijuana recently. The *Diagnostic and Statistical Manual* of the American Psychiatric Association (DSM-IV) lists them as criteria for a diagnosis of marijuana influence.

DRE training also acknowledges that the effects of drugs vary from one incident of use to another. A fingerprint-versus-signature analogy aptly illustrates the difference with drug effects being like a signature rather than being like a fingerprint. From birth to death, a fingerprint is unchanging and serves to positively identify an individual. A signature, on the other hand, differs slightly each time it is written. In fact, handwriting analysts believe they can discern a person's mood by variations in his or her signature from writing to writing. Certainly, signatures are affected by alcohol and drug influence.

C. Categories versus specific drug

The classification scheme focuses on a pattern of detectable, observable effects that DREs are trained to recognize as the signature pattern of a specific drug category. Within-category, however, effects are essentially the same, which means that it is not possible to discriminate between the various drugs within one category. Because drug effects do change over time, this limitation pertains only to a snapshot of an individual at a specific time. The time-related changes vary within category from one drug to another and sometimes enable the DRE to identify a specific substance.

Some states, such as California, have non-driving drug influence laws that require officers to specify a drug or drugs. Identification of a substance as a stimulant, for example, does not suffice, because the law requires that the arrest be made for the crime of being under the influence of a specific drug such as cocaine or methamphetamine. In those cases, other evidence must enter into the arrest decision, including such information as knowledge of drug-use trends in the community, the suspect's possession of a drug, differences in duration of effects, signs of method of drug administration, observations by witnesses, and the suspect's statements. Identification of a specific substance then must be confirmed by toxicological analysis of blood, urine, or other specimen.

An issue that frequently arises when analyzing a case for prosecution in court is that of effects on what is called the downside of drug influence. Briefly, each drug has a predictable, but not exact, continuum of effects. Starting in a state of relative sobriety, the user takes a substance that enters the bloodstream and is transported throughout the body, including the CNS and most importantly the brain. The initial buildup or onset of effects is the intoxicating slope of drug influence and can be thought of as the euphoric phase. Euphoria, of course, is positively reinforcing and encourages repeated use. When the effects begin to dissipate, the user enters the downward slope or dysphoric phase. Dysphoria can last substantially longer than euphoria. For example, the pleasurable effects of cocaine are relatively short-lived, whereas an addicted user may experience dysphoria as a result of abstinence from cocaine for weeks. In this phase, craving and withdrawal symptoms occur. These are negatively reinforcing and also encourage repeated use as the user now seeks to avoid negative effects. As an experienced drug user may explain, "I'm not trying to get high. I just don't want to get sick."

From the viewpoint of users, the effects of substances within a category feel similar or identical, making it very difficult to detect any differences between two drugs. In controlled laboratory studies at the Addiction

Research Center, U.S. National Institutes of Health (NIH) in which rats were given the opportunity to self-administer cocaine and methamphetamine, the rats appeared to be unable to discriminate between the two drugs. Although the drugs within a category may differ chemically, users experiences remarkably similar effects, possibly because the drugs are acting on the same neurotransmitter systems responsible for pleasure.

1.2 Drug Metabolism

The body's process of transforming a drug, metabolism, complicates issues of drug influence. The transformation sometimes produces non-psychoactive metabolites. For example, benzoylecgonine (BE), which is a metabolite of cocaine and serves as a marker of use within a defined time period, has no psychoactive properties. There are, however, psychoactive substances that also have psychoactive metabolites. In fact, certain parent drugs are produced as the psychoactive metabolites of other drugs. Amphetamine and methamphetamine both are parent drugs, but amphetamine also is a metabolite of methamphetamine. Therefore, when amphetamine is found in a specimen of urine, it may signal the use of either amphetamine or methamphetamine. Fortunately, laboratories have additional analytical and interpretive capabilities for determining which drug was taken.

The issue of psychoactive metabolites also applies to some widely prescribed medications, the benzodiazepines. These drugs, known as tranquilizers, induce tranquility or a state of calmness and also aid in relief of insomnia. Diazepam, sold as Valium®, possibly the best known of the tranquilizers, has entered the vernacular in the form of casual advice to an overly anxious person to "Take a Valium." This chemical family also includes Halcion, Xanax, Ativan, Rohypnol, Librium, Serax, and numerous others, with the drugs differing primarily in intensity, duration of effects, and dependency potential. In some cases, they may be both parent drug and metabolite. Serax (oxazepam), for example, is a parent drug and also a metabolite of Valium. When forensic urine testing identifies oxazepam in a specimen, it can be the result of ingestion of either Valium or Serax.

To further complicate this issue, certain metabolites occur as a result of the ingestion of two drugs. Cocaethylene (or ethylcocaine) occurs when both cocaine and alcohol are ingested. In this case, the body processes a depressant and a stimulant and produces cocaethylene. It is possible that this third substance, which is a marker for concurrent use of alcohol and cocaine, prolongs the effects of cocaine.

1.3 Development of Dependency

Chronic drug use leads to physical dependence. Simply described, over time the body adapts to a substance with the result that cessation of intake is followed by a withdrawal syndrome. John Lennon's "Cold Turkey" accurately portrays withdrawal from heroin. Beginning with influenza-like symptoms (runny nose, chills, general malaise), the syndrome progresses to vomiting, diarrhea and intense discomfort. Although severely uncomfortable, heroin withdrawal is not life-threatening. In time, there is relief from this acute abstinence syndrome. Prior to relief, of course, withdrawal can be stopped by administration of a different drug from the same category. Alcohol and the benzodiazepines are CNS depressants, and each will stop withdrawal from the other.

A corollary of dependency is cross-dependency within category. An individual who is dependent on one drug generally is predisposed to become dependent on other drugs in the same category. Another drug within a category that meets the dependent individual's need may in time move into the position of primary abused drug. This aspect of drug abuse has important implications for drug use trends. During the summer of 2001, the media focused attention on the narcotic analgesic, OxyContin, and on pharmacy robberies in which the robbers specifically demanded this drug. In the northeastern United States, the problem became so severe that some pharmacies elected to stop stocking OxyContin in violation of governmental regulations. Clearly, there are individuals who are dependent on OxyContin either as a primary drug of choice or as an alternative to other narcotic analgesics. If at some point in time, OxyContin becomes unavailable, they likely will seek another narcotic analgesic to forestall withdrawal. Since heroin will serve that purpose, it is possible that more rigorous control and reduced availability of OxyContin will lead to an increase in heroin use.

1.4 Development of Tolerance

Tolerance is an important aspect of drug abuse. The term is defined by two conditions: (1) a user needs more of a substance to obtain the desired effect, and (2) at a given dose, a user displays fewer effects than a non-tolerant individual. For example, the alcohol-tolerant individual needs more alcohol to achieve the desired level of inebriation, and he appears less impaired at a given blood alcohol concentration (BAC) than someone who is not alcohol-tolerant. Police officers and medical professionals frequently encounter drivers with BACs that are multiples of statutorily prohibited levels. Although these individuals may or may not appear grossly intoxicated, their driving skills are severely impaired and they cannot safely operate a motor vehicle. Tolerance is an imperfect adaptation to the presence of a psychoactive substance, and it develops on a continuum, gaining in strength with chronicity of use.

Individuals differ in the course of their development of tolerance to a drug, as can be illustrated with the course of certain disease processes. A person may have a genetic disposition for the development of diabetes but delay or prevent the actual onset of the disease with a healthy lifestyle. Conversely, an individual who lacks a genetic predisposition for diabetes may develop the disease as a result of poor nutrition, obesity, and lack of vigorous exercise. Similarly, drug tolerance emerges or fails to emerge as a function of the level and duration of exposure to alcohol or other drugs.

Tolerance also relates to the pharmacokinetics of a drug, that is, to the body's action on the drug. The body absorbs, distributes, metabolizes, and eliminates ingested substances, that is, the "ins, arounds, changes, and outs" of a drug. It is possible for chronic use to alter these body-drug processes. This can be easily illustrated for alcohol. The processes for other drugs tend to be both more complex and more variable.

A legally and scientifically accepted average alcohol metabolism (burn-off) rate is 0.015 percent per hour, although some alcohol experts believe this rate to be slightly low and use an average rate of 0.017 percent or 0.018 percent per hour. The entire range of rates spans at least 0.010 percent to 0.030 percent per hour with the higher rates being those of tolerant drinkers. Estimates of an individual's BAC over time are directly dependent on the estimate of his metabolism rate, among other variables. To illustrate, note the wide variations in estimates of the time to eliminate alcohol based on the extremes of metabolism. A drinker with a 0.10 percent BAC and a metabolism rate of 0.010 percent per hour will not reach a zero BAC until approximately ten hours have elapsed, whereas a highly tolerant drinker at the same alcohol level with a 0.03 percent per hour rate will be alcohol free in slightly more than three hours.

Alcohol tolerance signals a potential adverse health consequence. Although not inevitable, a chronic drinker is at risk of developing a fatty and cirrhotic liver. In effect, its vital life functions break down as result of overuse. A failing liver loses the ability to metabolize alcohol and may eventually lead to death.

The rapidity with which tolerance develops varies widely. The very quick and thorough development of tolerance with some substances discourages their frequent use. Nearly complete tolerance to the effects of LSD, a synthetic hallucinogen, develops within days, even over a weekend of use. Once a state of complete tolerance is reached, the user experiences no effects and, as a result, binge or prolonged use of LSD doesn't exist. In contrast, cocaine, particularly in smoked crack form, is often used continuously until the drug supply is exhausted, there is no money to purchase more, or the person is in a jail or a hospital.

Cross-tolerance is similar to cross-dependence. If an individual is not able to obtain a drug on which he is dependent, he may seek a drug from the same category to get high or to prevent withdrawal. Similarly, if a person is tolerant to one drug, he likely will be tolerant to other drugs in the same category even though he may never have used them.

Methadone, a synthetic narcotic analgesic, relieves the body's need for heroin at a neural level. Methadone maintenance programs are a mode of treatment for heroin addiction. A major advantage is that methadone is much longer-lasting drug than heroin. The duration of heroin is four to six hours, and to avoid withdrawal the dependent person needs four to six doses (or "hits") during a twenty-four-hour period. Since it is commonly administered intravenously, the multiple injections create risk of infection and other medical problems. In addition, the user must be vigilant to maintain an uninterrupted drug supply. Methadone, on the other hand, lasts about twenty-four hours. The user can take it once per day, go to work, return home, and engage in family activities without having to re-administer the drug. Because it is taken orally, the stigma and hazards of injection are avoided. Importantly, it doesn't cause behavioral impairment or produce euphoria unless an extremely high dose is taken.

Methadone prevents the negative reinforcement of withdrawal and avoids the positive reinforcement of a high. The highly heroin-dependent and heroin-tolerant person, who enrolls in a maintenance program, will require a higher dose of methadone than a less tolerant user. Methadone treatment professionals assess prospective patients' tolerance to determine the dose that will prevent withdrawal without producing impairment of such activities as driving. Prospective patients sometimes overstate their heroin use and obtain an inappropriately high dose, which then can be taken to achieve a psychoactive effect, can be hoarded, or can be diverted for cash, sex, or other drugs.

During a 1997 conference on heroin, sponsored by the U.S. National Institute on Drug Abuse (NIDA) and NIH, a researcher stated that a person maintained on methadone would not use heroin, because methadone completely satisfies his need for a fix. She reasoned further that to combat the spread of heroin use, methadone should be much more readily available as a matter of public policy. At the time of these statements, prosecutors in San Diego were preparing for the trial of an individual charged with murder-by-vehicle while under the influence of drugs. Both methadone and heroin had been found in the defendant's system.

When the researcher was informed of the facts of the San Diego case, including that the defendant was enrolled in a methadone maintenance program, she responded that if the methadone dose had been adequate, there would have been no need for the defendant to search out heroin. This view fails to take into account that drug users seek substances to produce pleasurable CNS effects. From a strictly neurochemical point of view, it is true that the methadone patient does not need to use heroin or any other opioid, because methadone prevents withdrawal. It does not, however, produce the desired euphoria. Heroin does. In the San Diego case, the defendant, who was found guilty of second degree murder, failed to obtain his methadone dose on the day of the incident and chose to use heroin.

1.5 Poly-Drug Use

A. General characteristics

Drug abusers sometimes use more than one drug, which may be legitimate substances and pharmaceutical preparations as well as illicit drugs. Concomitant or serial use of two or more drugs is termed poly-drug use, polypharmacy, multi-habituation, or pharmacological promiscuity. Multiple drugs intensify or prolong effects, introduce new effects, or moderate undesirable side effects. Some forms of poly-drug use, such as the combination of alcohol and caffeine, actually are common in modern society. Although alcohol is a depressant and caffeine is a stimulant, the two often are served together. Also, coffee is served as an antidote to the effects of alcohol. Its stimulant effects do offset the drowsiness and fatigue associated with alcohol, and a drinker may then feel alert and awake. It would be an error, however, for him to believe that the alcohol impairment is entirely reversed and that he can drive safely.

B. Four types of poly-drug use

Four concepts of poly-drug use—additive, antagonistic, overlapping, and null—help the DRE to determine whether an individual is under the influence of multiple drugs.

1. Additive

If substances taken together have additive effects, they enable users to achieve a higher, more intense state of intoxication. Intensification will occur with the simultaneous use of two drugs from the same category, such as alcohol and a minor tranquilizer. These combinations often underlie overdoses and suicides. The victim of a "Mickey Finn" ingests more drug than intended when someone surreptitiously adds a non-alcohol depressant to an alcohol beverage. Drugs currently used to incapacitate for purposes of robbery or sexual assault include benzodiazepines (diazepam, flunitrazepam, oxazepam), chloral hydrate, and gamma hydroxybutyrate (GHB). The latter two are known as date-rape drugs.

2. Antagonistic

If substances have antagonistic effects, one will moderate the undesirable effects of the other. Few substances exert uniform effects over time and even if initially positive, a drug's effects may become adverse over time. The user then is likely to seek relief from another substance. For example, when cocaine use is prolonged, the user has difficulty sleeping, develops paranoia, and experiences extremely rapid heartbeat. He then seeks drugs, usually depressants, to ease his discomfort. Conversely, an alcohol consumer may use cocaine in an attempt to counter fatigue after a drinking session.

"Speedball" refers to the concomitant use of heroin and cocaine. Each drug tempers some of the undesirable effects of the other, but remedy is incomplete. One drug cannot cure the effects of the other, although that argument is sometimes offered as a defense in court. Musicians in a symphony orchestra provide an analogy. If one violinist plays too fast, because he has taken cocaine, the music cannot be restored to harmony by a second violinist who takes heroin and plays slowly.

The results of poly-drug use are further complicated by the between-drug variations in duration of effects. Referring again to the speedball example, cocaine is a relatively short-acting drug, and a user may experience positive effects only for minutes. The effects of heroin, on the other hand, last four to six hours. If the user injects a second speedball as soon as the stimulant effects begin to dissipate, he then will have one cocaine dose and two heroin doses in his body. If he continues to readminister speedballs in this manner, an overdose will result from multiple doses of heroin. The widely publicized drug overdose of comedian John Belushi in 1982 in Los Angeles was believed to have occurred from the too frequent administration of speedballs.

A second drug can extend a high or introduce a different one and thereby help alleviate the crash that occurs when the effects of just one drug wear off. Phencyclidine (PCP) is also used with cocaine. Like heroin, the duration of PCP effects is four to six hours. Because it dissipates gradually, users say it prevents them from becoming depressed when the fast-acting cocaine wears off.

3. Overlapping

Another poly-drug effect is termed overlapping, describing the introduction by a second drug of an additional effect that neither intensifies nor antagonizes an effect of the first substance. An entirely new effect is layered onto the effects of the first drug, as can be illustrated by the results of adding alcohol to cocaine. Alcohol produces an eye-tracking dysfunction, horizontal gaze nystagmus (HGN), which is a gaze-evoked, lateral jerking of the eyeballs. Cocaine neither produces nor antagonizes HGN. When the person who has ingested cocaine also drinks alcohol in sufficient quantify, HGN will appear.

Pupil dilation is also an overlapping effect with combined cocaine and alcohol use. Consistent with the sympathomimetic actions of stimulants, cocaine produces elevated heart rate and blood pressure and also causes the pupils to dilate. Intoxicating levels of alcohol do not affect pupil size.

The consumption of alcohol, therefore, neither reinforces the dilated pupil effect of cocaine nor antagonizes it. When alcohol and cocaine are taken together, dilated pupils are an overlapping effect and are a key sign of concomitant use of the two drugs.

4. Null

The fourth poly-drug effect is the null effect or the absence of an effect by all of the drugs taken. Note that it means that there is no effect, not that effects have been nullified or cancelled. Returning to the speedball example, the absence of HGN is a null effect. Neither cocaine nor heroin produces HGN. Although two drugs from two different categories have been taken, the individual will not have HGN.

The additive, antagonistic, overlapping, and null concepts also assist in the more complicated analysis of drug cocktails with more than two drugs. In the combination of alcohol, cocaine, and heroin, HGN occurs due to the alcohol. Pupil dilation occurs initially due to the cocaine, but over time pupil constriction occurs because of the heroin. Thus, at any one point in time, the individual's pupils may be enlarged, constricted, or within a normal range. The latter condition does not mean that the eyes are functioning normally.

1.6 Drug Effects Defined and Described

A typical question in court cases involving drugs is, "What are the effects of this drug?" A complete answer requires extensive knowledge, training, and skill, but part of the correct answer is, "It depends." It depends on the substance. It depends on the subject who uses the substance, and it depends on the setting and the dynamic physical and psychological environments of use. These three "S's" of substance, subject, and setting provide a framework for understanding the complexity of drug effects.

A. Substance

The first "S" refers to the characteristics of the drug and includes factors such as quantity and potency. Illustrating the quantity/potency variable with alcohol, both a glass of wine and a liter of tequila contain alcohol, but the amount of alcohol in the larger bottle of a stronger beverage, tequila, far exceeds the amount in the smaller glass of wine. The drug is the same, but the effects will be grossly different, a statement which applies to other drugs of abuse. A large amount of cocaine will have qualitatively and quantitatively greater effects than a small amount of cocaine. It is, of course, much more difficult to determine quantities of illegal drugs than of alcohol or pharmaceuticals.

A pint of beer and a pint of tequila are equal in volume but not in potency. Because alcohol content is regulated, consumers know that tequila is 40 percent alcohol, and beer is approximately 5 percent alcohol. On the other hand, the purity and, therefore, the potency of illegal drugs are largely unknown to consumers time-to-time and dealer-to-dealer. Also, there is risk of contamination of a drug purchased in the illegal market.

Drugs can be taken into the body in a variety of ways, and their effects depend in part on which route of administration the user chooses. Cocaine, for example, can be taken orally, or it can be insufflated (snorted) for absorption via the nasal mucosa. It can be injected intravenously (I.V.), subcutaneously, and intramuscularly (I.M.). It can be vaporized and inhaled. The intake method is important, because it affects both the intensity and duration of effects. The faster a substance reaches the brain, the more intense the effects. Intense effects, or a rush, are usually of shorter duration than gradual effects.

The fastest route of administration is via smoking or inhaling vapors, which travel rapidly to the heart via the pulmonary vein, along with oxygen and other components of the air. The heart pumps the oxygenated blood, including the drug, throughout the body and to the CNS and, thus, to the brain. As any cigarette smoker knows, this entire process takes place within seconds. An advantage of the method is that it allows users to titrate the drug intake to achieve the desired high. A negative consequence of the intense but short-lived effects is the need for repeated use.

Intravenous injection (I.V.) is also a rapid administration method, which takes only slightly more time than smoking and also produces intense effects. Users can and do inject into any part of the body, the most commonly-used injection areas being the inner arms, between fingers, top of hands, neck, and back of ankles. They sometimes acquire and inject into tattoos in an attempt to hide the sites. Injection into skeletal muscles and injection under the skin, known as skin-popping, provide slower onset of effects with less intensity and longer duration than the I.V. method. Major drawbacks to any kind of injection are the risk of infection and the difficulty of titrating the dose. Because the entire quantity of drug is injected at once, overdoses are much more common with injections than with smoking.

Insufflation (snorting) is a popular method of intake for cocaine and some other drugs. It leads to relatively rapid absorption of the drug, which quickly travels to the brain. As with smoking or drinking, the user can titrate the dose to achieve the desired high without overdosing. Again, to deal with the short duration of effects, users readminister the drug frequently, and the consequences may include sores and ulcerations in the nasal cavity. Also, chronic constriction of blood flow by cocaine is eventually damaging. The nasal cavity is examined routinely during a DRE evaluation.

B. Subject

The second "S" refers to the subject, the drug user. As a medical advisor to the DRE program frequently emphasizes, individuals differ on the inside as well as on the outside. Bodies differ; so do minds.

A large individual has a larger blood volume than a small person. Muscle tissue has a larger blood supply than fatty tissue. The same drug amount in a larger blood supply is more dilute, and the diluted substance in the larger or muscular person will exert diluted effects. Again, alcohol provides a simple example. All other things being equal for a given amount of alcohol, a drinker of large body size will achieve a lower alcohol level than a smaller person, because the larger person has a larger blood volume into which the alcohol is distributed. For the same reason, a prescription for a medication may be written as quantity of drug per kilogram of body weight. Years ago, when medicines were dispensed as powders and liquids rather than tablets and capsules, the patient's size was critical to the preparation of potent drugs. A therapeutic dose for a very large person potentially is an overdose for a small person.

Since food in the stomach slows the absorption of alcohol into the bloodstream, drinkers are well advised to eat before and during alcohol consumption. Although eating after all the alcohol has been absorbed may make the drinker feel somewhat better, it will have no effect on BAC. Similarly, food in the digestive system slows the absorption of other drugs, the reason for specific prescription directions about how to take a medication in relation to meals. Food in the digestive system, of course, has no significant effect on injected or smoked drugs.

Mood states prior to and during drug ingestion are an additional factor with the second "S". A person who takes the same drug on different occasions may experience different effects because of different mood states. On celebratory occasions, alcohol likely will enhance participants' positive moods. Alcohol can also increase aggression or further deepen depression. Methamphetamine is a sympathomimetic that activates the sympathetic nervous system's fight or flight response. Those effects are unlikely to calm an angry participant in an argument. Police officers find that methamphetamine is a contributing fact in incidents of domestic violence, enraged behaviors, fighting, road rage, and other aggressive behavior.

Users' expectations concerning a drug's effects also impact the drug experience. An LSD user who expects pleasurable hallucinations is more likely to have a positive episode than someone who fears a "bad trip." An individual reported that he was introduced to LSD when he swallowed a pill he believed to be aspirin. He learned almost immediately that he had taken LSD, and a frightening twelve-hour trip ensued. He described it as a dissociative experience during which he saw himself in hell. Nonetheless, he persisted with LSD use and subsequently learned to control his psychedelic experiences by creating an environment of soft music, low lights, and generally reduced sensory stimulation.

During the 1960s and 1970s, the tetrahydrocannabinol (THC) content of marijuana was relatively low, and the role of expectation versus the drug's psychoactive properties was widely debated. At issue was whether marijuana actually produced a high or whether users felt high simply because they expected that effect. It is possible that during those years expectations were a large component of experienced effects. As the potency of marijuana has increased dramatically over the years, however, it can be assumed that the contribution of expectation to the user's high has decreased. Marijuana effects are no longer due solely, or even largely, to expectation.

Tolerance is another important factor with the "S" of subject. As discussed earlier, tolerance refers to the chronic user's need for more of the substance to achieve desired effects and to a reduction in overt signs of use. Tolerance does not mean that the individual is not experiencing or displaying any effects at all, nor does it mean that the performance of complex tasks such as driving has not been impaired. In a law enforcement setting, an individual's tolerance rarely is known, although it may be inferred in some cases. It is evidence of tolerance when an individual with a BAC of 0.15 percent or higher, for example, displays no overt signs of intoxication. The use of multiple drugs complicates the tolerance issue.

C. Setting

The third "S" refers to the dynamic physical and psychological environment. It is important from several perspectives, including that of officer safety. For example, the level of stimulation in the law enforcement setting is critical in dealing with PCP suspects. These individuals often are hostile and aggressive, and the anesthetic properties of the drug limit their response to the pain of a control hold. Officers learned through experience that the chance of a violent altercation is mitigated if sensory stimulation is minimized. Dimming lights, lowering voices, and avoiding sudden movement help to calm the person. Minimizing stimulation is also appropriate in managing suspects who are under the influence of hallucinogens and in medical settings when patients have been administered Ketamine, a dissociative anesthetic.

"White-coat" hypertension illustrates the impact of setting. It refers to an increase in blood pressure that occurs when measurements are made in a medical setting. The temporary elevation of pressure reflects the stress of undergoing medical procedures. In this case, the setting of a doctor's office changes the patient's physiology in a measurable way.

The impact of the setting in which drug evaluations occur can be tempered by the examiner's skill and demeanor. Even in a law enforcement facility, a skillful officer can gain the suspect's cooperation and, thereby, make it much more likely that drug influence will be accurately assessed.

Recently in a courtroom, an attorney stated that his client had displayed only subtle impairment. Subtle is a relative term, however, and it is possible that drug signs and symptoms that would not be apparent to a naive observer will be obvious to a trained examiner. In traffic enforcement, experienced officers who have had specialized training and who make DUI arrests regularly have become experts in identifying the signs and symptoms of impairment. In contrast, a new officer who lacks the experiential basis for recognizing impairment may fail to recognize the somewhat subtle signs of impairment.

The effects of setting also impact studies of drug effects. Although some drugs of abuse cannot be given to subjects either ethically or legally, others have been examined in well-designed, controlled studies. Experiments conducted in a laboratory with non-drug dependent, healthy adults provide important data about drug effects per se. Still, there are important differences between effects in a laboratory and effects in the real world. In a single example, consider the computer-based driving simulators that are used to create the visual environment and information processing demands of driving. They yield valid albeit limited data about drug effects on performance. A critical difference is that they cannot simulate risk. The simulator operator knows that he will not come to harm. Without real consequences, his performance is likely to differ from real world driving, with the result that the data may under- or overestimate the drug's effects on his performance.

In the early 1990s NIDA in cooperation with NHTSA undertook a study of DRE procedures at the Addiction Research Center in Baltimore. Recreational drug users were recruited to take certain drugs in a controlled, hospital-like setting. After they took drug(s) or placebo, DREs conducted abbreviated drug-influence assessments. In this setting, if a DRE determined that a subject was under the influence of a drug, there were no adverse consequences for the subject. Rather, study conditions provided positive consequences in the form of drugs and money. This contrasts with the law enforcement setting where the finding of drug influence leads to arrest, incarceration, and possibly conviction in a court proceeding. Interestingly, the impact of setting was apparent. Individuals who had smoked marijuana were relaxed, cooperative, and in a good mood during the assessment. In contrast, in circumstances of potential incarceration, individuals suspected of marijuana influence often are anxious and agitated. Although clinical manifestations of drug influence, such as bloodshot eyes, exist in both settings, mood and other behaviors differ markedly. The same drug and the same user in different settings result in very different behavior.

1.7 Seven Categories of Drugs

A. Cannabis

This category, which includes marijuana, hash, hash oil, and the synthetic drug dronabinol, is the most widely abused illicit drug. Although it has a popular reputation as a relatively benign drug, it is extremely impairing. It affects judgment, depth perception, and attention, as well as having effects on the cardiovascular system. It causes bloodshot eyes, tachycardia, muscle tremors, and forgetfulness. Unlike depressants, inhalants, and phencyclidine, it does not produce HGN.

B. CNS depressants

Eponymously, the substances in this category depress the activity of the central nervous system. They are classified in six subcategories.

1. Antianxiety, minor tranquilizers

The benzodiazepines (BZs) are efficacious treatment for anxiety and insomnia and are the most widely prescribed psychoactive medications. Although prevalence of use varies by region and country, those listed in Table 1.1 are commonly used and abused.

Table 1.1
Benzodiazepines

Valium	diazepam
Librium	chlordiazepoxide
Xanax	alprazolam
Halcion	triazolam
Rohypnol	flunitrazepam
Klonopin	clonazepam
Serax	oxazepam

2. Antipsychotics, or major tranquilizers

These medications are prescribed to treat major psychiatric disorders and are only rarely abused. The subcategory includes, among others, lithium, droperidol, haloperidol, and Thorazine.

3. Antidepressants, or mood elevators

The title of this category is somewhat confusing in that it suggests stimulant activity. Although the drugs do share some characteristics with CNS stimulants, they produce distinct behaviors that are unlike the frenzied activity induced by stimulants. The widely prescribed medications include the selective serotonin reuptake inhibitors (SSRIs) such as Prozac (fluoxetine). Others are Elavil (amitriptyline), Tofranil (imipramine), and

Sinequan (doxepin). Like the antipsychotics, these are rarely abused. They may be misused and taken inappropriately, but they are not taken for euphoric effects.

4. Barbiturates

Hundreds of these derivatives of barbiturate acid have been produced since they were first introduced in the mid-19th century. Phenobarbital, pentobarbital, amobarbital, and secobarbital are among the many barbiturates. Although still in use, they are not now the preferred drugs either for therapy or for abuse, due largely to the advent of the BZs.

5. Non-barbiturates

These substances have barbiturate-like effects but are not derivatives of barbiturate acid. Like the barbiturates, they are abused and they produce physical and psychological dependence. Chloral hydrate, which is known as a "Mickey Finn" or "knockout drops," is a non-barbiturate, which is still medically useful, as in dental surgery, but it is regularly abused. Other substances are glutethimide, methaqualone, carisoprodol, and gamma hydroxy butyrate (GHB).

6. Combinations

This subcategory should not be confused with the combinations of different substances for poly-drug abuse. These are pharmaceutical preparations containing more than one type of CNS depressant. An example of such a combination is Limbitrol, which contains Librium (chlordiazepoxide), a tranquilizer and Elavil (amitriptyline), an antidepressant. Percobarb is a combination of a barbiturate and a narcotic analgesic. Other therapeutic compounds cross drug category lines.

C. CNS stimulants

This category includes cocaine in its various forms, amphetamine, methamphetamine, ephedrine, Ritalin, certain diet pills, and other related substances. Known as "uppers," the effects mimic the body's fight or flight response, which is the autonomic nervous system's response to perceived danger. These effects include dilated pupils, elevated vital signs, hyperalertness, rapid and agitated body movements, and a diminished ability to filter environmental stimuli such as noise and movement. The user may overreact to seemingly minor events and view minor inconveniences as elaborate plots. As the effects wear off, he "crashes," going into a state that is nearly opposite to that of the active phase of drug influence. He sleeps for a long period, wakes voraciously hungry, and may be extremely dysphoric. Chronic heavy use of stimulants leads to extreme weight loss together with deteriorating health and hygiene. These drugs do not produce HGN.

D. Hallucinogens

These drugs distort sensory perceptions and produce hallucinations. They are closely related to CNS stimulants and, like stimulants, dilate pupils and elevate vital signs. They do not produce HGN. An individual under the influence of hallucinogens may experience synesthesia, a mixing of the senses in which visual stimuli such as colors are heard and sounds such as music are seen. LSD, psilocybin, mescaline, peyote, bufotenine, morning glory seeds, jimson weed, nutmeg, and the psychedelic amphetamines are in this category. The latter include ecstasy (MDMA or methylenedioxy methamphetamine).

E. Inhalants

This category includes volatile solvents, aerosols, and anesthetic gases. The category name is derived from the method of administration through inhalation of volatile fumes. The substances are pharmacologically similar to CNS depressants, and the behavior of users who are under the influence of inhalants mimics that of CNS depressant users. Telltale signs of inhalant use include the odor and remnants of the substance itself, such as paint specks on the person's hands and mouth.

The primary abused substances in this category, volatile solvents, evaporate rapidly and give off fumes that induce intoxication when inhaled in a concentrated fashion. Paint, gasoline, glue, thinner, parts cleaner, typewriter correction fluid, and many other substances are in this subcategory. A number of these are used in cleaning and household chores, and their presence in the home means they are available to youth who may experiment with them.

Aerosols are chemicals discharged from a pressurized container by the propellant force of a compressed gas. These are also found in the home in hair sprays, deodorants, insecticides and frying pan lubricants.

Medical/surgical usage is the origin of some of the anesthetic gases, including ether, chloroform, and nitrous oxide (laughing gas). Amyl nitrite, butyl nitrite and isobutyl nitrite are used medically to relieve heart-related chest pain.

F. Narcotic analgesics

Frequently termed opiates or opioids, this category includes morphine, codeine, percodan, heroin, meperidine, methadone, fentanyl, oxycodone, and others. These drugs relieve pain, sedate, constrict pupils, and depress vital signs. They do not produce HGN. An individual under the influence of a narcotic analgesic often will exhibit slow and deliberate movements and forgetfulness. These drugs frequently are injected, but because of the risk of contracting diseases through the sharing of needles, users also ingest them by means of insufflation and inhalation. The narcotic analgesics are known for their physically addicting properties, as well as for the extremely unpleasant, though not life-threatening, withdrawal syndrome.

G. Phencyclidine (PCP)

PCP is the acronym for phenyl cyclohexyl piperidine, which is classified as a hallucinogen in many texts as well as by law. Although it can induce distorted sensory perceptions or hallucinations, its effects are unique. Unlike true hallucinogens, it produces HGN. For this reason and others, PCP occupies a separate category. Note that ketamine, a related substance, is reported to be a widely abused substance in 2002.

The effects of PCP are elevated vital signs, both horizontal and vertical gaze nystagmus, rigid skeletal muscles, a blank stare, and hallucinations. Users are nonresponsive to pain. They can become suddenly violent and pose an extreme danger to police officers. Nonlethal control devices, such as taser dart guns, have been developed to aid officers who must subdue an individual under the influence of PCP.

Chapter 2

Pharmacology and Toxicology

Olaf H. Drummer

Synopsis

2.1 Introduction

As described in the previous chapter, the drug classification used by drug recognition experts (DREs) is based on the clinical manifestations of the drugs most commonly seen in drug-driving cases. Underlying these effects are, of course, their particular pharmacological properties. This chapter reviews the pharmacology of these drugs with particular attention to the mechanisms of drug actions, the likely consequences of the use of the drugs and certain combinations of these, and finally reviews aspects of their toxicology that are relevant to traffic medicine.

2.2 Mechanisms of Drug Action

With some exceptions, the drugs of interest in this book produce their adverse effects on safe driving by interfering with endogenous chemicals that act on specific recognition sites called receptors. Since many receptor systems are associated with nerves, many drugs affect proper nerve function. To understand how these drugs act, it is necessary to briefly explain how nerves work, and how receptors are important in regulating normal physiological processes.

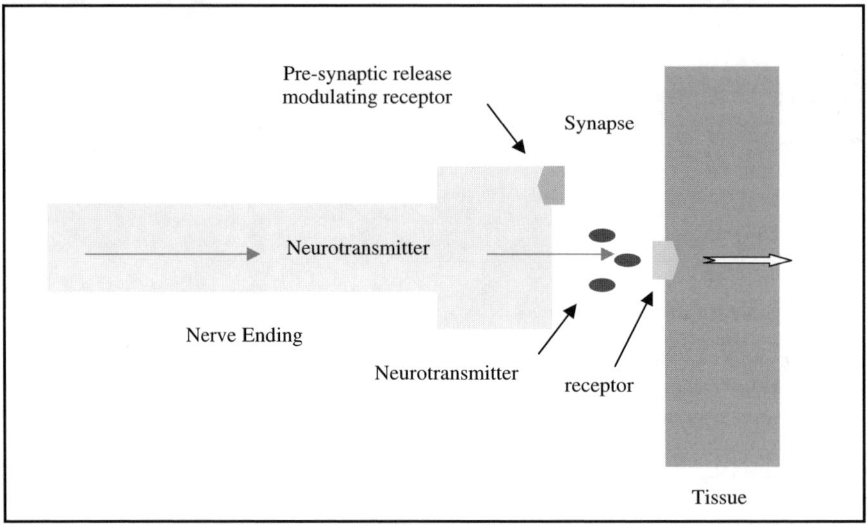

Figure 2.1 *Schematic representation of a neurotransmitter release from a nerve ending onto a target tissue*

Nerves are fibres that transmit signals from one part of the body to another. The best example is the spinal cord. This nerve is the main "trunk line" from the brain to the rest of the body. Any interference in the transmission of signals along this cord has profound effects. For example, severing of the cord at the level of the first thoracic vertebra will cause paraplegia (i.e. loss of all lower limb movements). Severing at the fourth cervical vertebra will cause quadriplegia.

The movement of signals along these nerves is caused by the migration of ions, somewhat akin to the movement of electrons along copper wire in electrical connections. At the nerve ending, known as the nerve terminal, transmission of the signal to the neighboring muscle, or another nerve, is caused by the release of chemicals. These chemicals are known as neurotransmitters. Common neurotransmitters include dopamine (DA), gamma-aminobutyrate (GABA), norepinephrine (NE), serotonin (also known as 5-HT), N-methyl-D-aspartate (NMDA), and acetylcholine

(ACh). The release of these chemicals at nerve terminals results in the activation of specific recognition sites at the target tissue in close proximity to the nerve terminal. These sites are termed receptors, and when activated, they elicit a chain of biochemical events that ultimately cause a response, such as a muscle contraction. The muscle contraction may result in actions such as a body movement, a breathing response, or an increase in heart rate (see Table 2.1).

In the brain, the target tissue is usually another nerve cell(s) and can result in behavioral changes often associated with drugs of abuse. These behavioral changes could be increased aggression and violence, or sedation and reduced cognitive performance.

A range of receptors present in brain tissue affects a range of physiological processes. Morphine-like drugs act on opiate-receptors that are involved in the regulation of pain (nociception). The minor tranquilizer benzodiazepines act on the GABA-receptor, an inhibitory neurotransmitter. The binding of the benzodiazepine on this receptor has the net effect of increasing movement of chloride through specific ion channels. This process reduces the stimulation of key areas in the brain involved in regulating a range of behaviors and physiological functions. These include anxiety, emotion and memory of events. CNS depressant drugs generally affect a number of receptor systems and nerve functions and produce unsteadiness on the feet (ataxia), reduce motor control manifesting in decreased control of lane position while driving, and slow information processing.

When a transmitter is released by the nerve terminal to produce a chemical signal, it is rapidly removed from the terminal junction (known as the synaptic cleft) by a combination of reuptake into the nerve terminal (presynaptic release modulating receptor), metabolism or diffusion into the surrounding blood supply. These mechanisms reduce the duration of the neurotransmitter response and reuse the neurotransmitter. Drugs can modify these processes and thereby reduce or enhance the effects of the neurotransmitters.

Some drugs mimic the actions of the transmitter at the receptor. This occurs with amphetamines that act on the same receptor as the neurotransmitter norepinephrine. Amphetamine and many of the weak non-amphetamine stimulants also act to facilitate release of more endogenous neurotransmitter.

Table 2.1
Sites of Action and Receptor Involvement of Selected Drug Classes

Drug Class / Drug	Principal Sites of Action	Receptor System
Amphetamines	CNS, muscles	Sympathetic system, adrenergic nerves and other nerve systems
Benzodiazepines	CNS	Inhibitory nerves utilising GABA
Cocaine	CNS, muscles	Sympathetic system, adrenergic nerves and others
Cannabis (THC)	CNS (main site, but also peripheral sites)	CB_1 cannabinoid receptor
PCP	CNS	Sigma-opiate antagonist and blocks NMDA-receptor ion channels, also affects dopamine system
Alcohol	CNS	Non specific depressant, also affects ACh, GABA, NMDA & 5-HT_3 receptors
Inhalants	CNS and heart	General anesthetic activity on nerve function; asphyxiant and pro-arrhythmic
LSD	CNS	Agonist on 5-HT_{1A}, 5-HT_{1C}, and 5-HT_2 receptors
Opioids (morphine, heroin)	CNS	Opioid (mu) receptor, and other opioid receptors
GHB	CNS	Inhibits reuptake of dopamine and weak agonist at the GABA receptor.

Drugs that inhibit the reuptake process cause an increased effect from a nerve signal since the neurotransmitter is present in the synaptic cleft longer. Liken this to a pianist who holds a note for a longer time. Drugs in this category include cocaine (inhibits reuptake of dopamine and norepinephrine) and the new generation of antidepressants known as serotonin reuptake inhibitors (e.g., fluoxetine, citalopram, etc.).

Some drugs affect the postsynaptic metabolism of neurotransmitters. These drugs include the monoamine oxidase inhibitors (MAOI) such as moclobemide, phenylzine and so on. The mild stimulant drugs caffeine and theophylline are weak inhibitors of the enzyme phosphodiesterase, which results in the elevation of biochemical mediators[1] of nerve functions.

2.3 Drug Classes

A. Amphetamines and cocaine

This groups includes amphetamine, methamphetamine, the designer amphetamines 2-CB, DOM, MDMA, MDA, MDE, MBDB, PMA and so forth, as well as the legally available but weaker stimulants such as ephedrine, *l*-desoxyephedrine and the anorexiants (diethyl propion, phentermine, benzphetamine, clobenzorex, fenproporex, fenetylline, mefenorex and mazindol). This group also includes cocaine[2], mescaline[3] and cathinone[4].

Amphetamines interact with nerves using norepinephrine, serotonin (or 5-hydroxy tryptamine, 5-HT) and dopamine to both replace the neurotransmitter in the nerve ending and act as a false neurotransmitter, as well as to facilitate the release of the endogenous neurotransmitter from the nerve endings.

Peripheral effects include raised heart rate and blood pressures, elevation of mood and reduction in effects of fatigue. Owing to the drug's stimulatory effects on the nervous system it will also cause persons to become agitated and talkative. Muscle tremor and rapid jerky movements are common symptoms of amphetamine usage. Users of strong stimulants tend to overestimate elapsed time. There is no effect on nystagmus, but at high doses pupil size may be enlarged.

MDMA (ecstasy) is also classed as a hallucinogen because of its profound effects on the CNS particularly on the dopamine and serotonin nerves.

Prolonged use of amphetamines, particularly MDMA, causes long lasting or even permanent nerve damage to dopamine and serotonin-containing nerves in the brain leading to stereotyped behaviors and paranoid psychosis. Long-term use of amphetamines is also associated with damage to heart muscle that can manifest as cardiac arrhythmias, although this may not be obvious from an external examination.

B. Cannabis

Cannabis includes a variety of products that originate from the plant Cannabis sativa. These include cigarettes made from dried leaves and flower heads, hashish, hash oil, sinsemilla[5] and other forms. The principal active component is (9-tetahydrocannabinol (THC), produced by the heating of precursor substances found in forms of marijuana. The legal form of THC, Marinol, is also available by prescription in the USA for regulated uses.

THC content in illicit supplies of cannabis usually ranges from 2–8 percent, although higher strengths are known. This typically yields THC doses of 5–30 mg through smoking, although the amount absorbed will depend on the amount of smoke inhaled.

Cannabis smoking produces a transient euphoria associated with emotional and cognitive changes. This effect distinguishes this drug from the CNS depressants. Persons under the influence of cannabis are relaxed, but show impairment of responses to visual signals and exhibit a reduced visual acuity (tunnel vision). In some persons (often repeatedly using high doses) acute psychoses may develop leading to characteristic behavioral changes. Novice users can experience unpleasant effects including anxiety, paranoia and panic attacks.

Cannabis produces increases in heart rate, blood pressure (largely systolic) and body temperature, although persons accustomed to the drug often experience less increase in these vital functions than novice users. In most cases, these effects are short-lived and return to normal within a few hours. Long-term use can impair short-term memory, overall learning capabilities and other cognitive processes.

Cannabis has observable effects on the eyes. Most obvious are red conjunctiva, but also present are small increases in the size of pupils. Other effects include a lowering in intraocular pressure and a reduction in tear formation, but there is no nystagmus. Users perceive a slowing of time. THC produces a reduction in skills required for safe driving, including an increase in reaction times, difficulty with single and divided attention tasks, poor tracking and lane control.

Orally consumed cannabis through "cookies" is less common and generally produces less profound effects than smoked cannabis. This is because of the relatively slow absorption and the much greater formation of 11-hydroxy metabolite of THC compared to smoked cannabis.

In acute users, blood concentrations of THC in excess of 2 ng/mL suggests recent use of cannabis, while in chronic users blood concentrations of THC may need to exceed 5 ng/mL to be reasonably sure of recent cannabis use. These blood concentrations translate to approximately 4 and 10 ng/mL in plasma or serum, respectively.

C. Central nervous system depressants

This is by far the biggest class of drugs. It includes alcohol (ethanol), and most of the minor tranquilizers including the benzodiazepines and barbiturates. GHB is also a CNS depressant. A number of other miscellaneous, but legally available, sedative drugs are included here. Of note are other depressants, including many of the older sedatives and hypnotics which are not included in the above classes, some anticonvulsant drugs, many antidepressants, the older sedating antihistamines and many of the antipsychotic drugs (see Table 2.2).

These drugs act as CNS depressants by interfering with one or more neuronal actions in the brain, sometimes in a nonspecific fashion. As the name of the class suggests these drugs, in sufficient doses, retard or depress nervous activity. They are often called "downers" to reflect their CNS depressant activity.

Paradoxical effects may be observed with benzodiazepines in some subjects. These effects result from disinhibition of normal control mechanisms and can result in aggression and bizarre behavioral changes. These reactions although not common can produce disturbing changes when benzodiazepines are abused. In extreme cases, subjects may not have any conscious control over their actions. Benzodiazepines such as alprazolam, clonazepam and flunitrazepam are known to cause these effects. It is likely that many other benzodiazepines can also exhibit these characteristics in susceptible persons. Alcohol is a common associated drug that intensifies these behavioral changes.

Drivers using a combination of CNS-depressant drugs are also more likely to exhibit adverse effects than when one such drug alone is consumed. Most commonly, this is associated with the combination of alcohol with one or other CNS-depressant drugs.

Abuse of CNS depressants gives rise to effects like those of alcohol. In fact, alcohol is the prototype drug in this group. Drunken behavior such as unsteady gait, slurred speech, and disorientation is expected. When abused, CNS depressants have serious adverse effects on driving skills. The depression of vital brain functions causes the impairment of psychomotor and cognitive skills. The slowed processing of information results in increased reaction times, poor lane control and tracking, and impaired divided attention tasks. Pupil size is not usually affected, but horizontal gaze nystagmus is present and vertical gaze nystagmus may also be present at higher doses.

GHB causes confusion, dizziness and loss of peripheral vision, as well as adverse effects on memory and probably a range of psychomotor functions. High doses can lead to a low body temperature, a low heart rate and low blood pressures. The drug will, therefore, cause significant impairment of the skills required for safe driving.

It is important to point out that many of the CNS depressant drugs, other than alcohol and the legal sedatives, can cause other effects particularly on the cardiorespiratory system. For example, propranolol lowers heart rate and blood pressures[6]. The older antidepressants and many of the antipsychotics can also lower blood pressure due to their effects on the cholinergic system as well as provide a range of behavioral changes. Consequently, no simple constellation of symptoms points to the use of these drugs.

The newer class of antidepressant drugs, serotonin reuptake inhibitors (e.g., fluoxetine, sertraline, etc.), mixed reuptake inhibitors (e.g., nefazodone, venlafaxine, etc.), and the reversible inhibitors of monoamine oxidase A (e.g., moclobemide) do not show significant CNS depressant actions, and are not usually of concern in drug driving cases. In some situations, however, persons using these drugs in combination exhibit profound behavioral changes that will impair their ability to drive safely. These include an altered conscious state, often associated with rigid movements, high body temperature and profuse sweating. This is known as the "serotonin syndrome," and occurs in persons misusing these drugs, or occasionally when combinations of psychiatric drugs are prescribed.

Table 2.2
Examples of CNS-Depressant Drugs

Drug Class	Prototype Drugs
Benzodiazepines	Alprazolam Bromazepam Clonazepam Diazepam / nordiazepam (or nordazepam) Flunitrazepam Flurazepam Lorazepam Nitrazepam Oxazepam Prazepam Temazepam Triazolam
Barbiturates	Amobabital (amylobarbital) Butalbital Pentobarbital Phenobarbital[1] Quinalbarbital (secobarbital)
Antidepressants[2]	Amitriptyline Doxepin Dothiepin Imipramine Clomipramine Trazodone Mianserin
Antipsychotics	Chlorpromazine Thioridazine Haloperidol Clozapine Olanzapine
Other drugs	Sedating anticonvulsants (e.g., phenytoin) Sedating cardiovascular drugs (e.g., propranolol) Sedating antihistamines(e.g., promethazine) Other sedatives (e.g. zopiclone, methaqualone) Cariosprodol,

[1] Mainly used as an anti-convulsant.
[2] These include the older sedating members of this class. The serotonin reuptake and mixed reuptake inhibitors, and the reversible monoamine oxidase inhibitor moclobemide showrelatively little impairment of psychomotor functions.

The anticonvulsant drugs of note that cause CNS depression are phenytoin, phenobarbital, methylphenobarbital, primidone and carbamazepine. Patients stabilized on these drugs tend not to show obvious symptoms of CNS depression (e.g., nystagmus) and providing their epilepsy is well controlled and they have therapeutic plasma concentrations, they are unlikely to present with impaired driving.

Abuse of sedating antihistamines could occur since some of these are available as over-the-counter preparations including syrups. Abuse, however, is rarely encountered. Modern antihistamines prescribed for allergies and related conditions are not markedly sedating and are less likely to cause impaired driving.

In practice, it is not common to find impaired drivers abusing these "miscellaneous" prescribed depressants. Alcohol and the benzodiazepines are by far the most common drugs detected of this class in drug-affected drivers.

D. Hallucinogens

Most of the hallucinogens are alkaloids obtained from plants and produce an altered perception of reality. One of the most common is LSD (lysergic acid diethylamide), often sold as "trips" or "tabs."[7] Other common hallucinogens include mescaline, psilocin/psilocybin and some of designer amphetamines such as MDMA (ecstasy). The amphetamines are also discussed in the amphetamine section of this chapter (see Table 2.3).

The serotonin system regulates emotions and thought processes and is affected by a range of drugs (e.g., antipsychotics and antidepressants). LSD is an antagonist of peripheral serotonin receptors, and an agonist at central serotonin receptors, particularly the subtypes 5-HT_{1A}, 5-HT_{1C} and 5-HT_{2}. LSD use leads to a distortion of sounds, smell and visual images. Subjects are often confused and exhibit illogical actions. Bad trips may result in bizarre behaviors, and paranoid delusions. Tolerance develops after three to six days of continuous use.

Mescaline causes pronounced visual distortions associated with unsteady gait, poor speech control, anxiety, panic attacks and emotional changes. Nausea, vomiting, diarrhea and sweating may also be present together with labile blood pressures and a high heart rate. Pupils may be dilated, but nystagmus is rarely present.

The consumption of "magic mushrooms" that contain psilocin/psilocybin alkaloids produces visual hallucinations and perceptual changes including vivid colors and off shapes. As with mescaline, physiological and psychological changes occur including anxiety, unsteady gait and dilated pupils. Compulsive movements and antisocial behavior are common for hallucinogens.

Table 2.3
Types and Sources of Common Hallucinogenics

Hallucinogen	Source
LSD	Synthetic derivative of the ergot alkaloid lysergic acid
Mescaline	Peyote cactus and related species, and synthetic
Psilocin / psilocybin	*Psilocybe* mushrooms
Ecstasy (MDMA etc.)	Synthetic designer derivatives of amphetamine

E. Narcotic analgesics

This group consists of opioids (e.g., heroin, morphine, oxycodone, hydromorphone, etc.) and synthetic opioid-like substances (e.g., methadone). In high doses weak analogs such as codeine and ethylmorphine can have similar effects to morphine. Less commonly available narcotics include etorphine, fentanyl and the designer fentanyls, and the short acting narcotics used in surgical settings alfentanil, remifentanil and sufentanil. All of these drugs act on the opioid receptors[8] in the brain to reduce the sensation of pain.

Intravenously used narcotics such as heroin (also known as diacetylmorphine) also produce an euphoric effect. This sensation produces a sudden elevation of mood and can be likened to an orgasm. The effects are associated with craving for further opioids.

As the narcotic name implies, these drugs cause sedation and drowsiness. It is this effect that is most important from a road safety perspective causing fatigue, or exacerbating fatigue caused by sleep deprivation, or from other causes. Sedation also affects cognition and slows reflexes, although tolerance to these effects can rapidly set in with continued use of narcotic analgesics. Apathy, reduced visual acuity, reduced physical activity and lethargy are also common.

Other side effects include respiratory depression, constriction of pupils (miosis) and reduction in motility of the gastrointestinal system (constipation). Nystagmus is not an effect of narcotic analgesics, but benzodiazepines which are often associated with use of narcotics may cause nystagmus in these cases.

Regular use of narcotics can cause psychological and physiological dependence usually associated with tolerance (see Section 2.5). In this situation, abrupt cessation of drug will cause marked withdrawal effects.

F. Phencyclidine

Phencyclidine (PCP) is a synthetic anesthetic drug that possesses a unique profile of activity and is therefore included as a separate category in the DRE classification of drugs. PCP analogs include thienyl cyclohexyl piperidine (TCP), phenyl cyclohexylpyrrolidine (PHP), phenyl cyclopentyl piperidine (PCPP) and cyclohexamine (PCE). Ketamine shares similar properties to PCP and is still used as an anesthetic in humans.

PCP is sold as a powder, flakes or a liquid. In any of these forms, it can be impregnated in tobacco or cannabis cigarettes, or leaf material. Street doses of PCP range from 1 to 10 mg. Ketamine is sold as solutions for injection, pills, powder or tab form. Ketamine is also commonly cut with cocaine, amphetamine and heroin. Common doses are 200–500 mg.

PCP blocks the N-methyl-D-aspartate (NMDA) receptor in the cortex and limbic regions of the brain, and it acts on the sigma-opioid receptor, and the dopamine-containing neurons in the brain. The effects on the dopamine system are primarily responsible for its effects on behavior.

PCP and its analogs are anesthetics that produce an altered conscious state leading to hallucinations and symptoms of dissociation. PCP has actions similar in some respects to LSD, in that it causes distortion of visual and other sensory signals. It also produces analgesia similar to opioids, and causes stereotyped behavior similar to amphetamines and cocaine. Subjects typically experience high heart rate and elevated blood pressures, dysphoria, numbness and sweating. Horizontal and vertical gaze nystagmus are present.

Users of PCP can experience acute psychotic episodes leading to reckless and dangerous action, and the drug, not surprisingly, is associated with violence and dissociated behavior.

G. Inhalants

These substances include a large range of volatile chemicals that are generally used recreationally by inhalation into the lungs. This kind of inhalant use is termed volatile substance abuse (VSA). Inhalation can occur directly from a spray can or indirectly from a bag containing inhalant placed over the face. "Chroming" is a term used in the street to define forms of VSA.

Hydrocarbons (aliphatic and aromatic) from gasoline, cigarette lighter refills, aerosol propellants, and from contact adhesives form the bulk of such volatile substances. Halogenated industrial solvents and related substances from fire extinguishers are also sometimes inhaled, as are volatile anesthetics.

Occasionally persons may be exposed to solvents from an inadvertent occupational exposure. This gives rise only in extreme cases of exposure to the significant adverse effects seen in cases of deliberate abuse.

Inhalation of inhalants into the lungs produces rapid effects, particularly on brain function, as a result of rapid absorption in the lungs and their generally high solubility in tissues.

Inhalants give rise to some degree of euphoria, but they are more associated with profound CNS disturbances similar to those caused by ethanol (alcohol). Typically such an affected person is disoriented, unsteady or dizzy and presents with slurred speech. Other manifestations include anorexia, abdominal pain, headache, lethargy, nausea, unproductive cough, runny nose, sore throat and bloodshot eyes. Auditory and visual hallucinations may occur. Pupil size is not affected, but horizontal gaze nystagmus is present, and at higher doses vertical gaze nystagmus may also be present.

Inhalants have serious adverse effects on driving skills associated with profound depression of the CNS.

Deprivation of oxygen during active volatile substance abuse can lead to serious medical emergencies including anoxia and cardiac arrhythmias. Long-term use often leads to permanent brain damage, and therefore, significant decrement of psychomotor and cognitive skills.

2.4 Drug Combinations

It is commonplace for drivers proven to be adversely affected by drugs to be using more than one drug. Clearly, the overall effects of drugs on a person will reflect their combined effect. It, therefore, sometimes becomes difficult for DREs to categorize the drug or drugs used if more than one drug is involved in producing behavioral changes.

Alcohol is the most common substance found in association with an impairing drug. At alcohol concentrations in excess of 0.10 gram/100 mL the effects of alcohol usually dominate over other substances. Thus, it may not always be possible to detect evidence of other drug use, particularly another CNS depressant drug such as a benzodiazepine. Cannabis is also frequently associated with the use of alcohol. Although cannabis is not classed as a CNS depressant it does share many features of CNS depressant drugs.

Attention deficits, poor lane control and increased reaction times will generally occur. These have been observed in open-road driving experiments with instrumented cars. Both alcohol and cannabis produce a measurable degree of impaired driving, and their combination produces an increased degree of impairment (see reading material).

With combinations of CNS depressant drugs and a stimulant, it becomes more difficult to predict the type and magnitude of behavioral changes. Although effects of both drug classes may be present, it is more likely that the range of skills required for safe driving will be worsened by their combination, rather than reduced. This occurs because all of these drugs act principally on the CNS and interfere with a range of proper nervous functions.

In many situations, the behavioral changes seen by a combination of drugs may mask the effect of any one drug, or confuse the correct classification of drug category. This can often be explained once the toxicology results are available when the likely effects of the drug combination can be properly considered.

2.5 Tolerance and Withdrawal

Users of essentially all of the drugs mentioned previously will exhibit tolerance if the drugs are used regularly. This applies particularly to the amphetamines, cocaine, and the narcotic analgesics, although users of cannabis and CNS depressants can show significant signs of drug dependence and tolerance if the drugs are misused. Chronic use of alcohol will also lead to dependence and tolerance.

Tolerance occurs as the human body becomes accustomed to the pharmacological and physiological effects of the drug. This is termed neuroadaptation. Drug users compensate by consuming larger amounts of drug. This is best illustrated with heroin and cocaine users. They will consume doses several fold higher during their active phase than when they first started using the drug. The phenomenon of tolerance occurs for a number of reasons. Desensitization and/or loss of receptors are the most common mechanisms when the body attempts to reduce the physiological effects of the drug. Tolerance can occur after days to weeks of use.

Although most of the abused drugs can produce tolerance, this physiological state can have both a chemical and psychological component. While the chemical component is associated with loss of receptors or a desensitization of receptor actions, the psychological component is far more complex. For example, heroin users will frequently have a greater psychological dependence than a chemical dependence if the drug is used sporadically. The net effect of tolerance is that blood concentrations associated with clinically significant impairment will have a much greater variation. Therefore, drug-dependent persons can tolerate much higher blood concentrations than drug-naive persons.

Drug-dependent persons will by definition not only exhibit drug-seeking behavior but will also show signs of withdrawal following abstinence from the drug. Withdrawal symptoms can often be more profound than symptoms exhibited by persons under the influence of drug.

For amphetamines and cocaine, abstinence symptoms important from a road safety perspective include fatigue, depression and suicidal behavior. This may also include paranoid psychoses and other mood disorders.

2.6 Therapeutic Use

It has been a world wide experience that persons using prescribed drugs properly are not likely to come under the attention of DREs. However, prescribed drugs are sometimes found in cases of drug-impaired driving. These drugs include the benzodiazepines, some stimulant drugs including nasal decongestants and anorexiants, narcotic analgesics and the psychiatric drugs. These cases can reflect misuse of prescribed drugs, or drugs obtained illegally, rather than persons taking their medications as prescribed by their physician.

The adverse effects of prescribed psychotropic drugs will wane as tolerance becomes established. For example, persons starting on medication for depression may become drowsy in the first weeks of treatment. Drowsiness (and often other side-effects) will disappear as tolerance sets in and their mood is elevated. This is also true for persons in methadone maintenance programs. Significant sedation is likely in the first weeks of treatment, but drivers eventually become accustomed to the sedating effects and are able to drive without exhibiting impairment, providing they do not abuse other drugs and the methadone dose has been controlled.

Glossary

Agonist Substance that is capable of eliciting a response from a receptor

Amphetamines Drugs related to amphetamine, including methamphetamine, ecstasy (MDMA) etc.

Autonomic nervous system The nervous system under involuntary control, which regulates breathing, heart muscle movements, hormone secretions, gastrointestinal movements etc.

Benzodiazepines A large family of minor tranquilizers with similar chemical structures and pharmacological properties.

Central nervous system The brain and spinal cord, abbreviated as CNS

Cholinergic system The parasympathetic nervous system (uses acetylcholine as neurotransmitter)

Cognition The process of thinking including judgment

Hallucinogens Drugs that affect perception of objects and time

Inhalants Volatile substances abused by inhalation

Neurotransmitters Chemical mediators used by nerves to transmit signals

Neurons Nerve fibres and endings

Opioids Drugs related to morphine, also known as opiates, including heroin, codeine, methadone, buprenorphine, meperidine, oxycodone, hydromorphone etc.

Periphery In this chapter, reference to parts of the body other than the CNS

Psychotropic Drugs capable of impairing psychomotor skills

Psychomotor skills Those skills that control hand eye coordination, lane control and reaction times

Receptor Specific recognition site that, when activated by a agonist, produces a physiological response

Sympathetic nerves Nerves utilizing norepinephrine as neurotransmitter

Parasympathetic nerves Nerves utilizing acetylcholine as neurotransmitter

Endnotes

1. These mediators include cyclic-AMP.

2. This includes both cocaine hydrochloride and the free base.

3. Psychoactive component of peyote cactus and certain other cactus species

4. Active component of the middle Eastern plant *Catha edulis*, better known as khat

5. Extract from the pollinated flowering tops of female plants

6. This drug is used to treat high blood pressure, angina, and other conditions.

7. Small pieces of patterned absorbent paper impregnated with LSD

8. There are at least three subtypes of opioid receptors, all of which produce different effects. For more details of these subtypes see a pharmacology textbook.

References

Adams, I.B., and Martin, B.R. (1996). "Cannabis: Pharmacology and toxicology in animals and humans." *Addiction*, 91, 1585-614.

Ashton, C.H. (1999). "Adverse effects of cannabis and cannabinoids." British Journal of *Anaesthesia*, 83, 637-49.

Baselt, R.C. (2001). *Drug Effects on Psychomotor Performance*. Foster City, CA.: Biochemical Publications.

Drummer, O.H., and Odell, M. (2001). *The Forensic Pharmacology of Drugs of Abuse*. London: Arnolds.

Goodman and Gilman's, *The Pharmacological Basis of Therapeutics*. (10th ed.) (2001). New York: Macmillan.

Katzung's Basic and Clinical Pharmacology (8th ed.). Stamford, CT: Appleton and Lange.

Mørland, J. (2000). "Driving under the influence of non-alcohol drugs." *Forensic Science Review*, 12, 79-105.

Robbe, H.W.J. (1994). *Influence of Marijuana on Driving*. Maastricht, The Netherlands. CIP-Data Koninklinik Bibliothek, The Hague.

Wills, S. (1998). "Side effects of cannabis use and abuse." In D.T. Brown (Ed.), *Cannabis: The Genus Cannabis*. London: Harwood Academic Press.

Chapter 3

Pharmacokinetics

Michael Corbett

Synopsis

3.1 Introduction

Kinetics is the scientific study of motion, and dynamics is the science of the forces associated with motion. Pharmacokinetics is the science of the movement of a chemical substance (Greek *pharmakon*) through a biological system such as a human body. Pharmacokinetics incorporates the processes of absorption, distribution, biotransformation (metabolism) and elimination of chemical substances.

Humans are exposed to a wide variety of chemical substances, by choice and by accident, such as food additives, environmental pollutants and therapeutic drugs.

A drug is broadly defined as any chemical agent that affects processes of the living (Benet, 1996). Absorption refers to the process of movement of a chemical substance, such as a drug, from a site of administration into the body's internal milieu. Distribution is the movement of the drug throughout the internal interstitial and cellular fluids and tissues. Biotransformation is the chemical alteration of an ingested drug into other related chemical substance(s), called metabolites, that are often more electrochemically polar and hydrophilic ("water loving") to facilitate their transfer from the body. Elimination, or excretion, is the transfer of drugs and metabolites out of the internal milieu into fluids such as urine, sweat, saliva and tears that are subsequently passed out of the body. Pharmacokinetics, therefore, is essentially the effect of the body upon chemical substances (Benet, 1996).

Pharmacokinetics is an important determinant of the pharmacological response of a drug substance. The concentrations of ingested drug substances and their metabolites can sometimes be related to the pharmacological response of the human or animal species at the time relevant biological specimens are sampled. Many times, however, the primary relevant specimen is not available, but a more convenient, related and appropriate specimen is available.

In the case of psychoactive drugs, that is, those that affect the mind, concentrations of the drugs and their metabolites in the brain and other tissues that contain the chemical receptors that such drugs seek, and physicochemically interact with, would be most relevant. The binding of drugs to brain tissues can be demonstrated using positron emission topography (PET) imagining methods along with labeled drugs and radiotracers in dedicated special clinical settings or in academic research laboratories (Fowler and Volkow, 1998). Specimens of brain tissue cannot be ethically obtained from living human subjects and, therefore, a substitute sample must be obtained from another location in the body. Blood is a biological fluid that is in physicochemical equilibrium with cerebral spinal fluid (CSF), which is in direct contact with brain tissue. In addition, blood specimens can be processed using liquid-liquid and solid-phase chemical extraction techniques that have been developed to selectively (cleanly) transfer and remove analytes (drug and metabolites) of interest into solvent extracts and leave or discard the undesired biological components that are not compatible with current analytical chromatography instruments and detectors.

The concentration-time (c(t)) profile of a drug and pharmacologically-active metabolites is important in elucidating the effect(s) of a drug upon a person involved in a medicolegal event. For a single acute ingestion of a fixed amount (dose) of drug, the first and early portion of the c(t) profile is known as the absorption phase in which the concentration of the drug is predominantly increasing. The second and later portion of the c(t) profile involves the concentration of the drug approaching and achieving a maximum concentration, and thereafter decreasing in concentration. This portion of the c(t) profile is the distribution phase in which drug concentration is governed by numerous equilibria that transfer the drug throughout fluid and tissue compartments of the body. The third and last phase of the c(t) profile is the elimination phase during which the concentration of drug is principally decreasing and will reach the baseline with zero concentration. The elimination phase is chiefly concerned with biotransformation (chemical alteration of a substance by a biological process) and excretion of the drug out of the accessioned site.

The pharmacokinetic processes of absorption, distribution, biotransformation and excretion occur simultaneously in each of the three phases of the drug's c(t) profile. In the absorption phase, the rate of the process of absorption exceeds the rates of its distribution and elimination and, therefore, the overall concentration of drug will increase. In the distribution phase, the rates of absorption and elimination are similar to each other and, therefore, the overall change in concentration of drug will be far less and may macroscopically appear not to change. Drugs, however, are always involved in a microscopic dynamic equilibrium within biological fluids and tissues.

A prolonged extension of the maximum concentration of a drug is sometimes described as a "plateau." During the plateau, the rate of the process of absorption is equal to the combined rates of the processes of distribution and elimination. In the elimination phase of the c(t) profile, the rate of elimination exceeds the rates of absorption and distribution, and governs the decrease in concentration of drug to the limit of no longer being found. Many drugs are chemically altered through biotransformation into metabolites that are more water-soluble than the administered drug. They then are more easily excreted into external fluids such as urine, sweat, saliva, tears, or through other means of departing from the body such as breath, hair, nails, skin or fecal matter.

The appearance of the c(t) profile will depend upon the nature of the biological specimen selected, and it may provide substantially different information depending upon the selected media. The most common specimens collected are blood and urine. The c(t) profile in blood may be related to the pharmacological effects whereas that in urine is indicative of an exposure.

There are many potential routes by which chemical substances enter the body, such as from the gastrointestinal tract (oral, sublingual or rectal administration), lungs (inhalation), skin (topical or subcutaneous injection), or other means of injections such as intramuscular, intrathecal or interperitoneal. The swallowing of a drug is a common human experience, but the process of absorption following oral ingestion is highly variable. The gastrointestinal tract is influenced by gastric/intestinal motility, the physicochemical environment of the stomach and small intestine, and the available surface areas and associated blood supplies (Rathbone and Hadgraft, 1991). Gastrointestinal diseases, systemic diseases with intestinal involvement, and gastrointestinal surgery can all modify the absorption process and increase variability in absorption beyond that of the general population (Milovic and Stein, 2000).

The rates of change in c(t) in the three pharmacokinetic phases may also be important determinants of the pharmacological response of the drug. In particular, the rapidly increasing rate of change of concentration of a psychoactive drug that affects the central nervous system (CNS), which incorporates the brain and spinal cord, may be of great importance to the overall effect of the drug (Van Dyke and Byck, 1982). For example, heroin is often rapidly introduced into the bloodstream of the human body by direct bolus intravenous injection after which it rapidly increases in concentration. The rapid increase is of paramount importance in producing the euphoric effects associated with the drug's abuse. In comparison, heroin is legally used in some countries for pain control for palliative care patients, especially those with overwhelming cancers. In these cases, heroin is administered slowly and continuously through an intravenous drip, and it does not produce euphoric effects as with bolus intravenous injection.

Heroin (diacetylmorphine) actually is a pharmacologically inactive chemical substance, but it rapidly evolves (half-life of three minutes) into metabolites of 6- and 3-monoacetylmorphine, and later morphine (half-life of 1.5 hours) and its gluronidated forms. These all combine to produce the psychoactive and physiological effects associated with heroin. There are substantial differences in concentrations of heroin, 6-MAM, and morphine between arterial and venous blood samples after intravenous administration (Rentsch et al., 2001). Heroin is completely metabolized to morphine. Thus, it may be described as a "prodrug," because its metabolites produce the known pharmacological effects.

In medicolegal applications, analytical methodologies concerning heroin focus on detection of the metabolites, rather than heroin, which is short-lived. For example, the rapidly formed metabolite of 6-monoacetylmorphine (6-MAM) is the focus of analytical confirmation methods for the urine samples (Smith et al., 2001) that are collected for employment-related drug testing, because 6-MAM is formed exclusively from heroin and, therefore, is a chemical marker of its use. In postmortem examinations, however, both 6-MAM and morphine (free and glucuronidated forms) are the focus of analytical confirmation methods for blood samples collected during medical examiner investigations.

Cocaine may be found in similar medicolegal applications as heroin. Introduction of cocaine by either direct intravenous injection or smoking gives rise to euphoric effects. Incidentally, smoking of heroin base also has been reported occasionally over the last decade, but that route of ingestion is far less frequent for heroin than for cocaine. Cocaine can be significantly absorbed from the gastrointestinal tract, but the rate of absorption is far slower than from intravenous or smoking routes, and that route of ingestion does not give rise to the euphoric effects found from the latter. Some countries approve the use of cocaine as a topical anesthetic for nasal and ocular surgery, and no euphoric effects are achieved with the low systemic concentrations achieved with topical application.

Absorption associated with intravenous injection of cocaine requires the use of the hydrochloride salt, which is far more water-soluble than the base form (crack or freebase depending upon the method of production) that is smoked. The base form of cocaine has a lower melting point than the hydrochloride salt form and does not decompose upon heating.

In medicolegal issues, the crucial variables are the immediacy, duration and magnitude of cocaine's effect, as well as the frequency and amount of cocaine used (Hatsukami and Fischman, 1996). The physiological and psychoactive effects of cocaine are somewhat similar for cocaine hydrochloride and cocaine base. Social and environmental factors such as the ease and convenience of smoking and avoidance of needle-transmitted disease may favor smoking cocaine base. In addition, some controlled studies on behavioral measures such as "good" drug effects and "liking" were higher by smoking than the intravenous route, although physiological changes were approximately equal at equivalent plasma concentrations of cocaine (Cone, 1995).

Cocaine is converted both in vivo (in the body) and in vitro (in solution) primarily to benzoylecgonine (BE), along with numerous other chemical substances. BE, which is considered to be pharmacologically inactive, is actually the target analyte in medicolegal applications such as employment-sponsored drug testing as a result of its chemical stability. In other medicolegal applications, such as medical examiner investigations, cocaine and BE would be analytically determined in cardiac and/or peripheral blood specimens (Corbett et al., 1994) along with other fluids (e.g., urine, stomach contents) and tissues (e.g., liver). Cocaine and some of its metabolites accumulate in the body as a result of chronic use resulting in a prolonged terminal elimination half-life (Jufer et al., 2000). Other metabolites such as cocaethylene and ecgonine methyl ester may also be analyzed in postmortem applications (Isenschmid et al., 1989).

Pharmacokinetics as a science combines (a) experimental data from the analytical toxicological determination of the concentration of a drug and its metabolites in various fluids and tissues with (b) mathematical models that incorporate numerical parameters. Experimental pharmacokinetic data from humans most often involves the analysis of blood or other fluids prepared from blood (such as serum or plasma). Studies also may use urine, saliva, sweat and hair specimens. Experimental data utilizing differing specimens will necessitate other numerical parameters in potentially differing mathematical models.

Many mathematical models with differing statistical analysis methods (Edler, 1999) may be applied in the science of pharmacokinetics, depending upon routes of administration of the drug and specimens of interest. The change in concentration of a drug with a constant amount of a drug per unit of time is known as zero-order kinetics. A change in concentration of drug with a constant fraction of a drug per unit of time is called first-order kinetics. These models aid in determination of the absorption, distribution, and especially the elimination phases of drugs. Pharmacokinetic numeric parameters such as bioavailability, clearance, volume of distribution and half-life have mathematical definitions, which may or may not have physiological meaning. Even the determination of the amount of drug that is available to the internal system within the body (bioavailability) is dependent upon an accurate determination of the purity and actual dose of the drug administered (Krstulovic and Lee, 1997).

The volume of distribution is the volume of fluid that would be required for all the drug in the body to be at the same concentration as drug in the blood (or plasma/serum). For drugs that are highly bound and sequestered in tissues, the numerical value of this volume parameter can greatly exceed the physiological volume of fluid within a human body. The numerical volume of distribution for a drug can be affected, however, by a myriad of physiological aspects such as the age of the human subject, gender, disease and body composition (Benet et al., 1996).

The rates of change in concentrations of drugs are often mathematically described in terms of the numerical concept of a half-life. In the elimination phase of the c(t) profile, the time for a drug to decrease in concentration by one-half (50 percent) is the half-life of the drug. The elimination phase of some drugs may be described by more than one half-life depending upon the portion of the elimination phase, early or late, and these differing half-lives are denoted with Greek letters such as alpha (α) for the first half-life, beta (β) for the second half-life, and others in the series.

Multiple half-lives are associated with mathematical modeling of distribution and elimination in two or more physiological compartments of the body. For example, the elimination of delta-9-tetrahydrocannabinol (Δ^9-THC), the principal pharmacologically active constituent of marijuana and hashish, may be described using two elimination half-lives. The longest half-life of Δ^9-THC is considered greater than 4.1 days, which is a combination of biotransformation, slow release of the drug from fat tissue, and enterohepatic recirculation (Huestis, 1999). However, after reaching maximum concentration from smoking and prior to the elimination phase, the concentration of Δ^9-THC in blood rapidly decreases due to its rapid distribution from fluid compartments into adipose (fat) tissue. That distribution phase also can be characterized by a half-life.

The half-life of a drug is perhaps the most easily understood pharmacokinetic parameter, and yet a calculation of half-life implies a linear, first-order, and time-invariant process. Although no drug perfectly obeys such assumptions, in practice the half-life often provides a valid approximation and useful quantitative information. It actually embodies other more exacting pharmacokinetic parameters such as clearance and volume of distribution.

The interpretation of pharmacokinetic parameters when there are multiple elimination phases is more challenging. Without information about dose history, such parameters actually are of little use. Statistical aspects of the estimation of half-life are often overlooked, but care must be taken to employ the half-life estimate appropriately in the context of dose history and clinically relevant pharmacodynamic end-points (Wright and Boddy, 2001).

For some drugs, it is possible to develop sophisticated mathematical models with several parameter values that describe the drugs' entire pharmacokinetic profile in a medium. These models are rarely used in court proceedings, however, especially those that involve viva voce evidence. The simpler concept of a half-life is more readily understood and accepted by a legal forum of nonscientists. Clarity of understanding generally is more relevant in such a forum than the ultimate in pure scientific and mathematical description.

In illustration, the nonlinear kinetics of ethanol elimination are well known, but existing nonlinear models appear to be inadequate for the usual medicolegal situation because of their complexity (Bruno et al., 1983). A mathematical model known as Michaelis-Menten kinetics globally describes the elimination phase of ethanol, but it is often approximated in medicolegal applications by using a rate of elimination independent of concentration (zero-order model). Ethanol elimination can be described overall by a two-compartment model that predicts a near constant elimination rate for blood ethanol concentrations (BACs) above 15 mg/dL. At those alcohol levels, complete saturation of some hepatic enzymes occurs (Levitt and Levitt, 1998). Some BAC calculations for medicolegal purposes assume ranges in the rates of elimination (Jones, 1993), whereas for other court proceedings the experimental determination of an individual's rate of elimination may be required.

Pharmacokinetics differs between different populations. For example, pharmacokinetics is very different in children, compared to adults, especially during the first year of life when body size, composition and organ function change rapidly (Yaffe, 2000, Kearns and Reid, 1989). The impact of developmental physiology in infants and children is different than in neonates. Comparing infants and children with neonates and young adults, the most notable drug disposition differences derive from alterations in body water and serum protein composition and the affinity or capacity for hepatic biotransformation of xenobiotics, or renal clearance (Seyffart, 1991).

The treatment of maternal diseases during pregnancy requires knowledge of the pharmacokinetics of drugs in pregnancy. Significant changes occur during pregnancy, as well as during the different phases of a woman's life cycle (Berg, 1997, Ritrovato and Dinella, 1995). The transfer of drugs from the mother to the fetus is an important consideration in terms of possible harm for the mother or the child, as well as therapeutic effects. This issue has been sparsely investigated for the first trimester of pregnancy when it is possible that maternal physiology affects drug pharmacokinetics in clinically relevant ways. For example, it is possible that a unique multicompartmental structure of the maternal-placental-fetal unity can trap drugs in the fetus. Methodological, ethical and legal problems make it difficult to acquire data concerning these issues, but the data are needed in order to prevent adverse and toxic effects both in the pregnant woman and in the fetus, and to attempt a therapy of fetus diseases in intrauterine life (Minora et al., 1990).

In adults, most physiological functions decline with increasing age, and there are substantial differences between biological and chronological ages. Pathologic conditions increase with advancing age (Ritschel, 1988).

A search of scientific and medical abstracts for pharmacokinetic(s) indexed by EMBASE indicated over one-quarter million citations involving pharmacokinetic(s) for the period since 1980. A similar search of MEDLINE located 130,000 citations. Clearly, the scientific and medical literature of pharmacokinetics is enormous. However, when additional literature search parameters included "forensic(s)" or "legal," fewer than 250 citations were located, many of which have little, if any, practical significance to legal aspects of the pharmacokinetics of drugs. Yet, the time-profile of the concentration of drugs and their metabolites indeed can have a profound influence upon the effect of a drug upon a person(s) (pharmacodynamics) and their involvement in matters that find their way into the judiciary and other regulatory forums.

Medical-legal drug issues often have roots within the field of (i) clinical therapeutics, which incorporates clinical pharmacokinetics. Two additional areas are (ii) human performance and (iii) employment, which may involve higher concentrations of drugs and other chemical substances than the concentrations commonly encountered in clinical therapeutics. Practices at (iv) poison control centers and hospital emergency departments, or (v) postmortem investigations conducted within medical examiner or coroner systems of investigations are also relevant.

Medical and scientific judgment in (i) may impact on the dose regimen prescribed for a patient, possibly with concern for (ii) or (iii), whereas judgments in (iv) may impact upon the course of emergency medical treatment of a patient. Pharmacokinetic considerations in (v) are concerned with formulating the medical decision as to manner and cause of a drug-related death.

Any one of the above areas (i through v) could easily generate a treatise. This chapter must however, be limited to some of the current aspects of the medicolegal applications of the five areas.

3.2 Clinical Therapeutics—Pharmacokinetics

Clinical pharmacokinetics as contained within the medical practice of clinical therapeutics may have several objectives depending upon the practice. It may be incorporated into the development of a drug, during which its study derives information about concentrations of drugs and metabolites in groups of human test subjects. Clinical pharmacokinetics may also be utilized in measuring concentrations of drugs in patients treated with legally approved applications of drugs to determine and confirm an effective dose regimen, or to adjust dosing to achieve an effective or optimal concentration of drug and metabolites. This latter practice, commonly described as therapeutic drug monitoring (TDM), can accumulate a vast amount of data from the actual treatment of patients with a diagnosed condition or disease.

Pharmacokinetic parameters such as half-life, volume of distribution, clearance and bioavailability are derived from the concentrations of analytes assayed in the biological samples collected at specified points in time. The capability of toxicologists and chemists to develop sensitive and specific analytical methods for the assay of lower concentrations of drugs and the ability to detect additional metabolites has contributed to advances in pharmacokinetics and its applications (Peng and Chiou, 1990).

Although current drug discovery and development practices are technologically sophisticated and highly efficient, the failure rate of compounds in both pre-clinical and clinical development is high (Spence, 1999). Only one in ten new chemical entities will successfully progress to the clinic. After drug discovery, the first phase of development involves pharmacokinetic investigations in animal and in-vitro testing. This testing plays a central part in the benefit/risk evaluation of new drugs (Kuhlmann, 1997).

Pharmacogenomics, the study of the association between genetics and drug response, is a rapidly evolving field (Norton, 2001). The molecular basis is associated with variations in genes responsible for absorption and metabolism of some drugs (March, 2000). Recent advances in combinatorial chemistry and pharmacogenomics have increased the number of early drug candidates by several orders of magnitude, and the role of pharmacokinetic studies in supporting drug discovery efforts is increasing (Sinko, 1999). Early knowledge of whether a polymorphic pathway is involved in drug metabolism and effects and its clinical relevance leads to a reduction of time and costs in new drug development (Zuhlsdorf, 1998).

In its later phases, drug development involves the integraton of pharmacokinetic modeling and testing in humans. This phase plays an important role in regulatory decision-making that affects the public and industry (Gobburu and Marroum, 2001). Computational methods are available to determine pharmacokinetic model parameters, but decisions about which methods to use have to be made in accordance with the goal of the drug discovery organization, the timeline for the project goals, and budgetary constraints (Podlogar et al., 2001, Gieschke and Steimer, 2001, Gabrielesson and Weiner, 1999). Some methods are particularly applicable to the production environment or a pharmaceutical project team where early pharmacokinetic information is sought to assist in drug design decisions and prioritization. In general, the pharmaceutical industry is committed to market safer drugs with fewer side effects and predictable pharmacokinetic properties (McGinnity and Riley, 2001).

After regulatory approvals, additional scientific and medical studies of human subjects may be undertaken with human subjects with differing physiological characteristics (e.g., age, sex, hepatic or renal function, disease states, nutrition/diet status, physical activity, drug interactions, as well as environmental factors (e.g., smoking)). Higher safety requirements have been suggested for human subjects involved in these clinical pharmacokinetic studies (Svensson, 1989). There is a need for TDM with patients to provide objective measures of drug concentrations in patients' blood to assist in optimizing therapeutic doses. Case reports may be relevant to medicolegal applications when published literature on a specific point of interest is lacking.

The measurement of pharmacokinetic parameters in human subjects almost always involves relatively small numbers of subjects (e.g., fewer than fifty). Study protocols actually may involve only five to twenty human subjects, from whom several dozen to hundreds of biological specimens are collected for drug concentration determinations. The specimens analyzed are usually plasma or serum, not whole blood. Therefore the use of experimental data from clinical studies for medicolegal applications involving other specimens, such as blood, requires additional information about the partitioning of the drug and its metabolites between serum or plasma and blood cells.

The study of the concentration ratio of drug and metabolites in plasma or serum to whole blood is often neglected. Despite the fact that medicolegal applications for ethanol have existed for decades, this issue was only recently addressed with a large number of subjects. A 1996 study examined the partitioning of ethanol between serum and red blood cells in over 200 human subjects (Charlebois et al., 1996). Previous studies of ethanol had been performed with the typically small numbers (five to twenty) of human subjects.

The number of human subjects included in clinical pharmacokinetic studies is far less than found in pre-market and post-market studies of a drug's effects, which may involve hundreds to tens of thousands of subjects. Altered drug response (e.g., therapeutic inefficacy) and pharmacological toxicity are frequently found in clinical applications of drugs, in part due to the differing activities of metabolic enzymes that may act as substrate inhibitors or inducers (Zuhlsdorf, 1998).

Many adverse drug-drug interactions that are pharmacokinetic in origin can be rationalized as alterations of cytochrome P450-catalyzed reactions (Clarke and Jones, 2002, Wrighton et al., 1996). As an example, warfarin is a long-standing, widely used anticoagulant that requires careful clinical management to balance the risks of over-anticoagulation and bleeding with those of underanticoagulation and clotting. Warfarin has a narrow therapeutic index and small changes in systemic concentration can lead to significant variation in pharmacodynamic response. Clinical pharmacokinetic studies are ongoing, as evidenced by the following synopsis of recent studies.

Higashi et al. (2002) found that mean maintenance doses of warfarin varied significantly among six genotype groups in a study of two hundred patients receiving long-term therapy, and that CYP2C9*2 and CYP2C9*3 polymorphisms are associated with an increased risk of over-anticoagulation and bleeding events among patients in a clinical practice. Their results suggest that screening for CYP2C9 variants may allow clinicians to develop dosing protocols to reduce the risk of adverse drug reactions (ADR) in patients receiving warfarin.

Hawk et al. (2002) followed two patients who were initially stable with warfarin anticoagulation and found that they developed elevated international normalized ratios (INR) that may be related to decreased metabolism of warfarin during stress. Lee and Thrasher (2001) reported on a patient receiving concomitant warfarin and rifampin to treat an intraventricular thrombus and a mycobacterial infection. A 233 percent increase in warfarin dose over four months was insufficient to attain a therapeutic INR during long-term rifampin therapy. After discontinuation of rifampin, a gradual 70 percent reduction in dose of warfarin over four to five weeks was required to maintain a therapeutic INR. Clearly, large changes in warfarin doses are required for therapy that includes concomitant use of rifampin.

Hope and Havrda (2001) presented two cases that demonstrate the potential for fluctuations in the INR when switching between generic and brand sources of warfarin while all other variables were kept consistent. Furthermore, management of warfarin drug interactions can be complicated by the lack of information about interactions with new drugs and herbal medicines (Wittkowsky, 2001).

In addition to physiological and medication conditions, there are additional analytical complexities associated with warfarin containing an asymmetric carbon atom. Clinically available warfarin preparations consist of a racemic mixture of equal amounts of two distinct S and R isomers, the former being four times more potent as an anticoagulant and more susceptible to drug interactions. The S isomer of warfarin has a half-life that is shorter than the R-isomer (Palareti and Legnani, 1996). Pharmacokinetic parameters can change with the stereoisomer form, as evidenced with the cardiac medication, metoprolol, where the S-isomer also has a shorter half-life than the R-isomer, but where female subjects were found to have greater drug exposure than males (Luzier et al., 1999). Much of the pharmacokinetics of stereoisomers has yet to be determined, which is surprising given that approximately one in four therapeutic agents are marketed as racemic mixtures of stereoisomers (Hutt and Tan, 1996).

These recent studies on warfarin affect the definition of an acceptable clinical standard of care that might have judicial consequences should an adverse drug reaction result in a loss or human death. The issue would be whether it could be established that the adverse reaction involved an element identified in these studies.

Pharmacokinetic approaches to clinical dosing have also been proposed for other drugs, such as anticancer agents, for which it has been reported that pharmacokinetically-guided administration yields lower interpatient variation in pharmacokinetic parameters (Van den Bongard et al., 2000). Traditional methods for the dose calculation of such agents are based upon body surface area, and given that oral bioavailability of many anticancer drugs is poor and highly variable (Schellens et al., 2000), a pharmacokinetic approach may be better able to account for interpatient variability. Pharmacokinetic tailoring, as a tool to ascertain analgesic and other effects of opioids at steady state, has also been applied to infusions of morphine and fentanyl (Hill et al., 1990).

Because the cytotoxicity of more than thirty anticancer drugs varies by more than 50 percent as a function of dosing time along the twenty-four-hour time scale, utilization of chemotherapy at the least toxic time of day usually achieves best antitumor efficacy in experimental models (Levi, 1999). In practice, this scheduling can be accomplished by using a computer-programmed multi-reservoir pump for drug delivery. The influence of circadian rhythms on pharmacokinetics is also an important consideration for increasing the effectiveness of drug therapy in the treatment of asthma (D'Alonzo et al., 1999).

One of the main objectives of population studies during drug development is to specify the population distributions of pharmacokinetic parameters. Statistical confidence intervals for population parameters are generally estimated by assuming asymptotic normality, which is a large-sample property that holds only if sample sizes are large enough. In actual clinical trials, sample sizes are significantly limited and, therefore, other statistical approaches may be more appropriate for the determination of population parameters (Yafune and Ishiguro, 1999).

Through the accumulation of clinical pharmacokinetic data from many small-scale studies, more reliable conclusions may evolve, and the significance of other pharmacokinetic aspects may become apparent. For example, in a recent extensive review of 199 studies involving drug-drug interactions between oral contraceptives and antibiotics (Dickinson et al., 2001), pooled results from relatively small samples showed that the oral antibiotic rifampin had a significant pharmacokinetic effect on the contraceptive components of ethinyl estadiol, levonorgestrel and norethindrone that can result in ovulation and pregnancy. Pharmacokinetic studies of other antibiotics have not shown any systematic interaction between antibiotic concentrations and oral contraceptive steroids, although individual patients do show large decreases in the plasma concentrations of ethinyl estadiol when they take other antibiotics, notably tetracycline and penicillin derivatives. Clearly, the occurrence of pregnancy in a woman who is taking oral contraceptives and then is prescribed rifampin could become a judicial issue, given the findings of this recent review.

Population pharmacokinetics has evolved from a discipline that was primarily applied to TDM to one that plays a significant role in clinical pharmacology and drug development (Williams and Ette, 2000). The US Food and Drug Administration recently issued a *Guidance for Industry Population Pharmacokinetics* to assist with mapping responses, explaining subgroup differences, developing and evaluating competing dose administration strategies, and as an aid in designing future studies (Sun et al., 1999).

In yet other areas within clinical therapy, medical practitioners should consider the potential harm to patients who may feign an illness, especially in the emergency room, in order to receive prescriptions for opioids, benzodiazepines, or stimulants for abuse (Withers, 2001). Deception is a common behavior of the addicted patient, and the ingestion of newly prescribed drugs may adversely interact pharmacokinetically or pharmacodynamically with those already in the patient's system, or result in additional drug-seeking behaviors that can lead to loss, injury or deaths. Drug abusers select chemical substances with particular pharmacokinetic properties such as rapid absorption, rapid entry in the central nervous system, high bioavailability, short half-life, small volume of distribution, and high free drug clearance. These properties predict a high potential for harmful use, because they increase positive reinforcement (Quinn et al., 1997). Rapid absorption and high lipid solubility are the most important factors contributing to early drug concentrations in the brain, and those with rapid elimination rates are associated with more self-administration and with early emergence of withdrawal symptoms (Farre and Cami, 1991). Objective analytical drug testing is required, especially with psychiatric outpatients, to establish the potential for a drug-drug interaction (Shearer et al., 1998). Interpretation of the drug test results requires knowledge of the performance characteristics of the analytical method, the route of administration, and the pharmacokinetics of the drug. In addition, physicians should consider pharmacokinetic factors such as the fact that benzodiazepines with longer half-lives are least likely to result in dependence (Van Valkenburg and Akiskal, 1999).

The clinical pharmacokinetics of different forms of pharmaceutical preparations may also be very important. For example, diltiazem, a cardiac antihypertensive medication, is available as regular, slow release and controlled-dose formulations, and each provides a very different concentration-time profile. The formulation of controlled-release preparations is a specialty within pharmaceutical research, and such formulations are designed to produce a slow and uniform absorption of drug. "Biorelevant dissolution" refers to a product's in vitro dissolution characteristics and pharmacokinetic parameters as described with pharmacokinetic modeling (Leeson et al., 1985).In practice, however, given significant interpatient variability in absorption, it is possible that the absorption profile may not be as long as expected. In fact, it may proceed quickly resulting in "dose dumping" that can result in toxicity when the total dose of drug is released within a much shorter time than expected. Alternatively, there has been a demand for the design of reliable fast-melting tablets, particularly for children and the elderly who have difficulty swallowing tablets and capsules (Dobetti, 2000). Again, the form of the preparation could result in very different absorption and distribution characteristics. A further consideration may be the physicochemical interactions between the medicine in a pharmaceutical preparation and the excipients that improve the characteristics of the pharmaceutical formulation (Kalinkova, 1999).

A controversial issue surrounding the approval of generic formulations is the reliance on the bioavailability data for the drug. Bioequivalence does not necessarily translate into therapeutic equivalence. Rigorous rules exist only for the approval of brand-name medications. With generic formulations, some patients may not receive adequate amounts of medication, while others may receive toxic doses. There are scientific, economic, social, and legal issues involved in generic drug use with particular emphasis on the psychotropic drugs (Diamond and Albrecht, 1987).

Some traditional drugs for TDM are digoxin, phenytoin (Valodia et al., 1999), carbamazepine (Calvo and Benitez, 1996), valproate (Hernandez-Fustes et al., 1999) and theophylline. As a result of a study of TDM involving a consortium of nine epilepsy clinics, doses were increased in 31.9 percent of patients and were reduced in 15.1 percent (Valodia et al., 1999). Subtherapeutic serum levels of carbamazepine and valproate were detected in 35 percent of sixty-six epileptic outpatients. Furthermore, there is large inter- and intra-individual variability in serum drug concentrations, and a single measurement does not reflect the reality of carbamazepine and valproic acid clinical kinetics. Three samples, at two, four and six hours after the last dose, are required to estimate a clinically useful pharmacokinetic profile (Hernandez-Fustes et al., 1999).

Asthma is a nocturnal disease in as many as 75 percent of those afflicted. Nonetheless, treatment typically relies on homeostatic considerations and on long-acting bronchodilator and other therapies to ensure near-constant levels of medication over twenty-four hours. In the clinical therapy of asthmatic children, it can be important to monitor other nonmedicinal substances. Knight et al. (1998) in a study of seventy-eight asthmatic children and eighty-six control children, who were all passively exposed to cigarette smoke, compared the manner in which their bodies handled nicotine. Parents of asthmatic children tended to report a lower daily number of cigarettes (7.4 versus 11.2, $p = 0.14$), which agreed with the trend of urinary cotinine corrected for creatinine (47 ng/mg versus 63 ng/mg). In comparison to the controls, the children with asthma had higher systemic nicotine, possibly due to a lower clearance rate. This may be evidence of pharmacokinetic predisposition to environmental tobacco smoke as an etiological factor in pediatric asthma.

In reviewing clinical therapy studies, it is evident that many factors can affect derived clinical pharmacokinetics and hence potential drug response, as a result of the unique physiology of the subject, presence of other drugs, the genetics of enzyme systems, chronobiology, stage of human growth and development, and the influence of the external environment. In clinical practice, the application of pharmacokinetics data obtained from studies of healthy subjects to patients, who have the condition or disease for which the drug is intended, may not be appropriate. Patients with the medical condition may respond differently than healthy young test subjects.

Pharmacokinetic modeling of the urinary excretion of methadone and EDDP, its primary metabolite, has been suggested for drug abusing individuals who are in a methadone maintenance program. The purpose would be to clearly establish compliance rather than contending with the uncertainty resulting from the inter-patient differences in measured concentrations (George and Braithwaite, 1999). For example, the steady-state plasma concentration of methadone in twenty long-term opiate addicts in a closed metabolic ward was found to range from 65 to 630 ng/mL, peak plasma concentrations ranged from 124 to 1255 ng/mL, and elimination half-lives ranged from 0.013 to 0.053/hr (de Vos et al., 1995).

It is a medicolegal requirement that pharmacokinetic information appear on pharmaceutical product labels, or package inserts, and in the "manual" for the safe and effective use of a drug (Marroum and Gobburu, 2002). Package inserts for older drugs should be updated to reflect new data and the proper dosage regimen, thereby enabling prescribers to optimize drug therapy and minimize possible adverse drug reactions. Failure to provide accurate or updated information could result in matters for the judiciary.

Reliance solely on pharmacokinetic calculations that have been determined by using pharmacokinetic software without associated therapeutic drug monitoring for the individual patient may also be fertile ground for a legal action. The liability associated with the software potentially extends to the physician, pharmacist, designer, manufacturer and seller of software. The programmer and manufacturer are responsible for verifying the program does what it purports to do, but the user must exercise due care in identifying any program limitations that might influence the accuracy of a calculation (Schwartz and Fink III, 1989).

In summary, it is evident that pharmacokinetic data obtained with selected groups of human test subjects in one study, or a combination of studies, cannot be extended to provide a 100 percent definitive conclusion about the responses of all people. Most importantly, the data may not support a conclusion about the actual person who is the focus of a judicial case. Informed expert opinions, however, based upon available and reproducible peer-reviewed studies can assist the judicial forum to arrive at a reasonable conclusion based on the state of knowledge from clinical therapeutics.

3.3 Human Performance Pharmacokinetics

Pharmacokinetics in medicolegal applications involving human performance are as diverse as those of clinical therapeutics. They range from the effects of drugs on the ability of people to perform exercises up to matters in the criminal justice system such as driving, sexual assaults and homicides.

Drug effects on exercise and sports performance has garnered much interest, and yet little is known about how the pharmacokinetics of a drug is influenced by exercise, application of physical agents, or massage (Sahin and Yakut, 2000). Such interventions may produce hemodynamic and physiological changes that can potentially alter drug disposition within the body. In general, exercise decreases absorption after oral administration, but increases it after intramuscular and subcutaneous administrations as the result of an increase blood flow to muscle tissue (Somani and Kamimori, 1996). Exercise can change the volume of distribution of some drugs. For example, it was increased by 25 percent for diazepam and decreased by 36 percent for caffeine. Acute exercise can decrease the blood flow to the liver and, therefore, increase the concentration of drugs such as morphine that have a high first pass effect. Exercise is expected to increase hepatic and renal elimination of capacity-limited drugs such as phenytoin and clonazepam but to decrease elimination of flow-limited drugs such as cocaine and diphenhydramine.

Caffeine is a common substance in the diets of many athletes, and it appears in such new products as energy drinks, sport gels, alcoholic beverages and diet aids. It increases speed and/or power output in simulated race conditions with durations ranging from 1 minute to 2 hours. The ingestion of caffeine as coffee appears to be ineffective compared to doping with pure caffeine. The pharmacokinetics of caffeine is similar for male and female athletes and is not altered by either exercise or dehydration. It may assist exercise performance, in part, by creating a more favorable intracellular ionic environment in active muscle that could facilitate force production by each motor unit (Graham, 2001).

A recent study of the effect of physical training on sulfamethazine, an antibiotic, found that 48 percent of a large subgroup of athletes ultra rapidly biotransformed sulfamethazine by acetylation, while the remaining 23 percent and 29 percent were rapid and slow acetylators. In contrast, an untrained control group had only a bimodal distribution of acetylators with 42 percent being rapid and 58 percent being slow (Abzalov et al., 2001). The ultra rapid acetylation phenotype was associated with the induction of Nacetyltransferase by adaptation to physical exercise.

A study with elderly subjects of the effects of physical exercise on antipyrine clearance found that salivary clearance was significantly increased by 17 percent and salivary half-life was reduced by 18 percent, but there were no significant changes in renal clearance (Mauriz et al., 2000). Antipyrine is a chemical test marker for oxidative metabolism.

Recent research reported that exercise performance was not influenced by the ingestion of fluoxetine (Meeusen et al., 2001) in healthy subjects. Pharmacokinetics of levodopa in parkinsonian patients was not altered by exercise (Reuter et al., 2000), or of digoxin in either young or old patients (Jessup et al., 2000).

The possible use of drugs to improve the performance of daily tasks has been investigated for some drugs. For example, Adrafinil is used primarily as a vigilance-enhancing drug, and clinical studies strongly indicate that it improves attention and memory, as well as other deficits that result from decreased vigilance. Adrafinil has two metabolites, modafinil and CR 40476, but little is known about the latter. Adrafinil and modafinil have very similar pharmacological effects, and the behavioral effects of adrafinil are closely tied to the pharmacokinetics of modafinil. One possible suggested use stemming from its ability to improve performance of psychometric tests and motor function is to treat "medically, neurologically, and psychiatrically healthy persons over fifty years of age who have experienced a gradual decline in the ability to perform certain tasks of daily life dependent on memory" (Milgram et al., 1999). It is possible that psychoactive drugs could be used to induce states that would influence a person's testimony when the drugs act through sedation, disinhibition, paradoxical reactions and alterations in memory (Lader, 1999).

Human performance issues in the criminal justice system often are related to the availability and use of widely available psychoactive drugs. Ethanol, marijuana and cocaine have been used for millennia and continue to be over-represented in emergency room statistics. Recent developments in production of the latter two have yielded potent products such as crack and hashish resin.

Ethanol is ubiquitous throughout society and is the drug that is most often analyzed in biological specimens in medicolegal applications (Garriott, 1996). Studies of ethanol as it relates to driving, include simple or complex isolated tasks in the laboratory, computer-based driving simulators, operation of actual motor vehicles in closed and open course driving courses, and large-scale epidemiological studies of motor vehicle crashes. The latter include control groups of drivers whose exposure has been similar to that of the crash drivers. No other drug has been studied (Baselt, 2001), or is likely to be studied, as extensively as ethanol. One reason for many studies of alcohol is its wide use throughout society, but another reason is the early development of reliable non-invasive breath-sampling instruments for alcohol measurement.

Forensic issues are often concerned with the pharmacokinetics of alcohol. Specimens of breath, blood or urine are nearly always collected some time after an incident. The subsequent calculation of the BAC at the time of the incident, called "retrograde extrapolation," is based on the measured concentration of alcohol in the obtained specimen. This is a frequently performed pharmacokinetic calculation. The opinion offered by the forensic toxicological expert then is based upon information and assumptions about the phase of the concentration profile and rates of elimination of alcohol from the blood. In one study of the rate of ethanol disappearance, the slowest rate was 9 mg/dL/hr in a healthy male after an overnight fast. The fastest rate was 36 mg/dL/hr in a male chronic alcoholic during detoxification (Jones, 1993). This fourfold difference must be considered when the pharmacokinetics of ethanol becomes an issue in judicial proceedings. An experimental reconstruction of the dosing scenario can, amongst other factors, determine the rate of elimination with greater precision that without the benefit of having such specific experimental test data. Testimony about the BAC typically is related to per se legal limits and to knowledge about alcohol impairment of the ability to operate a motor vehicle.

Technological aspects of breath alcohol testing have also been subjected to pharmacokinetic modeling. For example, oral cavity concentrations of ethanol after the consumption of alcoholic beverages are eliminated according to a model with a single term decaying exponential. Alcohol measurements do not accurately reflect BAC when breath specimens are collected within fifteen minutes after alcohol consumption (Gullberg 1992).

The most frequent analytical toxicological measurements in sexual assault and homicide cases are for alcohol. Again, a pharmacokinetic calculation of BAC at a previous time is often performed for the court, and the concentration may then be opined upon as to how it relates to human performance of either the accused or a complainant. In matters related to either bolus (Ditmar and Dorian, 1987) or chronic large ingestions (Zink and Reinhardt, 1984) of alcohol (e.g., >2.5 g/ kg body weight), appropriate pharmacokinetic models are required to provide a reliable opinion and estimate of ensuing blood alcohol concentrations.

Analyses for THC and related metabolites in biological fluids are also frequently performed in driving, sexual assaults and homicides cases. As a result of pharmacokinetic and chemical differences between marijuana and ethanol, the model developed for ethanol cannot be used as a model for relating drug concentrations to effects for marijuana. The patterns of distribution to and elimination from active sites of ethanol and THC are very different. Pharmacokinetic models that account for the dispositional differences (Huestis et al., 1992) of THC will be more successful in defining blood concentrations that are better associated with the psychoactive effects of THC (Huestis, 1999).

The simultaneous use of cocaine and alcohol produces both a pharmacodynamic and pharmacokinetic interaction in the biosynthesis of a newly formed active metabolite, cocaethylene. The metabolite then is biotransformed along the same pathway as cocaine, but it has a longer half-life. The longer elimination half-life of cocaethylene is believed to explain the longer-lasting effects of the alcohol-cocaine combination (Cami et al., 1998).

Pharmacokinetic data are important in assessing the effects of drugs other than alcohol upon the ability to operate motor vehicles and machinery (Baselt, 2001). Studies of the effects of drugs (legal and illicit) on psychomotor performance require the selection of appropriate doses and formulations and a consideration of the c(t) profiles. Many studies of psychomotor performance, unfortunately, have not collected c(t) profile data for the subjects being studied, relying instead on psychomotor tests as a function of dose. Consultations between psychopharmacologists and forensic toxicologists are attempting to address this gap in collection of c (t) data.

Per se limits for driving have been established for some drugs in some European Union countries, for example in Germany. Such concentration limits have been derived from analytical measurements in isolation without consideration of the evidence of impairment associated with the drug. Not all drugs and driving issues are related to performance decrements. A recently developed, slow-release caffeine formulation has been suggested as a countermeasure for the drowsiness induced by partial sleep deprivation. It reportedly decreased lane drifting as measured by a 45 minute driving task on a simulator (De Valck and Cluydts, 2001).

Over the past decade, there has been a dramatic increase in mass media reports about sexual assault victims who described being "knocked out" or incapacitated by drugs (LeBeau and Mozayani, 2001), and some case reports have appeared in forensic journals (Stark and Wells, 1999). Alcohol is the drug used most often in sexual assaults. Other drugs are likely to become an issue more frequently in judicial matters as the ability to detect drugs increases and more pharmacokinetic information about drug doses becomes available. From the perspective of complainants, the purpose of drugs in sexual assaults is (a) to decrease the ability of the complainants to physically and mentally protect themselves from the accused, (b) to render the complainants unconscious, thereby chemically removing their physical and mental defenses against the accused, and/or (c) to alter their state of consciousness for the purpose of impairing or eliminating memory of the sexual assault. From the perspective of the accused, pharmacokinetics may be considered in the choice of drug. A drug with a short half-life might be chosen, for example, specifically because it would enable the perpetrator to elude a criminal investigation.

3.4 Employment-Related Pharmacokinetics

Workers are exposed to a wide variety of chemical substances, whether by accident or by choice. They may be suddenly and unexpectedly exposed to the release of chemicals that previously had been isolated and contained, or they may be chronically exposed to environmental pollutants during the course of their duties at the workplace. Workers may also be under the active care of a physician with treatment that requires their use of therapeutic drugs. They also may choose to use or abuse alcohol and psychoactive illicit drugs in a manner that is incompatible with safety and performance at the workplace, as well as with corporate profile and image.

The exposure of workers to chemical substances in the workplace can involve several disciplines, including occupational/industrial medicine, industrial toxicology, regulatory toxicology, industrial hygiene, and/or occupational health and safety. Because information about chemical exposure is most often based upon animal studies, physiologically based pharmacokinetic models (PBPK) (Thrall et al., 2000) must be used to estimate parameter values for humans under exposure conditions. However, human subject differences, which can influence response to workplace toxicants, should be delineated when setting regulatory standards to protect workers from potentially hazardous workplace environments. Anatomical and physiological parameters include body composition (surface area, volumes of blood, organ and tissues), metabolism, and organ structure and function (cardiovascular, pulmonary, gastrointestinal and renal) (Silvaggio and Mattison, 1994).

Information from human subjects may be available from those that participate in a predesigned study prior to exposure. For example, the development of protection respirators were based upon actual dosing of human subjects with Freon-113 in a closed chamber, followed by end-exhaled breath sampling from the human subjects, pharmacokinetic modeling, and test subject characterization (Coffey et al., 1998).

The volatility and lipophilicity of organic solvents are distinct from other chemical substances and constitute a characteristic pharmacokinetic feature (Sato and Nakajima, 1987). PBPK modeling may indicate that concern is merited, but the acquisition of experimental data may be very difficult, if not impossible. For example, PBPK modeling indicates that infants can be exposed to elevated levels of perchloroethylene, a dry-cleaning solvent, through breast milk due to their mother's inhalation at the workplace (Schreiber, 1993). The substantiation of estimated large increases in cancer risks for infants under certain exposure scenarios requires analytical data, but it is hard to conceive of knowledgeable mothers who would be willing to participate in such an experimental study.

Very recent pharmacokinetic studies using urine specimens have assessed the exposure of workers to butylbenzyl phthalate, a volatile silicone found in commercial and consumer products (Martens and Martens,

2002), ethylbenzene, a solvent used in paints and the metal industry (Jang et al., 2001), and N, N-dimethylformamide, a solvent used in the polyacrylic fibre industry (Kafferlein et al., 2000). Others involved acetone, a solvent used in the microelectronics fabrication industry (Hallock et al., 1993), styrene, a solvent used in polyester manufacturing (Guillemin et al., 1982), mercury, which is used in chloralkali manufacturing (Mattiussi et al., 1982), and methylene chloride, which is used in industry and commerce (DiVencenzo and Kaplan, 1981).

Sparse and heterogeneous data can be obtained from isolated case reports of individuals who sustained acute injury or death, or developed adverse medical conditions that resulted in premature death. Pharmacokinetically based risk assessments have been developed for the assessment of workplace exposure to benzene, which has been linked to occupational lifetime cancer risk estimates. The estimates have been confirmed by epidemiological data showing 10 to 175 leukemia cases per 1000 workers (Beliles and Totman, 1989). Acute experimental human exposure has ascertained that there are three or four distinct compartments retaining benzene, and yet pharmacokinetic modeling of the system can provide reasonably accurate accounts of the measurement of conjugated phenol, a principal metabolite of benzene, determined from biological monitoring (Sherwood, 1988).

Even though the risk associated with workers' exposure to chemicals may be perceived as cause for acute concerns, the overall cost of monitoring may be unwanted. Monitoring for the contamination of medical facilities with nitrous oxide is obligatory in Germany, and the additional cost of analytical monitoring may serve as an incentive to use other forms of anesthesia (Baum et al., 2000). Environmental tobacco smoke (ETS) has been determined by U.S. environmental and occupational health authorities to be a human carcinogen. It is possible to validate estimates for exposure to ETS by pharmacokinetic modeling (Repace and Lowrey, 1993) using cotinine, a metabolite of nicotine, which can be readily measured in plasma and urine. This and other studies have led to the establishment of workplace polices providing "smoke free" environments.

Pharmacokinetic data may also be available for populations that have been occupationally or otherwise exposed to chemical substances such as pesticides. Biological monitoring that evaluates people in agricultural and industrial environments who have been exposed accidentally or by voluntary contact serves to establish pharmacokinetic information (Aprea et al., 2001).

Each year, physicians in the United States write more than 1.5 billion prescriptions for their patients. Some of the medicines will be taken by people while they are at work. Both the therapeutic and adverse consequences of such drug use potentially may compromise safety in the workplace. Furthermore, the conditions of the job or work environment may adversely alter the expected pharmacokinetics of some agents. The effects of drugs on job skills and the persistence of such effects are particularly important for hypnotics and other psychoactive medications. Pharmacokinetic factors are an important consideration that determines the persistence of action of these drugs (Nicholson, 1990).

The focus of employment-sponsored drug testing, however, is not on performance issues. Instead, drug-testing programs are designed to deter the use of selected drugs/drug classes (amphetamines, cocaine, opioids, phencyclidine and cannabinoids). This is evident when one considers that not all employees are tested all the time at work to determine "fitness for duty." Typically, only five to twenty-five percent of employees are tested on a random basis on a previously unannounced day on one day of the year. In contrast, pre-employment drug screening is widely applied to potential employees in some companies with a view to assisting in the selection process of suitable candidates, and this testing may search for additional drugs such as nicotine (Jacob et al., 1999). The term "drug screening" is a misnomer since it implies screening for all drugs, which is not possible (Hammett-Stabler, 2002).

In employment-sponsored drug testing, pharmacokinetic considerations are a factor in establishing the various drug cutoff levels. A medical review officer (MRO) is available to consult with the employer in the interpretation of a positive urine drug test result (St. Clair, 1998; Schulz, 1998; Upfal and Markell, 1992). The interpretation considers whether the positive finding could have arisen from approved medical treatment or other acceptable exposure scenarios, or whether it reflects a lifestyle of drug abuse that is not consistent with corporate policy. Pharmacokinetic considerations may be a factor in assessing the accuracy of an alleged exposure. Issues of well-known contention in some cases have been the ingestion of poppy seeds and passive inhalation of marijuana or cocaine smoke. Another pharmacokinetic consideration exists with the oral ingestion of codeine that metabolizes to morphine. In urine, the ratio between total recovered morphine and urine increases with time and is about unity in one to two days which is similar to the detection time by EMIT assays. Elimination rates for morphine are slower than codeine, which is also the case for the respective glucuronidate metabolites of M3G and C6G (Lafolie et al., 1996). This pharmacokinetic characteristic must be considered by the MRO when interpreting the presence of opioids and other drugs such as cocaine (Osterloh, 1993) during employment-sponsored testing.

It is possible that employers will become interested in testing for other specific drugs. Ketamine, an anesthetic agent used in the short-term induction of anesthesia in humans and in veterinary medicine, has gained in popularity in the Rave scene of all-night dance clubs. Requests from the U.S. Department of Defense (DOD) for ketamine analysis increased from 1 in 1997 to 116 in 2000 at the Armed Forces Institute of Pathology laboratory, and yet there was very little information regarding the pharmacokinetics of ketamine in urine as it relates to the parent drug and its metabolites of norketamine and dehydroketamine (Moore et al., 2001). In a study of the metabolism of enantiomers of ketamine, Williams and Wainer (2002) found a significant and stereo-selective decrease in ketamine and norketamine metabolism in protein-calorie malnourished rats. Environmental factors (smoking, alcohol use, diet) and drug interactions may impact upon the pharmacokinetic profiles of enantiomeric chemical substances. Analytical methodologies of pharmacokinetic studies can use chiral stationary phases in HPLC or GC (Williams and Wainer, 2002) or chirial capillary electrophoresis (Zaugg and Thorman, 2000). Similarly, the DOD has developed an analytical method (Grieshaber et al., 2001) for the detection in urine of psilocin, the active ingredient in some species of hallucinogenic "magic" mushrooms. Psilocin is rarely determined in forensic laboratories as a result of its chemical instability.

Research involving alcohol and drug use continues to advance and provide additional tests to assist with the interpretation of results, and those additional tests can be particularly helpful in some situations. For example with alcohol, Helander and Jones (1995) found that measuring the concentration of methanol and the ratio of 5-hydroxytryptophol to 5-hydroxyindoleacetic acid in urine was a more sensitive way to monitor recent drinking, because their concentrations remained above the endogenous levels at eight hours post-infusion despite urinary ethanol no longer being measurable (<0.01 g/L).

In the case of marijuana, monitoring the ratio of major cannabinoid metabolite (Δ^9-THCCOOH) to creatinine (M/C) has been used to predict new drug use. According to Huestis and Cone, the best accuracy (85.4 percent) for predicting new marijuana use was a ratio of ≥0.5 from two urine specimens collected at least twenty-four hours apart, whereas Manno et al. recommended an M/C ratio of ≥1.5. These two pharmacokinetic models were tested in a study with 826 urine specimens from twenty-six individuals. In a clinical setting, the Huestis and Cone ratio is recommended because of a lower false-negative rate (7.4 percent) than the Manno et al. false-negative rate (24 percent). However, in legal situations, the Manno et al. ratio is recommended because of its lower false-positive ratio (0.1 percent) as stated by Huestis and Cone. (Fraser and Worth, 1999).

Heroin is a major target of workplace drug-testing programs because of its history of abuse, liability and negative social impact. In a recent study of 11 male subjects, urine concentrations varied greatly between and within subjects with time after dosing but become more predictable when reported as amount of drug per unit of creatinine (Smith et al., 2001).

The time of drug elimination is highly dependent upon the nature of the subjects, the nature of the sample, and the testing methodology. In urine, total codeine was detected up to 123 hours and free codeine up to 97.5 hours, while in serum, total codeine was detected up to twenty-nine hours and free codeine up to 6.3 hours (Reiter et al., 2001). Knowledge of the state of distribution and elimination of active and inactive opioid metabolites and glucuronidates offers new possibilities in forensic interpretation of analytic results. For example, the use of dihydrocodeine as a prescribed heroin substitute in Germany was shown to pose a risk for proper dosage in patients who are either poor or extensive metabolizers.

Further developments in pre-employment testing of drugs of abuse may see an increase in the use of alternative matrices such as hair, and nails (Palmeri et al., 2000). These specimens increase the time frame for the detection of abuse of some drugs.

A final area of interest in employment drug testing is related to competitive athletics that are prohibited from using numerous substances.

Stimulants, narcotics, anabolic agents, diuretics, and peptide and glycoprotein hormones and analogues are among the prohibited substances (Segura et al., 1998). In 1995, twenty-four laboratories that were accredited by the International Olympic Committee (IOC) analyzed more than 90,000 urine samples from athletes and found a total positive testing rate of 1.6 percent, with anabolic steroids accounting for 65 percent of the positive tests. The consumption of such chemical substances is believed by the athletes to be associated with improvement in their performance, but the premise of drug testing of athletes is similar to other employment-related urine drug testing programs. In both environments, the detection of a prohibited substance can have severe consequences including restricting or prohibiting the performance of the athlete or worker.

3.5 Poison Control Center/Medical Emergency Department—Pharmacokinetics

Many jurisdictions have some form of a Poison Control Center (PCC) with personnel who have specialized knowledge, training and resources in the properties of chemical substances and are able, therefore, to provide timely and potentially lifesaving information to people who have been accidentally or intentionally exposed to chemical substance(s). In addition to providing a poison and drug information service to the public, the PCC may be affiliated with the medical emergency department (MED) that provides direct medical care and treatment to people exposed to and injured by chemical substances. The main functions of a PCC are to provide information and advice to the general public, to assist in qualitative evaluation of the exposure, to provide basic techniques to reduce the exposure, and to advise on application of first aid measures and when and where to seek appropriate medical treatments. The PCC may also serve as a resource to health care professionals, assist with teaching, conducting research and developing new therapies. The PCC provides advice to government and other regulatory bodies on prevention strategies to reduce accidental and occupational poisoning. The actual role of the PCC varies in different jurisdictions depending upon the size of the population served and the available financial and technical resources.

Overall there are about 5 million cases of poisoning per year in the United States, and a minority (perhaps 40 percent) are reported to the American Association of Poison Center Toxic Exposure Surveillance System (AAPCC-TESS). Many cases of poisoning, recognized or not, go unreported. The diversity of chemical substances that may be encountered at the PCC far exceeds those within the previous areas of this chapter on clinical therapeutics, human performance and employment issues.

Intoxications from drugs of abuse and other pharmaceutical products may not be substantiated with analytical toxicological test results. An axiom in practice of medical toxicology is to treat the symptoms, and not the drug. Emergency medical toxicologists, however, may find that when they include salicylate, acetaminophen and ethanol, drug test results assist them in the course of treatment.

Pharmacokinetic considerations are an important element in the advice imparted by the PCC and may impact upon the course of emergency medical treatment within the hospital medical emergency department. The primary concern with pharmacokinetics relates to the absorption phase of the chemical substance. Information about the identity of the chemical substance, along with the route, amount and duration of the exposure, is important in the assessment by PCC staff of the need and urgency for medical treatment. That information is also important to treatment decisions and efforts by the emergency staff at a hospital or medical center.

Knowledge about the toxicological profiles of chemical substances that an individual has encountered continue to accumulate over time, and may eventually indicate new concerns or aspects of the poisoning that had hitherto not been considered. For example, phenol is a general protoplastic poison that has been used in medicine and industry for decades. It is readily absorbed through the skin and causes local and systemic toxicity. A recent case report (Bentur et al., 1998) concerned a person who spilled a 90 percent phenol solution over his foot (less than 4 percent of the body area) and experienced significant toxicological effects. The rate of elimination associated with the exposure was found to be considerably longer than previously reported. The prolonged elimination may be explained by extensive tissue distribution or by "slow-release reservoir" properties of phenol (Bentur et al., 1998).

A long-standing, traditional medical emergency treatment to reduce the absorption of a chemical substance has involved the use of activated charcoal to bind the chemical substance or drug that has been ingested. The European and American position statement on the use of activated charcoal recommends its administration within one hour of ingestion of a charcoal-binding poison, but in reality, this time limit is difficult to follow for the majority of poisoned patients. In one recent study at a teaching hospital in London, England (Karim et al., 2001), the median time of arrival at the facility after an oral overdose was 136 minutes, and only 15 of 63 patients presented within one hour. These results are likely to be exaggerated in rural hospitals unless activated charcoal can be safely administered to appropriate patients in the pre-hospital environment, as advised by the PCC. The literature suggests a general approach that can be followed until there is evidence supporting a different strategy.

Acetaminophen overdose results in more calls to poison control centers in the U.S. than overdose with any other pharmacological substance. Optimal management strategy remains controversial. A single dose of activated charcoal should be administered within one hour of acetaminophen overdose. Other means of gastric decontamination are not warranted, given the known metabolic pathway of acetaminophen in producing a toxic metabolite that is responsible for the longer hepatotoxicity associated with overdoses. Acetylcysteine is an antidote that can be used to treat severe overdoses of acetaminophen. The long-standing established treatment is guided by determining the concentration of acetaminophen in serum, followed by another measurement several hours later. A comparison of the two concentrations can be related to a clinical pharmacokinetic elimination graph known as the Rumack-Matthew nomogram, which is the pharmacokinetic profile best known to toxicologists. Treatment is indicated if the measured concentrations are greater than the line on the nomogram. If the concentration is below the treatment line, another acetaminophen concentration should be determined four to six hours later (Zed and Krenzelok, 1999).

Chemical substances can also be used as antidotes to enhance elimination of the unchanged poison. In acute carbon monoxide poisoning, oxygen can be used to enhance elimination by the lungs. In acute iron poisoning, deferoxamine will enhance elimination by the kidneys. Antidotes that activate metabolic pathways responsible for inactivation of the poison include N-acetylcysteine in acute acetaminophen poisoning and methylene blue in toxic methemoglobinemia. Ethanol and 4-methylpyrazole are antidotes that inhibit metabolic pathways responsible for activation of the poison in acute methanol or ethylene glycol poisoning. Fab fragment antibodies serve as antidotes that modify distribution of the poison in acute digitalis poisoning (Lapostolle et al., 1999).

The treatment of severe overdoses of some chemical substances can create chemical events that are not found in the practice of clinical therapeutics. For example, the overdose of some drug substances, such as calcium channel blocking agents, can form bezoars or a clumping of the medication within the gastrointestinal tract. This can substantially delay absorption and then later unexpectedly break apart within the body, giving rise to unexpected toxicities. Such events cannot be predicted from the pharmacokinetic models and parameter values determined from clinical therapeutics.

The great diversity of pharmacokinetic considerations at the PCC or medical emergency department is similar to that other of areas covered in this chapter. As a further example, a diagnosis of Munchausen syndrome by proxy can be made by the application of pharmacokinetics with analytical identification and determination of the concentration of xenobiotic or otherwise unexpected chemical substances found in patients admitted to hospital (Mahesh et al., 1988).

3.6 Postmortem Investigations—Pharmacokinetics

In postmortem biological exhibits, pharmacokinetics may be an important consideration in interpreting the concentration of chemical substances and its relation to the cause and manner of death. However, if events that lead up to a death are prolonged, perhaps in a hospital, profound changes in physiological functions can affect the pharmacokinetics of drug disposition. Poor kidney and liver function, low serum albumen, general malaise, and interactions between these factors and other drugs can alter the pharmacokinetics from those expected in normal clinical therapeutics. (Uges and Greijdanus, 1990).

Compared to other areas covered in this chapter, postmortem investigations differ substantially in the nature of the samples that are collected. Pharmacokinetic information in postmortem investigations is ascertained by analyzing concentrations of drugs and metabolites in diverse fluids and tissues collected at autopsy. Biological samples commonly collected at the autopsy include blood (central and peripheral), urine, stomach contents, liver, vitreous humor, bile, kidney and lung. Additional specimens such as brain, muscle, spleen, lung, bone, hair, nails, meconium, and even insects may also be collected.

It is important to ascertain the exact nature of the specimens collected. For example, the collection of a blood sample may appear to be straightforward, but in fact, is not so. The technique used to actually collect blood samples is highly varied amongst those who conduct medicolegal autopsies. Furthermore, specification of the site is not always provided to the toxicologist to assist with interpretation of the findings. Blood should be collected from at least two locations such as central (heart) and peripheral (femoral vein) sites, and the exact sites of collection should be appropriately documented. Blood may also be collected from subdermal hematomas when present on the body and may in some circumstances provide information about a sample of blood that has been isolated from circulation by the body as a result of the injury. In the case of severe trauma, blood is often collected from the chest cavity, a less reliable source.

After collection of the specimens from autopsy, it is also important to ascertain how the nature of these samples may have changed since the actual time of death. For drugs with high volumes of distribution, such as the tricyclic antidepressants, the drug and metabolite that had been sequestered in tissue (for example, in the heart) may be released into the blood and fluids that are in contact with tissue collected for analysis. This phenomenon, known as postmortem redistribution (Anderson and Prouty, 1990), can cause the artifact of significantly higher concentrations of the drug and metabolite in the blood specimen and lead to an incorrect interpretation. In addition, other factors may require consideration. For example, in addition to age and weight, other factors that may influence tissue concentrations of digoxin in infants and children include duration of treatment, route of administration, sampling time, time of last dose, and the death-autopsy interval (Hastreiter and Horst, 1984).

The analysis of different specimens provides a "snapshot" at one particular time of different portions of the c(t) profiles associated with drugs and their metabolites. This assumes that no change in the concentration of the drug and metabolite occurred between the time of death and time of analysis. In a study of four benzodiazepines (clonazepam, midazolam, flunitrazepam and oxazepam) stored at 40° C, Mahjoub and Staub (2000) found a 90–100 percent decrease in concentration for low concentrations and from 50–80 percent decrease for high concentrations. Therefore, optimal storage conditions are essential in forensic cases. Zopiclone was not detectable after one month at 250° C, whereas at 40° C, 55 percent remained after two months and 8 percent after six months (Pepin et al., 1998). The decrease in diltiazem concentrations in stored postmortem blood was highly variable, varying from complete to negligible in a period of ninety-two days (Koves and Lawrence, 1998).

Another issue with postmortem examinations is the stability of the drug and its metabolites in the collected samples, which may not be analyzed for weeks to months after the collection. The time scale for analyzing specimens and reporting toxicology results in postmortem investigations may be orders of magnitude longer than in other areas such as medical emergency departments or even employment-related testing where timely reporting is critical. In the absence of preservatives, cocaine chemically breaks down to benzoylecgonine both in vivo and in vitro. There were no consistent patterns of site-specific differences for any of the cocaine analytes, and the central compartment showed both higher and lower concentrations than the peripheral. There were no consistent patterns of direction or magnitude of change in the concentrations with respect to time for any of the analytes. This is consistent with anecdotal reports and is believed to be a result of competing processes of tissue release and chemical and enzymatic degradation of the analytes (Logan, 1997).

The distribution ratios of cannabinoids between whole blood and serum in postmortem cases is scattered over a larger range of values than those determined in living people (Giroud et al., 2001). Even in living people, the blood to serum ratio needs to be determined for a large group of human subjects.

The blood to plasma concentration ratio for morphine (average 0.58) was unaffected by variations in hematocrit and water content, whereas the corresponding ratios for M3G and M5G were strongly influenced. The blood to plasma concentration ratio for M3G and M6G were 0.27 and 0.28 respectively for a hematocrit of 71 percent, whereas they were 0.81 and 0.89, respectively, for a hematocrit of 10 percent. Therefore, it is important to realize that conclusions drawn from pharmacokinetic studies and transferred to parent drug-to-metabolite ratios for forensic blood samples may be biased by the particular biological matrix under investigation (Skopp et al., 1988).

To relate the concentration of a chemical obtained postmortem to pharmacokinetic aspects of the drug requires an appropriate selection of a diversity of biological and other specimens related to the body, and knowledge about the physiological stability of the analytes in the matrix of interest, and the chemical stability of analytes both in vivo and in vitro. Additional information obtained from investigators at the scene and other locations, including the medicolegal autopsy, can then assist in ascertaining pharmacokinetic aspects as may be related to the death, which in turn may aid in determining the cause and manner of death.

References

Abzalov, R.A., Nigmatullina, R.R., Khairullina, G.N., Garmonov, S.U., Shakirova, L.S. (2001). "Effect of physical training on sulfamethazine acetylation rate." *Bull Exp Biolog Med*, 130, 12, 1141–1143.

Aderjan, R.E., and Skopp, G. (1998). "Formation and clearance of active and inactive metabolites of opiates in humans." *Ther Drug Monit*, 20, 5, 561–569.

Aprea, C., Sciarra, G., Lunghini, L., and Bozzi, N. (2001). "Biological monitoring of pesticide exposure: Occupationally exposed workers and general population." *Ann Dell Sup Sanit*, 37, 2, 259-174.

Barbone, F., McMahon, A.D., Davey, P.G., Morris, A.D., Ried, I.C., McDevitt, D.G., et al. (19998). "Association of road-traffic accidents with benzodiazepine use." *Lancet*, 352, 9137, 1331–1336.

Baselt, R.C. (2001). Drug Effects on Psychomotor Performance. Foster City, CA: Biomedical Publications.

Baum, J., Sievert, B., Stanke, H.G., and Sachs, G. (2000). "Low flow anaesthesia without nitrous oxide." *Anaesth Reanim*, 25, 3, 60–67.

Beliles, R.P., and Totman, L.C. (1989). "Pharmacokinetically-based risk assessment of workplace exposure to benzene." *Reg Tox Pharmacol*, 9, 2, 186–196.

Benet, L.Z. (1995). "General Principles," In P.B. Molinoff and R.W.Ruddon (Eds.), *Goodman and Gilman's The Pharmacological Basis of Therapeutics*, (9th ed.). New York: McGraw-Hill.

Benet, L.Z., Kroetz, D.L., and Sheiner, L.B. (1995). "Pharmacokinetics: Drug absorption, distribution and elimination," In P.B. Molinoff, and R.W.

Ruddon (Eds.), *Goodman and Gillman's The Pharmacological Basis of Therapeutics* (9th ed.) (Chapter 1). New York: McGraw Hill.

Bentur, Y., Shoshani, O., Tabak, A., Bin-Nun, A., Ramon, Y., Ulman, Y., et al. (1998). "Prolonged elimination half-life of phenol after dermal exposure." J *Tox Clin Tox*, 36, 7, 707–711.

Berg, M.J. (1997). "Status of research on gender differences." *J Am Pharm Assoc*, 37, 1, 43–56.

Bruno, R., Iliadis, A., and Treffot, M.J. (1983). "Non-linear kinetics of ethanol elimination in man: Medico-legal applications of the terminal concentration-time data analysis." *For Sci Int*, 21, 3, 207–213.

Calvo, M., and Benitez, E. (1996). "Clinical pharmacokinetics of carbamazepine." *Rev Soc Esp Quim Clin*, 15, 1, 6–12.

Cami, J., Farre, M., Gonzalez, M.L., Segura, J., and de la Torre, R. (1998). "Cocaine metabolism in humans after use of alcohol: Clinical and research implications." *Recent Dev Alcohol*, 14, 437–455.

Charlebois, R.C., Corbett, M.R., and Wigmore, J.G. (1996). "The determination of ethanol in blood, serum and blood cells for forensic application." *J Anal Tox*, 20, 3, 171–178.

Clarke, S.E., and Jones, B.C. (2002). "Human cytochromes P450 and their role in metabolism-based drug-drug interactions," In A.D. Rodrigues (Ed.), *Drug-Drug Interactions*. Marcel Dekker.

Coffey, C.C., Campbell, D.L., Myers, W.R., Zhuange, Z., and Das, S. (1998). "Comparison of six respirator fit-test methods with an actual measurement of exposure in a simulated health care environment: Part I—protocol development." *Am Indust Hyg Assoc J*, 59, 12, 852–861.

Cone, E.J. (1995). "Pharmacokinetics and pharmacodynamics of cocaine." *J Anal Tox*, 19, 6, 459–478.

Corbett, M.R., and Koves, E.M. (1994). "Gas-chromatography-mass spectrometry for the determination of cocaine and benzoylecgonine in postmortem blood." *J For Sci*, 39, 1, 136–149.

D'Alonzo, G.E., Crocetti, J.G., and Smolensky, M.H. (1999). "Circadian rhythms in the pharmacokinetics and clinical effects of beta-agonist, theophylline, and anticholinergic medications in the treatment of nocturnal asthma." *Chronobiol Internat*, 16, 5, 663–682.

DeHart, R.L. (1990). "Medication and the work environment." *J Occup Med*, 32, 4, 310–312.

De Valck, E., and Cluydts, R. (2001). "Slow-release caffeine as a countermeasure to driver sleepiness induced by partial sleep deprivation." *J Sleep Res*, 10, 3, 203–209.

de Vos, J.W., Geerlings, P.J., van den Brink, W., Ufkes, J.G. and van Wilgenburg, H. (1995). "Pharmacokinetics of methadone and its primary metabolite in 20 opiate addicts." *Eur J Clin Pharmacol*, 48, 5, 361–366.

Diamond, B.I., and Albrecht, J.W. (1987) "Medical and psychiatric implications of generic drugs." *Psychopath*, 20, Suppl 1, 92–98.

Dickinson, B.D., Altman, R.D., Nielsen, H.N., and Sterling, M.L. (2001). "Drug interactions between oral contraceptives and antibiotics." *Obstet Gynec*, 98, 5, 853–860.

Dittmar, E.A., and Dorian, V. (1987). "Ethanol absorption after bolus ingestion of an alcoholic beverage. A medico-legal problem." *Can J For Sci*, 20, 2, 61–69.

DiVincenzo, G.D., and Kaplan, C.J. (1981). "Uptake, metabolism, and elimination of methylene chloride vapor by humans." *Tox Appl Pharmacol*, 59, 1, 130–140.

Dobetti, L. (2000). "Fast-melting tablets: Developments and technologies." *Pharm Tech Int*, 12, 9, 32–42.

Edler, L. (1999). "Uncertainty in biomonitoring and kinetic modeling." *Ann New York Acad Sci*, 859, 80–100.

El Mahjoub, A., and Staub, C. (2000). "Stability of benzodiazepines in whole blood samples stored at varying temperatures." *J Pharm Biomed Analys*, 23, 6, 1057–1063.

Farre, M., and Carmi, J. (1991). "Pharmacokinetic considerations in abuse liability evaluation." *Br J Addict*, 86, 12, 1601–1606.

Fowler, J.S., and Volkow, N.D. (1998). "PET imaging studies of drugs of abuse." *J Tox Clin Tox* 36, 3, 163–174.

Fraser, A.D., and Worth, D. (1999). "Urinary excretion profiles of 11-nor-9-carboxy-Delta-9-tetrahydrocannabinol: A Delta-9-THCCOOH to creatinine ratio study." *J Anal Tox*, 23, 6, 531–534.

Gabrielsson, J.L., and Weiner, D.L. (1999). "Methodology for pharmacokinetic/pharmacodynamic data analysis." *Pharm Sci Tech Today*, 2, 6, 244–252.

Galloway, G.P., Frederick-Osborne, S.L., Seymjour, R., Contini, S.E., and Smith, D.E. (2000). "Abuse and therapeutic potential of gamma-hydroxybutyric acid." *Alcohol*, 20, 3, 263–269.

Garriott, J.C. (Ed.). (1996). *Medicolegal Aspects of Alcohol.* Tucson: Lawyers & Judges Publishing Co.

George, S., and Braithwaite, R.A. (1999). "A pilot study to determine the usefulness of the urinary excretion of methadone and its primary metabolite (EDDP) as potential markers of compliance in methadone detoxification programs." *J Anal Tox,* 23, 2, 85–85.

Gieschke, R., and Steimer, J.L. (2000). "Pharmacometrics: Modeling and simulation tools to improve decision making in clinical drug development." *Eur J Drug Metab Pharmacokin*, 25, 1, 49–58.

Giroud, C., Menetrey, A., Augsburger, M., Buclin, T., Sanchez-Mazas, P., and Mangin, P. (2001). "Delta-9-THC, 11-OH-Delta-9-THC, and Delta-9-THC-THCCOOH plasma or serum to whole blood concentrations distribution ratio in blood samples taken from living and dead people." *For Sci Int*, 123, 2-3, 159–164.

Gobburu, J.V.S., and Marroum, P.J. (2001). "Utilization of pharmacokinetic-pharmacodynamic modeling and simulation in regulatory decision-making." *Clin Pharmacokin*, 40, 12, 883–892.

Graham, T.E. (2001). "Caffeine and exercise metabolism, endurance and performance." Sports Med, 31, 11, 785-807.

Graves, N.M., Brundage, R.C., Wen, Y., Cascino, G., So, E., Ahman, P., et al. (1998). "Population pharmacokinetics of carbamazepine in adults with epilepsy." *Pharmacotherapy*, 18, 2, 273–281.

Grieshaber, A.F., Moore, K.A., and Levine, B. (2001). "The detection of psilocin in human urine." *J For Sci*, 46, 3, 627–630.

Guillemin, M.P., Bauer, D., Martin, B., and Marazzi, A. (1982). "Human exposure to Styrene. IV. Industrial hygiene investigations and biological monitoring in the polyester industry." *Int Arch Occup Environ Health*, 51, 2, 139–150.

Gullberg, R.G. (1992). " The elimination rate of mouth alcohol: Mathematical modeling and implications in breath alcohol analysis." *J For Sci*, 37, 5, 1363–1372.

Hallock, M.F., Hammond, S.K., Kenyon, E., Smith, T.J., and Smith, E.R. (1993). "Assessment of task and peak exposures to solvents in the microelectronics fabrication industry." *Appl Occup Environ Hyg*, 8, 11, 945–954.

Hammett-Stabler, C.A., Pesce, A.J., and Cannon, D.J. (2002). "Urine drug screening in the medical setting." *Clin Chim Acta*, 315, 1–2, 125–135.

Hastreiter, A.R., and van der Horst, R.L. (1984). "Tissue concentrations at autopsy in infants and children receiving therapeutic digoxin." *J For Sci*, 29, 1, 139–146.

Hatsukami, D.K., and Fischman, M.W. (1996). "Crack cocaine and cocaine hydrochloride: Are the differences myth or reality? *J Am Med Assoc*, 276, 19, 1580–1588.

Hawk, T.L., Havrda, D.E., Rivera-Miranda, G., and Parent, M. (2002). "Effect of stress on international normalized ration during warfarin therapy." *Ann Pharmacotherapy*, 36, 4, 617–620.

Hearn, W.L. (Ed.). (1998). "Postmortem Toxicology," In S. Karch (Ed.), *Drug Abuse Handbook* (Chapter 12). Boca Raton, FL: CRC Press, Boca Raton.

Heath, A., Ahlmen, J., and Branegard, B. (1983). "Thallium poisoning—Toxin elimination and therapy in three cases." *J Tox Clin Tox*, 20, 5, 451–463.

Helanderm A., Beck, O., and Jones, A.W. (1995). "Distinguishing ingested ethanol from microbial formation by analysis of urinary 5-hydroxytryptophol and 5-hydroxyindoleacetic acid." *J For Sci*, 40, 1, 95–98.

Hernandez-Fustes, O.J., Marcourakis, T. and De Bittencourt, P.R.M. (1999). "The clinical relevance of serial determinations of plasma concentrations of carbamazepine and sodium valproate." *Rev Neurol*, 28, 11, 1043–1047.

Higashi, M.K., Veenstra, K.L., Kondo, L.M., Wittkowsky, A.K., Srinouanprachanh, S.L., Farin F.M., et al. (2002). "Association between CYP2C9 genetic variants and anticoagulation-related outcomes during warfarin therapy." *JAMA*, 287, 13,1690–1698.

Hill, H.F., Saeger, L., Bjurstrom, R., Donaldson, G., Chapman, C.R. and Jacobson, R. (1990). "Steady-state infusions of opioids in human volunteers. I. Pharmacokinetic tailoring." *Pain*, 43, 1, 57–67.

Hope, K.A., and Havrda, D.E. (2001). "Subtherapeutic INR values associated with a switch to generic warfarin." *Ann Pharmacotherap*, 35, 2, 183–187.

Huestis, M.A. (1999). "Marijuana," In B. Levine (Ed.), *Principles of Forensic Toxicology* (Chapter 14). Am Assoc Clin Chem.

Huestis, M.A., Henningfield, J.E., and Cone, E.J. (1992). "Blood cannabinoids. I. Absorption of THC and formation of 11-OH-THC and THCCOOH during and after smoking marijuana." *J Anal Tox* ,16, 5, 276–282.

Hutt, A.J., and Tan, S.C. (1996). "Drug chirality and its clinical significance." *Drugs*, 52, Supp 5, 112.

Isenschmid, D.S., Levine, B.S., and Caplan, Y.H. (1989). "A comprehensive study of the stability of cocaine and its metabolites." *J Anal Tox*, 13, 5, 250–256.

Jacob, III, P., Yu, L., and Benowitz, N.L. (1999). "Minor tobacco alkaloids as biomarkers for tobacco use: Comparison of users of cigarettes, smokeless tobacco, cigars and pipers." *Am J Pub Health*, 89, 5, 731–736.

Jang, J.Y., Droz, P.O., and Kim S. (2001). "Biological monitoring of workers exposed to ethylbenzene and co-exposed to Xylene." *Int Arch Occup Environ Health*, 74, 1, 31–37.

Jessup, J.V., Lowenthal, D.T., Pollock, M.L., Williams, L., and Ruiz, J. (2000). "The effects of exercise training on the pharmacokinetics of digoxin." *J Cardiopulm Rehab*, 20, 2, 89–95.

Jones, A.W. (1993). (1993). "Disappearance rate of ethanol from the blood of human subjects: Implications in forensic toxicology." *J For Sci*, 38, 1,104–118.

Jufer, R.A., Wstadik, A., Walsh, S.L., Bevine, B.S., and Cone, E.J. (2000). "Elimination of cocaine and metabolites in plasma, saliva, and urine following repeated oral administration to human volunteers." *J Anal Tox*, 24, 7, 467–477.

Kafferliein, H.U., Goen, T., Muller, J., Wribitzky, R., and Angerer, J. (2000). "Biological monitoring of workers exposed to N, N-Dimethylformamide in the synthetic fibre industry." *Int Arch Occup Environ Health*, 73, 2, 113–120.

Levitt, M.D., and Levitt, D.G. (1998). "Use of a two-compartment model to assess the pharmacokinetics of human ethanol metabolism." *Alcoholism: Clin Exp Res*, 22, 8, 1680–1688.

Kalinkova, G.N. (1999). "Studies of beneficial interactions between active medicaments and excipients in pharmaceutical formulations." *Int J Pharm*, 187, 1, 1–15.

Karim, A., Ivatts, S., Dargan, P., and Jones, A. (2001). "How feasible is it to conform to the European guidelines on administration of activated charcoal within one hour of an overdose?" *Emerg Med J*, 18, 5, 390–392.

Kearns, G.L., and Reed, M.D. (1989). "Clinical pharmacokinetics in infants and children: A reappraisal." *Clin Pharmacokinet*, 17, Supp 1, 29–67.

Knight, J.M., Eliopoulos, C., Klein, J., Greenwald, M., and Koren, G. (1998). "Pharmacokinetic predisposition to nicotine from environmental tobacco smoke: A risk factor for pediatric asthma." *J Asthma*, 35, 1, 113–117.

Koves, E.M., and Lawrence, K. (1998). "Stability of diltiazem in whole blood: Forensic implications." *J For Sci*, 43, 3, 587–597.

Kraemer, T., and Maurer, H.H. (2002). "Toxicokinetics of amphetamines: Metabolism and toxicokinetic data of designer drugs, amphetamine, methamphetamine and their N-alkyl derivatives." *Ther Drug Monit*, 24, 2, 277–289.

Krstulovic, A.M., and Lee, C.R. (1997). "Defining drug purity through chromatographic and related methods: Current status and perspectives." *J Chromat B: Biomed Applic*, 689, 1, 137–153.

Kuhlmann, J. (1997). "Drug research: From the idea to the product." *Int J Clin Pharmacol Therap*, 35, 12, 541–552.

Lader, M. (1999). "The influence of drugs upon testimony." *Med Sci Law*, 39, 2, 99–105.

Lafolie, P., Beck, O., Lin, Z., Albertioni, F., and Boreus, L.(1996). "Urine and plasma pharmacokinetics of codeine in healthy volunteers: Implications for drugs-of-abuse testing." *J Anal Tox*, 20, 7, 541–546.

Lapostolle, F., Bismuth, C., and Baud, F. (1999). "Classification of antidotes based on mechanism of action. Part 1." *Sem Hopit*, 75, 1–2, 45–52.

LeBeau, M.A., and Mozayani, A. (Eds.). (2001). *Drug-Facilitated Sexual Assault*. New York: Academic Press.

Lee, C.R., and Thrasher, K.R. (2001). "Difficulties in anticoagulation management during coadministration of warfarin and rifampin." *Pharmacotherapy*, 21,10 I, 1240–1246.

Leeson, L.J., Adair, D., Clevenger, J., and Chiang, N. (1985). "The in vitro development of extendedrelease solid oral dosing forms." *J Pharmacokin Biopharm*, 13, 5, 493–514.

Levi, F. (1999). "Cancer chronotherapy." *J Pharm Pharmaco*l, 51, 8, 891–898.

Logan, B.K., Smirnow, D., and Gullberg, R.G. (1997). "Lack of predictable site-dependent differences and time-dependent changes in postmortem concentrations of cocaine, benzoylecgonine, and cocaethylene in humans." *J Anal Tox*, 21, 1, 23–31.

Luzier, A.B., Killian, A., Wilton, J.H., Wilson, M.F., Forrest, A., and Kazierad, D.J (1999). "Genderrelated effects of metoprolol pharmacokinetics and pharmacodynamics in healthy volunteers." *Clin Pharmacol Therap*, 66, 6, 594–601.

Mahesh, V.K., Stern, H.P., Kearns, G.L., and Stroh, S.E. (1988). "Application of pharmacokinetics in the diagnosis of chemical abuse in Munchausen Syndrome by Proxy." *Clin Ped*, 27, 5, 243–246.

March, R. (2000). "Pharmacogenomics: The genomics of drug response." *Comp Funct Genomics* 17, 1, 16–21.

Marroum, P.J., and Gobburu, J. (2002). "The product label: How pharmacokinetics and pharmacodynamics reach the prescriber." *Clin Pharmacokinet*, 41, 3, 161–169.

Martens, F., and Martens, M. (2002). "Analysis of the monoester metabolites of butylbenzyl phthalate by GC-MS in urine of exposed workers." *Acta Clin Belg*, 57, Supp 1, 16–23.

Mattiussi, R., Armeli, G., and Bareggi, V. (1982). "Statistical study of the correlation between mercury exposure (TWA) and urinary mercury concentrations in chloralkali workers." *Am J Indust Med*, 3, 3, 335–339.

Mauriz, J.L., Taberno, B., Garcia-Lopez, J., Jorquera, F., Villa, J.G., Gonzalez-Gallego, J. (2000). "Physical exercise and improvement of liver oxidative metabolism in the elderly." *Eur J App Physiol Occup Physiol*, 81,1–2, 62–66.

McGinnity, D.F., and Riley, R.J. (2001). "Predicting drug pharmacokinetics in humans from in vitro metabolism studies." *Biochem Soc Trans*, 29, 2, 135–139.

Meeusen, R., Piacentini, M.F., Van Den Eynde, S., and De Meirleir, K. (2001). "Exercise performance is not influenced by a 5-HT reuptake inhibitor." *Int J Sports Med*, 22, 5, 329–336.

Milgram, N.W., Callahan, H., and Siwak, C. (1999). "Adrafinil: A novel vigilance promoting agent." *CNS Drug Reviews*, 5, 3, 193–212.

Milovic, V., and Stein, J. (2000). "Gastrointestinal disease and dosage form performance," In J.B. Dressman, and H. Lenneras (Eds.), *Oral Drug Absorption: Prediction and Assessment*. Marcel Dekker, 2000.

Minora, T., Ventresca, G.P., and Mariani, L. (1990). "Problems of pharmacokinetics in pregnancy. A bibliographic review." *Ann Ostet Gin Medic Perin* 111, 3,159–173.

Moore, K.A., Sklerov, J., Levine, B., and Jacobs, A.J. (2001). "Urine concentrations of ketamine and norketamine following illegal consumption." *J Anal Tox*, 25, 7, 583–588.

Nicholson, A.N. (1990). "Hypnotics and occupational medicine." *J Occup Med*, 32, 4, 335–341.

Norton, R.M. (2001). "Clinical pharmacogenomics: Applications in pharmaceutical R and D." *Drug Discov Today*, 6, 4, 180–185.

Osterloh, J. (1993). "Testing for drugs of Abuse. Pharmacokinetic considerations for cocaine in urine." *Clin Pharmacokinet*, 24, 5, 355–361.

Palareti, G., and Legnani, C. (1996). "Warfarin withdrawal. Pharmacokinetic-pharmacodynamic considerations." *Clin Pharmacokin*, 30, 4, 300–313.

Palmeri, A., Pichini, S., Pacifici, R., Zuccaro, P., and Lopez, A. (2000). "Drugs in nails. Physiology, pharmacokinetics and forensic toxicology." *Clin Pharmacokin*, 38, 2, 95–110.

Peng, G.W., and Chiou, W.L. (1990). "Analysis of drugs and other toxic substances in biological samples for pharmacokinetic studies." *J Chromat Biomed Appl*, 531, 3–50.

Pepin, G., Dubourvieux, N., and Gaillard, Y. (1998). Difficulty of interpretation of rates concerning benzodiazepines and other anxiolytic molecules in post mortem blood taken during autopsy: Study of their degradation in vitro after 6-months storage at different temperatures." *J Medec Leg Droit Medic*, 41, 5, 341–353.

Podlogar, B.L., Muegge, I., and Brice, L.J. (2001). "Computational methods to estimate drug development parameters." *Curr Opin Drug Discov Develop*, 4, 1, 102–109.

Poetsch, L., and Skopp, G. (2001). "Discussion on morphine data in post mortem blood after palliative pain treatment." *Rechtsmedizin*, 11, 5, 205–211.

Pragst, F., Spiegel, K., Leuschner, U. and Hager, A. (1999). "Detection of 6-Acetylmorphine in vitreous humor and cerebrospinal fluid—Comparison with urinary analysis for proving heroin administration in opiate fatalities." *J Anal Tox*, 23, 3, 168–172.

Prouty, R.W., and Anderson, W.H. (1990). "The forensic science implications of site and temporal influences on postmortem blood-drug concentrations." *J For Sci,* 35, 2, 243–70.

Quinn, D.I., Wokak, A., and Day, R.O. (1997). "Pharmacokinetic and pharmacodynamic principles of illicit drug use and treatment of illicit drug users." *Clin Pharmacokinet*, 33, 5, 344–400.

Rathbone, M.J., and Hadgraft, J. (1991). "Absorption of drugs from the human oral cavity." *Int J Pharmaceut,* 74, 9–24.

Reiter, A., Hake, J., Meissner, C., Rohwer, J., Friedrich, H.J., and Oehmichen, M. (2001). "Time of drug elimination in chronic drug abusers: Case study of 52 patients in a "low-step" detoxification ward." *For Sci Int*, 119, 2, 248–253.

Rentsch, K.M., Kullak-Ublick, G.A., Reichel, C., Meier, P.J., and Fattinger, K. (2001). "Arterial and venous pharmacokinetics of intravenous heroin in subjects who are addicted to narcotics." *Clin Pharmacol Therap*, 70, 3, 237–46.

Repace, J.L., and Lowrey, A.H. (1993). "An enforceable indoor air quality standard for environmental tobacco smoke in the workplace." *Risk Analysis*, 13, 4, 463–475.

Reuter, I., Harder, S., Engelhardt, M., and Baas, H. (2000). "The effect of exercise on pharmacokinetics and pharmacodynamics of levodopa." *Movement Disorders,* 15, 5, 862-868.

Ritrovato, C.A., and Dinella, C. (1995). "The representation of women in clinical drug trials." *Drug Info J*, 29, 1, 147–154.

Ritschel, W.A. (1988). *Gerontokinetics: The Pharmacokinetics of Drugs in the Elderly*. Caldwell, NJ: The Telford Press.

Sahin, S., and Yakut, E. (2000). "Effects of physical therapy interventions on pharmacokinetic parameters." *FABAD J Pharm Sci*, 25, 2, 75–82.

Sato, A., and Nakajima, T. (1987). "Pharmacokinetics of organic solvent vapors in relation to the toxicity." *Scand J Work Environ Health*, 13, 2, 81–93.

Schellens, J.H.M., Malingre, M.M., Kruijtzer, C.M.F., Bardelmeijer, H.A., Van Tellingen, O., Schinkel, A.H., et al. (2000). "Modulation of oral bioavailability of anticancer drugs: From mouse to man." *Eur J Pharm Sci,* 12, 2, 103–110.

Schreiber, J.S. (1993). "Predicted infant exposure to tetrachloroethylene in human breast milk." *Risk Analysis*, 13, 5, 515–524.

Schultz, T.F. (1998). "Current legal issues of workplace drug testing," In S. Karch (Ed.), *Drug Abuse Handbook* (Chapter 13.1). Boca Raton, FL: CRC Press.

Schwartz, J.I., and Fink, III, J.L. (1989). "Legal issues associated with pharmacokinetic software." *Am J Hosp Pharm,* 46, 1, 120–124.

Segura, J. (1998). "Sports," In S. Karch (Ed.), *Drug Abuse Handbook* (Chapter 9). Boca Raton, FL: CRC Press.

Seyffart, G. (1991). *Drug Dosage in Renal Insufficiency*. Boston: Kluwer Academic Publishers.

Shearer, D.S., Baciewicz, G.J., and Kwong, T.C. (1998). "Drugs of abuse testing in psychiatric outpatient service." *Clin Lab Med*, 18, 4, 713–726.

Sherwood, R.J. (1988). "Pharmacokinetics of benzene in a human after exposure at about the permissible limit." *Ann New York Acad Sci*, 534, 635–647.

Silvaggio, T., and Mattison, D.R. (1994). "Setting occupational health standards: Toxicokinetic differences among and between men and women." *J Occup Med*, 36, 8, 849–854.

Sinko, P.J. (1999). "Drug selection in early drug development: Screening for acceptable pharmacokinetic properties using combined in vitro and computational approaches." *Curr Opin Drug Discov Devel*, 2, 1, 42–48.

Skopp, G., Potsch, L., Ganssmann, B., Aderjan, R., and Mattern, R. (1998). "A preliminary study on the distribution of morphine and its glucuronides in the subcompartments of blood." *J Anal Tox*, 22, 4, 261–264.

Smith, M., Shimomura, E., Summers, J., Paul, B., Jenkins, A.J., Darwin, W.D., et al. (2001). "Urinary excretion profiles for total morphine, free morphine and 6-acetylmorphine following smoked and intravenous heroin." *J Anal Tox*, 25, 7, 504–514.

Somani, S.S., and Kamimori, G.H. (1996). "The effects of exercise on absorption, distribution, metabolism, excretion, and pharmacokinetics of drugs," In S.M. Somani (Ed.), *Pharmacology in Exercise and Sports*. CRC Press.

Spence, P. (1999). "From genome to drug—Optimising the drug discovery process." *Prog Drug Res,* 53, 157–191.

St. Clair, S. (1998). "The role of the medical review officer: Current issues," In S. Karch (Ed.), *Drug Abuse Handbook* (Chapter 10.5). Boca Raton, FL: CRC Press.

Stark, M.M., and Wells, D. (1999). "Drug-mediated sexual assault." *J Clin For Med*, 6, 1, 53–55.

Sun, H., Fadiran, E., Jones, C., Lesko, L., Huang, S., Higgins, K., et al. (1999). "Population pharmacokinetics: A regulatory perspective." *Clin Pharmacokinet*, 37, 1, 41–58.

Svensson, C.K. (1989). "Ethical considerations in the conduct of clinical pharmacokinetic studies." *Clin Pharmacokin*, 17, 4, 217–222.

Tenenbein, M. (1998). "Toxicokinetics and toxicodynamics of iron poisoning." *Tox Lett*, 102-103, 653–656.

Thrall, K., Poet, T., Corley, R., Tanojo, H., Edwards, J., Weitz, K., et al. (2000). "A real-time in-vivo method for studying the percutaneous absorption of volatile chemicals." *Int J Occup Environ Health*, 6, 2, 96–103.

Uges, D.R.A., Greijdanus, B. (1990). "Euthanasia: A challenge for the forensic toxicologist." *J For Sci*, 35, 6, 1424–1430.

Upfal, M.J., and Markell, B. (1992). "Training and proficiency in the medical review of job applicant drug screens." *J Occup Med*, 34, 12, 1189–1196.

Valodia, P.N., Seymour, M.A., Kies, B.M., and Folb, P. (1999). "Optimization of phenytoin therapy in adults with epilepsy in the Western Cape, South Africa." *J Clin Pharm Therap*, 24, 5, 381–385.

Van den Bongard, H.J.G.D., Mathod, R.A.A., Beijnen, J.H., and Schellens, J.H.M. (2000). Pharmacokinetically-guided administration of chemotherapeutic agents." *Clin Pharmacokinet*, 39, 5, 345–367.

Van Dyke, C., and Byck, R. (1982). "Cocaine." *Science*, 246, 82, 128–141.

Van Valkenburg, C., and Akiskal, H.S. (1999). "Which patients presenting with clinical anxiety will abuse benzodiazepines?" *Hum Psychopharmacol,* 14, Supp 1, S45–S51.

Williams, M.L., and Wainer, I.W. (2002). "Role of chiral chromatography in therapeutic drug monitoring and in clinical and forensic toxicology." *Ther Drug Monit*, 24, 2, 290–296.

Williams, P.J., and Ette, E.I. (2000). "The role of population pharmacokinetics in drug development in light of the Food and Drug Administration's 'Guidance for industry: Population pharmacokinetics'." *Clin Pharmacokinet*, 39, 6, 385–395.

Withers, N.W. (2001). "Deceptions in addiction psychiatry." *Am J For Psych*, 22, 4, 7–28.

Wittkowsky, A.K. (2001). "Drug interactions update: Drugs, herbs and oral anticoagulation." *J Thromb Throbol*, 12, 1, 67–71.

Wright, J.G., and Boddy, A.V. (2001). "All half-lives are wrong, but some half-lives are useful." *Clin Pharmacokinet*, 40, 4, 237–244.

Wrighton, S.A., VandenBranden, M., and Ring, B.J. (1996). "The human drug metabolizing cytochromes P450." *J Pharmacokinet Biopharm*, 24, 5, 461–473.

Yaffe, S. (Ed.). (2000). *Rational Therapeutics for Infants and Children*. Washington, D.C.: National Academy Press.

Yafune, A., and Ishiguro, M. (1999). "Bootstrap approach for constructing confidence intervals for population pharmacokinetic parameters. I: A use of bootstrap standard error." *Stat Med*, 18, 5, 581–599.

Zaugg, S., and Thorman, W. (2000). "Enantioselective determination of drugs in body fluids by capillary electrophoresis." *J Chromat A*, 875, 1–2, 27–41.

Zed, P.J., and Krenzelok, E.P. (1999). "Treatment of acetaminophen overdose." *Am J Health Sys Pharm*, 56, 11, 1081–1093.

Zink, P., and Reinhardt, G. (1984). "Der Verlauf der Blutalkoholkurve bei groben Trinkmengen." *Blutalkohol*, 21, 422–442.

Zuhlsdorf, M.T. (1998). "Relevance of pheno- and genotyping in clinical drug development." *Int J Clin Pharmacol Therap*, 36, 11, 607–612.

Chapter 4

Laboratory Issues

Wayne Jeffrey

Synopsis

4.1 Introduction

A laboratory deals with many issues prior to undertaking any analysis and interpreting analytical results. The toxicologist asks the following questions. What drugs or poisons are to be looked for? What samples have been collected? How have they been preserved? Which samples will be analyzed? What screening, confirmation and quantitation technology will be used? What quality controls will be used, and how will the data be interpreted?

4.2 Analysis of Samples Obtained from Living Subjects

In the living subject, the fluids that can be collected are blood, serum, plasma, urine, saliva, sweat and hair. Formerly, toxicologists debated about whether blood or urine was the best sample. Now other matrices such as saliva, sweat and hair may be considered, depending upon the situation. Toxicologists' first choice frequently is blood, because it provides evidence of drug use, and data are available about therapeutic, toxic and lethal levels. Also, because the circulating blood transports the drugs to the receptors, the presence and concentration of drugs and/or metabolites provide information about impairment.

Blood also has disadvantages. Legal issues may make it difficult to obtain the sample. The trained personnel, who are required to take samples, may not be available at the time and place they are needed. A drug may be difficult to detect in blood due to a low level or extensive metabolism. It is generally more difficult and expensive to analyze, and the small amount drawn from a living subject may not be sufficient for all types of analysis.

Plasma and serum sometime are collected. Plasma is part of the extra cellular fluid of the body, and serum is the plasma expressed from the clot. The amount of protein in either of these two fluids differs from the amount of protein in blood. Because drugs bind to protein, the interpretation of the results of drug analyses of plasma or serum will be different than the interpretation of analyses of whole blood.

Urine has several advantages as a sample. It is easy to obtain, and it provides evidence of past drug use. Because drugs and metabolites are concentrated and remain in the urine longer than in blood, detection usually is easier. Also, urine can be analyzed at a reasonable cost, compared to blood.

Urine has the following disadvantages as a sample. The presence of drugs has minimal or no relationship to impairment, which limits interpretation of results. Subjects may be able to manipulate the sample and alter the validity of results. Certain drugs may be present for weeks after psychoactive effects have ended, and some drugs are extremely difficult to detect or may not be excreted in the urine.

The use of other biological specimens for the detection and quantification of drugs has attracted considerable interest in recent years. Oral fluid (saliva), for example offers the advantage of noninvasive collection. Since samples can be collected under direct observation, concerns about their adulteration and or questions about their identity are eliminated. Saliva is a blood filtrate and relatively free of blood constituents. Therefore, it is easily processed by conventional drug screening and confirmation methods. The distribution of drugs into saliva (oral cavity) may occur from remnants of oral, nasal, or ingestion by smoking, as well as by redistribution from circulation.

In a comprehensive review of studies of the use of saliva for illegal drug tests, Cone (1993, 1997) concluded that saliva tests provide valuable information. The detection time in saliva, however, is relatively short (approximately 12–24 hours), which means the tests provide information only about very recent usage. The time limit may be an advantage or disadvantage, depending on the circumstances that led to testing. Peel, Perrigo, and Mikhael (1984) first investigated the detection of drugs in the saliva of impaired drivers.

Several problems have been demonstrated with saliva. Drug concentrations are lower in saliva than in urine, and differences in collection protocols can produce variable results. Saliva usually contains the parent drug, whereas most immunoassays are based on the metabolites. There is limited information relating drug concentration in saliva to the effects of the drug. Collection can be difficult if salivary flow has been decreased, as it can be by psychological factors, heavy smoking, and the use of certain drugs with anticholinergic effects (antidepressants, neuroleptics) or adrenergic effects (amphetamines). The level of opioids, in oral fluids does appear to parallel blood levels (Niedbal et al., 2001).

Recently, sweat has been studied for the analysis of illicit drugs in impaired drivers (Samyn and van Haeren, 2000). The "Drugwipe" (Securetec, Germany) has been used to screen for amphetamine, cocaine, THC and opiates, and the reported results are encouraging. The major advantage of sweat is that the specimens can be collected under close supervision without embarrassment, and they are not subject to evasive maneuvers.

The principal advantages of hair analysis, which has been reviewed extensively (Klintz, 1996), is that hair provides a long-term record, and drugs and their metabolites are stable in hair for an extended period of time. Also, by segmenting the hair samples, it is possible to differentiate chronic and sporadic uptake. The disadvantages of hair analysis are tedious sample preparation, poor reproducibility, difficult quantitation, possible external contamination, and lack of reference material.

4.3 Analysis of Postmortem Samples

In postmortem toxicology, blood, urine, and vitreous samples, as well as liver, kidney, brain and lung samples, can be collected. Which will be the sample or samples of choice depends on the type of case, what drugs are to be looked for, and the state of the body's decomposition. Hair, nails, and bone also may be used if other samples are unavailable. For a number of reasons, the concentration of drugs in biological samples can change significantly after death. Changes may occur due to postmortem redistribution (Pounder and Jones, 1990), as a result of chemical instability in a biological fluid, or as a result of metabolic activity (Robertson and Drummer, 1995). An understanding of these methods of drug loss is essential for the toxicologist to accurately interpret drug level.

The use of vitreous fluid as an alternative sample to blood or urine in postmortem toxicology is of particular interest when the body has undergone considerable bleeding, decomposition, or burning. Vitreous fluid is thought to be much less susceptible to postmortem changes than blood. Scott and Oliver (2001) studied the analysis of benzodiazepines in vitreous fluid.

Other samples are sometimes collected: the stomach contents when an acute poisoning is suspected, the liver (when no blood or urine is available), the kidney when poisoning by heavy metals is suspected, and the lungs when volatiles are suspected. If decomposition has set in, the only possible samples may be the nails, bone or hair.

A thorough understanding of tissue distribution and postmortem stability of drugs is essential in order for a forensic toxicologist to select the most appropriate specimen for analysis and to determine the severity of the poisoning by drugs (Moriya and Hashimoto, 1997). Postmortem redistribution occurs when drugs diffuse from sites having high concentrations, (liver and lung) into the blood. It is postulated that the extent of postmortem release of drugs from tissues is associated with the volume of distribution. The larger the volume of distribution, the larger should be the amount of extravascular drug serving as a depot for release. Apple in 1988 and Pounder and coworkers (1990a, 1990b, 1994, 1996a, 1996b) in the early 1990s were the first to report this phenomenon.

The influence of postmortem diffusion would be lessened if the autopsy sampling technique were standardized, specifying that blood is to be taken from a ligated peripheral vein (preferably femoral or external iliac), and liver is to be taken from deep within the right lobe (Pounder, 1996). When heart blood is screened for drugs and metabolites and found positive, then if both the heart blood and a venous blood sample are quantified, similar results from both can rule out postmortem diffusion. Studies of postmortem are summarized in Table 4.1.

Table 4.1
Studies of Post-Mortem Drug Diffusion

Drug	Diffusion	Study
Barbiturates	Yes	Pounder (9)
Carbamazepine	No change	Tomson et al. (2)
Cocaine	Decrease due to breakdown	Moriya and Hashimoto(3), Hearn et al. (14)
Cocaethylene	More stable than cocaine	Moriya and Hashimoto(3), Hearn et al. (14)
Codeine	Yes	Jones (13)
Diphenylhydantoin	35–65% decrease	Tomson et al. (2)
Fluvoxamine	Unknown	Kunsman et al. (4)
Morphine	Site dependent	Moriya and Hashimoto(5), Skopp et al. (16)
Methamphetamine	Site dependent	Miyazaki, Moriya (5)
Methadone	Yes	Levine (12)
Tricyclic Antidepressants	Yes	Pounder (9, 10, 15)
Zopiclone	Yes	Pounder (8)
Nitrobenzodiazepines	Some changes	Robertson (17)

It appears that the nonspecific hydrolysis of conjugated morphine to free morphine does not occur in corpses at least for a few days after death (Moriya and Hashimoto, 1997). Staub, Jeanmond, and Fryc (1990) reported that a mean of 76 percent of total morphine in blood was present as the free base in individuals who died rapidly from heroin injection, whereas a mean of 31 percent of the total morphine existed as unconjugated morphine in individuals who survived for a period of time.

Femoral vein blood is considered to be the most accurate representation of drug concentration at the time of death (Patterson, 1993).

4.4 Drug Stability in Biological Products.

Some drugs are stable in biological samples but some are not, and knowing the fate of different drugs stored under different conditions is of prime importance for the correct interpretation of analytic results. Drug stability is influenced by temperature, pH, storage time, light, drug concentration, and type of biological fluid. Levine and Smith (1990) summarized the stability of barbiturates, benzodiazepines, cannabinoids and cocaine in biological fluids.

It is well known that cocaine in blood will break down rapidly unless the sample is at a specific pH (acidic) and contains the proper preservatives. It is degraded spontaneously under alkaline condition to benzoylecgonine and to ecognine methyl ester by plasma pseudocholinesterase. The following is known about the breakdown of cocaine in biological fluids (Levine and Smith, 1990):

1. Cocaine hydrolysis is independent of concentration.
2. Cocaine hydrolysis in unpreserved blood occurs more rapidly as the temperature and pH of the blood increases.
3. The greatest stability is obtained with preservation of the fluid with fluorides or organophosphates at pH5.

The stability of benzodiazepines in whole blood has been studied extensively. Mahjoub and Staub (2000) found that clonazepam, midazolam, flunitrazepam and oxazepam were stable when stored at –800° C, but that a significant decrease occurred when stored at 200° C. Temazepam was found to be stable over a twelve-month period when stored at –200° C, but samples stored at 50° and 250° C showed a significant decrease (Levine et al., 1983). Diazepam, nordiazepam and flurazepam are relatively stable in blood when stored at 40° C, but chlordiazepoxide decomposes rapidly in whole blood (Levine et al., 1983). Skopp, Potsch, Konig and Mattern (1998) found that after 240 days the concentration of benzodiazepines stored at 40° C decreased by at least 60 percent. Although most benzodiazepines are relatively stable in biological fluids, those with a nitrogen bonded to an oxygen show instability (Levine and Smith, 1990). Flunitrazepam and its metabolite were shown to disappear completely when stored at room temperature (Kloenig et al., 1997).

Morphine and buprenorphine (Al-Hadidi and Oliver, 1998), and trihexylphenidyl (Battah and Hadidi, 1998) have also been found to be stable in blood products stored at –250°. K. Al-Hadidi (1998) found that phenytoin, phenobarbital, and carbamazepine were reasonably stable after fifteen months when stored at –200° C. The concentrations of some drugs in blood and urine stored at –200° C showed no significant changes during a one year period, and that finding extended to two or three years for other drugs (Moody et al., 1999).

The rapid enzymatic breakdown of drugs in blood samples even while being transported to the laboratory is a well-known problem. The use of grey-top Vacutainer tubes (Becton Dickinson), which contain the anticoagulant potassium oxalate and the cholinesterase inhibitor sodium fluoride, has been shown to prevent or delay cocaine catabolism for certain periods of time (Isenschmid et al., 1989). Toennes and Kauert (2001) found that the cannabinoid immunoassay was susceptible to hemolysis in fluoride containing samples. Also, the GC-MS assay revealed lower concentration of THCCOOH in the fluoride-preserved sample. The plasticizer tri (butoxyethyl) phosphate (TBEP) was previously used in the plastic caps of blood collection tubes, but it was found that TBEP, which leached out into the blood samples, displaced basic drugs such as imipramine, alprenolol, propranolol, lidocaine and quinine. The released drugs were then re-equilibrated and distributed into the red blood cells causing their measurement to be erroneously low in the separated plasma or serum samples. The use of TBEP has now been discontinued.

It also is well known that drugs adsorb onto glassware during storage and sample preparation, especially at low concentrations. Silianization to deactivate the glass adsorption can often alleviate this problem. The subject of permeation, leaching, and sorption from plastic surfaces has been reviewed (Autian, 1963a, 1963b).

4.5 Screening and Confirmation

Table 4.2
Recommended Screening and Confirmation Limits for Drugs in the Workplace Testing (46)

	Screening	Confirmation
Depressants		
Inhalants		μg/ml level [?]
Phencyclidine	25	μg/ml level [?]
Cannabis	50	15
BZE	150–300	100–150
Amphetamines	300–500	250–500
Methamphetamine		250–500
MDA, MDMA, MDEA		250–500
Hallucinogens (psilocin)		μg/ml level (50) [?]
Morphine	300–2000	200–2000
Acetylmorphine		10
Dihydrocodeine		300

4.6 Drug Detection Times

Factors that affect drug excretion times in bodily fluids include dose, health of the individual, gender, and poly drug use. Detection times in blood are affected by all of these factors as well as by a drug's half-life. For most illegal drugs, the detection time in urine is approximately seventy-two hours (Cone, 1993). Saliva has a much shorter time of 12–24 hours. Table 4.3 summarizes detection times for some of the most common drugs found in toxicological analysis.

Table 4.3
Drug Detection Times

	Specimen		
Drug	**Saliva**	**Blood**	**Urine**
Amphetamine			20–50 hours (14)
Methamphetamine			24 hours
THC	5–10 hours		13 hrs ± 3 1–24 (19)
THCCOOH	74.3(1)	433 hours (1)	
Cocaine	5–10 hrs	0.19	12 hours (42)
Benzoylecgonine		5.6	2–24 hours (14)
Ecgonine methylester (EME)		0.68	
Heroin	minutes		4–5 hours (14)
Morphine	121 hrs (1)	270(1)	4–24 hours (42)
6-monoacetylmorphine		34.5 h (1)	
Codeine	29 (free 6.3)(1)	123*(free 95)(1)	24–36 hours (14)
Methadone			24 hours (14)
Flunitrazepam	72 hrs (32)	9 hrs (33)	

Reiter (2001) analyzed the blood and urine in chronic users undergoing detoxification and found that certain drugs were detected for a long period of time. Huestis, Mitchell and Cone (1995) studied the detection times of cannabis metabolites in urine by GC-MS and immunoassay. The sensitivity and specificity of the immunoassay is essential, as significant difference exist between current immunoassay products. Longer detection times were observed at the higher marijuana dose. Mean detection times were less than one day with a 100 ng/ml cutoff, and less than two days with a 50 ng/ml cutoff. When a 20 ng/ml assay was used, detection times increased 7.8 and 2.7 times compared with the 100 and 50 ng/ml assays, respectively. Samyn, Verstraete, van Haeren, and Kintz (1999) studied detection time in saliva, and reported that drugs can be detected as long as

12–26 hours with different durations for different drugs. Table 4.4 lists durations of observable effects.

Table 4.4
Duration of Drug Effects

Drug Category		Duration (observable)
CNS depressants	barbiturates	1–16 hours
	tranquilizers	4–8 hours
	methaqualone	4–8 hours
Inhalants	most volatile solvents	6–8 hours
	anesthetic gases	very short
	aerosols	very short
	phencyclidine (PCP)	4–6 hours
	cannabis	2–5 hours
CNS stimulants	cocaine	90 minutes
	amphetamines	48 hours
	methamphetamine	12 hours
Hallucinogens		highly variable
Narcotic analgesics	heroin	4–6 hours

4.7 Conclusion

The reliability of the results of laboratory analyses of biological samples is dependent upon the accuracy and precision of the analytical methods employed. Factors that affect the integrity of the bioanalytical data must, therefore, be controlled. It is essential for a laboratory to develop and implement protocols for site sampling, type of containers, and testing methodology. Importantly, it must be demonstrated that the analytical methods have been validated.

References

Al-Hadidi, K. (1995). "Stability of temazepam in blood." *Science and Justice*, 35, 105–108.

Al-Hadidi, K.A., and Oliver J.S. (1990). "Stability of some drugs of forensic interest in whole blood stored at different conditions." Twenty-seventh TIAFT Meeting, Perth Australia October 1990, (pp. 325–335).

Al-Hadidi, K., and Oliver, J.S. (1998). "Stability of morphine and buprenorphine in whole blood." *International Journal of Legal Medicin*e, 111, 165–167.

Apple, F.S., and Bandt, C.M. (1988). "Liver and blood postmortem tricyclic antidepressant concentrations." *American Journal of Clinical Pathology*, 89, 794–796.

Autian, J. (1963a). "Plastics in pharmaceutical practice and related fields, part one." *J Pharm Sci*, 52, 1.

Autian, J. (1963b). Plastics in pharmaceutical practice and related fields, part two." *J Pharm Sci*, 52, 105.

Battah, A.H., and Al-Hadidi, K.A. (1998). "Stability of trihexylphenidy in stored blood and urine specimens." *International Journal of Legal Medicine*, 111, 111–114.

Cone, E.J. (1993). "Saliva testing for drugs of abuse." In D.Malamud and L.Tabak (Eds.). *Saliva as a Diagnostic Fluid*, Annals of the New York Academy of Sciences; Vol. 694.

Cone, E.J. (1997). "New developments in biological measures of drug prevalence." In L. Harrison and A. Hughes (Eds.). *The Validity of Self-Reported Drug Use: Improving the Accuracy of Survey Estimates*. Rockville Maryland: U.S. Department of Health and Human Services.

ElSohly, M.A., Feng, S., Salamone, S.J., and Wu, R. (1995). "A Sensitive GC-MS procedure for the analysis of flunitrazepam and its metabolites in urine." J Analytical Toxicology, 21, 335–40.

ElSohly, M.A., Feng, S., Salamone, S.J., and Brenneisen. (1999). "GC-MS determination of flunitrazepam and its major metabolites in whole blood and plasma." *J of Analytical Toxicology*, 23, 486–489.

ElSohly, M.A., and Jones, A.B. (1995). "Origin of morphine and codeine in biological fluids." In R.H. Liu, and B.A.Goldberg, *Handbook of Workplace Drug Testing* (225–237). Washington, D.C.: AACC Press.

Hearn, W.L., Keran, E.E., Wie, H., and Hime. G. (1991). "Site dependence changes in blood cocaine concentrations." *Journal of Forensic Science,* 36, 673-684.

Huestis, M.A., Mitchell, J.M., and Cone. E.J. (1995). "Detection times of marijuana metabolites in urine by immunoassay and GC-MS." *J of Analytical Toxicology,* 19, 443–449.

Isenschmid, D.S., Levine, B.S., and Caplan, Y.H. (1989). "A comprehensive study of the stability of cocaine and its metabolites." *J Analytical Toxicology,* 13, 250–256.

Jenkins, A.J., Oyler, J.M., and Cone, E.J. (1995). "Comparison of heroin and cocaine concentrations in saliva with concentration in blood and plasma." *J of Analytical Toxicology*, 19, 359–374.

Jones, G.R., and Pounder, D.J. (1987). "Site dependence of drug concentrations in post-mortem blood." *Journal of Analytical Toxicology*, 11, 186–190.

Kintz, P. (1996). *Drug Testing in Hair.* Boca Raton: CRC Press.

Kloenig, I., Skopp, G., Schmitt, G., and Mattern, R. (1997)."The stability of flunitrazepam, flurazepam, diazepam and metabolites in blood and plasma." *Archives Kriminol*, 200, 17–24.

Kunsman, G.W., Rodriguez, R., and Rodriguez, R. (1999). "Fluvoxamine distribution in postmortem cases." *The American Journal of Forensic Medicine and Pathology*, 20, 1, 78–83.

Levine, B.S., Blanke, R.V., and Valentour, J.C. (1983). "Post mortem stability of benzodiazepine in blood and tissues." *Journal of Forensic Science*, 102–115.

Levine, B., and Smith, M.L. (1990). "Stability of drug of abuse in biological specimens." *Forensic Science Review*, 2, 147–156.

Levine, B., Wu, S.C., Dixon, A., and Vern, B.A. (1995). "Site dependence of postmortem blood methadone concentrations." *American Journal of Forensic Medicine and Pathology*, 16, 97–100.

Mahjoub, A.E., and Staub, C. (2000). "Stability of benzodiazepines in whole blood samples stored at varying temperatures." *Journal of Pharmaceutical and Biomedical Analysis*, 23,1057–1063.

Miyazaki, T.N, Kojima, T., Yashiki, M. Wakamoto, H., Iwasaki, Y. and Taniguchi, T. (1993). "Site dependence of methamphetamine concentrations in blood samples collected from cadavers of people who had been methamphetamine users." *American Journal of Forensic Medicine and Pathology*, 14, 2,121–124.

Moody, D.E., Monti, K.M., and Spanbauer, A.C. (1999). "Long-term stability of abused drugs and antiabuse chemotherapeutical agents stored at –20° C." *J of Analytical Toxicology*, 23, 535–540.

Moriya, F., and Hashimoto, Y. (1996). "Postmortem stability of cocaine and cocaethylene in blood and tissues of humans and rabbits." *Journal of Forensic Sciences*, 41, 612–616.

Moriya, F., and Hashimoto, Y. (1997). "Distribution of free and conjugated morphine in blood fluids and tissue in a fatal heroin overdose: Is conjugated morphine stable in postmortem specimens?" *Journal of Forensic Science*, 42, 736–740.

Niedbala, R.S., Kardos, K.W., Fritch, D.F., Kardos, S., Fries, T., and Wafa, J. (2001). "Detection of use by oral fluid and urine analysis following single-dose administration of smoked and oral marijuana." *Journal of Analytical Toxicology*, 25, 289–302.

Niedbal, R.S., Kardos, K., Waga, J., Fritch, D., Yeager, L., Doddamane, S., et al. (2001). "Laboratory analysis of remotely collected oral fluid specimens for opiates by immunoassay." *Journal of Analytical Toxicology*, 25, 310–315.

Patterson. S. (1993). "Drugs and decomposition." *Medicine Science and the Law*, 33, 103–9.

Peel, H.W., Perrigo, B.J., and Mikhael, N.Z. (1984). "Detection of drugs in saliva of impaired drivers." *J Forensic Science*, 29, 185–189.

Pounder, D.J., Adams, E., Fuke, C., and Langford, A.M. (1996). "Site to site variability of postmortem drug concentrations in liver and lung." *Journal of Forensic Science*, 41, 6, 927–932.

Pounder, D.J., and Davies, J.I. (1994). "Zopiclone poisoning: Tissue distribution and potential for postmortem diffusion." *Forensic Science International*, 65, 177–83.

Pounder, D.J., Fuke, C., Cox, D.E., Smith, D. and Kuroda, N. (1996). "Postmortem diffusion of drugs from gastric residue: An experimental study." *American Journal of Forensic Medicine and Pathology*, 17, 1, 1–7.

Pounder, D.J., and Jones, G.R. (1990). "Postmortem drug redistribution—A toxicological nightmare." *Forensic Science International*, 45, 253–263.

Pounder, D.L., Owen, V., and Quigley, J. (1994). "Postmortem changes in blood amitryptyline concentrations." *American Journal of Forensic Medicine and Pathology*, 15, 224–230

Reiter, A., Hake, J., Meissner, C., Rohwer, J., Friedrich, J.H. and Oehmichen, M. (2001). "Time of drug elimination in chronic drug abusers. Case study of 52 patients in a low-step detoxification ward." *Forensic Science International*, 119, 2, 248–253.

Robertson, M.D., and Drummer, O.H. (1995). "Postmortem metabolism by bacteria." *Journal of Forensic Science*, 40, 282–286.

Robertson, M.D., and Drummer, O.H. (1998). "Postmortem distribution of nitrobenzodiazepines in man." *Journal of Forensic Science*, 43, 9–13.

Samyn, N., and van Haeren, C. (2000). "On-site testing of saliva and sweat with drugwipe and determination of concentrations of drugs of abuse in saliva, plasma, and urine of suspected users." *International Journal of Legal Medicine*, 113, 150–154.

Samyn, G., Verstraete, A., van Haeren, C., and Kintz, P. (1999). "Analysis of Drugs of Abuse in Saliva." *Forensic Science Review*, 11, 1–14.

Scott, K.S., and Oliver, J.S. (2001). "The use of vitreous humor as an alternative to whole blood for the analysis of benzodiazepines." *J Forensic Science*, 46, 694–697.

Skopp, G., Lutz, Ganbmann B., Mattern, R., and Aderjan, R. (1996). "Postmortem distribution of morphine and morphine glucuronides in heroin overdoses." *International Journal of Legal Medicine*, 109, 118–124.

Skopp, G., Potsch, L., Konig, I., and Mattern, R. (1998). "A preliminary study of benzodiazepines in blood and plasma stored at 4° C." *International Journal of Legal Medicine*, 111, 1–5.

Staub, C., Jeanmond, R., and Fryc, O. (1990). "Morphine in postmortem blood: Its importance for the diagnosis of deaths associated with opiate addiction." *International Journal of Legal Medicine*, 104, 39–42.

Sticht, G., and Kaferstein, H. (2000). "Detection of psilocin in body fluids." *Forensic Science International*, 113, 403–407.

Toennes, S.W., and Kauert, G.F. (2001). "Importance of vacutainer selection in forensic toxicological analysis of drugs of abuse." *J Analytical Toxicology*, 25, 339–343.

Tomson, T., Skold, A.C., Holmgen, P., Nilsson, L. and Danielsson, B. (1998). "Postmortem changes in blood concentrations of phenytoin and carbamazepine. An experimental study." *Therapeutic Drug Monitoring*, 20, 3, 309–312.

Verstraete, A.G., and Pierce, A. (2001)."Workplace drug testing in Europe." *Forensic Science International*, 121, 2–6.

Chapter 5

Laboratory Technology

Laurent Rivier

Synopsis

5.1 Introduction

In forensic toxicology, analysis of a biological specimen is the necessary step in determining whether or not an individual has been impregnated with any substance that might have influenced his or her behavior. Providing evidence of illegal drug abuse, or of a murder by poisoning are just two important tasks, as is the determination of psychoactive drugs in blood which may reduce the responsibility of a criminal as well as the fitness to drive a car, a train, or an airplane. Doping controls in sport are also illustrations of the tasks of forensic toxicology. It is important to note that most of the time, the toxicologist does not know what chemicals he has to look for. The analyst, as a first step, has to identify correctly the compound(s) of interest and, therefore, has to take into account a vast number of relevant substances. This makes the task difficult and challenging. For example, since a single immunoassay or chromatographic technique made on a unique biological sample will never provide unequivocal identification, suitable techniques, screening tests, and confirmatory analysis have to be used side-by-side (Rivier and Saugy, 1995). The final identification is achieved when the results from all the applied techniques match each other. Then, quantification of the most relevant substances is necessary in order to evaluate the importance of the body's impregnation at the "juridical relevant time." Consequently, the limitations and advantages of each technique must be addressed so that the correct combination of procedures can be chosen to provide the required identification power.

Procedures for screening, identification, and/or quantification for xenobiotics are numerous, and it is difficult to judge from outside the laboratory which one might be best. The newest technology and latest instrument developments definitely can add significant benefit to the overall efficacy of the analytical strategy. The most advanced analytical approaches have been reviewed recently in a special volume of the Journal of Chromatography, and many tables list all the procedures known to have practical utility (Maurer, 1999; Drummer, 1999; Polettini, 1999; Bogusz, 1999). It is not the purpose of the present chapter to give further indications about which analytical procedure to select, and the reader can refer directly to these excellent papers to find the best technical solution for a particular problem. The aim of the present paper is to explain the general technical requirements in the forensic toxicology laboratory, and how they are so specific in the demonstration of the proof of exposure to chemicals, drugs, and/or poisons.

We are surrounded by thousand of potentially toxic chemicals, such as drugs pesticides, herbicides, bactericides, household products, cosmetics, and doping agents, not to speak of the numerous natural substances found in food or in our environment. Ingesting significant quantities of these chemicals can bring a toxic reaction of the body's physiology and change the normal behavior of the individual. When abnormal situations arise, it is important for the justice system to document and evaluate these for an objective analysis of the person's responsibility. The task of the forensic toxicologist is to bring unequivocal evidence of the presence of chemically well-defined substances in specified bio-matrices, to quantify them, and to interpret the outcome in regard to the reason for carrying out the analysis (de Zeeuw and Franke, 2000).

The analytical methods used must be sensitive to the broad spectrum of relevant substances from antidepressants to stimulants, keeping in mind that variations in use and abuse behavior evolve continually. A rough estimate states now that more than six million substances are known to man, originating from either natural or synthetic sources. Those chemicals that might have a significant toxic effect at low concentrations amount to approximately 60,000. Furthermore, only a minority is available in a specific location (e.g., in Western countries). For example, in more than 40,000 intoxication cases investigated at the poison Center in Munich, just more than 8,000 different chemicals were involved.

For instrumental and economical conveniences, the majority of forensic toxicologists distinguish seven categories of toxic chemicals (Table 5.1) for implementing their analytical strategy. Most of them are routinely searched for during systematic toxicological analysis.

Table 5.1
Classes of Toxic Chemicals That are Looked at During Systematic Toxicological Analysis.

Classes	Screening	No. of substances	Reference
Gases	No	25	
Volatiles	GC-FID	40	
Lipophillic agents	GC-MS	>6000	Maurer, 1999
Non-lipophillic agents	HPLC-UV and LC-MS	> 1200	Marquet & Lachâtre,1999
Metals	ICP-MS	70	
Ions	No	120	
Varia	(No) LC-MS	Undetermined	

Gases comprise carbon monoxide, methane, ethane and other natural gases, hydro-cyanic acid and its salts, for example. The laboratory is asked to screen for gases when the circumstances require doing so. On the other hand, volatiles are always screened for. Volatiles cover most organic solvents. Alcohols, and ethanol and acetone as items of special importance, may require immediate quantification. Lipophillic agents are so named due to the solubility property of these molecules into organic non-polar solvents like diethyl ether or toluene. They are not easily soluble in water, at least as parent drug. It is the largest class because the majority of pharmaceutical agents, psychoactive drugs, and drug of abuse belong to the category. The non-lipophillic molecules, on the other hand, can dissolve into water and other polar solvents. They are difficult to screen for because of extraction problems from biological fluids with ordinary solvents. Special technology is required like LC-MS but it is not available in most laboratories yet. Quaternary ammonium salts, compounds of the Curare type or scopolamine derivatives belong to this category. Only specialized professionals (pharmacists, surgeons, anesthesiologists, nurses, etc.) handle these preparations. Screening for these chemicals is usually performed on specific indication from the inquiry, or because the specific context of the case indicates the possible accessibility and use of such specialized compounds. For metals (Mercury, Thallium, Selenium, Lead, and others), acute poisoning can generally be seen at autopsy, and forensic pathologists request the laboratory to confirm their diagnosis. Long-term exposure to metals is more an occupational medicine problem rather than a forensic one. Finally, ions are usually closely related to specific jobs, as they are not accessible to the general public. Galvanic baths, revelation or fixative preparations are restricted, for example, to the silver industry or photographers. Here again, the specific circumstances will guide the laboratory concerning the necessity to perform that screening.

5.2 Context of Analyzing—Systematic Toxicological Analysis

Owing to the proliferation of pharmaceuticals during the last forty years, it has become difficult for the forensic analyst to keep up with new drug developments. Even before new pharmacologically active substances are introduced on the market, whether for human or veterinary uses, they may appear in samples submitted for analysis: designer drugs are typical in this context. Comparing the work of the scientist who has to analyze urine and/or blood samples from forensic samples with analysts dealing with clinical ones shows obvious differences. In forensic toxicology, the laboratory receives sealed and coded samples with the indication of the case type. If not advised to look for a particular class of drug because evidence such as apparent intoxication is lacking, the laboratory should collect all information available. If a xenobiotic has been taken, the amount in blood is most unlikely to be within the normal therapeutic range of concentration, but the notion of normality is not necessarily applicable. Obviously, we may encounter drug concentrations ranging from low levels where mixtures may show synergic interactions to overdose cases where large concentrations of the drug or metabolites are present. A review of techniques used to screen biological specimens for the presence of drugs with particular reference to systematic toxicological analysis has been published recently (Drummer, 1999). This paper presents an excellent summary of extractability of selected drugs, as well as of published GC, HPLC, and TLC methods.

A limited volume of urine or blood is provided, typically between 40 and 50 ml and for the large majority of the cases there will be no opportunity to obtain a second sample. Nevertheless, the exact identity of any xenobiotic substance present in the sample must be stated unequivocally. If results are to be released within strict time limits, it is usually specified in the contract agreed with the authorities.

Since most samples are positive, i.e. are found to contain a substance of toxicology relevance, and since confirmatory tests are relatively complex, time-consuming, and expensive, all samples are first submitted to a range of screening tests. The screening tests usually rely on one or several of the following techniques: thin layer chromatography (TLC), gas chromatography (GC), high performance liquid chromatography (HPLC), mass spectrometry usually coupled with GC (GCMS) or HPLC (LC-MS), and immunoassays (RIA or ELISA, for example). Only those samples that fail screening tests are then submitted to confirmatory testing. The screening tests are designed to be sensitive, and typically 80 percent of the samples require some form of confirmatory tests. The confirmatory test relies heavily on GC-MS or LC-MS together with the use of chemical derivatization or chemical ionization to improve both GC and MS characteristics of the substance. Very often, the laboratory identifies metabolites of the substance, especially when the parent compound is undetectable.

A. The need for large spectra extraction and high specificity detection

For toxicologists to provide a comprehensive screening service, it is clear that no one single chromatographic system can provide a sufficiently exhaustive coverage of relevant chemicals and their metabolites. GC-MS can provide reasonable coverage depending on the number of extraction systems used. Indeed, one single liquid-liquid or solid-phase extraction system cannot extract most compounds of interest. Acids and neutrals, on one hand, basic and neutrals on the other hand, both extracts might be combined to reduce chromatography time, although derivatization is required to detect any polar drug by GC. HPLC can pass moderate and very polar substances, but its actual chromatography resolution is still not as good as that achieved with capillary GC, even when using 1 mm diameter columns.

The signal of the detector should give high confidence of the specificity of the result. In short, the detector should be able to see only the compound of interest at a chromatography retention time. This can be best achieved with mass spectrometry. It is assumed here that the reader has basic knowledge of the principle and practice of GC-MS, which is now considered as the "gold standard" in analytical toxicology. If the reader wants to become more knowledgeable about GCMS analysis, *GC/MS in Clinical Chemistry*, (Gerhards et al., 1996) is recommended. This book provides explanations of the fundamentals of gas chromatography and mass spectrometry, potential applications in the field of working medicine, and drug analysis in a simple and practical form are given.

B. The need for non-specialization

Some drugs of forensic importance are not easily detected by chromatographic screening techniques. (For example, many of the potent benzodiazepines, opiates, neuroleptics, fentanyl and its designer variations, a number of cardiovascular drugs, many plant-derived substances, peptidic drugs, chloral hydrate and its metabolites.) Any techniques currently applied in the laboratory should be checked for their ability or failure to detect these additional substances. To be as complete as possible, the laboratory should thus perform additional targeted testing, typically screening for LSD, psilocybin, fentanyls, and opioids like buprenorphine, and so on

If a sample is found positive by immunoassay, targeted confirmation must be conducted by GC-MS or LC-MS.

Validated technique or analytical approaches used for screening purposes should acknowledge the list of drugs that can be detected at a specified level. Such performance must be communicated to the mandate, if not in the report itself, at least when establishing the first contacts.

C. Extracting the analytes of interest

The conduct of an efficient and extensive toxicological screening is essential for forensic cases to either detect substances or exclude their involvement in a particular situation. Unfortunately, not all substances can be extracted and detected with a single drug screening. The presence of acidic, neutral and basic properties in toxic compounds and their overall lipophilicity affect the ability to extract substances of interest from biological matrices. The choice of hydrolysis conditions for glucuronide conjugates depends very much on the drug or drug metabolite. A review of the conditions required for benzodiazepines has been published (Drummer, 1998). Acid hydrolysis (heating with concentrated HCl for thirty minutes) has been used to liberate conjugates and to improve recovery for highly protein-bound drugs. Enzymatic incubation (glucuronidase one hour at 55° C) might be preferred, as it does not give rise to production of so many artifacts.

With few exceptions, chromatographic techniques require some form of isolation procedure to separate and concentrate the drugs from the biological matrix. These procedures can be distinguished into three distinct types:

1. Liquid-liquid extraction
2. Solid-phase extraction
3. Others

Liquid-liquid extraction techniques have been the traditional method for isolating xenobiotics from biological specimens. It is very simple and fast and does not require specialized glassware or equipment. Many solid-phase extraction techniques on small columns or disks are proposed for many analytes or groups of substances. The possibility of automating the whole process, high recovery and cleanness of the extracts make it very attractive for routine drug screening in STA (Chen et al., 1993). Other procedures include direct injection or solid-phase micro-extraction (SPME) and have been restricted so far to HPLC on a limited range of compounds. None of them has yet been described for successful STA.

D. Criteria for a successful determination

For any screening system, there are limitations with respect to the ability to detect drugs and other poisons. Awareness of the strengths and limitations is of critical importance in any systematic analysis of specimens for the presence of xenobiotics and should be communicated to the mandate. Thermal stability of the extracted substances, their polarity, and the detector sensitivity affect the detectability of drugs in chromatographic systems. Impurities detected by one method may not be seen by another when based on a completely different physico-chemical detection approach (i.e., LC with UV detection and GC with NPD detection). The final choice of a combination of several procedures is the responsibility of the laboratory. Its reputation will depend on its success in correctly detecting xenobiotics in a large variety of cases. Inter-laboratory comparisons and proficiency tests proposed at various time intervals by professional societies or associations are very useful in providing the necessary credibility of the laboratory.

5.3 The Analytical Strategy

General guidelines can be offered based on my practical experiences in "systematic toxicological analysis" and other related fields like "general unknown analyses" in forensic toxicology and human doping analyses.

1. Screening urine samples with immunoassays is quite common and laboratories may use more than fifteen different drug immunoassays. These are always used in combination with at least one other chromatographic technique for confirmation.
2. Most laboratories perform one to five (average two) different extraction procedures on the biological samples, mainly urine and blood, before using one or more chromatographic techniques to detect various groups of drugs and metabolites. The total volume of urine used for the extractions averages 10 ml and ranged from 3 to 20 ml. The

derivatization of the extracts is obtained most of the time with Acetate anhydride, TFA, TMS or methylation reagents.

3. It appears that there has been a decrease over the years in the use of TLC and an increase in the use of HPLC/DAD and GC/MS. When using TLC, mostly on Silica Gel GF 254, several developing solvent combinations are used together with various visualization reagents, noting that multiple visualizations are not overlaid on the same TLC plate. In many cases, more than one TLC system is used on the same urine extract with different visualization techniques used on each plate.
4. In HPLC/DAD screening, reverse phase systems with aqueous acid / organic mobile phases and solvent programming are used to analyze acidic extracts for polar compounds like the antiinflammatory drugs. Computer programs allow reviewing of the data in respect to their respective retention and UV spectra data. LC-MS screening is still in its infancy, and each laboratory has to build its own collection of reference mass spectra. To date, no commercially available reference MS database exists.
5. A few laboratories use GC/NPD analysis, mostly on basic extracts with no derivatization. The analyses are performed on capillary columns with temperature programming, and the limited list of compounds that are detected is well documented.
6. Automated GC/MS screening is made possible with rather simple and economic instruments equipped with suitable automatic injection devices and comparison with adequate reference mass spectra databases. Dedicated collections of MS are available from various commercial sources, but none is specifically dedicated to forensic toxicology and doping, except that of PMW that was updated last year (Pfleger, Maurer and Weber, 2000).

A. Basic requirement of the techniques

With the many instrument-based procedures, the laboratory should be able to extract reliable results. Excellent knowledge of the fundamentals and of the practices of the techniques must be assured. Normally, each laboratory monitors the performance of the apparatus daily (i.e., specificity and limit of detection) and checks the good practice of laboratory technical workers by introducing several internal quality controls (QCs) in between the samples. Such QCs can be bought from commercial sources but are better made in-house. They are very important, as controls can indicate when the protocol is not working properly. The faulty part must be immediately identified and corrected. The mistake can originate from various sources: sample preparation, derivatization, chromatographic separation, and/or tuning the detector. Clerical mistakes are also detected when the internal QC is blind (i.e., the operator doesn't know that a specific sample is a control). If a significant fault is detected, all samples belonging to the batch must, of course, be re-analyzed. The laboratory must have an open information policy with its mandates, explaining in detail the nature of the QC samples and how often they are introduced into the everyday work.

On the other hand, the mandate can itself submit QC samples as real samples to the laboratory. A few can contain xenobiotics at concentrations close or lower than what the laboratory claims to be able to detect. The difficulty of obtaining biological samples from external sources and the relatively high costs make this practice infrequent. In serious doping programs in sport, however, the rate of QC samples can be as high as 10 percent of the total samples submitted to the laboratory. The mandate can then be absolutely sure that the laboratory is maintaining the level of requested performance while analyzing their samples.

B. Requirement for identification

Toxicology screening has several unique requirements relative to the other areas where toxicological analysis is performed. It must encompass a broad range approach to the correct identification of all possible drugs or drug combinations able to produce the observed physiological effect. Identification should be objective and reliable, not depending on the subjective interpretation of the operator. External experts should review all data for possible cross-examination. This may be difficult if the procedure is highly automated.

In general, positive findings in qualitative analysis follow two different kinds of methods: screening and confirmation. During the screening step, a fast and economical method is used to distinguish negatives from "presumptive" positive samples. For confirmation purposes, several instrumental approaches are used to demonstrate the presence of a substance in the sample "beyond any reasonable doubt". Excellent sources of data on toxicologically relevant substances have been published on the most frequently used methods, including TLC, HPLC GC and GC-MS. The preferred technique is GC-MS, which is considered "the least likely to be challenged in court."

According to de Zeeuw and Franke (2000), the following criteria are crucial in the selection of suitable analytical techniques for differentiation and detection, as well as for subsequent identification.

1. The substances measured in the analytical systems should cover the total range and be evenly distributed over that range (i.e., for GC-MS the RT of the standard substances ranges from three to thirty minutes).
2. The standard deviations of measurements should be as small as possible and the values (i.e., RT) must be standardized in such a way that good reproducibility is obtained on an inter-laboratory scale.
3. When more than one system or technique is used, there should be low correlation between these systems or techniques.

In order to fulfill these criteria, several mathematical approaches have been proposed such as the Mean List Length (MLL, de Zeeuw and Franke, 2000). Examples of these approaches can be found in their respective references, but recognize that none of them are used routinely and they remain more on the theoretical rather than the practical side. This uncomfortable position will change drastically with the advent of the ISO 17025 requirements (ISO 17025, 1998) as more and more laboratories have to adopt them in the near future.

C. The information needed

The general criteria for any procedure are simple: the method has to be able to distinguish between the analyte and all known interfering materials that may possibly occur in the relevant matrix, and the physical and chemical behavior of the analyte during the analysis has to be distinguishable from that of the corresponding standard material (reference substance) in the corresponding matrix. This means that detailed information about the molecular structure of the analyte is essential. Each analytical technique possesses an identification power (IP) of its own (Moffat, 1978). Obviously, retention index in TLC will offer less information about the identity of a substance than retention time in capillary GC combined with a mass spectrum. On the basis of IP, the best methods of identification can be selected (de Zeeuw and Franke, 2000). The total information obtained is the sum of each piece of information derived from each individual analytical step of the method, ranging from partition coefficient to fragmentation pattern in mass spectroscopy.

For known compounds, the requirements for the several chromatographic techniques used in systematic toxicological analysis are:

1. TLC. Co-chromatography of the analyte and the reference substance on the same plate and color matching of the spots are mandatory.
2. GC and LC. Co-chromatography is mandatory on two closely related runs of the analyte and the reference substance. The retention time of the analyte should match that of a standard with a tolerance of $\pm 5\ \sigma$ on capillary columns. When using an internal standard, the relative retention time of the analyte must match that of the reference substance with a tolerance of 5/A, where A is the absolute retention time of the internal standard in σ. The nearest peak maximum should be separated from the analyte peak by at least one full width at half maximum peak height.
3. GC-MS. At least three, preferably more diagnostic ions should be monitored (the molecular ion has to be included if relevant). All ions from the analyte should appear at the same retention time as the reference substance. Relative intensities as a percentage of the base ion should be within ≤ 20 percent in the chemical ionization mode and ≤ 10 percent in the electron impact mode with respect to the standard analyte.

For substances where no reference standards are available, and no official criteria have ever been established, it is the expertise of the professionals involved in each specialized analytical field that become crucial. Published mass spectra can be used. The correct use of reference mass spectra databases is, however, of utmost importance. Various mathematical algorithms, which have been developed for automatic spectra comparison (called "library searching") with identification probability in %, make the task relatively easy to perform. Yet some drawbacks inherent to such systems have to be described:

1. A typical library does not always contain complete mass spectra, and only a few ions are retained.
2. Instrumental differences produce different ions' intensities, which can result in poor matching.
3. Impurities co-eluting with the compound of interest may give mismatching.
4. Number and type of substances present in libraries are finite.

The algorithms used by the different commercially available systems are not similar, and any retrieval system tends to give poor results when the unknown substance is not in the reference computer library. Another valuable approach is the use of structure-orientated databases and mathematical procedures able to interpret unknown mass spectra. Although this is a very promising field, the full identification of the analyte still requires direct comparison with authentic reference compounds and ad hoc synthesis must sometimes be initiated to cover the specific requirements of the forensic field.

Scientific probability is difficult to explain to courts, and an expert analytical toxicologist may be requested to testify with statements "beyond a reasonable doubt" (Furst, 1997). Does it mean 90% probability level, or even 95%, or only 51% as can be accepted as "more probable than not" in some civil suits? The problem of providing sufficient proofs may require the analyst to evaluate the amount of data provided by his or her laboratory as well as related information obtained from the scientific literature and reports from real cases presented at courts. Unfortunately, forensic toxicologists may not be familiar with the outcome of these interesting cases. Professional associations like the Society of Forensic Toxicologists (SOFT) can play an important role in bringing these specific points to the attention of their members. Finally, the analytical toxicologist should be aware of so called junk science when attempting to determine identity of a compound. Gross mistakes in the characterization of so-called "new metabolites" have been published in renowned international scientific reviews and journals. A simple but essential rule is to refer to two rather than just one published reference.

D. Requirement for quantification

In some cases, the quantitative determination of the xenobiotic may be needed (i.e., for driving under the influence of drugs cases). Ethanol is the oldest example, and extensive laboratory rules govern the way it has to be quantified. Abused drugs like tetrahydrocannabinol (acid and delta-9 metabolite) can also display regulatory limits of concentration in blood or other body fluids. Adequate methodology using pure standards and, as far as possible, biological blank samples, has to be implemented. Deuterated internal standards are recommended. Linearity, recovery rates, limit of quantification, and all related uncertainties must be known before any real forensic sample can be analyzed. Results from triplicates should be presented with the mean value and the corresponding standard variation for evaluating the dispersion of the dosage.

E. Validation of the method and quality assurance in the laboratory

Validation is an old concept, and any good toxicologist validates an analytical method before using it for routine work! Equipment has been tested before it has been used for measurements. But, in reality, several problems are frequently encountered (Huber, 1999):

1. Often, there is a lack of documented procedures and documented validation results. For example, when asked for calibration plots or for the exact procedure they used that very day, the laboratory may not be able to provide the corresponding documentation.
2. Only part of the total analytical procedure has been validated, not the complete procedure. For example, the analytical steps themselves are validated, but not the sample preparation steps, which very often contribute most to the overall error.
3. Accessories and materials used are not qualified. For example, there are no controls on the calibrated glassware introduced in the laboratory when received from the manufacturer.
4. Performance parameters and acceptance limits are loosely defined or not applied when necessary.
5. Qualification and validation are done at just one particular point of time. However, these are ongoing processes and should cover the complete lifetime of a method or equipment.

The suitability of the methods chosen by the laboratory cannot be assessed without running several internal control samples. These biological samples are produced from blank blood or urine to which definite amounts of xenobiotics are added. These samples are then run through the normal procedures, and results must correspond to what has been added within a certain error margin. Such validation should be repeated at regular intervals depending on the complexity and stability of the procedures. It is important for the laboratory to document these tests, as they can be very useful during court examination to give the best evidence of the state of excellence of the laboratory when a sensitive sample was submitted for analysis.

To extend these controls further, an external quantity assurance scheme can be implemented. This is an inter-laboratory testing system based on both qualitative and quantitative determination limited either to one country or international. Several institutions are now organizing these inter-laboratory tests at regular intervals

Due to the widely recognized need in industrial countries, many organizations now promote the evaluation of performance of laboratories.

Table 5.2
Performance Levels of Analytical Methods (uncertainty) in Relation to Validation (adapted from Aderjan, 2000)

Action/level	Deviations due to instruments and methods	Power of the method	Testing of the method	Inter-laboratory comparison
Measurement of physical parameters	Calibration			
Identification	Measurement precision	Selectivity		Selectivity
Measurement of physico-chemical parameters	Measurement and method precisions	Robustness/ ruggedness	Linearity, precision, accuracy	Accuracy
Qualitative trace analysis (one substance or more)	Measurement and method precisions	Selectivity, robustness/ ruggedness	Limit of detection, limit of identification	Selectivity, completeness of detection and identification
Content, quantitative trace determination	Measurement and method precisions	Selectivity, robustness/ ruggedness	Possible range of measurement, precision, accuracy, limit of detection, limit of identification, limit of quantification	Reproducibility, accuracy

Quality assurance principles of testing laboratories are now generally accepted. In order to give guidance in forensic quality terms, professional organizations like The International Association of Forensic Toxicologists (TIAFT), SOFT, and others have formulated guidelines for testing in forensic and analytical toxicological laboratories, based on scientific and quality aspects. Recently, the International Laboratory Accreditation Conference (ILAC) proposed guidelines for forensic laboratories with management and technical requirements. Future agreements with authorities submitting samples for forensic toxicology analyses will require the laboratory to present a minimum requirement for quality and performance. This will be done in accordance with the newest ISO 17025 regulations (previously called ISO guide 25) entitled "General Requirements for the Competence of Testing and Calibration Laboratories," and any supplementary document containing more specific instructions that professional associations might rely on in the future.

In short, the laboratory must demonstrate the quality of its structure (staff, management and technical direction, facilities, equipment and supplies). Then each procedure has to be described, correctly implemented, and maintained after validation. During the validation, the robustness/ruggedness of the analytical procedure should also be checked (Vander Heyden et al., 2001). This measure of the capacity of an analytical procedure to remain unaffected by small, but deliberate variations in method parameters provides an indication of its reliability during subsequent normal usage. In summary, the critical points to review in a procedure are:

1. It must not miss any substance present at or above the limit of detection, and possibly at or above a selected threshold limit concentration.
2. It must not report false positive results.
3. There must be a documented validation that the extraction procedure removes compounds of interest from the sample matrix and that the analytical (chromatographic part) assay is also able to detect the same substances.
4. For quantitative determinations, the recovery of the analyte must be 50 to 100 percent with a coefficient of variation of < 20 percent.

5. Values found and corrected for recovery must agree within 20 percent with the recovery corrected values obtained by the "official or reference method" if existing.

Figures may vary from one application to the other, and these performance tests should have acceptance limits suitable for the intended use (Huber, 1999). For example, precision of peak retention times in GC, after five repeated injections of one standard can be < 1 percent of the relative standard deviation, but if an internal standard is used, this figure may be not relevant and is replaced by the relative retention index. It is the responsibility of the head of the laboratory to determine these figures and make certain they are applied throughout the procedures. Whenever asked to give explanations about how the analyses have been performed, he or she should be able to provide the necessary details. In forensic toxicology laboratories, these aspects are often not faced with the seriousness they deserve, but major changes are expected to occur with the introduction of ISO norms and related quality assurance regulations.

F. Second analysis or confirmatory analysis

At times, it is necessary to perform a confirmatory analysis either in the same laboratory or in another one that is able to perform similar instrumental tests. In doping controls, such requirements are mandatory except when the athlete declines to use his or her right to such control analysis. No matter who does the experiment, complete records must be kept. Unimportant details may become important points later in an open court. Every observation, every calculation, and every measurement must be recorded. Each item that has been handled must be recorded, and a note must be made to assure that no person substituted any agent during or after the experiment was completed.

Qualitative results from experiment one and two must be superimposable but not necessarily identical. Because the storage time was different for sample A and sample B, the quantities of parent drugs and their metabolites will not always be the same even though the samples were kept at low temperature. In short, small discrepancies between the two results are acceptable. For dosages, statistical considerations have to be introduced and standard errors of the mean determined in order to appreciate whether two results are similar or not. Finally, a logical step is to consider the value that is acting in favor of the accused person.

G. The economics of the methodological approach

The running costs of a forensic toxicology laboratory are high. They depend on the analysis required and on the viewpoint of the mandate. For example, in clinical toxicology, GC/MS is not a viable method for determining cannabis from urine in drug screening, as a separate sample treatment is necessary here. A request for analysis can usually be dealt with adequately in the hospital from both economic and quality aspects by an immunological test. This does not apply at all to a comprehensive screening for toxic substances. GC/MS analysis clearly gives results with a higher information content compared to immunoassays. Single substances and/or their metabolites are always determined, so that information about accompanying medication can be gathered, provided the correct combination of extracts - derivatization is made.

5.4 Drug Screening

The technology of drug screening has greatly improved during the two past decades. Ideally, a screening test for doping controls should be rapid (a short turnaround time), highly specific (without false-positive results), highly sensitive (allowing the detection of very low concentration of the drug in the specimen), reliable (same result from one laboratory to another for a given specimen), easily performed technically, and inexpensive. Since none of the available analytical technology meets all of these requirements perfectly, doping screening is usually achieved by means of the combination of two different techniques in order either to extend the screening test to a larger group of substances not detectable by a single method or to confirm a result. As a matter of fact, screening tests are designed for maximum sensitivity at the expense of selectivity. Confirmatory analyses are often just as sensitive (if not more so), but additionally they provide the requisite specificity. It is important, however, to point out that screening procedures must not give false-negative results, because this terminates the testing process. False-positives at this stage are acceptable, because all presumptive samples are to be re-analyzed by a confirmatory technique like high resolution or high selectivity GC-MS (Rivier and Saugy, 1995; Gerhards et al., 1999; de Zeeuw and Franke, 2000).

The methods most frequently employed for forensic toxicology cases, drug of abuse as well as doping screenings, are immunoassays, thin layer, gas or liquid chromatography and capillary electrophoresis (sometimes). Both serum (or blood) and urine can be analyzed by these techniques.

A. Immunoassays

Immunological techniques are now the most widely used screening procedures in drug of abuse testing. Advantages include high sensitivity, no extraction steps, and applicability to a large number of samples. Popular versions of these tests are represented by radioimmunoassay (RIA), enzyme-multiplied immunoassay technique (EMIT), enzyme-linked immuno-sorbent assay (ELISA) and fluorescent polarization immunoassay (FPIA) (Miyaishi, 1995). These techniques use antibodies specific to the drug being assayed and a labeled form of the same drug. The label itself may be a radioactive isotope (RIA), an active enzyme (EMIT and ELISA) or a fluorescent label (FPIA) that is incorporated synthetically. A fixed quantity of antibody and labeled drug are added to the test sample. The binding sites on the antibody attract both labeled drug and the unlabeled drug in the sample. The amount of labeled drug bound is inversely proportional to the number of unlabeled drug molecules present. RIA kits are available for opiates, barbiturates, amphetamines, cocaine, phencyclidine, cannabinoids and LSD. Drawbacks of RIA include the necessity for training personnel to handle radioactive reagents, the fact that only one sample at a time may be assayed and the high false negativity rate if the sample has been adulterated (Montagne et al., 1988).

In EMIT and FPIA testing, the analytical measurement is based on an optically detected change such as UV absorption, fluorescence, or luminescence. These systems avoid the use of radioactive isotopes but also have reduced sensitivity when compared to RIA, because the optical signal is measured in the presence of the original biological fluid. EMIT kits are available for opiate, barbiturates, cocaine, amphetamines, benzodiazepines, methaqualone, methadone, phencyclidine, cannabinoids and LSD. The advantages of EMIT as a screening technique include its rapidity, semi-quantification and its ability to detect a number of drugs. Disadvantages include the expense of its reagents and its susceptibility to both false-positives and false-negatives, so that confirmation by an alternative methodology is mandatory for confirming positive and even negative results (Baselt, 1984). FPIA is both sensitive and specific; however, the equipment is expensive and susceptible to sample alteration affecting its accuracy. The application of FPIA technique to forensic blood work and to alternative specimens such as hair or bile has been described (Gerde et al., 1990). Additional antibody kits are also available expanding the uses of these systems (Montagne et al., 1988).

A few ELISA kits are available for testing anabolic agents like anabolic steroids and beta-2 agonists, as well as beta-blockers in horse urines. Transposition of the use of these kits to human samples can be done, but full evaluation of their exact performance is still lacking.

B. Thin-layer chromatography

Thin-layer chromatography (TLC) is one of the simplest tests, and it is still a widely used technique for the separation and identification of drugs. Essentially, the drug is extracted from urine and concentrated onto a silica plate. The plate is then placed in a solvent tank of chosen polarity. As the solvent rises up the plate, it elutes the drugs and carries them to various distances depending upon the affinity of the drug for the plate and for the solvent (mobile phase). The plate is then sprayed with suitable reagents that allow the drugs to be identified by color and specific positioning relative to drug standards. Although TLC is low-cost, relatively simple, and offers many choices of stationary and mobile phases making complex separations possible, the result is only qualitative and dependent on the freshness of the reagents used, as well as the technical proficiency of the operator who performs and visually interprets the test. Disadvantages include misinterpretation due to interference from endogenous substances, fading of the plate and stains that makes archiving a permanent record of the results difficult. Additionally TLC occasionally fails to detect drugs known to be present in a sample (e.g., cocaine) for a variety of technical reasons, often including inadequate migration (Kelly, 1988).

For several years, this technology has been improved with the introduction of automatic TLC samplers, in situ UV detection by scanning densitometers equipped with workstations and UV spectrum libraries making possible instrumental measurement for identification and quantification. In doping analyses, TLC is mostly used by horse doping control laboratories in the U.S.A. This technique lacks sensitivity for many individual substances. Thus, additional characterization of any suspicious sample by a more informative technique like GC-MS is mandatory.

C. High-performance liquid chromatography

High-performance liquid chromatography (HPLC) allows the separation of nonvolatile substances from an extraction residue. When a mixture of substances is injected onto the column, each component is partitioned between the stationary phase (column) and the liquid (mobile) phase. Molecules with greater affinity for the column spend more time in that phase and, therefore, take longer to reach the detector. The time taken from injection to the peak maximum is known as the retention time. The detector responds in direct proportion to the concentration of material passing through it, hence peak heights and area shown on the chromatogram are directly related to the concentration of each analyte.

HPLC shows good sensitivity and high specificity depending upon the detection system used. The most common detectors utilize absorption of UV. A diode array detector will allow recording of a full UV spectrum of the analyte. This can be compared to references' spectra, and identification is then based both on retention time and UV spectra. Most instruments also include the ability to obtain first and second derivative spectra to provide an additional means of identification. Postcolumn reactions for increased sensitivity have also been described. Due to its qualities, HPLC can be used to screen a sample for many doping agents. The use of mass spectrometry as HPLC detector (LC-MS) is becoming more common in toxicological laboratories. Accumulation of individual reference mass spectra for each solvent combination is needed in order to set up an accurate screening like what can be done with GC-MS. The technique is very sensitive and can be extended to many polar and thermo-labile substances. The drawbacks of HPLC include its expense, the high expertise necessary for operation of the equipment, and the need for sample extraction (Moore, 1996).

D. Gas chromatography

Capillary-gas chromatography (GC) is also a method of separating substances of great analytical interest (Rivier and Saugy, 1995; Moore, 1996). It is one of the most sensitive techniques available for detecting drugs in body fluids. The separation is carried out on an analytical column containing a stationary phase (liquid or solid, depending on temperature) that is maintained at a given temperature inside an oven. The whole GC system comprises six components: gas supply and flow controllers, injector, oven, column, detector and recording device. In drug testing, GC capillary (rather than packed) columns are commonly used. A compound is identified by matching its retention time with that of a drug standard under the same conditions. The use of more sensitive and selective detectors such as electron capture (ECD), nitrogen-phosphorus (NPD) detectors or a mass spectrometer (GC-MS, Gerhards et al., 1999) has greatly improved the reliability of GC. Drawbacks include the time necessary to prepare the specimen and to thermo-stabilize it by chemical derivatization.

E. Capillary electrophoresis

During the past decade, capillary electrophoresis (CE) emerged as a promising, effective, and economic approach for separation of a large variety of substances including those encountered in forensic toxicology. CE comprises a family of electro-kinetic separation techniques that separate compounds based upon differences in electrophoretic mobility, phase partitioning, isoelectric point, molecular size, or a combination of one or several of these properties. Electro-kinetic capillary methods employed for forensic toxicology include capillary zone electrophoresis (CZE) and an electro-kinetic capillary chromatography technique called micellar electro-kinetic capillary chromatography (MECC). In CZE, a few nanoliters of sample are applied to the beginning of a fused-silica capillary filled with buffer. On application of a high-voltage direct current field, charged solutes begin to separate and are swept through the capillary by the combined action of electrophoresis and electro-osmotic bulk flow and are on-column detected towards the capillary end. In MECC, the buffer contains charged micelles (dodecyl sulfate micelles). Both uncharged and charged solutes separate based on differential partitioning between the micelles and the surrounding buffer and, if charged, also by differential charge effects, including electrophoresis. Using on-column UV absorbency or MS detection, CE is well suited for toxicological drug screening, although its sensitivity is not always high enough. Compared with HPLC and GC, this technology has distinct advantages, including automation, small sample size, minimal sample preparation, use of very small amounts of organic solvents, and low cost of capillary columns (Von Heerren and Thormann, 1997).

F. Drug confirmation

A drug's identity confirmation is based upon the use of at least two different techniques, each confirming the other's results (de Zeeuw and Franke, 2000). In this respect, the combination of two of the previously mentioned techniques adds confidence in the accuracy of the result (Rivier and Saugy, 1995).

On the other hand, the introduction of the mass spectrometry detection method has revolutionized analytical toxicology in providing the capacity of an absolute identification. GC-MS has become the gold standard of forensic drug testing. After separation by GC, the compounds are bombarded with high-energy electrons causing them to break apart. The fragments produced are separated on the basis of their mass to charge ratio. Under the same conditions, a molecule will fragment in exactly the same pattern every time, producing the same spectrum. This spectrum constitutes a virtual " fingerprint " for the particular chemical compound. Detection sensitivity may be as low as in ng/ml amounts of drug. Automated GC-MS is considered the method of choice for drug identification (Polletini et al., 1998).

Other confirmatory techniques include high performance liquid chromatography coupled with mass spectrometry (LC-MS) that constitutes a straightforward method for the analyses of polar or thermo labile compounds without a derivatization step as required in GC-MS and gas chromatography. GC or HPLC coupled with tandem or ion trap mass spectrometers (GC-MS/MS and LC-MS/MS) will both enhance the selectivity and the sensitivity of the detection by producing secondary fragmentations of selected ions obtained by the first fragmentation. All of these sophisticated techniques can offer valuable additional information, but they are extremely expensive to run, as they require highly skilled operators to produce quality data (Moore, 1996; Polettini, 1999).

5.5 Pitfalls and Limitations of Drug Screens

The rapid growth and development of drug testing technology has created a number of testing methodologies that can assess a range of biological specimens not only to provide evidence of recent drug use but also to indicate the pattern of drug use (i.e., route, frequency, dose and time of last use), the degree of impairment, and the extent of drug dependence of the individual. Many of these specimens, especially in doping controls, must be used with special attention because of the potential for false-positive results due to their contamination during passive environmental exposure.

For the forensic physicians or administrators, the broad range of drug test accuracy, coupled with the confusing rubric "toxic screen," often leads to confusion about what, in fact, a test is able to detect. All toxic screen methods have in common, however, a basic design which maximizes sensitivity while making compromises in specificity.

Immunoassays generally are less sensitive than GC-MS although both are capable of detecting very low quantities of drugs. The duration of a test positive depends in part on the sensitivity of the test and also on the circumstances of abuse. Multiple doses of a drug taken chronically can redistribute to deep body compartments with slow release back into the blood compartment, prolonging significantly the pharmacokinetics of elimination. This is particularly true for cannabinoids, methaqualone, and phencyclidine. Therefore, issues in drug pharmacokinetics and testing methodologies can easily lead to false-positive and false-negative tests, both with significant consequences.

A. Causes of false-positive drug screens

The two major causes of false positive drug results concern immunoassay tests and contaminations by environmental exposure to drugs. All immunoassay tests are susceptible to false-positive results due to antibody cross-reactivity with substances bearing some structural similarity to the drugs to be detected (Liu, 1994). Included among these are poppy seeds that may contain opium congeners resulting in a drug screen that is positive for opiates. Also common is the ability of nasal decongestants such as ephedrine or phenylpropanolamine to produce a urine drug screen that is positive for amphetamines. Newer immunoassays for amphetamines have begun to use a monoclonal antibody assay that theoretically has a higher specificity for the amphetamine core. Even with the monoclonal assay, however, cross-reactivity may still occur; phenmetrazine and l-ephedrine may produce such a positive result. Dextromethorphan and diphenhydramine, which are commonly used over-the-counter agents, also have the potential to produce a positive urine test result for phencyclidine. Household and commercial adulterants can produce false-negative results for some drugs and false-positive results for others depending on the type of immunoassay that might be used (Liu, 1994). Cross-reactive substances shown to produce false-positive immunological drug screening in urine have been listed recently (Moore, 1996).

Although it arguably may represent genuine exposure and, therefore, not a false-positive result, environmental exposure to drugs such as marijuana smoke may produce a positive urine specimen. The problem of external contamination is more crucial concerning hair testing (Kidwell and Blank, 1996). In situations where drugs are known to be present in the environment, it is clear that passive exposure can produce positive hair analysis results. In this respect, it has been reported that in the unwashed hair of non-smokers the nicotine level overlapped that of smokers (Haley and Hoffmann, 1985). In contrast, cotinine (the nicotine metabolite) does appear to be a marker of tobacco use in the smoker population (Kintz et al., 1992). For children living in a family where cocaine (crack) was used and thus present as smoke in the environment, 85 percent of the children tested positive for cocaine and benzoylecgonine in their hair (Smith and Kidwell, 1996). In this study, it was assumed that children of three to ten years of age were unlikely to be self-administering cocaine, so that any cocaine in their hair must have come from passive exposure. This was confirmed by the fact that skin wipes obtained from the children by wiping their foreheads with a cotton swab were also positive for cocaine, indicating extensive surface contact. Saliva testing was negative in most of the children showing that ingestion of cocaine was not likely a source of the cocaine in the hair.

The problem of hair contamination by environmental exposure to drug is subject to more complexity since experts disagree, some claiming that external contamination can be removed by washing through several kinds of decontamination procedures, others claiming that washing removes drugs from inside the hair shaft and does not completely remove external contaminants (Blank and Kidwell, 1995). Cautiousness, until better decontamination procedures are established, should restrict tests to short hair lengths near the scalp to limit environmental exposure. Of course, such a limitation reduces the potential advantage of hair analysis to provide long-term drug use history for an individual.

B. Causes of false-negative drug screens

Equally problematic in drug screening testing are situations where a drug test fails to identify the athlete who has, in fact, recently used doping drug. The reasons for a false-negative test can be divided into three general categories: technological shortcomings, pharmacokinetic characteristics, and intentional specimen alteration or adulteration.

1. Technological shortcomings

One of the most common reasons for a negative doping screen result despite obvious drug abuse is that the clinician or the scientist fails to recognize that the particular screen being used is incapable of detecting the substance in question (Woolf and Shannon, 1995). For example, some new chemicals abused by sport athletes cannot be detected by routine screening of urine by commercially available immunoassays or any of routine GC-MS based screening procedure. LCMS screening might actually offer a better picture than GC-MS, the dimension of which is still not yet completely evaluated. Without prior knowledge of what the test specifically seeks, the diagnosis may be missed. Similarly, although immunological drug screens commonly identify all members of a drug family, structural differences of specific drugs within the family may limit their detection (e.g., fentanyl and its analogues in an opiate screen, or clonazepam in a benzodiazepine screen).

2. Pharmacokinetic characteristics

The pharmacokinetic characteristics of drugs have an important influence on drug detection, particularly if the wrong biological specimen is examined or if the wrong technology is used. Another pharmacokinetic characteristic, elimination half-life, also has important implications for drug detection capability. With drugs that have a short elimination half-life (e.g., cocaine) the parent compound may be undetectable in blood within eight hours; however, cocaine metabolites can be detected in urine for several days after a significant exposure because of the drug excretory pattern. Also, pharmacokinetics of certain drugs varies according to the individual. As a general rule, urine remains the best biological specimen for drug testing, because it takes advantage of the fact that kidneys are the primary excretory organs for most drugs.

3. Intentional specimen alteration or adulteration

Biological specimens, particularly urine, can also be intentionally altered or adulterated to produce a false-negative result (Mikkelsen and Ash, 1988). Patients who believe that samples taken from them will show positive analytical results frequently attempt to interfere with the analysis procedure by adding various substances to the urine or less frequently to the blood in order to mask the detection of the drugs. Immunological methods can sometimes even give false positive results after such manipulation which, in the absence of a confirmatory procedure, can cast doubt on the selected method and weaken the credibility of the testing. Methods are numerous and varied, ranging from simple dilution of the collected specimen to actual substitution of sample, with the individual giving the examiner a sample of his or her urine that was produced before any drug use occurred, or providing a fluid that resembles urine (Warner, 1989; Cody and Schwarzhoff, 1989). Another commonly used method consists of drinking large amount of fluid or even using a diuretic to reduce the concentration of drug in urine, so that it falls below the detection threshold of the assay. Moreover, adulteration of the collected specimen with chemical agents is the method chosen by many users because it requires little sophistication and can be easily accomplished in unobserved collection conditions. Although well-designed collection procedures can minimize the opportunity for sample adulteration, and laboratory tests exist that may detect certain types of adulterants (temperature, specific gravity, pH measurement of the sample and measurement of urinary creatinine), no system is absolutely foolproof (Soper, 1996).

5.6 Summary

The medical-legal consensus states that a positive case is chemically established by the unequivocal detection of a forbidden parent molecule and/or any of its metabolite(s) in urine, no matter the amounts which were administered or when the drug was taken. Screening is accomplished most of the time by using immunoassays and GC-MS procedures on urine samples. These have been optimized to detect most if not all of the forbidden compounds that are on the list. Identification criteria have to be selected to provide a high probability level. The quality and quantity are decided by the head of the laboratory comparing with what has been accepted in similar situations. Concentrations of most toxic agents is much lower in blood than in urine, and their detection requires highly efficient methodology. These procedures must be validated on a regular basis and inter-laboratory proficiency testing should be conducted to insure the correct evaluation of the laboratory's performances. The costs of these analyses are higher for blood than the corresponding ones for urine. However, all of the requirements for quality are justified in view of the possible major consequences from a social, economic, or political viewpoint of any forensic toxicological analysis error.

References

Baselt, R.C. (1984). "Urine drug screening by immunoassay: interpretation of results," In R.C. Baselt (Ed.), *Advances in Analytical Toxicology* (pp. 81–123). Foster City, CA: Biomedical Publications.

Blank D.L., and Kidwell, D.A. (1995). "Decontamination procedures for drugs of abuse in hair: Are they sufficient?" *Forensic Science International* 70, 13–38.

Bogusz, M.J. (1999). "Hyphenated liquid chromatographic techniques in forensic toxicology." *J Chromatog*r, B 733, 65–91.

Chen, X.H., Franke, J.P., Ensing, K., Wijsbeek, J., and de Zeeuw, R.A.J. (1993). "Pitfalls and solutions in the development of a fully automated solid-phase extraction method for drug screening purposes in plasma and whole blood." *Journal of Analytical Toxicology*, 17, 7, 421–26.

Cody, J.I., and Schwarzhoff, H. (1989). "Impact of adulterants on RIA analysis of urine for drugs of abuse." *Journal of Analytical Toxicology*, 13, 277–284.

de Zeeuw, R.A., and Franke, J.P. (2000). "General unknown analysis," In M.J. Bogusz (Ed.) *Handbook of Analytical Separations, Vol. 2: Forensic Science* (pp. 567–599).

Drummer, O.H. (1998). "Methods for the measurement of benzodiazepines in biological samples—Review." *Journal of Chromatography* B, 713, 1, 201–225.

Drummer, O.H. (1999). "Chromatographic screening techniques in systematic toxicological analysis." *J Chromatogr*, B 733, 27–45.

Furst, A. (1996). *The Toxicologist as Expert Witness. A Hint Book for Courtroom Procedure*, (p. 106). Washington, Bristol and London: Taylor and Francis.

Gerhards, P., Bons, U., Sawazki, J., Szigan, J., and Wertmann, A. (1999). *GC/MS in Clinical Chemistry* (p. 241). Weinheim, New York, Chichester, Brisbane, Singapore and Toronto: WileyVCH.

Gjerde, H., Christophersen, A.S., Skuterud, B., Klemeisen, K. and Morland, J. (1990). "Screening for drugs in forensic blood samples using EMIT urine assays." *Forensic Science Internationa*l, 44, 179–185.

Haley, N.J., and Hoffmann, D. (1985). "Analysis for nicotine and cotinine in hair to determine cigarette smoker status." *Clinical Chemistry*, 31, 1598–1600.

Huber, L. (1999). *Validation and Qualification in Analytical Laboratories*, (p. 318). Buffalo Grove, USA: Interpharm Press.

ISO 17025. *General Requirements for the Competence of Testing and Calibration Laboratorie*s. 1998.

Kelly, K. (1988). "The accuracy and reliability of tests for drugs of abuse in urine samples." *Pharmacotherapy*, 8, 263–275.

Kidwell, D.A., and Blank, D.L. (1996). "Environmental exposure: The stumbling block of hair testing," In P. Kintz (Ed.), *Drug Testing in Hair* (pp. 17–68). Boca Raton, FL: CRC Press.

Kintz, P., Ludes, B., and Mangin, P. (1992). "Evaluation of nicotine and cotinine in human hair." *Journal of Forensic Sciences*, 37, 72–76.

Liu, R.H. (1994). "Comparison of common immunoassay kits for effective application in workplace drug analysis." *Forensic Science Review*, 6, 20–57.

Maurer, H.H. (1999). "Systematic toxicological analysis procedure for acidic drugs and/or metabolites relevant to clinical and forensic toxicology and/or doping control." *J Chromatogr*, B 733, 3–25.

Mikkelsen, S.L., and Ash, K.D. (1988). "Adulterants causing false negatives in illicit drug testing." *Clinical Chemistry*, 34, 2333–2336.

Miyaishi, S. (1995). "Immunoassays: Theory and instrumentation, techniques, applications," In *Encyclopaedia of Analytical Sciences* (pp. 2049–2108). London (U.K.): Academic Press.

Montagne, M., Pugh, C.B., and Fink, J.L. (1988). "Testing for drug use, part 1: Analytical methods." *American Journal of Hospital Pharmacy*, 45, 1297–1305.

Moore, C.M. (1996). "Drug testing in the '90s," In S.B. Leikin, and F.P. Paloucek (Eds.), *Poisoning and Toxicology Handbook* (2nd ed.) (pp. 1162–1175). Hudson (Cleveland): Lexi-Comp Inc. and American Pharmaceutical Association.

Polettini, A. (1999). "Systematic toxicological analysis of drugs and poisons in biosamples by hyphenated chromatographic and spectroscopic techniques." *J Chromatogr*, B 733, 47–63.

Polettini, A., Groppi, A., Vignali, C. and Montagna, M. J. (1998). *Chromatogr*, B 713, 265–279.

Rivier, L., and Saugy, M. "Systematic drug identification," In *Encyclopaedia of Forensic Sciences* (pp. 1594–1606). London (U.K.): Academic Press.

Smith, F.P., and Kidwell, D.A. (1996). "Cocaine in hair, saliva, skin swabs and urine of cocaine users'children." *Forensic Science International,* 83, 179–189.

Soper, J.W., and Canfield, V. (1996). "Description of a screening assay system to detect adulteration of urine samples." *Journal of Analytical Toxicology*, 20, 77.

Vander Heyden, Y., Nijhuis, A., Smeyers-Verbeke, J., Vandeginste, B.G.M., and Massart, D.L. (2001). "Guidance for robustness/ruggedness tests in method validation." *J Pharmaceutical Biomed Anal*, 24, 723–753.

Von Heeren, F., and Thormann, W. (1997). "Capillary electrophoresis in clinical and forensic analysis." *Electrophoresis*, 18, 2415–2426.

Warner, A. (1989). "Interference of common household chemicals in immunoassay methods for drugs of abuse." *Clinical Chemistry*, 35, 648–651.

Woolf, A.D., and Shannon, M.W. (1995). "Clinical toxicology for the paediatrician." *Paediatric Clinics of North America*, 42, 317–333.

Chapter 6

Performance and Behavioral Effects of Illicit Drugs

Jeroen A. J. Schmitt, Caroline T. J. Lamers,
Johannes G. Ramaekers and Wim J. Riedel

Synopsis

6.1 Introduction

It is estimated that in the year 2000 fourteen million Americans used illicit drugs, which constitutes 6.3 percent of the population above twelve years of age (Substance Abuse and Mental Health Services Administration

(SAMHSA), 2001). Needless to say, abuse of illicit drugs is a serious and widespread problem in our society. The term illicit drugs refers to a variety of compounds such as marijuana, cocaine, amphetamines, heroin, and various hallucinogens, including PCP and LSD, which are generally obtained through illegal channels. In addition, drug abuse also includes the nonmedical use of prescription drugs, such as tranquillizers and sedatives, medicinal stimulants and analgesics, as well as the abuse of psychoactive compounds found in common household or industrial products (e.g., inhalants). Alcohol and nicotine, although illegal for youths, are not considered illicit drugs.

Illicit drugs can impair behavior and mental performance in various ways. They may cause sedation or over-activation. They can blur or distort perception, compromise a clear judgment of situations, impair decision-making and responding. The behavioral toxicity of a drug can be ascertained through a variety of methods, ranging from subjectively reported experiences to various kinds of epidemiological surveys and controlled experimental studies. Adverse behavioral effects may even be predicted solely on the basis of a drug's pharmacological properties (Riedel et al., 1998; Schmitt et al., 2001). Each method has its advantages and limitations. For example, the assessment of drug-induced changes with laboratory tests of specific cognitive and psychomotor functions in a controlled and supervised setting may have limited predictive value for real-life complex behaviors such as driving (Moran, 1999). Conversely, with a methodologically sound experimental design, any observed effects can be attributed to a clear factor, notably the administered drug, thus establishing a causal link between performance and use of a drug at a certain dose. Causality is particularly difficult to ascertain in cross-sectional epidemiological studies comparing groups of drug abusers to normal controls, since the influence of factors other than drug use is unknown. For example, pre-existing differences in characteristics and lifestyle cannot be excluded as potential discriminating factors.

The combined picture emerging from various viewpoints and research lines can provide insight into a drug's potential behavioral toxicity. Unfortunately, for many drugs, and particularly for illicit drugs, the data on effects on mental performance and potential risk are incomplete. Existing data are limited to narrow dose ranges, selected research subjects (often young healthy volunteers) and specific behavioral outcome parameters. Although effects in other circumstances may be inferred based on existing information, the actual demonstration of such behavioral effects, for example on driving capacity, remains essential.

This chapter provides an overview of the known behavioral and performance effects of the most commonly abused illicit drugs. It will focus on the effects of acute drug intoxication, occurring at the time when the psychoactive substance is present in the body and exerting its pharmacological effects in the central nervous system (CNS). Such long-term sequelae of drug abuse as behavioral changes that are the result of structural and irreversible brain damage from long-term exposure to neurotoxic compounds do not fall within the scope of this chapter. The cognitive, emotional, and social effects of prolonged drug abuse are addressed in reviews, articles and book sections on various illicit drugs, e.g. cocaine (Brown et al. 1992), ecstasy (Morgan, 2000), stimulants (Ornstein et al., 2000; Simon et al., 2000), marijuana (Adams and Martin, 1996; Ameri, 1999), inhalants (Marelich, 1997; Sharp and Rosenberg, 1997), hallucinogens (Halpern and Pope, 1999) and heroin (Darke et al., 2000).

6.2 Psychostimulants

Psychostimulants boost users' confidence and temporally enhance feelings of well being and euphoria. The fatigue-counteracting capabilities of these drugs also make them popular among truck drivers and other who perform demanding jobs (Crouch et al., 1993). The three most used psychostimulants are cocaine, amphetamines (including methamphetamine) and ecstasy. Cocaine was the first widely used psychostimulant. Amphetamines soon followed, and different amphetamine analogues became available, including methamphetamine and dextro-amphetamine. Amphetamines often are used as a substitute for cocaine. The effects are similar, but amphetamines are cheaper and more available, and their effects are longer lasting. Ecstasy is popular among people in the dance and club scene. Ecstasy can rely for its effect on several derivatives, including MDA and MDE, but the original psychoactive substance of the drug, MDMA, is still the most popular.

A. Cocaine

Cocaine raises levels of dopamine and norepinephrine by inhibiting their reuptake into presynaptic terminals and to a lesser degree by acting as direct agonists. The influence of cocaine on the dopamine system seems to play a prominent role in the drug's psychostimulant properties (Feldman et al., 1997; Gawin, 1991; Izenwasser, 1998).

Cocaine increases pulse rate, body temperature, glucose availability, pupil size, vasoconstriction, alertness, motor activity, and restlessness, and it counteracts sleep (Rush et al., 1999; Stillman et al., 1993). The drug heightens energy levels and enhances consciousness, talkativeness, feelings of euphoria and self-confidence (Higgins and Katz, 1998). The cocaine "high" often is followed by a fatigue rebound with a period of anxiety, depression, and paranoia (Higgins and Katz, 1998). After higher doses, tremors, convulsions, and a severe loss of coordination can occur (Feldman et al., 1997). High doses also can produce sleeplessness, anxiety, paranoia, psychosis, hypervigilance, hyperreactivity, increased impulsivity, compulsive behavior and increased aggression (Higgins and Katz, 1998; Licata et al., 1993).

Cocaine administration under experimental conditions has produced contrasting findings. Some investigators reported improved reaction time, performance speed, enhanced attention and information processing (Farre et al., 1993; Higgins et al., 1990; Higgins et al., 1993); Johnson et al., 1998; Stillman, et al., 1993). Others found no effect of a single dose of cocaine on information processing, learning, recognition memory, simple and choice reaction time, concentration, and central nervous system processing capacity (Farre et al., 1993; Foltin et al., 1993; Higgins et al., 1990; Johnson et al., 1998; Rush et al., 1999).

Combined use of cocaine and alcohol is very common among cocaine abusers (Grant and Harford, 1990). When cocaine and alcohol have been administered together under experimental conditions, cocaine compensated for the impaired task performance that was observed with alcohol alone, including reaction speed and information processing (Farre et al., 1993; Higgins et al., 1993).

The influence of cocaine on actual driving performance has not been studied. In traffic situations, however, increased self-confidence, impulsivity and aggression could result in overestimation of one's driving performance and in higher risk acceptance. Another expected problem for adequate driving performance is the rebound of sleep during withdrawal. In this stage, cocaine abusers can experience extreme fatigue, lack of concentration, and anxiety. This impairs focus of attention, and therefore would impair driving performance. A combination of cocaine and ethanol use has been frequently identified in fatally injured drivers (Marzuk et al., 1990). This finding suggests that the reduction of alcohol-induced sedation does not lead to safer driving performance.

B. Amphetamine

Amphetamine acts to release newly synthesized dopamine and norepinephrine and inhibit their reuptake (Feldman et al., 1997; King and Ellinwood, 1997). Under experimental conditions, small doses of amphetamines (5–20 mg) have been shown to increase arousal and improve task performance in fatigued, as well as non-fatigued, subjects. The effects include increases in reaction speed, vigilance, accuracy in a spatial delay response task, verbal reasoning, coordination and cognitive processing speed (Fleming et al., 1995; Koelega, 1993; Newhouse et al., 1989). Enhanced memory was observed after 10 mg *d*-amphetamine due to improved consolidation of new material (Soetens et al., 1995). Data from other studies, however, show that amphetamines did not affect task performance, including information processing and mental set shifting (Pickworth et al., 1997). The amounts administered in experiments resemble therapeutic dosages (2.5–60 mg), but amphetamine abusers often take much higher doses (50–300 mg) and multiple doses (Logan, 1996; Newhouse et al., 1989; Pickworth et al., 1997).

In one study, methamphetamine abusers had used their regular dose of the drug during the seventy-two hours prior to assessment (Simon et al., 2000). The exact time between drug consumption and assessment was not given, but only 55 percent of subjects reported using methamphetamine on the day of assessment. Therefore, many possibly were in withdrawal while being tested. They had problems manipulating information and were less able to combine information in new ways. They also had difficulty focusing on the task at hand, because they lacked the capacity to ignore irrelevant information. These observed impairing effects may indicate either reduced processing resources or reduced processing rate (Simon et al., 2000).

Methamphetamine abusers admitted to trauma centers were most likely to have been injured in traffic accidents, whereas cocaine abusers' primary causes for admission were injuries caused by violence, such as gunshot or stab wounds and assaults (Schermer and Wisner, 1999). This does not necessarily indicate safer driving after cocaine, in comparison to methamphetamine. Instead, it may reflect a relatively higher rate of traffic participation after the use of methamphetamine as seems to be confirmed by field studies. Although only two percent of voluntarily tested truck drivers tested positive for methamphetamine, 12 percent refused participation. The actual number of questioned truck drivers who had used methamphetamine, therefore, may be higher (Lund et al., 1988). In another study, methamphetamine was found in seven percent of fatally injured truck drivers (Crouch et al., 1993). Complex behavioral tasks, such as driving, require rapid processing of incoming information and correct decision making in regard to other traffic and traffic signaling. Thus, incorrect or slowed information processing can be expected to reduce traffic safety.

Other impairing effects of amphetamines during withdrawal include extreme exhaustion (amphetamine abusers can go without sleep for up to a week), loss of concentration, paranoia, and anxiety (Logan, 1996). Typical amphetamine-related driving behaviors, which lead to arrest, accidents, or fatal car crash, include drifting in and out of lane of travel, weaving, drifting off the road, speeding, high speed collisions, and erratic driving (Logan, 1996).

In conclusion, a therapeutic dose of amphetamine generally will not severely reduce task performance and traffic safety. High doses, however, can impair driving performance during the acute phase by inducing hallucinations, panicky behavior, and increased risk taking. During withdrawal the reduced capacity to ignore irrelevant information, manipulate and combine information, together with extreme exhaustion and confusion, mediate misinterpretation of information, wrong decision making, reduced attention, risk taking and dangerous driving.

C. Ecstasy (MDMA)

± 3,4-Methylenedioxymethamphetamine (MDMA) is a phenethylamine, structurally related to amphetamine and mescaline (De Man, 1994; Morgan, 2000). MDMA is a monoaminergic agonist that releases and inhibits reuptake of serotonin (Rudnick and Wall, 1992; White et al., 1996) and to a lesser extent of dopamine (Battaglia et al., 1988; Shankaran and Gudelsky, 1998).

In some studies, single doses of MDMA (range 0.9–1.9 mg/kg) were not found to impair task performance, including selective attention, visual search, planning or retrieval from semantic memory (Downing, 1986; Vollenweider et al., 1998a). In a study with MDMA doses of 75 and 125 mg, esophoria (squinting) was observed after the higher dose, but there was no effect on simple reaction time (Cami et al., 2000). After 75 mg, however, dissociative effects were observed on perceptual performance under divided attention conditions; i.e., compensatory tracking and movement speed, and object movement estimation was impaired. This latter task measured the subjects' ability to correctly estimate the time-to-collision of a moving dot with a central target under various conditions of occlusion. The reduction in timing ability, as indicated in this task, may become of crucial importance in certain traffic situations (Lamers et al., submitted).

Little is known about participation in complex operations such as driving while under the influence of ecstasy or MDMA. Although some aspects of vehicle control, such as tracking capacity, appear to improve after a single dose of MDMA, traffic safety may be seriously compromised nonetheless as a result of the user's inability to perceive and adapt to the behavior of other traffic participants (Lamers et al., submitted). In addition, impaired coordination, concentration difficulties, and hallucinations have been observed in people while under the influence of MDMA (Downing, 1986; Schifano, 1995; Vollenweider et al., 1998a).

Any cognitive or psychomotor impairment can compromise driving performance. Therefore, any combination of the various impairing effects of MDMA is likely to seriously impair driving performance. The drug's use has already been linked to sometimes-fatal car crashes (Henry et al., 1992; Moeller and Hartung, 1997; Morland, 2000; Schifano, 1995). Furthermore, in real life, MDMA doses may be higher than those administered under experimental conditions, and it may be combined with sedative psychoactive substances such as marijuana and alcohol. In a recent review of studies of MDMA effects on motor skills and of the relationship between dose and blood concentrations, and studies and case reports of the specific effects on driving, it was concluded that MDMA use is not consistent with safe driving, and that impairment of various types persist for a considerable time after last use (Logan and Couper, 2001). In conclusion, the driving skills of persons under the influence of MDMA may be seriously impaired as indicated by its effects on object movement estimation, coordination, concentration, and esophoria.

6.3 Cannabis

Cannabis sativa contains more than 400 chemical compounds, of which about sixty are cannabinoids. The cannabinoid primarily responsible for the drug's physiological and psychological effects is Δ9-tetrahydrocannabinol (THC). When entering the systemic circulation, THC is rapidly distributed in fatty tissues, including the brain, and full elimination from the body can take several days to weeks. Consequently, THC metabolites can be present in urine for an extended period after the last drug intake. To date, two cannabinoid receptors, CB1 and CB2, have been identified. Cannabinoid receptors are involved in analgesia, cognition, memory, motor activity, control of appetite and vomiting. THC is generally used for recreational purposes because of its psychotropic properties, but it is also indicated in the medical treatment of pain, inflammation, glaucoma, and the nausea associated with cancer therapy (Voth and Schwartz, 1997).

THC is rapidly absorbed during cannabis smoking, and its peak effects appear after thirty to sixty minutes. Acute subjective effects are dose dependent, and their duration is two to four hours. Subjectively, the principal psychological effect of THC is euphoria or a "high." This state is sometimes accompanied by a mild state of anxiety, tension, and confusion. Acute consumption of cannabis is associated with impairment of a variety of cognitive and psychomotor tasks, including memory, sense of time, motor coordination, and reaction speed. Memory impairment is the most consistently reported cognitive deficit. The acquisition or consolidation of newly learned information and work seems particularly impaired after an acute dose of THC (Ameri, 1999; Robbe, 1994).

Numerous experimental studies have investigated the effects of THC on isolated psychological functions and skills related to driving performance. These have generally shown that THC amounts between 40 and 300 μg/kg cause a dose dependent reduction in performance of laboratory tasks of attention, reaction time, tracking, or motor control (Robbe, 1994). Results from driving simulator and closed-course studies of THC doses up to 250 μg/kg have generally failed to demonstrate severe effects (Attwood et al., 1981; Casswell, 1977; Peck et al., 1986; Smiley et al., 1981; Stein et al., 1983). Results of these studies have shown differences between the effects of alcohol and the effects of THC. Alcohol leads to an increase in driving speed whereas THC leads to a decrease in speed. THC subjects drive in a more conservative manner, i.e., in the studies, they maintained a longer headway and refused more opportunities to pass whereas the opposite was the case following alcohol. THC did, however, increase reaction time and the standard deviation of lateral position (SDLP), although the magnitude of impairment was generally small. There were also no significant interactions between alcohol and marijuana effects on performance, indicating that the combined effects of the drugs are additive.

A series of driving studies in actual traffic was conducted by a group of researchers at Maastricht University, The Netherlands. Robbe (1998) investigated the effects of THC 0, 100, 200 and 300 μg/kg on performance in a one-hour road-tracking test and a thirty-minute car-following test on a primary highway, and the effect of alcohol and THC 100 μg/kg on a city driving test.

The combined effects of THC and alcohol were further investigated in two subsequent studies with subjects who were recreational users of marijuana. The first assessed the effects of THC 0, 100 and 200 μg/kg with and without a low dose of alcohol on road tracking and car-following performance (Robbe, 1998; Ramaekers et al., 2000). In the second study, during a city driving test a licensed driving instructor used a standardized questionnaire to rate the effects of THC 0 and 100 μg/kg with and without a low alcohol dose (BAC <0.05 g/dl) on general driving proficiency (Lamers and Ramaekers, 2001). In addition, the subjects' visual search for traffic at intersections was recorded by means of head-mounted cameras that registered the subject's eye and direction of gaze.

In these studies, THC produced a dose-related increment in SDLP, which is a measure of "weaving," during the road-tracking test. Reaction time to the speed accelerations/ decelerations of a lead vehicle in the car-following test and general driving proficiency in the city driving test were not affected by THC. Blood concentrations of THC and THC-COOH were not related to the degree of impairment. The effects of THC on SDLP were comparable to those of alcohol at a BAC of 0.05 g/dl, the legal limit for driving in most European countries. THC in combination with a low dose of alcohol, however, produced severe performance impairment in the road-tracking test, and to lesser extents also in the car-following and city driving test. There were no significant interactions between alcohol and THC, indicating that the effects were additive. When compared to a previously established alcohol calibration curve (Louwerens et al., 1987), the combination of THC 100 and 200 μg/kg with alcohol produced a rise in mean SDLP equal to that associated with BACs of 0.09 g/dl and 0.14 g/dl, respectively.

In summary, experimental studies indicate that THC impairs cognition, psychomotor performance and driving performance in a dose-related manner. The degrees of impairment observed in simulated or actual driving tests after THC doses up to 300 μg/kg are mild to moderate and comparable to the effects of an alcohol dose producing 05 g/dl BAC. It has been argued, however, that most THC doses in experimental research have been less than those used for recreational purposes. In this regard, in a dose-finding study (Robbe, 1994) twenty-three recreational users of THC indicated that they had achieved their desired effects after smoking a mean dose of 300 μg/kg THC1. The range of this preferred dose varied, however, between 194–524 μg/kg THC indicating considerable inter-individual variation. It is thus likely that drivers in the general population will at times use doses that are higher than the ones that have been studied. It can be predicted from currently available data that the use of higher doses of THC (> 300 μg/kg) will be associated with severe driving impairment. It is absolutely clear also that THC in combination with alcohol always produces severe driving impairment, even at low doses.

6.4 Hallucinogens

A wide variety of pharmacological substances produce so-called hallucinogenic effects. Briefly, a psychiatric definition of a hallucination is 'sensory perception without external stimulus of the relevant sensory organ' (DSM III-R 1987, American Psychiatric Association). There are no systematic epidemiological studies of hallucinogen use by drivers or laboratory studies of the effects of hallucinogens on skills related to driving. Visual disturbances while driving, even more than ten hours after drug use, have been reported in individual cases (Woody, 1970). Delayed visual hallucinations appearing days to months after the use of LSD potentially could impair driving ability (Seppälä et al., 1979).

Many substances that are discussed in other sections of this chapter, such as cannabis, amphetamines and MDMA, are said to possess hallucinogenic properties. This, however, appears not to be their primary characteristic. Therefore, this section focuses on substances, which are used primarily for their hallucinogenic effects. They are categorized according to their primary pharmacological mechanisms of action.

A. Glutamatergic hallucinogens (NMDA receptor antagonists)

Phencyclidine (PCP) and ketamine are noncompetitive NMDA glutamate receptor antagonists. PCP can induce a broad range of psychological symptoms in non-schizophrenic subjects that resemble the symptoms observed in schizophrenia (Ellison, 1995; Krystal et al., 1994; Oranje et al., 2000), including hallucinations, delusions, idiosyncratic and illogical thinking, poverty of speech and thought, agitation, disturbances of emotion, withdrawal, decreased motivation, and dissociation (Newcomer et al., 1999). Ketamine, a PCP analog still used in human anesthesia, has been reported to cause reactions similar to but not as severe as those caused by PCP, including brief, reversible "positive" and "negative" schizophrenia-like symptoms (Krystal et al., 1994; Newcomer et al., 1999). Both PCP and ketamine can exacerbate the psychosis in schizophrenia (Newcomer et al., 1999)

B. Ketamine

The most important adverse effects of the anaesthetic ketamine are hallucinations and excessive increases in blood pressure and heart rate (Moran, 1999). These reactions can be attenuated or avoided by combining ketamine with sedative or hypnotic drugs (Adams and Werner, 1977). A standard recreational dose of ketamine is typically 1/8 g, usually taken intranasally with effects lasting for approximately one hour. It is one of the drugs consumed regularly among members of the new dance culture. At present, the long-term consequences of ketamine use, including addictive potential, are not known (Moran, 1999).

Subanaesthetic doses of ketamine can produce psychedelic effects in healthy volunteers. Several investigators have studied the effects of ketamine in volunteers to model cognitive deficits in schizophrenia, memory impairment and dementia. These studies have shown that NMDA antagonists produce a broad range of symptoms, behaviors, and cognitive deficits that resemble aspects of endogenous psychoses and thought disorder, particularly schizophrenia and dissociative states (Adler et al., 1998;

Adler et al., 1999; Bowdle et al., 19998; Breier et al., 1997; Duncan et al., 2001; Hetem et al., 2000; Lahti et al., 2001; Newcomer et al., 1999; Van Berckel et al., 1998; Vollenweider et al., 1997a; Vollenweider et al., 1997b).

C. PCP

Phencyclidine (PCP) or "angel dust" is a dissociative anaesthetic with notoriety as an abused substance. A derivative of the anaesthetic ketamine, PCP is the predominant member of the arylhexylamine class of designer drugs (Buchanan and Brown, 1988). States of florid psychosis lasting for days can follow a brief encounter with PCP (Isaacs et al., 1986). Observations of many investigators have shown that the acute effects of PCP following several routes of administration are dose-related (Pradhan, 1984). High doses produce acute intoxication with disturbing manifestations including psychosis, numbness, light-headedness, vertigo, ataxia, and nystagmus. Furthermore, some subjects in these studies became irritable, argumentative or negative under conditions of social stress and demanding tasks. In addition to a variety of central actions, PCP has also been shown to affect cardiovascular function, heat storage, and exercise performance. It can induce, although rarely, psychotic episodes in psychotic and pre-psychotic personalities. Tolerance, but not physical dependence, develops to the effects of PCP. Psychological dependence as indicated by craving for the drug has, however, been reported. The elicitation of violent or psychotic behavior by phencyclidine is well documented (Moran, 1999).

D. Serotonergic hallucinogens

The classic hallucinogens, such as LSD, DMT, mescaline or psilocibin, are all characterized by a serotonergic pharmacology; all display agonist activity at 5-HT2 receptors, and there is evidence that some may interact with other 5-HT receptor subtypes as well, such as 5-HT1A receptors (McKenna, 1996). Chemically, they tend to fall into one of three categories: phenylethylamine derivatives (mescaline and synthetic analogues), lysergamides (LSD, morning glory seeds) and tryptamine derivatives (psilocybin, psilocin, DMT) (McKenna, 1996).

E. LSD (lysergide)

LSD, familiarly called "acid," is the synthetic version of ergotamine, produced by ergot, which is a parasite of rice or rye (Maes et al., 1999). It is the diethylamide of lysergic acid. After its discovery, LSD was misused very quickly for its hallucinogenic effects, because the active dose of this hallucinogenic is so small that the drug can be delivered in many forms, including microtablets, window panes, or stamps (Maes et al., 1999).

The most likely mechanism to account for LSD-induced hallucinations is the increase of neocortical glutamatergic neurotransmission through an initial partial agonistic action at 5-HT2 receptors, predominantly 5-HT2A receptors (Aghajanian and Marek, 1999). The effects appear fifteen minutes to one hour after ingestion and last six to eight hours. Tolerance develops after only a few days of use. Cardiac frequency, blood pressure and temperature increase, and spatiotemporal distortion and depersonalization are frequently reported. Reaction time is significantly increased. Users can become so fearful that they will make suicide attempts. LSD induces a solid psychic dependence (Maes et al., 1999).

F. Magic mushrooms: psilocybin and psilocin

Magic mushrooms belong essentially to three groups: psilocybe, panaeolus and conocybe. The psychoactive hallucinogenic substances are psilocybin and psilocin, chemically similar to LSD. Effects can be obtained with 10 to 60 mg, and last five to six hours. First, the user is affected by nausea, and then sensations affecting eyes, hearing and consciousness occur. These products seem to induce less panic than LSD (Maes et al., 1999), but their effects are similar. With psilocibin, 5HT2A agonism has been demonstrated as the mechanism to induce symptoms (Vollenweider et al., 1998b).

G. Ayahuasca (DMT)

Ayahuasca is a South American psychoactive beverage that contains the naturally occurring psychedelic agent N, N- dimethyltryptamine (DMT) (Riba et al., 2001). This "tea" has been used for centuries in religious and medicinal contexts in the rain forest areas of South America, and it is presently gaining the attention of psychedelic users in North America and Europe. Tea brewed of encapsulated freeze-dried ayahuasca in a dose range of 0.5, 0.75, and 1.0 mg DMT/kg body weight produces psychological effects including hallucinatory sensations. The effects begin within thirty to sixty minutes, peak between sixty and 120 minutes, and last until about 240 minutes. Ayahuasca effects are of longer duration and milder intensity than those previously reported for intravenously administered DMT. DMT and hence ayahuasca, like LSD, has affinity for 5-HT2A receptors (Riba et al., 2001).

H. Mescaline (peyote cactus *Lophophora Williamsii*)

Mescaline is the active compound extracted from the peyote, a cactus from Central America. The chemical structure is 3,4,5-trimethoxy-phenethylamine. After oral ingestion, 66 percent can be absorbed (Maes et al., 1999). The effects are very similar to LSD, with reinforcement of color vision. Users call mescaline the "mellow LSD", but real hallucinations are more frequent than with LSD. Tachycardia, hypertension, hyperthermia, hypersalivation and tremor are the most frequent side effects. Mescaline induces tolerance and psychic dependence, and may sometimes produce physical dependence (Maes et al., 1999). Synthetic derivatives of phenethylamine are substances like DOM (2,5-dimethoxy-4-methylamphetamine), and MDA (3,4-methylenedioxyamphetamine) that are structurally similar to the amphetamines (Christopherson, 2000; DeBruin et al., 1998).

I. Hallucinogen effects on driving performance

The incidence of the use of hallucinogens is not well documented. Taken from a database containing 44,000 records of persons registered in an addiction care unit in The Netherlands, it appeared that there were twenty-nine cases reporting frequent LSD use. For comparison, 328 reported frequent use of MDMA (DeBruin et al., 1998).

There are no data from studies of hallucinogen effects on driving behavior, but the many observations from experimental studies with healthy volunteers provide evidence that hallucinogen use and traffic participation do not mix in a safe manner. The reason for this is the primary motive for the use of hallucinogenic substances, which is to alter or distort the perception of reality.

6.5 Inhalants

The term inhalant refers to a broad range of gases and vapors that can be inhaled to induce a psychoactive or mind-altering effect. Inhalants are inexpensive, readily available, and often abused by children, adolescents, and young adults (Kurtzman et al., 2001; SAMHSA, 2001). Based on their pharmacological and behavioral effects, they can be categorized in three main groups: (1) volatile solvents and fuels, (2) nitrous oxide and (3) alkyl nitrites (Balster, 1998).

A. Volatile solvents and fuels

Volatile solvents are liquids that vaporize at room temperature. They are abundantly found in household and industrial products, including thinners, paint, nail polish remover, and correction fluids (acetone, toluene, methylene chloride, methanol), dry-cleaning fluids and degreasers (tetrachloroethylene, trichloroethane), gasoline and glues (toluene, hexane, ethyl acetate, trichloroethylene), and felt-tip marker fluids (toluene). Aerosols, including hairspray, deodorants and air fresheners, contain propellants (propane, butane, fluorocarbons ["freons"]), whereas paint and shoeshine sprays may contain solvents (toluene).

The majority of solvents have behavioral effects that are similar to that of the classic CNS depressants, i.e., alcohol, barbiturates and benzodiazepines (Balster, 1998; Bowen et al., 1996a; Evans and Balster, 1991). The neuronal mechanisms underlying the CNS effects have not yet been identified, but they may include enhancement of GABA and inhibition of NMDA neurotransmission (Balster, 1998). Inhalation of solvents produces a very rapid intoxicated state that resembles alcohol intoxication in many respects (Bowen et al., 1996a; Bowen et al., 1996b; Sharp and Rosenberg, 1997) including the psychomotor and cognitive effects (Echeverria et al., 1991). The symptoms include initial excitation turning to drowsiness, euphoria, disinhibition, lightheadedness and agitation. Increasing intoxication can lead to ataxia, slurred speech, delusions, dizziness and disorientation, and further intoxication may induce signs of sleeplessness, general muscle weakness, nystagmus, and occasionally hallucinations (Dinwiddie, 1994; Kurtzman et al., 2001; Sharp and Rosenberg, 1997). In extreme cases, stupor develops and may progress to seizures, coma, cardiopulmonary arrest or, not uncommonly, death. Abusers may feel invulnerable and engage in high-risk, impulsive behaviors (Sharp and Rosenberg, 1997).

Although intoxication is characterized by a rapid onset and equally rapid recovery, a "high" can be maintained for several hours by repeated sniffing (Meredith et al., 1989). As a result, performance can be impaired for extended periods of time and may thus present a safety hazard. To illustrate the potential risk, almost a quarter of related fatalities studied recently in Virginia were associated with sniffing while driving, riding or sitting in a motor vehicle (Bowen et al., 1999). Also, the use of the propellant difluorethane while driving was related to a fatal car accident (Broussard et al., 1997). Therefore, although no experimental data are available on solvent intoxication and driving capacity, impairment that is qualitatively and quantitatively comparable to that of alcohol may be expected.

B. Nitrous oxide

Nitrous oxide or "laughing gas" is the most abused of the gases. Because nitrous oxide is commonly used as an analgesic in medicine and dentistry, medical personnel sometimes abuse it. It is also used as a propellant in whipped cream dispensers.

There is a wealth of information documenting that extended nitrous oxide inhalation (minutes to more than an hour) impairs psychomotor and cognitive functioning (Armstrong et al., 1995; Cheam et al., 1995; Fagan et al., 1994; File et al., 1992; Janiszewski et al., 1999; Walker and Zacny, 2001; Zacny et al., 1994a; Zacny et al., 1999). However, nitrous oxide is most commonly abused via inhalation of higher concentrations for a very brief period of time (i.e., one or several breaths). The behavioral effects, including those on psychomotor performance, peak approximately thirty seconds after bolus inhalation and gradually subside over the time course of about five minutes. Nonetheless, even brief inhalation (four breaths) of 80 percent nitrous oxide has been shown to produce memory deficits as well as psychomotor impairment. Higher concentrations of nitrous oxide (100 percent) produce hypoxia, which may also add to the behavioral sequelae (Zacny et al., 1994b).

C. Alkyl nitrites

Alkyl nitrites act primarily to dilate blood vessels and relax smooth muscle tissue through the release of endogenous nitric oxide. Most abused compounds are amyl nitrite (used medically for the treatment of angina), butyl nitrite and cyclohexyl nitrite. The latter is present in room odorizers, whereas amyl nitrite and butyl nitrite are sold in ampules or bottles and are called "poppers," "snappers" or "rush." Alkyl nitrites are used as a euphoriant and as a sexual enhancer (Chalmers, 1991). The use of nitric inhalants can acutely produce dizziness and headache from orthostatic hypotension. Nitrites increase global cerebral blood flow and have been noted to decrease anger, fatigue and depression (Mathew et al., 1989). As with solvents and alcohol, biphasic effects on activity (activation followed by inactivation at higher dosages) are seen with amyl nitrite in animal studies (Bowen and Balster, 1998). Users report a variety of short-term effects that are consistent with CNS depression, including lack of coordination and balance, blurred vision, short-term memory loss, and lethargy (French and Power, 1997).

6.6 Opioids

The opioids are a group of compounds that includes natural opium derivates (morphine, codeine), semisynthetic substances, the most notorious being heroin (diacetylmorphine), and synthetic drugs. The characteristic common to all opioids is that they exert their action by binding to specific opioid receptors, which are widely distributed throughout the brain and peripheral nervous system. Three main receptor subtypes have been identified: mu, delta and kappa receptors (Reisine and Pasternak, 1996). Based on their affinity and actions on these receptors, opioids can be categorized into prototypical mu-agonists (morphine, heroin, methadone), partial mu-agonists (codeine) and mixed agonists-antagonists (buprenorphine) (Jaffe and Martin, 1990; Zacny, 1995).

Opioids are potent analgesics and opioid drugs are extensively used for the management of moderate to severe pain, and chronic pain in cancer patients (Joranson et al., 2000). They produce altered mood (often euphoria), decreased anxiety, respiratory depression, inhibition of gastrointestinal motility, inhibition of certain spinal reflexes, suppression of cough and a reduction of pupil size (miosis). They can also produce pruritus (itching), nausea, and vomiting (Jaffe et al., 1997). The development of tolerance and physical dependence is a classic feature of all opioid drugs (Reisine and Pasternak, 1996).

The primary opioid drug of abuse is heroin. However, among medical professionals who have ready access to them, other morphine-like agonists such as fentanyl and meperidine may also be abused. Methadone, a morphine-like agonist, is used to treat heroin abuse. Its longer action, availability as an oral preparation, and ability to blunt the craving for other opioids make methadone the most effective treatment for opioid abuse currently used.

The current general consensus with regard to the cognitive and psychomotor effects of opioids is that, although some impairment of performance may occur following a single administration, the debilitating effects soon wear off with continued administration of a fixed dose. Tolerance usually develops within days. As a result, people who are on stable doses of opioids for an extended time period, show little if any treatment-related cognitive impairment (Zacny, 1995; Zacny, 1996). Patients who are on chronic opioid therapy, including methadone treatment for heroin abuse, are considered fit to drive and work (Chapman, 2001; Galski et al., 2000; Hanks, 1995; Smith, 1996; Vainio et al., 1995; Zacny, 1996). However, sudden dose increments may result in the temporary reappearance of impaired performance. For example, Bruera et al. (1989) demonstrated that after receiving their opioid medication (usually morphine or hydromorphone) cancer patients on stable opioid therapy experience no performance decrements, whereas patients who had a dose increment of at least 30 percent in the last three days showed impaired psychomotor, memory and arithmetic performance compared to pre-drug assessments.

A. Morphine

Identification of the cognitive and psychomotor effects of opioid drugs is largely based on studies with morphine. Zacny (1995) published a comprehensive review of these studies dating back to the 1940s 1950s and 1960s. In opioid-naive healthy volunteers, morphine in acute dosages up to 30 mg has been shown to impair a variety of functions, including reaction time, tracking, information processing, attention, and memory (Zacny, 1995; Cleeland et al., 1996; Hanks et al., 1995; Walker and Zacny, 1999; Zacny et al., 1998). This broad pattern of impairment is consistent with a mild dearousing effect (sedation), which is also apparent from subjective reports of mental clouding, confusion, grogginess and light-headedness. Generally, speed rather than accuracy is reduced (Zacny, 1996). It must be noted that the observed detrimental effects are generally very mild when compared, for example, to those of low dosages of benzodiazepines (Hanks et al., 1995), and most often performance is found to be unchanged (Zacny, 1995; Hill and Zacny, 2000; Walker and Zacny, 1998, 1999; Zacny et al., 1998; Zacny et al., 1994c) or may even be improved (O'Neill et al., 2000). As mentioned above, in opioid-dependent users the cognitive effects are even less pronounced as a result of tolerance (Zacny, 1995).

B. Heroin

Given the highly addictive profile of heroin, major ethical objections prevent studies of it in an experimental setting. Hence, scant experimental data are available on the performance effects of heroin. Nevertheless, two remarkable studies conducted in the early 1960s describe the effect of both acute and sub-chronic administration of heroin in non-dependent opioid abusers (Fraser et al., 1963, 1964). The subjects were incarcerated men with a history of opioid abuse, but they were not dependent at the start of the experiment. In two double-blind experiments, the subjects initially received placebo (saline) injections for thirty days (phase 1), with an exception of day seventeen, at which time saline was replaced by 8 mg heroin. Psychomotor (eye-hand coordination) performance was somewhat lower compared to the previous day, but performance on a twelve-minute number cancellation task was not affected by the acute heroin administration. In the next phase, which lasted sixty days, the subjects received heroin four times a day in an incremental dosing regimen (10 to 95 mg), and they became physically dependent. During this time, psychomotor performance showed a small but significant decline for the first twelve days but returned to normal (phase 1) levels for the remainder of the study. These results clearly demonstrate that, similar to other opioids, tolerance develops for the performance degrading effects of heroin.

The scantiness of experimental heroin studies allows no specific statement as to its performance effects. However, there is marked similarity between heroin and morphine in terms of their efficacy and at the mu-receptor, their ability to produce physical dependence. There also is similarity in their subjective, reinforcing and discriminative stimulus effects. Thus, one may predict minimal, if any, impairing effects of heroin in opioid-dependent users (Zacny, 1995).

C. Methadone

In a recent study by Curran et al. (2001), opioid dependent abusers who underwent a methadone treatment program received their normal dose (10–50 mg) or a doubled dose according to a crossover design. Diminished long-term memory functioning was seen following the double dose but not the normal dose. Information processing, attention, and psychomotor speed remained unchanged. Reviewing the experimental data, Zacny (1995) concludes that the orally administered doses used for methadone maintenance would not impair cognitive or psychomotor performance. Again, in nonusers (Rothenberg et al., 1977) and in users following a sharp dose increase, there is a greater risk of mild impairment.

In conclusion, impairment of cognitive ability by opioid drugs is not necessarily or specifically linked to absolute dosage levels. Although there appears to be a rather straightforward dose-response relation in drug-naive users (Walker and Zacny, 1999; Zacny et al., 1994c), prolonged opioid users become insensitive to the adverse cognitive effects of even quite high fixed doses (Zacny, 1995). In the practical setting of drug abuse, however, opioid doses for an individual are likely to show considerable variation. Heroin content may vary greatly from dose to dose and the prevalence of nonlethal heroin overdose is extremely high (McGregor et al., 1998). This incidental exposure to higher than normal dosages is likely to produce diminished psychomotor and cognitive abilities. Also, in certain specific situations impairment may occur despite apparent habituation. For example under conditions of low light, the miotic effect to which no tolerance develops (Reissinne and Pasternak, 1996) may impair performance that is dependent on visual acuity, such as night driving. Furthermore, opioids are known to alter mood, attitude and most likely risk assessment, changes which may ultimately result in careless, indifferent and risky behavior and increase the likelihood of traffic accidents. Epidemiological data, however, do not indicate that opioid use is associated with increased accident risk (Zacny, 1995). This supports the notion that stable doses are safe and also may indicate that those who abuse opioids are not likely to engage in traffic.

6.7 Gamma Hydroxybutyric Acid (GHB)

Gamma hydroxybutyric acid is a substance akin to Gamma-Amino-Butyric-Acid (GABA) that is naturally present in mammal species. It is used as an anaesthetic agent, but other indications have been suggested, such as the treatment of insomnia, alcohol, opiate withdrawal, and many cerebrovascular disorders. After oral absorption, the GHB peak is reached in serum after twenty to forty-five minutes, and the half-life is proportional to the amount ingested (more or less twenty minutes). Metabolism occurs in the liver with oxidation in CO_2. Urinary elimination is very limited (1 to 5 percent of the absorbed quantity) (Maes et al., 1999).

GHB is abused for its euphoric, sedative and anabolic (bodybuilding) effects. An "amphetamine like" sensation is obtained after 20 to 30 mg/kg, and with 10 mg/kg, amnesia and muscular relaxation can be observed. These properties have led to its use as a rape drug. Physical dependence occurs. Side effects are nausea, vomiting, vertigo, sleepiness, bradycardia, and respiratory depression. Coma and seizures have been reported following GHB abuse. Patients regain consciousness spontaneously within a few hours after ingestion. Ingestion in combination with alcohol or other psychoactive drugs is very dangerous.

In one study, the effects of GHB on human psychomotor performance and subjective feelings important for the safety of skilled performance, such as driving, were investigated (Ferrara et al., 1999). After single doses of 12.5 and 25 mg/kg (therapeutic doses in alcohol addiction treatments), GHB did not induce changes in psychomotor performance and, therefore, the drug did not seem to influence the ability to drive or work (Ferrara et al., 1999). However, repeated reports of the abuse of GHB and its use in treating ethyl alcohol addiction indicate that it may play an "agonist-like" role, which means that it should only be used under close medical supervision (Ferrara et al., 1999).

6.8 Conclusions

Without exception, all illicit drugs have the potential to impair the cognitive and behavioral skills that allow a person to engage in normal daily activities, such as driving and working. A person's ability to interact optimally with the environment may be compromised by a distorted perception of the world due to the effects of hallucinogens, marijuana or psychostimulant drugs. Miotic or mydriatic effects of opioids and psychostimulants, respectively, prevent optimal adaptation to changing environmental light intensities. On a more global level, drugs such as opioids and inhalants produce CNS depressant effects and may cause sedation, leading to reduced accuracy and responsivity as well as overall dysfunction over a wide range of cognitive domains. In contrast, psychostimulants can induce a state of over-activation in which premature and inaccurate responding may occur. In addition, most drugs produce mood and attitude changes, diminish a person's judgment, quality of decision-making and risk assessment, and produce disinhibition. Most notable are the feelings of overconfidence and increased aggression following stimulant abuse and consequent exposure to risky and dangerous situations. Thus, despite their apparent performance-enhancing effects in certain controlled laboratory tasks, stimulants are likely to impair performance in real life.

If, and to what extent, impairment will actually occur with a drug is dependent on certain additional factors besides its potential behavioral effects. Drug dosage, of course, is an important determinant as many behavioral effects are dose-dependent. However, the development of tolerance or sensitization, or metabolic differences leading to unusually high or low blood drug levels, can modify an individual's response to a particular dose. Environmental cues may also play an important role.

It must also be noted that the dosage and purity of a street drug is often unclear, and illicit drug formulations may contain numerous, potentially toxic constituents, the combined effects of which are largely unknown. Furthermore, poly-drug use is a common, rather than exceptional, practice among drug abusers. Interaction effects between various illicit drugs, as well as co-use of alcohol, can produce additive and potentiated behavioral effects, which are not often investigated and thus are unknown.

References

Adams, I.B., and Martin, B.R. (1996). "Cannabis: Pharmacology and toxicology in animals and humans." *Addiction*, 91, 1585–1614.

Adams, H.A., and Werner, C. (1997). "From the racemate to the eutomer: (S)-ketamine. Renaissance of a substance?" *Anaesthesist*, 46, 1026–1042.

Adler, C.M., Goldberg, T.E., Malhotra, A.K., Pickar, D., and Breier, A. (1998). "Effects of ketamine on thought disorder, working memory, and semantic memory in healthy volunteers." *Bioi Psychiatry*, 43, 811–816.

Adler, C.M., Malhotra, A.K., Elman, I., Goldberg, T., Egan, M., Pickar, D., et al. (1999). "Comparison of ketamine-induced thought disorder in healthy volunteers and thought disorder in schizophrenia." *Am J Psychiatry*, 156, 1646–1649.

Aghajanian, G.K., and Marek, G.J. (1999). "Serotonin and hallucinogens." *Neuropsychopharmacology*, 21, 16S–23S.

Ameri, A. (1999). "The effects of cannabinoids on the brain." *Prog Neurobiol*, 58, 315–348.

American Psychiatric Association. (1987). *Diagnostic and Statistical Manual of Mental Disorders, DSM-III-R.* Washington, D.C.: American Psychiatric Association.

Armstrong, P.J., Morton, C., Sinclair, W., and Tiplady, B. (1995). "Effects of nitrous oxide on psychological performance. A dose-response study using inhalation of concentrations up to 15%." *Psychopharmacology*, 117, 486–490.

Attwood, D.A., Williams, R.D., McBurney, L.J., and Frecker, R.C. (1981). "Cannabis alcohol and driving: Effect on selected closed-course tasks." *Alcohol Drugs and Traffic Safety*. Stockholm: Almqvist and Witsell International.

Balster, RL. (1998). "Neural basis of inhalant abuse." *Drug Alcohol Depend*, 51, 207–214.

Battaglia, G., Brooks, B.P., Kulsakdinun, C., and De Souza, E.B. (1988) "Pharmacologic profile of MDMA (3,4-methylenedioxymetharnphetamine) at various brain recognition sites." *Eur J Pharmacol*, 149, 159–163.

Bowdle, T.A., Radant, A.D., Cowley, D.S., Kharasch, E.D., Strassman, R.J., and Roy-Byrne, P.P. (1998). "Psychedelic effects of ketamine in healthy volunteers: Relationship to steady-state plasma concentrations." *Anesthesiology*, 88, 82–88.

Bowen, S.E., and Balster, R.L. (1998). "A direct comparison of inhalant effects on locomotor activity and schedule-controlled behavior in mice." *Experimental and Clinical Psychopharmacology*, 6, 235–247.

Bowen. S.E., Daniel, J., and Balster, R.L. (1999). "Deaths associated with inhalant abuse in Virginia from 1987 to 1996." *Drug Alcohol Depend*, 53, 239–245.

Bowen. S.E., Wiley, J.L., and Balster, R.L. (1996a). "The effects of abused inhalants on mouse behavior in an elevated plus-maze." *EurJ Pharmacol*, 312, 131–136.

Bowen, S.E., Wiley, J.L., Evans, E.B., Tokarz, M.E., and Balster, R.L. (1996b). "Functional observational battery comparing effects of ethanol, 1,1, I-trichloroethane, ether, and flurothyl." *Neurotoxicol Teratol*, 18, 577–585.

Breier, A., Malhotra, A.K., Pinals, D.A., Weisenfeld, N.I., and Pickar, D. (1997). "Association of ketamine-induced psychosis with focal activation of the prefrontal cortex in healthy volunteers." *AmJ Psychiatry*, 154, 805–811.

Broussard, L.A., Brustowicz, T., Pittman, T., Atkins, K.D. and Presley, L. (1997). "Two traffic fatalities related to the use of difluoroethane." *Journal of Forensic Sciences*, 42, 1186–1187.

Brown, E., Prager, J., Lee, H.Y., and Ramsey, R.G. (1992). "CNS complications of cocaine abuse: prevalence, pathophysiology, and neuroradiology." *AJR AmJ Roentgenol*, 159, 137–147.

Bruera, E., Macmillan, K., Hanson, J., and MacDonald, R.N. (1989). "The cognitive effects of the administration of narcotic analgetics in patients with cancer pain." *Pain*, 39, 13–16.

Buchanan, J.F., and Brown, C.R. (1988). "Designer drugs. A problem in clinical toxicology." *Med Toxicol Adverse Drug Exp*, 3, 1–17.

Cami, J., Farre, M., Mas, M., Roset, P .N., Poudevida, S., Mas, A., et al. (2000). "Human pharmacology of 3,4-methylenedioxymethamphetamine ("ecstasy"): Psychomotor performance and subjective effects." *J Clin Psychopharmacol*, 20, 455–466.

Casswell, S. (1977). "Cannabis and alcohol: Effects on closed course driving behaviour." In I. Johnson (Ed.), *Seventh International Conference on Alcohol Drugs and Traffic Safety*, Melbourne, Australia.

Chalmers, E.M. (1991). "Volatile substance abuse." *Med J Aust*, 154, 269–74.

Chapman, S. (2001). "The effects of opioids on driving ability in patients with chronic pain." *APS Bulletin*, 11.

Cheam, E. W., Dob, D.P., Skelly, A.M., and Lockwood, G.G. (1995). "The effect of nitrous oxide on the performance of psychomotor tests. A dose-response study." *Anaesthesia*, 50, 764–768.

Christophersen, A.S. (2000). "Amphetamine designer drugs—An overview and epidemiology." *Toxicol Lett*, 112–113,127–131.

Cleeland, C.S., Nakamura, Y., Howland, E. W., Morgan, N.R., Edwards, K.R., and Backonja, M. (1996). "Effects of oral morphine on cold pressor tolerance time and neuropsychological performance." *Neuropsychopharmacology*, 15, 252–262.

Crouch, D.J., Birky, M.M., Gust, S.W., Rollins, D.E., Walsh, J.M., Moulden, J.V., et a1. (1993). "The prevalence of drugs and alcohol in fatally injured truck drivers." *J Forensic Sci*, 38, 1342–1353.

Curran, H. V., Kleckham, J., Bearn, J., Strang, J., and Wanigaratne, S. (2001). "Effects of methadone on cognition, mood and craving in detoxifying opiate addicts: A dose-response study." *Psychopharmacology (Berl)*, 154, 53–60.

Darke, S., Sims, J., McDonald, S., and Wickes, W. (2000). "Cognitive impairment among methadone maintenance patients." *Addiction*, 95, 687–695.

De Bruin, A., Vuurman, E.F.P.M., and Riedel, W.J. (1998). *Gedragseffecten vangeneesmiddelen en (ll) legale genotmiddelen als risicofactor bij verkeersdeelname: een literatuuroverzicht*. lnstituut Hersenen and Gedrag, Universiteit Maastricht.

De Man, R.A. (1994). "Morbiditeit en sterfie als gevolg van ecstacygebruik." *Ned Tijdschr Geneeskd* 138, 1850–1855.

Dinwiddie, S.H. (1994). "Abuse of inhalants: A review." *Addiction*, 89, 925–939.

Downing, J. (1986). "The psychological and physiological effects of MDMA on normal volunteers." *J Psychoactive Drugs*, 18, 335–340.

Duncan, E.J., Madonick, S.H., Parwani, A., Angrist, B., Rajan, R., Chakravorty. S., et al. (2001). "Clinical and sensorimotor gating effects of ketamine in normals." *Neuropsychopharmacology*, 25, 72–83.

Echeverria, D., Fine, L., Langolf, G., Schork, T., and Sampaio, C. (1991). "Acute behavioral comparisons of toluene and ethanol in human subjects." *Br J lnd Med*, 48, 750–761.

Ellison, G. (1995). "The N-methyl-D-aspartate antagonists phencyclidine, ketamine and dizocilpine as both behavioral and anatomical models of the dementias." *Brain Res Rev*, 20, 250–267.

Evans, E.B., and Balster, R.L. (1991). "CNS depressant effects of volatile organic solvents." *Neurosci Biobehav Rev*, 15, 233–241.

Fagan, D., Paul, D.L., Tiplady, B., and Scott, D.B. (1994). "A dose-response study of the effects of inhaled nitrous oxide on psychological performance and mood." Psychopharmacology, 116, 333-338.

Farre, M., de la Torre, R., Llorente, M., Lamas, X., Ugena, B., Segura, J., et al. (1993) "Alcohol and cocaine interactions in humans." *J Pharmacol Exp Ther*, 266, 1364–1373.

Feldman, R.S., Meyer, J.S., and Quenzer, L.F. (1997). *Principles of Neuropyschopharmacology*. Sinauer Associates, Inc.

Ferrara, S.D., Giorgetti, R., Zancaner, S., Orlando, R, Tagliabracci, A., Cavarzeran, F., et al. (1999). "Effects of single dose of gamma-hydroxybutyric acid and lorazepam on psychomotor performance and subjective feelings in healthy volunteers." *European Journal of Clinical Pharmacology*, 54, 821–827.

File, S.E., Balakrishnan, J., Murray, A., Harris, A., and Skelly, A.M. (1992). "Effects of nitrous oxide on memory for instructions in dental patients." Hum *Psychopharmacol*, 7, 37–44.

Fleming, K., Bigelow, L.B., Weinberger, D.R., and Goldberg, T.E. (1995). "Neuropsychological effects of amphetamine may correlate with personality characteristics." *Psychopharmacol Bull*, 31, 357–362.

Foltin, R. W., Fischman, M. W., Pippen, P.A., and Kelly, T.H. (1993). "Behavioral effects of cocaine alone and in combination with ethanol or marijuana in humans." *Drug Alcohol Depend*, 32, 93–106.

Fraser, H. F., Jones, B.E., Rosenberg, D.E., and Thompson, A.K. (1963). "Effects of addiction to intravenous heroin on patterns of physical activity in man." *Clinical Pharmacology and Therapeutics*, 188–196.

Fraser, H.F., Jones, B.E., Rosenberg, D.E., and Thompson, A.K. (1964). "Effect of a cycle of addiction to intravenous heroin on certain physiological measurements." *Bulletin of Narcotics*, 16, 17–23.

French, R.S., and Power, R. (1997). "Self-reported effects of alkyl nitrite use: A qualitative study amongst targeted groups." *Addiction Research*, 5, 519–548.

Galski, T., Williams, J .B., and Ehle, H. T. (2000). "Effects of opioids on driving ability." *Journal of Pain and Symptom Management*, 19, 200–208.

Gawin, F.H. (1991). "Cocaine addiction: Psychology and neurophysiology." *Science*, 251, 1580–1586.

Grant, B.F., and Harford, T.C. (1990). "Concurrent and simultaneous use of alcohol with cocaine: Results of national survey." *Drug Alcohol Depend*, 25, 97–104.

Halpern, J.H., and Pope, H.G. (1999). "Do hallucinogens cause residual neuropsychological toxicity?" *Drug Alcohol Depend*, 53, 247–256.

Hanks, G. W. (1995). "Morphine sans morpheus." *Lancet*, 346, 652–653.

Hanks, G.W., O'Neill, W.M., Simpson, P., and Wesnes, K. (1995). "The cognitive and psychomotor effects of opioid analgesics. II. A randomized controlled trial of single doses of morphine, lorazepam and placebo in healthy subjects." *Eur J Clin Pharmacol*, 48, 455–460.

Henry, J.A., Jeffreys, K.J., and Dawling, S. (1992). "Toxicity and deaths from 3,4- methylenedioxymethamphetamine ("ecstasy")." *Lancet*, 340, 384–387.

Hetem, L.A.B., Danion, J.M., Diemunsch, P., and Brandt, C. (2000). "Effect of a subanesthetic dose of ketamine on memory and conscious awareness in healthy volunteers." *Psychopharmacology*, 152, 283–288.

Higgins, S.T., Bickel, W.K., Hughes, J.R, Lynn, M., Capeless, M.A., Fenwick, J.W. (1990). "Effects of intranasal cocaine on human learning, performance and physiology." *Psychopharmacology*, 102, 451–458.

Higgins, S. T., and Katz, J.L. (1998). *Cocaine Abuse: Behavior, Pharmacology and Clinical Applications*. San Diego: Academic Press.

Higgins, S.T., Rush, C.R, Bickel, W.K., Hughes, J.R., Lynn, M., Capeless, M.A. (1993). "Acute behavioral and cardiac effects of cocaine and alcohol combinations in humans." *Psychopharmacology*, 111, 285–294.

Hill, J.L., and Zacny, J.P. (2000). "Comparing the subjective, psychomotor, and physiological effects of intravenous hydromorphone and morphine in healthy volunteers." *Psychopharmacology (Berl)*, 152, 31–39.

Isaacs, S.O., Martin, P., and Washington, J.A., Jr. (1986). "Phencyclidine (PCP) abuse. A close-up look at a growing problem." *Oral Surg Oral Med Oral Pathol*, 61, 126–129.

Izenwasser, S. (1998). "Basic pharmacological mechanisms of cocaine." In S.T. Higgins and J.L. Katz (Eds.), *Cocaine Abuse: Behavior, Pharmacology and Clinical Applications* (pp. 1–20). San Diego: Academic Press.

Jaffe, J.H., Knapp, C.M., and Ciraulo, D.A. (1997). "Opiates: Clinical aspects." In J.H. Lowinson, P. Ruiz, R.B. Millman, and J.G. Langrod (Eds.) *Substance Abuse: A Comprehensive Textbook* (pp. 158–166). Baltimore: Williams and Wilkins.

Jaffe, J.H., and Martin, W.R. (1990). "Opioid analgesic and antagonists." In A.G. Gilman, T.W. RaIl, A.S. Nies, and P. Taylor. (Eds.) *Goodman and Gilman's: The Pharmacological Basis of Therapeutics* (pp. 485–521). New York: Pergamon Press.

Janiszewski, D.J., Galinkin, J.L., Klock, P.A., Coalson, D. W., Pardo, H., and Zacny, J.P. (1999). "The effects of subanesthetic concentrations of sevoflurane and nitrous oxide, alone and in combination, on analgesia, mood, and psychomotor performance in healthy volunteers." *Anesth Analg*, 88, 1149–1154.

Johnson, B., Overton, D., Wells, L., Kenny, P., Abramson, D., Dhother, S., et al. (1998). "Effects of acute intravenous cocaine on cardiovascular function, human learning, and performance in cocaine addicts." *Psychiatry Res*, 77, 35–42.

Joranson, D.E., Ryan, K.M., Gilson, A.M., and Dahl, J.L. (2000). "Trends in medical use and abuse of opioid analgesics." *JAMA*, 283, 1710–1741.

King, C.R., and Ellinwood, E.H. (1997). "Amphetamines and other stimulants." In J.H. Lowinson, P. Ruiz, RB. Millman, and J.G. Langrod (Eds.) *Substance Abuse: A Comprehensive Textbook* (pp. 207–223). Baltimore: Williams and Wilkins.

Koelega, H.S. (1993). "Stimulant drugs and vigilance performance: A review." *Psychopharmacology*, 111, 1–16.

Krystal, J.H., Karper, L.P., Seibyl, J.P., Freeman, O.K., Delaney, R., Bremner, J.D., et al. (1994). "Subanesthetic effects of the noncompetitive NMDA antagonist, ketamine, in humans. Psychotomimetic, perceptual, cognitive, and neuroendocrine responses." *Arch Gen Psychiatry,* 51, 199–214.

Kurtzman, T.L., Otsuka, K.N., and Wahl, R.A. (2001). "Inhalant abuse by adolescents." *J Adolesc Health*, 28, 170–180.

Lahti, A.C., Weiler, M.A., Michaelidis, T., Parwani, A., and Tamminga, C.A. (2001). "Effects of ketamine in normal and schizophrenic volunteers." *Neuropsychopharmacology*, 25, 455–467.

Lamers, C. T .J., and Ramaekers, J. G. (2001). "Visual search and urban city driving under the influence of marijuana and alcohol." *Human Psychopharmacology*, 16, 393–401.

Lamers, C.T.J., Ramaekers, J.G., Muntjewerff, N.D., Sikkema, K., Samijn, N., Read, N.L., et al. (submitted) "Dissociable effects of a single dose of MDMA on psychomotor skills and attentional performance."

Licata, A., Taylor, S., Bennan, M., and Cranston, J. (1993). "Effects of cocaine on human aggression." *Pharmacol Biochem Behav*, 45, 549–552.

Logan, B.K. (1996). "Methamphetamine and driving impairment." *J Forensic Sci*, 41, 457–464.

Logan, B.K., and Couper, F.J. (2001). 3,4-Methylenedioxymethamphetamine (MDMA, ecstasy) and driving impairment. *J Forensic Sci*, 46, 1426–33.

Louwerens, J.W., Gloerich, A.B.M., Vries, G., Brookhuis, K.A., and O'Hanlon, J.F. (1987). "The relationship between drivers' blood alcohol concentration (BAC) and actual driving performance during high speed travel." In P.C. Noordzij and R. Roszback (Eds.), *Alcohol, Drugs and Traffic Safety*-T86 (pp.183–186). Amsterdam: Elsevier.

Lund, A.K., Preusser, D.F., Blomberg, R.D., and Williams, A.F. (1988). "Drug use by tractor-trailer drivers." *J Forensic Sci*, 33, 648–661.

Maes, V., Charlier, C., Grenez, 0., and Verstraete, A. (1999). *Drugs and Medicines That Are Suspected to Have a Detrimental Impact on Road User Performance*. Gent: The Toxicological Society of Belgium and Luxembourg (BLT) as subcontractor of University of Gent (RUG).

Marelich, G.P. (1997). "Volatile substance abuse." *Clinical Reviews in Allergy and Immunology*, 15, 271–289.

Marzuk, P.M., Tardiff, K., Leon, A.C., Stajic, M., Morgan, E.B., and Mann, J.J. (1990). "Prevalence of recent cocaine use among motor vehicle fatalities in New York City." *JAMA*, 263, 250–256.

Mathew, R.J., Wilson, W.H., and Tant, S.R (1989). "Regional cerebral blood flow changes associated with amyl nitrite inhalation." *Br J Addict*, 84, 293–299.

McGregor, C., Darke, S., Ali, R., and Christie, P. (1998). "Experience of non-fatal overdose among heroin users in Adelaide, Australia: Circumstances and risk perceptions." *Addiction*, 93, 701–711.

McKenna, D.J. (1996). "Plant hallucinogens: springboards for psychotherapeutic drug discovery." *Behav Brain Res*, 73, 109–116.

Meredith, T.J., Ruprah, M., Liddle, A., and Flanagan, R.J. (1989). "Diagnosis and treatment of acute poisoning with volatile substances." *Hum Toxicol*, 8, 277–286.

Moeller, M.R., and Hartung, M. (1997). "Ecstasy and related substances-serum levels in impaired drivers." *Journal of Analytical Toxicology*, 21, 591.

Moran, R. (1999). *Literature Review on the Relation between Drug Use, Impaired Driving and Traffic Accidents*. EMCDDA/HRB, Health Research Board, Drugs Misuse Research Division, Tel. 00 353 1 6761176, e-mail rmoran@hrb.ie, Dublin.

Morgan, M.J. (2000). "Ecstasy (MDMA): A review of its possible persistent psychological effects." *Psychopharmacology (Berl)*, 152, 230–248.

Morland, J. (2000). "Toxicity of drug abuse-amphetamine designer drugs (ecstasy): Mental effects and consequences of single dose use." *Toxicol Lett*, 112–113, 147–152.

Newcomer, J. W., Farber, N.B., Jevtovic-Todorovic, V., Selke, G., Melson, A.K, Hershey, et al. (1999). "Ketamine-induced NMDA receptor hypofunction as a model of memory impairment and psychosis." *Neuropsychopharmacology*, 20, 106–118.

Newhouse, P.A., Belenky, G., Thomas, M., Thome, D., Sing, H.C., and Fertig, J. (1989)." The effects of d-amphetamine on arousal, cognition, and mood after prolonged total sleep deprivation." *Neuropsychopharmacology*, 2, 153–164.

O'Neill, W.M., Hanks, G.W., Simpson, P., Fallon, M.T., Jenkins, E., and Wesnes, K. (2000). "The cognitive and psychomotor effects of morphine in healthy subjects: A randomized controlled trial of repeated (four) oral doses of dextropropoxyphene, morphine, lorazepam and placebo." *Pain*, 85, 209–215.

Oranje, B., van Berckel, B.N., Kemner, C., van Ree, J.M., Kahn, R.S., and Verbaten, M.N. (2000). "The effects of a sub-anaesthetic dose of ketamine on human selective attention." *Neuropsychopharmacology*, 22, 293–302.

Ornstein, T .J., Iddon, J.L., Baldacchino, A.M., Sahakian, B.J., London, M., Everitt, B.J., et al. (2000). "Profiles of cognitive dysfunction in chronic amphetamine and heroin abusers." *Neuropsychopharmacology*, 23, 113–126.

Peck, R.C., Biasotti, A., Boland, P .N., and Malloy, C. (1986). "The effects of marijuana and alcohol on actual driving performance." *Alcohol, Drugs and Driv*ing, 2, 135–154.

Pickworth, W.B., Rohrer, M.S., and Fant, R.V. (1997). "Effects of abused drugs on psychomotor performance." *Exp Clin Psychopharmacol*, 5, 235–241.

Pradhan, S.N. (1984). "Phencyclidine (PCP): Some human studies." *Neurosci Biobehav Rev*, 8, 493–501.

Ramaekers, J.G., Robbe, H. W.J., and O'Hanlon, J.F. (2000). "Marijuana, alcohol, and actual driving performance." *Hum Psychopharmacol*, 15, 551–558.

Reisine, T., Pasternak, G. (1996). "Opioid analgesic and antagonists." In A.Gilman Goodman, L.S. Goodman, A.Gilman, J.G. Hardman, P .B. Molinoff, R.W. Ruddon, et al. (Eds.), *Goodman and Gilman's The Pharmacological Basis of Therapeutics* (pp. 521–555). New York: McGraw-Hill.

Riba, J., Rodriguez-Fomells, A., Urbano, G., Morte, A., Antonijoan, R., Montero, M., et al. (2001). "Subjective effects and tolerability of the South American psychoactive beverage Ayahuasca in healthy volunteers." *Psychopharmacology (Berl)*, 154, 85–95.

Riedel, W.J., Vermeeren, A., Van Boxtel, M.P.J., Vuurman, E.F.P.M., Verhey, F.R.J., Jolles, J., et al. (1998). "Mechanisms of drug-induced driving impairment: A dimensional approach." *Human Psychopharmacolog*y, 13, S49–S63.

Robbe, H.W.J. (1994). "Influence of Marijuana on Driving." Datawyse, Datawyse.

Robbe, H.W.J. (1998). "Marijuana's impairing effects on driving are moderate when taken alone but severe when combined with alcohol." *Human Psychopharmacology*, 13, S70–78.

Rothenberg, S., Schottenfeld, S., Gross, K., and Selkoe, D. (1977). "Performance differences between addicts and non-addicts." *Psychopharmacology*, 52, 299–306.

Rudnick, G., and Wall, S.C. (1992). "The molecular mechanism of "ecstasy" [3.4- methylenedioxymethamphetamine (MDMA)]: Serotonin transporters are targets for MDMA-induced serotonin release." *Proceedings of the National Academy of Sciences of the United States of America*, 89,1817–1821.

Rush, C.R., Baker, R. W., and Wright, K. (1999). "Acute physiological and behavioral effects of oral cocaine in humans: A dose-response analysis." *Drug Alcohol Depend*, 55, 1–12.

Schermer, C.R., and Wisner, D.H. (1999). "Methamphetamine use in trauma patients: A populationbased study." *J Am Coli Surg*, 189, 442–449.

Schifano, F. (1995). "Dangerous driving and MDMA ('ecstasy') abuse." *Journal of Serotonin Research*, 1, 53–57.

Schmitt, J.A.J., Kruizinga, M., and Riedel, W.J. (2001). "Non-serotonergic pharmacological profiles and associated cognitive effects of serotonin reuptake inhibitors." *Journal of Psychopharmacology,* 15, 173–179.

Selby, M.J., Azrin, R.L. (1998). "Neuropsychological functioning in drug abusers." *Drug Alcohol Depend,* 50, 39–45.

Seppälä, T., Linnoila, M., Mattila, M.J. (1979), "Drugs, alcohol and driving." *Drugs*, 17, 389–408.

Shankaran. M., Gudelsky, G.A. (1998). "Effect of 3,4-methylenedioxymethamphetamine (MDMA) on hippocampal dopamine and serotonin." *Pharmacol Biochem Behav*, 61, 361–366.

Sharp, C. W., and Rosenberg, N.L. (1997). "Inhalants." In J.H. Lowinson, P. Ruiz, R.B. Millman, and J.G. Langrod (Eds.), *Substance Abuse: A Comprehensive Textbook* (pp. 246–258). Baltimore: Williams and Wilkins.

Simon, S.L., Domier, C., Carnell, J., Brethen, P., Rawson, R., and Ling, W. (2000). "Cognitive impairment in individuals currently using methamphetamine." *Am J Addict*, 9, 222–231.

Smiley, A.M., Moskowitz, H., and Ziedman, K. (1981). "Driving simulator studies of marijuana alone and in combination with alcohol." Twenty-fifth Conference of the American Association of Automotive Medicine. (pp.107–116).

Smith, A.M. (1996). "Patients taking stable doses of morphine may drive." *BMJ*, 312, 56–57.

Soetens, E., Casaer, S., D'Hooge, R., and Hueting, J.E. (1995). "Effect of amphetamine on long-term retention of verbal material." *Psychopharmacology*, 119, 155–162.

Stein, A.C., Allen, R. W., Cook, M.L., and Karl, R.L. (1983). *A Simulator Study of the Combined Effects of Alcohol and Marihuana on Driving Behavior*. National Highway Safety Traffic Administration; Systems Technology, Inc., Hawthorne, California.

Stillman, R., Jones, R. T., Moore, D., Walker, J., and Welm, S. (1993). "Improved performance four hours after cocaine." *Psychopharmacology*, 110, 415–20.

Substance Abuse and Mental Health Services Administration. (2001). *Summary of Findings from the 2000 National Household Survey on Drug Abuse*. SAMSHA.

Vainio, A., Ollila, J., Matikainen, E., Rosenberg, P., and Kalso, E. (1995). "Driving ability in cancer patients receiving long-term morphine analgesia." *Lancet*, 346, 667–670.

Van Berckel, B.N.M., Oranje, B., van Ree, J.M., Verbaten, M.N., and Kahn, R.S. (1998). "The effects of low dose ketamine on sensory gating, neuroendocrine secretion, and behavior in healthy human subjects." *Psychopharmacology*, 137, 271–281.

Vollenweider, F.X., Gamma, A., Liechti, M., and Huber, T. (1998a). "Psychological and cardiovascular effects and short-term sequelae of MDMA ("ecstasy") in MDMA-naive healthy volunteers." *Neuropsychopharmacology*, 19, 241–251.

Vollenweider, F.X., Leenders, K.L., Oye, I., Hell, D., and Angst, J. (1997a). "Differential psychopathology and patterns of cerebral glucose utilisation produced by (S)- and (R)-ketamine in healthy volunteers using positron emission tomography (PET)." *Eur Neuropsychopharmacol*, 7, 25–38.

Vollenweider, F.X., Leenders, K.L., Scharfetter, C., Antonini, A., Maguire, P., Missimer, J., et al. (1997b)."Metabolic hyperfrontality and psychopathology in the ketamine model of psychosis using positron emission tomography (PET) and [18F] fluorodeoxyglucose (FDG)." *Eur Neuropsychopharmacol*, 7, 9–24.

Vollenweider, F.X., Vollenweider-Scherpenhuyzen, M.F., Babler, A., Vogel, H., and Hell, D. (1998b). "Psilocybin induces schizophrenia-like psychosis in humans via a serotonin-2 agonist action." *Neuroreport*, 9, 3897–3902.

Voth, E.A., Schwartz, RH. (1997). "Medicinal applications of delta-9-tetrahydrocannabinol and marijuana." *Ann Intern Med*, 126, 791–798.

Walker, D.J., Zacny, J.P. (1998). "Subjective, psychomotor, and analgesic effects of oral codeine and morphine in healthy volunteers." *Psychopharmacology (Berl)*, 140, 191–201.

Walker, D.J., Zacny, J.P. (1999). "Subjective, psychomotor, and physiological effects of cumulative doses of opioid mu agonists in healthy volunteers." *J Pharmacol Exp The*r, 289, 1454–1464.

Walker, D.J., Zacny, J.P. (2001). "Within- and between-subject variability in the reinforcing and subjective effects of nitrous oxide in healthy volunteers." *Drug Alcohol Depend*, 64, 85–96.

White, S.R., Obradovic, T., Imel, K.M., Wheaton, M.J. (1996). "The effects of methylenedioxymethamphetamine (MDMA, "ecstasy") on monoaminergic neurotransmission in the central nervous system." *ProgNeurobiol*, 49, 455–479.

Woody, G.E. (1970). "Visual disturbances experienced by hallucinogenic drug abusers while driving." *Am J Psychiatry*, 127, 683–686.

Zacny, J.P. (1995). "A review of the effects of opioids on psychomotor and cognitive functioning in humans." *Experimental and Clinical Psychopharmacology*, 3, 432–466.

Zacny, J.P. (1996). "Should people taking opioids for medical reasons be allowed to work and drive?" *Addiction*, 91, 1581–1584.

Zacny, J.P., Coalson, D.W., Lichtor, J.L., Yajnik, S., and Thapar, P. (1994a). "Effects of naloxone on the subjective and psychomotor effects of nitrous oxide in humans." *Pharmacol Biochem Behav*, 49, 573–578.

Zacny, J.P., Hill, J.L., Black, M.L., and Sadeghi, P. (1998). "Comparing the subjective, psychomotor and physiological effects of intravenous pentazocine and morphine in normal volunteers." *J PharmacolExp Ther*, 286, 1197–1207.

Zacny, J.P., Janiszewski, D., Sadeghi, P., and Black, M.L. (1999). "Reinforcing, subjective, and psychomotor effects of sevoflurane and nitrous oxide in moderate-drinking healthy volunteers." *Addiction*, 94, 1817–1828.

Zacny, J.P., Lichtor J.L., Coalson, D.W., Apfelbaum, J.L., Flemming, D., Foster, V. (1994b). "Time course of effects of brief inhalations of nitrous oxide in normal volunteers." *Addiction*, 89, 831–839.

Zacny, J.P., Lichtor, J.L., Flemming, D., Coalson, D.W., and Thompson, W.K. (1994c). "A dose- response analysis of the subjective, psychomotor, and physiological effects of intravenous morphine in healthy volunteers." *J Pharmacol Exp Ther*, 268, 1–9.

Chapter 7

Performance and Behavioral Effects of Medicinal Drugs

Johannes G. Ramaekers

Synopsis

7.1 Introduction

The choice to prescribe a particular drug should be made in the light of possible behavioral effects of available drug therapies. Medicinal drugs, of course, are intended to ameliorate symptoms or to cure a disease. Yet in addition to a therapeutic effect, they can also have disadvantages that can limit their clinical usefulness. These include primary toxic reactions such as cardiotoxicity, liver or kidney injury, bone marrow depression, and a range of central nervous system (CNS) side effects such as sedation, sleep disturbances, motor and emotional disturbances, and lethargy. The term "side effects" is often used in the literature to describe reactions that are subordinate to the therapeutic response and implies that these may not be severe. Yet at the behavioral level these side effects may cause impairment of thought processing, attention deficits, indecisiveness, or psychomotor impairment. In many patients, these behavioral deficits are superimposed on preexisting ones. Consequently, past and present researchers in the field of psychopharmacology have repeatedly pointed out that CNS side effects can reduce a patient's ability to cope with the psychomotor, intellectual, and cognitive demands of everyday living. Such detrimental drug effects on human performance have been described previously in terms of behavioral toxicity. (Cole, 1960; Fingl and Woodbury, 1964; Dimascio and Shader, 1968; Hindmarch and Kerr, 1992; O'Hanlon and Freeman, 1995; Ramaekers, 1998).

7.2 Behavioral Toxicity: Problem Definition

Each year many new drugs are introduced to the market. Their registration in various countries is contingent upon their demonstrated efficacy in large, well-controlled clinical trials. Unfortunately, it is not so common to investigate the effects of new agents on everyday performance even though impairment can sometimes be anticipated beforehand on the basis of their specific pharmacological characteristics. Still, the profile of behavioral side effects of a medicinal drug is of crucial importance for the well being and safety of its users, particularly in ambulant patients who continue their daily activities within a social, domestic, work, and traffic environment.

Use of medicinal drugs such as benzodiazepines and tricyclic antidepressants has been shown to more than double the risk of involvement in injurious falls and traffic accidents (Ray et al., 1987, 1992; Neutel, 1995; Barbone et al., 1998). Traffic accidents resulting in 50,000 fatalities and 1.5 million injuries cost European society over 70 billion Euro (De Gier, 1995). The contribution of medicinal drugs to that cost is currently unknown, but it may be substantial since an average of ten percent of the adult population is using a drug or drugs at any given time. At a very conservative estimate, if ten percent of the adult population is driving under the influence of behaviorally toxic drugs, thus incurring twice the risk of being involved in a traffic accident, those drugs are causing 4,500 deaths, 135,000 injuries and 6.3 billion Euro damage to society each year (De Gier, 1995). In the U.S., findings from the 1996 *National Household Survey of Drug Abuse* suggested that 3.8 million Americans (approximately 2.2 percent of the population ages sixteen and older) occasionally drive after medicinal and non-medicinal use of barbiturates, sedatives and stimulants (Townshend et al., 1998). The percentage of drivers who reported using behaviorally toxic medicinal drugs would probably have been much higher if questions concerning all potentially impairing medicinal drugs had been included in the survey.

The relative lack of interest in the behavioral toxicity of medicinal drugs becomes more surprising given that the extent of performance impairment varies greatly between them, even if they belong to the same therapeutic class. Many novel drugs that have been introduced to the market over recent years produce fewer behavioral side effects than their predecessors because of their more selective activities within the brain. Sometimes, the difference in the level of behavioral toxicity is their only distinction. Clearly, information pertaining to such differences would provide physicians with a better rationale for choosing a particular drug. The amount of drug-related accidents could be expected to decrease dramatically if only the least impairing drugs were to be prescribed. Even if a severely impairing drug has to be prescribed for lack of a better alternative, the recognition of its potential effects on performance could increase the patient's awareness of those situations in which the drug poses the biggest risk to his or her safety (e.g., traffic). Behavioral toxicity of medicinal drugs should, therefore, always be assessed in experimental performance studies before they enter the market in the same way that their efficacy is always evaluated in clinical trials.

7.3 Assessment of Behavioral Toxicity

Determination of a drug's level of behavioral toxicity has been based largely on information provided by the field of psychopharmacology, a distinct coalescence of behavioral pharmacology, biological psychiatry, and experimental psychology. Over the last thirty years this discipline has aided in the development of more efficacious drugs and in the identification of their adverse behavioral side effects. Psychopharmacologists have devised a large number of experimental performance tasks for measuring the behavioral effects of medicinal drugs. The earliest were taken from existing psychometric test batteries (e.g., the Digit Symbol Substitution Test (DSST) from the Wechsler Adult Intelligence Scale). Other early tests were those developed for diagnosing neurological, ophthalmological, and vestibular disorders (e.g., respectively, Wisconsin Card Sorting, Maddox Wing, Body Sway). Later, psychomotor tests characterized by contingent motor responding to an imposed discrete or continuous signal were applied (e.g., reaction time (RT), tracking, and critical flicker fusion

(CFF)). Cognitive tests were added for measuring, primarily, various mnemonic functions but also deductive reasoning. Finally, tests were developed to measure some aspects of real-life performance, such as driving in a simulator, staged driving maneuvers on a course closed to other traffic, or driving on public roads in actual traffic. All of these tests have been applied in single or multiple-dose, double-blind studies, usually with healthy volunteers but sometimes with patients. They have followed both parallel group and crossover designs, most with both placebo and active drug (i.e., verum) controls.

The great advantage of the empirical approach is its ability to determine the intrinsic pharmacological effects of drugs on performance without the confounding factors that obscure or exaggerate the effects in the natural environment. Moreover, experimental studies can be undertaken with drugs in all phases of clinical development and with doses that extend beyond the therapeutic range. They are particularly valuable for identifying and controlling problematic drugs. However, the empirical approach has limitations as well. All tests employed in experimental studies are more or less artificial. No one knows how to fully translate the results they provide into conclusions about the safety-relevant performance impairment of patients in their normal daily living activities. There are just enough comparative data to know that both volunteers and patients experience similar side effects of psychoactive drugs (van Laar et al., 1992; O'Hanlon et al., 1995; Ramaekers et al., 1997a), but there is much less information about effects of these drugs that might improve patients' performance (Freeman and O'Hanlon, 1995). In short, it is not generally possible to predict the net effect of psychoactive drugs on patients' performance from results obtained in experimental studies. Finally, the relatively small numbers (i.e., < 30) often employed in these studies may be insufficient for observing extreme or unusual reactions, particularly those that inhibit spontaneous behavior or provoke grossly aberrant behavior. Such unusual reactions are only reported in clinical case studies. Though somewhat anecdotal, these reports must be regarded seriously. The phenomena they describe are often the most severe kinds of behavioral toxicity afflicting individual patients. Any review of this topic would be incomplete without mentioning them.

7.4 Anxiolytics and Hypnotics

GABA is a major inhibitory and widely distributed neurotransmitter in the mammalian CNS, which is released by a web of short-axon interneurons occupying some 40 percent of all synapses. Benzodiazepine (BZD) ligands affect inhibitory GABA neurotransmission by allosterically modulating the neurotransmitter's ability to open chloride channels at the GABAA/BZD receptor complex. The classic BZD anxiolytics and hypnotics act as agonists and achieve their anxiolytic, anticonvulsant and sedative effects through potentiation of GABA stimulated chloride flux.

Previous reviews of pharmacodynamic studies with healthy volunteers and patients have generally shown that BZD agonists can cause severe impairment in tests designed to measure psychomotor and driving performance (Saletu, 1987a; Koelega, 1989; Woods et al., 1992; Van Laar and Volkerts, 1998). Among psychomotor tasks, measures of CFF, DSST, tracking, and RT were particularly sensitive to the sedative effects of BZDs. The data generally indicate that BZDs cause a reduction in users' overall speed of information processing and motor response. In addition, performance impairment may still be present to a certain degree the morning after drug ingestion. These longerlasting side effects are generally referred to as the "hangover" or "residual" effects of benzodiazepines.

The practical relevance of psychomotor impairment by BZDs has been amply demonstrated in a long series of driving studies employing a standardized test (O'Hanlon et al., 1982, 1986, 1995a; O'Hanlon, 1984; O'Hanlon and Volkerts, 1986; Volkerts and O'Hanlon, 1986; Brookhuis and Borgman, 1988; Riedel et al., 1988; Brookhuis et al., 1990; Van Laar et al., 1992, 2001; Volkerts et al., 1991, 1992; Vermeeren et al., 1998a). The test involves operating a specially instrumented vehicle at a constant speed and with a steady lateral position over a 100 km (61 mi) circuit on a primary highway in actual traffic. Standard deviation of lateral position (SDLP), a measure of tracking error, is its primary performance measure. Subjects included both healthy volunteers and anxious patients, and no essential difference was noted in their reactions to the same drugs. Typically, their driving performance deteriorated in a dose-related manner to same day treatment with anxiolytics and on days following hypnotic treatment. Almost all commonly used BZDs have been tested, and practically none has failed to seriously impair driving performance. BZD hypnotics that produced serious hangover effects on driving impairment after one or several nights of dosing included flunitrazepam 2 mg, flurazepam 15 and 30 mg, lormetazepam 2 mg, nitrazepam 10 mg, loprazolam 2 mg and oxazepam 50 mg. In general, no residual driving impairment occurred in subjects treated with short acting BZDs (midazolam 15 mg and temazepam 20 mg) or with single, low doses of BZDs with intermediate or long half-lives (lormetazepam 1mg and nitrazepam 5 mg). Because of drug accumulation, however, use of the latter should still be avoided when a daily regimen is indicated. BZD anxiolytics found to impair driving performance when given in single and repeated doses over the day included lorazepam 2 mg and diazepam 5 and 10 mg. The maximum effect was seen after the initial doses of lorazepam, and after repeated doses of diazepam because of its slow rate of elimination. The drugs' adverse effects on driving diminished over time but were still significant for up to three weeks of continued dosing

BZD agonists are also known to produce anterograde amnesia in healthy volunteers and patients (reviews: Curren, 1986; Woods et al., 1992). It is thought that the specific amnesic effect is somewhat independent of the general sedative effect responsible for psychomotor impairment (Kirk et al., 1990; Derschwitz et al., 1991; Curran et al., 1991; Curran and Birch, 1991; Hommer et al., 1993) and that the former may outlast the latter (Pomara et al., 1989; Gorenstein, 1994). There is increasing evidence that most BZDs affect explicit memory systems involved in recall of specific events but not implicit memory systems involved in knowledge of language, procedures and motor skills that do not require deliberate recollection (Danion et al., 1989; Weingarter et al., 1992; Curran and Gorenstein, 1993; Polster et al., 1993; Bishop et al., 1996).

The practical implication of the specific amnesic effect of BZDs may be best illustrated by a number of case reports reviewed by Woods et al. (1992). All patients suffered from transient anterograde amnesia after taking initial doses of midazolam or triazolam. They were perfectly capable of routinely performing their daily, occupational activities while in this state, but they were completely unable to recall any events occurring for up to twenty-four hours after ingesting the medication. Other case reports have related BZD-impaired cognitive functions in anxious but otherwise healthy individuals to degrees commonly observed in demented patients (review: Starr and Whalley, 1994). Moreover, BZDs occasionally provoked aberrant behavior, such as hostility, and in some cases overt aggression, self-harming behavior and mania (review: Cole and Kando, 1993). The practical importance of these case reports cannot easily be disregarded. Similar case reports were the reason for triazolam's forced withdrawal from the market in several countries.

Recognition of the detrimental effects of BZDs on performance has led to the development of newer drugs expected to achieve anxiolysis without concomitant sedation. The first was buspirone, a 5-HT1A receptor partial agonist (review: O'Hanlon, 1991; Van Laar et al., 1992). Other new classes of BZD-like drugs acting as partial agonists at the GABAA receptor complex such as the cyclopyrollones, zopiclone and suriclone, and the imidazopyridines, such as alpidem, were less successful in achieving that goal. All had detrimental effects on performance similar to those seen for classic benzodiazepines (Fairweather et al., 1992; Balkin et al., 1992; Allain et al., 1995; Roehrs et al., 1994; Vermeeren et al., 1995; O'Hanlon et al., 1995a; O'Hanlon et al., 1995b; Patat et al., 1995a; Vermeeren et al., 1998; Vermeeren et al., 2000).

Development of a safer hypnotic may have been achieved with the recent introduction of zaleplon. This drug is a novel pyrazolopyrimidine hypnotic that binds selectively as an agonist at the omega1 receptor at the GABAA receptor complex. Zaleplon doses of 10 and 20 mg did produce psychomotor and cognitive impairment at peak concentrations between one and 1.5 hours after administration, but these detrimental effects rapidly diminished over time (review: Patat et al., 2001). Zaleplon has a very short elimination half-life of approximately one hour and is more rapidly eliminated than any hypnotic currently in use in clinical practice. No residual impairment of psychomotor and actual driving performance was observed after zaleplon 10 and 20 mg taken in the evening or in the middle of the night up to four hrs before driving (Vermeeren et al., 1998, 2002, Volkerts et al., 2000). The same doses also failed to produce any residual effects on memory function when given in the evening, and produced only minor impairment of short-term memory when given in the middle of the night at four hrs before testing (Vermeeren et al., 1998; Stone et al., 2000). Current experimental evidence thus suggests that zaleplon 10 and 20 mg can be taken at bedtime or in the middle of the night without serious risks of hangover effects the following morning.

In summary, empirical studies have consistently demonstrated that behavioral toxicity occurs with benzodiazepine administration. Short-acting BZDs affect psychomotor performance in the same way as long-acting BZDs and do not necessarily represent an advantage in avoiding behavioral impairment. Clearly, impairment is less persistent for short-acting BZDs, but this may be irrelevant to patients who receive multiple doses of short acting BZD anxiolytics for achieving steady state plasma concentrations. Similarly, none of the newer BZD receptor ligands appear to be devoid of behavioral toxicity, although nocturnal doses of zaleplon were found to be free of residual impairment during the day.

7.5 Antidepressants

Most antidepressants are thought to achieve their efficacy by increasing postsynaptic concentrations of monoamines (Leonard, 1997). Tricyclic antidepressants (TCAs) relieve depression by inhibiting the reuptake of NA and 5-HT, whereas second-generation antidepressants such as selective serotonin reuptake inhibitors (SSRIs) preferably inhibit reuptake of 5-HT. Other antidepressants, such as mianserin and mirtazapine, enhance noradrenergic release by blocking presynaptic $alpha_2$ receptors or increase monoamine release by inhibition of MAO-A as with moclobemide. Apart from reversible inhibitors of MAO-A and some SSRIs, most of these antidepressants possess binding affinities for postsynaptic adrenergic ($alpha_1$) or histaminergic (H1) receptors that are thought to play a major role in the development of sedation-causing cognitive, psychomotor and driving impairment (Rickelson, 1996; Simons, 1994; Coccaro and Siever, 1985; Deptula and Pomara, 1990; Freeman and O' Hanlon, 1995). TCAs antagonize muscarinic acetylcholine receptors as well and may cause amnesia (review: Thompson, 1991). Among TCAs, impairment is most pronounced for the tertiary amines (clomipramine, amitriptyline, doxepin, imipramine, dothiepin) and less for secondary amines (desipramine, nortriptyline) that possess very modest anticholinergic activity (review: Riedel and Van Praag, 1996).

Psychomotor and cognitive deficiencies are present in most patients suffering from major depression. Whenever compared to normal controls using conventional tests of psychomotor performance and cognition, the former scored worse than the latter (Seppällä et al., 1978; Cohen et al., 1982; Weckowicz et al., 1982; Peselow et al., 1991; Austin et al., 1992). The degree of impairment in both types of performance tests correlated significantly with the severity of depression (Cohen et al., 1992; Austin et al., 1992). Psychomotor and cognitive abilities of depressed patients, who responded favorably to antidepressant treatment, have been shown to improve to levels seen in normal controls, whereas performance of non-responders remained impaired (Hobi et al., 1982; Siegfried and O'Connoly, 1986; Moon and Davey, 1988; Peselow et al., 1991; Austin et al., 1992). Together these data indicate that depression per se is responsible for cognitive and psychomotor impairment, and that there exists a causal relation between relief from depression and improved mental functioning.

For most patients, the therapeutic response occurs between two and six weeks after initiation of antidepressant treatment, but there is a small fraction of non-responders in whom it never occurs. Side effects of antidepressants are predominant after one or several doses and may be superimposed on behavioral disturbances related to depression itself during the first weeks of treatment. Numerous experimental studies have demonstrated that sedative antidepressants such as TCAs severely impair psychomotor and cognitive functions of healthy volunteers or patients after single doses (reviews: Deptula and Pomara, 1990; Freeman and O'Hanlon, 1995). These side effects are generally expected to dissipate after two to four weeks of treatment, which is about the same time that therapeutic effects begin.

Most studies indicate that tolerance to the acute sedative effects of amitriptyline, imipramine, mianserin, doxepin, and maprotiline on psychomotor and actual driving performance develops in both healthy volunteers and patients within one to three weeks of treatment (Curran and Lader, 1986b; Seppälä et al., 1975, 1984; Dijen et al., 1989; Stromberg et al., 1988; Moon and Jesinger, 1991, Robbe et al., 1995; Ramaekers et al., 1994; Van Laar et al., 1995). Acute effects of sedating antidepressants also can be reduced by administration of nocturnal doses. A number of studies demonstrated that daytime driving and psychomotor performance during subchronic treatment with nocturnal doses of amitriptyline, dothiepin, mianserin and mirtazepine was virtually indistinguishable from that during placebo treatment (Lader et al., 1986; Allen et al., 1988; Stille and Herberg, 1989; Ramaekers et al., 1995, 1998; Wilson et al., 2000). It is not clear, however, whether tolerance completely abolishes the initial deficits, or whether tolerance develops at the same rate for every sedative antidepressant during the course of chronic antidepressant therapy. The persistence of certain kinds of performance impairment has been shown in several empirical studies with both volunteers and depressed patients receiving sedative antidepressants (Ramaekers et al., 1992, 1995; Hindmarch et al., 1990; Fairweather et al., 1993a; Hale and Pinninti, 1995). In particular, anticholinergic effects of antidepressants on memory functions seem resistant to tolerance (Sakulsiprong et al., 1991; Spring et al., 1992).

The latest generation of antidepressants, such as the reversible inhibitors of MAO-A, moclobemide and befloxatone, SSRIs, or venlafaxine have no or little affinity for histaminergic, adrenergic, or muscarinic receptors. This is mainly why therapeutic doses of reversible MAO-A inhibitors have never been shown to adversely affect cognitive and psychomotor function (Ramaekers et al., 1992, 1994, 1996; Patat et al., 1995b; Hindmarch and Kerr, 1992; Allain et al., 1992). Generally, SSRIs have little effect on performance as well (Robbe and O'Hanlon 1994; Fairweather et al., 1993a; Hindmarch et al., 1990; Fairweather et al., 1993b). Mild psychomotor and memory impairment is most likely to occur for those possessing some affinity for muscarinic receptors, such as paroxetine and fluvoxamine (Herberg and Menke, 1981; Hindmarch and Harrison, 1988; Dijen et al., 1989; Kerr et al., 1992; Robbe and O'Hanlon, 1994; Weinstein et al., 1996; Schmitt et al., 2001) or for $alpha_1$ receptors, like nefazodone (Frewer et al., 1993; Van Laar et al., 1995). This is not to say that performance impairment can never occur with the more selective reuptake inhibitors that have no specific affinities for muscarinic, adrenergic, or histamine receptors, as in the case of venlafaxine and fluoxetine. Serotonergic drugs such as buspirone, fluoxetine, paroxetine, sertraline and venlafaxine have all been shown to selectively impair sustained attention in laboratory-based vigilance tests but to have no or little effect on actual driving or psychomotor performance (Ramaekers et al., 1995; O'Hanlon et al., 1998; Schmitt et al., 2002). The relevance of this finding is unknown, but it cannot be disregarded too soon. Fluoxetine concentrations are known to accumulate over four to eight weeks before steady state is achieved (Farid et al., 1991; Newhouse et al., 1996). Accumulation over time might produce a belated emergence of adverse events.

A number of case reports have associated the chronic use of SSRIs with unusual adverse behavioral reactions. The most likely reason that most of them implicate fluoxetine is that it is the most widely prescribed. Anxiety, insomnia, and agitation have been most frequently reported for patients taking fluoxetine (Beasley et al., 1991; 1992; Mander et al., 1994;

Meghji, 1994; Coulter and Pillians, 1995; Haenel et al., 1995), sometimes in combination with confusion and amnesia (Betschy and Vandel, 1993; Ruiz, 1994; Singh et al., 1995). Inhibitory reactions such as apathy, indifference, and loss of initiative have been reported with both fluoxetine and fluvoxamine (Hoehn-Saric et al., 1990). In another case, a sixty-year-old women retired as a piano teacher when she failed to learn piano pieces and a foreign language in preparation for a trip. Withdrawal of fluoxetine resulted in her being able to resume her career as a piano teacher and learn the language she had been unable to master (Mirow, 1991). Fluoxetine has also been reported to provoke aberrant behavior such as paranoia, hostility, and aggression (Mandalos and Szarek, 1990; Grounds et al., 1995; Wilkinson, 1999). Cessation of fluoxetine resulted in an abatement of the problems, which usually returned on re-challenge.

In summary, experimental data consistently demonstrate that most sedative antidepressants impair psychomotor or memory function and diminish their users' driving performance, as measured in a standard driving test. Impairment is most prominent during the first days of treatment or after a significant dose increment, but it gradually decreases over time as a result of tolerance. Initial impairment can be reduced by administration of sedative antidepressants in nocturnal doses. Impairment is most pronounced for antidepressants that possess multiple antagonistic affinities for histaminergic, adrenergic, and muscarinic receptors, such as with the TCAs. They generally produce greater sedation than antidepressants with selective affinity for the 5-HT and NA transporters. Yet even in the absence of sedation, behavioral toxicity can still occur with the latter, as shown by their selective effects on vigilance and the adverse motivational and emotional reactions noted in case reports.

7.6 Antipsychotics

Phenothiazines, such as thioridazine and chlorpromazine, were the first D2 receptor antagonists used in the treatment of schizophrenia. Most produce profound sedation by blocking dopamine neurotransmission required for sustaining arousal. Additional blockade of histaminergic, anticholinergic and -adrenergic neurotransmission also contributes to the sedative potential of phenothiazines and results in a high prevalence of concentration difficulties, fatigue, and daytime sleepiness (Bhavnani and Levin, 1996). Studies to examine the effects of phenothiazines on psychomotor performance have not been conducted often, but those that have been conducted confirm the expected detrimental effects on psychomotor performance and wakefulness (McClelland et al., 1990; Hindmarch, 1994; Wylie et al., 1993; King, 1993; Quigley et al., 1996).

Since their introduction in the 1950s, more selective and potent dopaminergic drugs such as haloperidol have largely replaced these drugs. Like any dopaminergic receptor antagonists, in empirical studies with patients or healthy volunteers, haloperidol also produced sedation responsible for psychomotor impairment (review: King, 1993). Yet sedation produced by selective dopaminergic antipsychotics is less profound and less capable of affecting a variety of mental functions and dependent behaviors, as compared to antipsychotics that also block postsynaptic receptors within other monoamine systems. This was repeatedly demonstrated for the substituted benzamides, which selectively block dopaminergic neurotransmission at D_2/D_3 receptors. The first of its kind, sulpiride, produced only minimal psychomotor and cognitive impairment in conventional tests (Liljequist et al., 1975; Bartfai and Wiesel, 1986; McClelland et al., 1990). Therapeutic doses of its successors, remoxepride and amisulpride, consistently impaired psychomotor performance in healthy volunteers, but generally less than subtherapeutic doses of chlorpromazine or haloperidol (Fagan et al., 1988; Mattila et al., 1988, 1996; King et al., 1995; Rammsayer and Gallhofer, 1995; Ramaekers et al., 1999).

Reappraisal of clozapine treatment, has led to the development of a new generation of comparable antipsychotics that, besides affinity for dopaminergic receptors, possess multiple mechanisms of action. Clozapine, risperidone, olanzepine, and seroquel are potent antagonists of the $5HT_{2A}$, H1 and $alpha_1$ receptor, and in the case of clozapine and olanzapine, the muscarinic acetylcholine receptor as well. Sertindole was shown to possess strong antagonistic activity at the $alpha_1$ receptors (Jackson et al., 1994; Leysen et al., 1996; Kinon and Lieberman, 1996). None of these antipsychotics has been extensively investigated in studies designed to examine effects on psychomotor and cognitive function. Yet in theory all of them should produce deficits in performance comparable to those observed for the earlier phenothiazines. Clozapine, for example, was shown to cause changes in EEG indicative of sedation (Saletu et al., 1987b). Another indication came from a multi-center clinical trial that evaluated the effectiveness of five doses (1, 4, 8, 12 and 16 mg) of risperidone in over 1,300 patients (Peuskens et al., 1995). At the lowest dose, 23.5 to 28.8 percent of the patients complained of concentration difficulties, increased fatigue, and sedation and 19 percent complained of memory problems. At the highest dose, these percentages rose to 42 to 48 percent and 34 percent, respectively. Studies conducted in healthy volunteers confirmed risperidone's and olanzapine's impairing potential. Psychomotor impairment and sedation assessed in healthy subjects were of greater severity and duration after a single oral dose of risperidone 2 mg as compared to a single dose of chlorpromazine 50 mg (Hughes et al., 1999). Likewise, four days of repeated dosing with olanzapine 3mg and haloperidol 3 mg produced comparable patterns of attention, memory and motor control impairment in healthy elderly volunteers. Olanzapine's detrimental effects were slightly smaller in magnitude than those of haloperidol (Beuzen et al., 1999).

Cognitive impairment has been intrinsically linked to schizophrenia and has been described in many cognitive domains, including attention, executive functioning, verbal recall, visiospatial abilities, and motor skills (Palmer et al., 1997). Traditional antipsychotics have no efficacy in the treatment of cognitive impairment beyond occasional improvement in attention, and they generally exacerbate preexisting deficits (reviews: Spohn and Strauss, 1989; Cassens et al., 1990). There is some indication, however, that cognitive performance may improve in patients treated with novel antipsychotics (reviews: Sharma, 1999; Meltzer and McGurk, 1999). Patients receiving risperidone or olanzapine demonstrated better performance on cognitive test batteries as compared to patients treated with haloperidol (Green et al., 1997; Weiser et al., 2000; Purdon et al., 2000). Whether these findings reflect a direct and beneficial drug effect of risperidone and olanzapine, or the presence of confounding factors such as the higher incidence of extrapyramidal symptoms and anticholinergic comedication during haloperidol treatment, remains to be established. Improvements in cognitive scores during treatment with risperidone and olanzepine did not correlate with improvements in clinical syndrome scores (Purdon et al., 2000). Caution in the generalization of the results from these studies thus seems warranted.

Antipsychotics may also induce additional inhibitory behavioral reactions such as psychic indifference, and diminished conation, affect, and motivation by blocking central D2 receptors (Levander, 1994; King, 1994). These mental side effects, nowadays referred to as neuroleptic induced deficit syndrome (NIDS) (Lader, 1994), are among the most neglected in schizophrenic patients because of their similarity to the negative symptoms of schizophrenia. As a consequence, the former may easily be mistaken for the latter and remain undetected in patients. This apparently confounding situation contributed to the currently growing belief that the principal action of antipsychotics may be best studied in healthy volunteers (King, 1997). The latter do not suffer negative symptoms and thus serve as a better sample for establishing the existence of NIDS. Up to now, only one group of investigators (Ramaekers et al., 1999) followed this approach for demonstrating NIDS. They treated seventeen volunteers for five days with haloperidol 4 mg, amisulpride 50 and 400 mg, and placebo to investigate affective function and other effects. Affective function was assessed with the Positive and Negative Symptom Scale (PANSS) and Naber's Subjective Well-being under Antipsychotics (SWN) scale. Haloperidol, but not amisulpride, significantly elevated negative symptoms, general psychopathology ratings on the PANSS, and reduced feelings of well being on the SWN scale. Since both haloperidol and amisulpride are selective D2 receptors antagonists, the absence of negative symptoms during amisulpride treatment was remarkable. It may be explained by evidence suggesting that amisulpride preferably attaches to receptors in the limbic rather than striatal system, whereas haloperidol does not discriminate between regional subpopulations of dopamine receptors (Schoemaker et al., 1997; Perrault et al., 1997).

Perhaps the clearest demonstration of the potentially toxic behavioral effects of antipsychotics comes from the unethical use of these drugs in former Soviet psychiatry (Koryagin, 1981). Dissenters of the Soviet regime, who were in good mental condition, were sometimes confined to special clinics and subjected to psychiatric repression for the political purpose of punishing, restraining, and isolating those with anti-Soviet tendencies. They received high doses of antipsychotics (e.g., haloperidol) while being forced to renounce their beliefs and opinions. Thus, they were subjected to punishment by "treatment."

In summary, empirical studies have demonstrated the ability of antipsychotic drugs to produce profound sedation and disrupt psychomotor and cognitive function through blockade of central dopaminergic receptors.

Their adverse effects on performance may further increase if neurotransmission within other monoamine or cholinergic systems is blocked simultaneously. Other dopamine-regulated adverse reactions such as mental disturbances may additionally diminish a patient's ability or motivation to initiate behavior. These adverse reactions seem least likely to occur during treatment with the substituted benzamides, though the amount of comparative data is rather limited.

7.7 Antihistamines

Histamine is a neurotransmitter responsible for the maintenance of arousal. First-generation antihistamines, such as diphenhydramine, triprolidine, clemastine and chlorpheniramine, are strong antagonists of muscarinic and H1 receptors. All first-generation antihistamines induce somnolence and repeatedly have been demonstrated to seriously diminish cognitive, psychomotor, and driving performance in healthy volunteers (reviews: Simons, 1994; Rombaud and Hindmarch, 1994; O'Hanlon and Ramaekers, 1995). Impairment might be of even greater clinical significance in patients when the allergic disorder per se adversely affects CNS function, as suggested by studies in which a reduction in learning ability of children and young adults with allergic rhinitis was exacerbated by diphenhydramine (Vuurman et al., 1993, 1996).

Second-generation antihistamines are less lipophilic and cross the blood-brain barrier more slowly than their predecessors. Their potential to produce sedation and affect psychomotor performance and cognition is generally much less than that of first-generation antihistamines (reviews: Adelsberg, 1997; Nolen, 1997; Mattila and Paakkari, 1999). Second- generation antihistamines are often referred to as non-sedating antihistamines, but that classification has never been fully justified by the most relevant findings from experimental studies or from general practice (Ramaekers and Vermeeren, 2000; Mann et al., 2000).

The impairing properties of second-generation antihistamines have been extensively assessed using the standardized actual driving test previously described, usually after both single and repeated doses in amounts up to four times those currently recommended. Most of these driving studies were conducted between 1989 and 1994 (review: O'Hanlon and Ramaekers, 1995), and several others have followed later (Vermeeren et al., 2002; Theunissen et al., 2002). Results show that the extent to which these antihistamines cause sedation varies with the drug, its dose, and the chronicity of dosing. Several (acrivastine, cetirizine, mizolastine and emedastine) mildly affected driving performance when given in therapeutic doses. Others (ebastine, loratadine, mequitazine and terfenadine) did not have significant effects after recommended doses but had at least measurable effects after doses that were twice as high. Together these results indicate that not all second-generation antihistamines possess the same low tendency to produce sedation. Mann et al. (2000) recently came to the same conclusion based on the frequency with which sedation was reported in post-marketing surveillance studies of four non-sedating antihistamines. The odds ratios and confidence intervals (CI) for the incidence of sedation were 0.63 (CI: 0.36–1.1) for fexofenadine, 2.79 (CI: 1.69–4.58) for acrivastine, and 3.53 (CI: 2.07–5.42) for cetirizine compared with loratadine. In response, some drug manufactures have marketed products that combine the second-generation histamine with the decongestant sympathomimetic pseudoephedrine. Mild impairment is sometimes overcome by this combination (O'Hanlon and Ramaekers, 1995; Stanley et al., 1996), but it may also be associated with a higher frequency of insomnia and other symptoms of CNS stimulation (Simons, 1994).

Recently, the term "third generation" has emerged in the antihistamine literature. Third-generation drugs are being developed from the active metabolites of second-generation drugs. They retain the activity of the parent compound but allegedly have better tolerability and pharmacokinetics. In the antihistamine drug class, terfenadine has been replaced by fexofenadine; and norastemizole is being developed from astemizole, desloratadine from loratadine, and levocetirizine from cetirizine. To date, fexofenadine is the only one that has been marketed in the US and Europe. Others are expected to follow soon as they currently are being filed for registration or are in their final stage of development.

Enhanced safety profiles may be achieved in terms of drug interactions, because these new drugs are the product, not the substrate, for the cytochrome P-450 system. However, whether the third-generation antihistamines pose any advantage over the second-generation antihistamines in terms of their direct effects on performance will need to be established. Only a few studies have investigated the effects of third-generation antihistamines on performance. Fexofenadine in single doses of 60 to 240 mg has been shown not to impair actual and simulated driving performance and performance in psychometric tests (Vermeeren et al., 1998; Hindmarch et al., 1999; Weiler et al., 2000; Nicholson et al., 2000). Likewise, single 5-mg doses of desloratadine did not impair actual driving and psychomotor performance (Vuurman et al., 2000), nor did it exacerbate the detrimental effects of alcohol (Rikken et al., 2000). Some tests even suggested a beneficial effect of fexofenadine and desloratadine on performance. In comparison to placebo, the former improved performance of a laboratory based tracking task (Vermeeren et al., 1998), whereas the latter improved brake reaction time in an actual driving test (Vuurman et al., 2000). The clinical significance of these findings is yet unclear, but they may show that fexofenadine and desloratadine do enter the brain. Available data thus suggest that fexofenadine at the current licensed doses of 120 and 180 mg, and desloratadine 5 mg should be generally safe in individuals performing skilled operations. Before it can be safely concluded that these drugs are truly non-sedating, however, there is a specific need to further investigate their effects on performance after higher doses and after prolonged administration.

In summary, from empirical studies it can be concluded that the second- and third-generation antihistamines possess a major advantage over first-generation antihistamines in that they produce considerably less behavioral toxicity. The differences between the second-generation antihistamines should not be exaggerated but cannot be ignored. Regulatory authorities from Europe and the United States recognized these differences and have required appropriate warnings for some of the second-generation antihistamines. Recent studies indicate that third-generation antihistamines do not impair performance at therapeutic doses, but whether they are free of CNS effects at any dose still needs to be determined.

7.8 Antiepileptic Drugs

A deficiency in brain GABA levels is known to cause convulsions or epilepsy. Consequently, drugs that increase the amount of GABA available in the brain for neurotransmission have the potential to become antiepileptic agents. Drugs that are known to act at these sites include phenobarbital, valproic acid, vigabatrin, tiagabine, gabapentin and all benzodiazapines. A second group of antiepileptics act on sodium channels and modify the conduction of nerve impulses. These include phenytoin, carbamazepine and oxcarbazepine. Felbamate and lamotrigine belong to a third group of antiepileptics, which decrease the activity of excitatory aminoacids such as glutamate and aspartate (review: Emilien and Maloteaux, 1995).

The major established drugs in the management of epilepsy are carbamazepine, phenytoin, valproate, phenobarbital and benzodiazepines. Patients taking these drugs often complain of decreased alertness. Sedation and drowsiness are common adverse reactions in about 30–40 percent of patients during the first months of treatment. Other side effects may include dizziness, amnesia and agitation. The frequency and severity of side effects vary with dose, method of administration, and co-administration of other drugs, but they generally decrease over time as a result of tolerance (Mattson et al., 1989, 1992; Salinsky et al., 1995; Heller et al., 1995; Chadwick, 1999). CNS side effects may hamper patients' skilled and cognitive performance during antiepileptic treatment. Unfortunately, research to assess the effects of antiepileptic drugs on cognition and psychomotor function has been scarce and often flawed by methodological limitations (review: Drane and Meador, 1995).

Practically all studies have been conducted to assess the side effects of conventional antiepileptics. Their results generally show that carbamazepine produces impairment of cognitive and psychomotor functions during chronic treatment, particularly in combination with other antiepileptics (MacPhee et al., 1986; Aldenkamp et al., 1987, 1998; Gillham et al., 1988; Meador et al., 1990; Bawden et al., 1999). In healthy volunteers, carbamazepine decreased cognitive and psychomotor functions after single doses of 600 mg (MacPhee et al., 1986; Kuitunen et al., 1990; Hamilton et al., 1993) and during four to five weeks of treatment with therapeutic doses (Meador et al., 1991, 1993). Daily doses of carbamazapine 400-to-600 mg also impaired road tracking, time to speed adaptation, and brake reaction time performance of healthy volunteers in actual driving tests during twelve days of treatment with incremental dosing regimens (Ramaekers et al., 2002). Studies comparing carbamazapine's effects on cognition and performance to those of valproate and phenytoin in patients and healthy volunteers generally found no difference between these drugs (Meador et al., 1990, 1991, 1993, 1995; Prevey et al., 1996).

The effects of carbamazepine, valproate and phenytoin on performance appear modest when dosages are kept within therapeutic ranges and polypharmacy is avoided. Violation of these conditions increases the risk of detrimental changes in attention, concentration, memory, and motor speed. Furthermore, the evidence suggests that a more global and severe depression of cognitive and psychomotor function can be expected after treatment with GABA-ergic drugs such as phenobarbital or benzodiazepines. In studies comparing the cognitive and psychomotor performance of patients treated with phenobarbital with the performance of patients treated with carbamazepine, valpraote or phenytoin, the former always performed worse (Meador et al., 1990; Manni et al., 1993). A group of investigators rated driving ability of epileptic patients in practical driving tests and reported severe performance impairment in patients receiving polytherapy that included phenobarbital (Barcs et al., 1997).

Antiepileptics have also been associated with psychiatric adverse reactions such as depression, hyperactivity, mania and psychosis (Wong et al., 1997). Clinical trials, observational studies, and case reports suggest that patients exposed to phenobarbital and vigabatrin are at the highest risk of developing adverse psychiatric reactions. Hyperactivity has been reported to occur in 20 to 50 percent of pediatric patients treated with phenobarbital, whereas depression and psychosis are reported in about 2 percent of patients treated with vigabatrin. Carbamazepine, phenytoin and valproate have also been reported to cause adverse psychiatric reactions but at lower rates.

In summary, all antiepileptic drugs may cause impairment of psychomotor and cognitive functions in patients. Detrimental effects of carbamazapine, valproate and phenytoin appear to be modest when taken in therapeutic doses and as monotherapy. Higher doses of the same drug or coadministration with another drug, however, may produce severe performance deficits. Performance impairment is more severe and behavioral adverse reactions more frequent for GABA-ergic drugs when compared to other major antiepileptics.

7.9 Other Drugs

Other classes of drugs are known to cause adverse behavioral reactions in individual cases. It is generally accepted that beta-blockers can cause depression and that frequent adverse events such as fatigue, somnolence, and dizziness diminish the patient's quality of life (Patten and Love, 1994; Gleiter and Decker, 1996). Anticholinergic agents, opioids, NSAIDS, antihypertensives and H2 antagonists all have been implicated in disturbance of consciousness and changes in cognition that are indicative of drug induced delirium or dementia (Starr and Whalley, 1994; Carter et al., 1996). Manic reactions have been associated with anti-Parkinsonian agents, antimalarials and sympathomimetics (Peet and Peters, 1995). Stimulant drugs (e.g., dextroamphetamine and methylphenidate) that are prescribed for a number of health conditions including narcolepsy and attention-deficit hyperactivity disorder can lead to feelings of paranoia and hostility, particularly at high doses (Froley et al., 2000).

7.10 Drug Interactions

Various studies have shown that it is common for elderly patients to take seven or eight prescription drugs daily (Lamy et al., 1992; Broderick, 1997). Obviously, these patients are at increased risk for experiencing adverse drug reactions (Jones, 1997). Unfortunately, it is not so common for polypharmacy to be carefully monitored (Stuck et al., 1994; Apparasu and Fliginger, 1997; Langdorf et al., 2000). The consequence can be severe as illustrated by Larson et al. (1988) who identified thirty-five cases of drug-induced cognitive impairment among 308 outpatients who were evaluated for suspected dementia. Twenty-seven patients were taking at least one drug known to cause cognitive impairment, and the others were taking two or three such drugs. BZDs were implicated in nearly half the cases, with antihypertensives and major tranquillizers as the other main offenders. The number of differential drugs prescribed was a main risk factor in those suffering from drug-induced cognitive impairment as compared to the rest of the sample. In all cases, cognition improved when the drugs were withdrawn.

It has become increasingly clear that the effects of drugs given concurrently are not necessarily predictable on the basis of their effects when given alone. When physicians prescribe several drugs concurrently, they face the problem of knowing whether a specific combination of drugs causes an interaction. A drug interaction refers to the possibility that one drug may alter the intensity of the pharmacological effects of another drug taken concurrently. The net results may be enhanced or diminished effects of one or both drugs or the appearance of a new effect that has not been observed with either drug alone. Interactions may be either pharmacokinetic or pharmacodynamic. The latter are interactions between agonists and antagonist at the receptor level. There are numerous examples of drugs that interact at a common receptor site or that have additive or inhibitory effects due to actions at different sites. The former describe interactions at any point during the processes of absorption, distribution, metabolism or excretion of drugs. The result may be an increase or decrease in the concentration of a drug, which produces a quantitative or qualitative change in the patient's response. Most often, the response is a known dose-dependent effect of the affected drug that occurs unexpectedly at an unusual dose due to the alteration in clearance. For example, impaired clearance of a benzodiazepine might cause excessive sedation.

The pharmacokinetic process of metabolism or biotransformation has been an exceptionally active and productive area of research over the last decade. The cytochrome P450 enzymes are proteins that are responsible for the oxidative metabolism of many drugs. A number of distinct P450 subfamilies that have been identified have specific affinities for different subgroups of drugs or chemicals. The liver is the most important site of cytochrome P450 activity, although significant amounts of subfamilies are present in the gastrointestinal tract as well. Several subfamilies among the P450 cytochrome enzymes appear to be particularly important for the metabolism of commonly used medications. These can act as substrate for one or more of the subfamilies, but they may also serve as inhibitor or inducer of the same or other enzymes. Hence, medicinal drugs can be the target and/or the cause of pharmacokinetic drug-drug interactions.

CYP2D6 is one of the major subfamilies of the cytochrome P450 system that is of clinical importance. It is implicated in the metabolism of TCAs (desipramine, imipramine, amitriptyline) and several antipsychotics (clozapine, thioridazine, haloperidol), and it also controls the metabolism of several non-psychotropic drugs including beta-blockers and codeine. Interest in CYP2D6 began to increase when several SSRIs (fluoxetine, sertraline, paroxetine and fluvoxamine) were shown to inhibit these enzymes.

A second cytochrome subfamily of clinical importance is the CYP3A subfamily that mediates the metabolism of many benzodiazepines (triazolam, alprazolam, midazolam, diazepam), TCAs (imipramine, amitriptyline), antiepileptics (carbamazapine), opioids and antihistamines (astemizole, terfenadine, loratadine). Macrolite antibiotics and grapefruit inhibit this cytochrome. SSRIs also inhibit the CYP3A subfamily, but their inhibiting potency is less than for CYP2D6. The antiepileptics carbamazapine and phenytoin were furthermore shown to induce the activity of CYP3A. Other major subfamilies implicated in drug metabolism include CYP1A2, CYP2C9 and CYP2C19. (reviews: Moltke et al., 1994; Brøsen, 1996; Sproule et al., 1997).

Many more drugs and chemicals now have been identified either as a substrate, inhibitor, or inducer of P450 cytochromes, and many more can be expected to be added to the list in the near future. A concerted effort is currently underway to establish the actions of all available medicinal drugs at the P450 cytochrome system. This is an important development that will enable physicians to predict potential interactions between combinations of drugs and adjust individual drug regimens accordingly.

Despite the enormous amount of data that has been gathered on cytochrome P450 enzyme function, only a few experimental studies have been conducted to assess the practical implications of pharmacokinetic drug interactions for the cognitive and psychomotor performance of patients receiving combination drug therapy. Those that have been conducted all focused on combination treatments that included antidepressants, SSRIs in particular. The reason, of course, was the discovery of the potential of these drugs to inhibit certain cytochrome P450 subfamilies. The studies showed that the combination of CYP3A inhibitors fluoxetine and nefazodone, with alprazolam, a well known benzodiazepine substate of CYP3A, results in the latter's accumulation in plasma and progressive psychomotor impairment in healthy volunteers (Lasher et al., 1991; Kroboth et al., 1995). Another study assessed the effects of antidepressant treatment with moclobemide or fluoxetine combined with benzodiazepine on actual driving performance (Ramaekers et al., 1997). Moclobemide is a potent inhibitor of CYP2C19 implicated in the demethylation of diazepam and the hydroxylation of its metabolite, nordiazepam. Driving performance of a group of depressed outpatients treated with fluoxetine or moclobemide deteriorated over six weeks of treatment for those using a BZD co-medication that is metabolized by a cytochrome P450 isozyme subject to inhibition by their particular antidepressant. Incompatible BZDs included substrates of CYP3A, i.e. bromazepam and alprazolam, in the fluoxetine group, and the CYP2C19 substrates diazepam, prazepam, cloxazolam, clotiazepam and clorazepate (i.e., BZDs that are metabolized to nordiazepam) in the moclobemide group. Patients had been taking

BZDs chronically for at least three months before entering the study and continued to do so during antidepressant treatment. Though not assessed, it was assumed that concurrent use of antidepressants elevated plasma levels of BZDs to supratherapeutic levels, which in turn caused profound sedation.

The increasing knowledge of the mechanisms of drug interactions has an important bearing on the relevance of single drug studies for predicting side effects during polypharmacy. In clinical practice only a minority of patients is treated with a single drug. Most patients receive two or more treatments concurrently and at times switch to other medications in the absence of a therapeutic response or due to unusual sensitivity to a particular drug. The potential and risks for drug interactions during the course of treatment with medicinal drugs thus are manifold. These may not always be acknowledged when determining the side effect profile of medicinal drugs in studies comparing monotherapies, which can introduce a conservative bias concerning a drug's effect in the presence of another.

7.11 Conclusion

Behavioral toxicity is relatively common among medicinal drug users. Results from experimental performance studies all converge on the fact that drugs frequently produce side effects that prevent their users from performing everyday tasks in an efficient or normal manner. As a consequence, they are at higher risk of becoming involved in accidents, which in turn may lead to injury and death. Unfortunately, behavioral toxicity often goes unnoticed by both the users and their prescribing physician. Clearly, more effort from regulatory authorities is needed for increasing patients' and physicians' awareness of detrimental drug effects on behavior in general, and of differences between the effects of different drugs and different doses of the same drug. Much of this information can be gained from experimental literature comparing individual drug effects on performance. Yet this is presently incomplete since most existing research examined monotherapies, whereas in clinical practice patients often receive multiple drugs and may experience drug interactions. Several drug classes have not been properly investigated yet, though they are suspected or known to decrease a patient's quality of life. In the interest of patients, it should be the responsibility of drug manufactures and drug regulators, to always identify a drug's potential for producing behaviorally toxic side effects.

References

Adelsberg, B.R. (1997). "Sedation and performance issues in the treatment of allergic conditions." *Archives of Internal Medicine*, 157, 494–500.

Aldenkamp, A.P., Alpherts, W.C., Moerland, M.C., Ottevanger, N., and Van Parys, J.A. (1987). "Controlled release carbamazepine: Cognitive side effects in patients with epilepsy." *Epilepsia*, 28, 507–14.

Aldenkamp, A.P., Rentmeester, T., Hulsman, J., Majoie, M., Doelman, J., Diepman, L., et al. (1998)." Pharmacokinetics and cognitive effects of carbamazepine formulations with different dissolution rates." *European Journal of Clinical Pharmacology*, 54, 185–92.

Allain, H., Lieury, A., Brunet–Bourgin, F., Mirabaud, C., Trebon, P., et al. (1992). "Antidepressants and cognition: Comparative effects of moclobemide, viloxazine and maprotaline." *Psychopharmacology,* 106, S56–S61.

Allain, H., Patat, A., Lieury, A., Le Coz, F., Janus, C., Menard, G., et al. (1995). "Comparative study of the effects of zopiclone (7.5 mg), zolpidem, flunitrazepam and a placebo on nocturnal cognitive performance in healthy subjects, in relation to pharmacokinetics." *European Psychiatry*, 10, 129s-136s.

Allen, D., Lader, M., and Curran, V. (1988). "A comparative study of the interactions of alcohol with amitriptyline, fluoxetine and placebo in normal subjects." *Progress in Neuropsychopharmacology and Biological Psychiatry*, 12, 63–80.

Aparasu, R.R., and Fliginger, S.E. (1997). "Inappropriate medication prescription for the elderly by office–based physicians." *Annals of Pharmacotherapy,* 31, 823–829.

Austin, M.P., Ross, M., Murray, C., O'Carrol, R.E., Ebmeier, K.P., et al. (1992). "Cognitive function in major depression." *Journal of Affective Disorders*, 25, 21–30.

Balkin, T.J., O'Donnell, V.M., Wesensten, N., McCann, U., Belenky, G. (1992). "Comparison of the daytime sleep and performance effects of zolpidem versus triazolam." *Psychopharmacology*, 107, 83–88.

Barbone, F., McMahon, A.D., Davey, P.G., Morris, A.D., Reid, I.C., McDevitt, D.G., et al. (1998). "Association of road–traffic accidents with benzodiazepine use." *Lancet*, 352, 9137, 1331–1336.

Barcs, G., Vitrai, J., and Halasz, P. (1997). "Investigation of vehicle driving ability in two diagnostic groups of epileptic patients with special neuropsychological approach." *Medicine and Law,* 16, 277–287.

Bartfai, A., and Wiesel, F.A. (1986). "Effects of sulpiride on vigilance in healthy subjects." *International Journal of Psychophysiology,* 4, 1–5.

Bawden, H.N., Camfield, C.S., Camfield, P.R., Cunningham, C., Darwish, H., Dooley, J.M., et al. (1999). "The cognitive and behavioural effects of clobazam and standard monotherapy are comparable." *Epilepsy Research* 33, 133–43.

Beasley, C.M., Sayler, M.E., Bosomworth, J.C., and Wernicke, J.F. (1991). "High dose fluoxetine: Efficacy and activating–sedating effects in agitated and retarded depression." *Journal of Clinical Psychopharmacology*, 11, 166–174.

Beasley, C.M., Sayler, M.E., Weiss, A.M., and Potvin, J.H. (1992). "Fluoxetine: Activating and sedating effects at multiple fixed doses." *Journal of Clinical Psychopharmacology*, 12, 328–333.

Betschy, G., Vandel, S. (1993). "Fluoxetine related indifference and akathesia. A case report." *Therapie*, 48, 158–159.

Beuzen, J.N., Taylor, N., Wesnes, K., Wood, A. (1999). "A comparison of the effects of olanzapine, haloperidol and placebo on cognitive and psychomotor functions in healthy elderly volunteers." J*ournal of Psychopharmacology*, 13, 152–158.

Bhavnani, S.M., and Levin, G.M. (1996). "Antipsychotic agents: A survey of the prevalence, severity and burden of side effects." *International Clinical Psychopharmacology,* 11, 1–12.

Bishop, K.I., Curran, H.V., and Lader, M. (1996). "Do scopolamine and lorazepam have dissociable effects on human memory systems? A dose response study with normal volunteers." *Experimental and Clinical Psychopharmacology,* 4, 292–299.

Blake, A.J., Morgan, K., Bendall, M.J., Dallosso, H., Ebrahim, S.B.J., et al. (1988). "Falls by elderly people at home: Prevalence and associated factors." *Age and Aging*, 17, 365–372.

Broderick, E. (1997). "Prescribing patterns for nursing home residents in the U.S. The reality and the vision." *Drugs and Aging*, 11, 255–260.

Brookhuis, K.A., and Borgman, A.E. (1988). "The effects of some anxiolytics on driving performance." *TGO Tijdschrift voorTherapie, Geneesmiddel, en Onderzoek*, 13, 228–231.

Brookhuis, K.A., Volkerts, E.R., O'Hanlon, J.F. (1990). "Repeated dose effects of lormetazepam and flurazepam upon driving performance." *European Journal of Clinical Pharmacology*, 39, 83–87.

Brøsen, K. (1996). "Are pharmacokinetic drug interactions with the SSRIs an issue?" *International Clinical Pharmacology*, 11, 23–27.

Carter, G.L., Dawson, A.H., and Lopert, R. (1996). "Drug-induced delirium. Incidence, management and prevention." *Drug Safety*, 15, 291–301.

Cassens, G., Inglis, A.K., Appelbaum, P.S., and Gutheil, T.G. (1990). "Neuroleptics: Effects on neuropsychological functioning in chronic schizophrenic patients." *Schizophrenia Bulletin*, 16, 477–499.

Chadwick, D. (1999). "Safety and efficacy of vigabatrin and carbamazepine in newly diagnosed epilepsy: A multi-center randomized double-blind study. Vigabatrin European Monotherapy Study Group." *Lancet*, 354, 13–19.

Coccaro, E.F., and Siever, L.J. (1985). "Second generation antidepressants: A comparative review." *Journal of Clinical Pharmacology,* 25, 241–260.

Cohen, R.M., Weingartner, H., Smallberg, S.A., Pickar, D., and Murphy, D.L. (1982). "Effort and cognition in depression." *Archives of General Psychiatry*, 39, 593–597.

Cole, J.O. (1960). "Behavioral toxicity." In L. Uhr, and J.G. Miller (Eds.), *Drugs and Behavior* (p.375). New York: John Wiley and Sons.

Cole, J.O., and Kando, J.C. (1993). "Adverse behavioral events reported in patients taking alprazolam and other benzodiazepines." *Journal of Clinical Psychiatry*, 54, s49–s61.

Coulter, D.M., Pillians, P.I. (1995). "Fluoxetine and extrapyramidal side effects." *American Journal of Psychiatry*, 152, 122–125.

Curran, H.V. (1986). "Tranquillizing memories: A review of the effects of benzodiazepines on human performance." *Biological Psychology*, 23, 179–213.

Curran, H.V., and Birch, B. (1991). "Differentiating the sedative, psychomotor and amnestic effects of benzodiazepines: a study with midazolam and the benzodiazepine antagonist, flumazenil." *Psychopharmacology*, 103, 519–523.

Curran, H.V., and Gorenstein, G. (1993). "Differential effects of lorazepam and oxazepam on priming." *International Clinical Psychopharmacology*, 8, 37–42.

Curran, H.V., and Lader, M. (1986). "The pharmacological effects of repeated doses of fluvoxamine, mianserin and placebo in healthy human subjects." *European Journal of Clinical Pharmacology*, 29, 601–607.

Curran, H.V., Shifano, F., and Lader, M. (1991). "Models of memory dysfunction? A comparison of the effects of scopolamine and lorazepam on memory, psychomotor performance and mood." *Psychopharmacology*, 103, 83–90.

Currie, D., Hashemi, K., Fothergill, J., Findlay, A., Harris, A. et al. (1995). "The use of antidepressants and benzodiazepines in the perpetrators and victims of accidents." *Occupational Medicine*, 45, 323–325.

Danion, J.M., Zimmerman, M.A., Willard–Schroeder, D., Grange, D., and Singer, L. (1989). "Diazepam induces a dissociation between explicit and implicit memory." *Psychopharmacology*, 99, 238–243.

De Gier, J.J. (1995). *Drugs Other than Alcohol and Driving in the European Union.* Technical Report, Institute for Human Psychopharmacology, (pp. 95–54). The Netherlands: Maastricht University.

Deptula, D., and Pomara, N. (1990). "Effects of antidepressants on human performance: A review." *Journal of Clinical Psychopharmacology,* 10, 105–110.

Dershwitz, M., Rosowm C.E., Dibiase, P.M., and Zaslavky, A. (1991). "Comparison of the sedative effects of butorphanol and midazolam." *Anesthesiology*, 74, 717–724.

Dijen, J.B., Loriaux, S.M., Orlebeke, J.F., and De Vries, J. (1989). "Effects of paroxetine and maprotiline on mood, perceptual-motor skills and eye movements in healthy volunteers." *Journal of Psychopharmacology*, 3, 149–155.

Dimascio, A., and Shader, R.I. (1968). "Behavioral toxicity of psychotropic drugs: I Definition; II Toxic effects on psychomotor functions." *Connecticut Medicine*, 32, 617–620.

Drane, D.L., and Meador, K.J. (1995). "Epilepsy, anticonvulsant drugs and cognition." *Bailliere's Clinical Neurology*, 5, 877–885.

Emilien, G., and Maloteaux, J.M. (1998). "Pharmacological management of epilepsy. Mechansims of action, pharmacokinetic drug interactions, and new drug discovery possibilities." *International Journal of Clinical Pharmacology and Therapeutics*, 36, 181–194.

Fagan, D., Scott, D.B., Mitchell, M., and Tiplady, B. (1991). "Effects of remoxipride on measures of psychological performance in healthy volunteers." *Psychopharmacology*, 105, 225–229.

Fairweather, D.B., Kerr, K.S., Harrison, D.A., Moon, C.A., and Hindmarch, I. (1993a). "A double blind comparison of fluoxetine and amitriptyline on cognitive function in elderly depressed patients." *Human Psychopharmacology*, 8, 41–47.

Fairweather, D.B., Kerr, J.S., and Hindmarch, I. (1992). "The effects of acute and repeated doses of zolpidem on subjective sleep, psychomotor performance and cognitive function in elderly volunteers." *European Journal of Clinical Pharmacology*, 43, 597–601.

Fairweather, D.B., Kerr, J.S., and Hindmarch, I. (1993b). "The effects of moclobemide on psychomotor performance and cognitive function." *International Clinical Pharmacology*, 8, 43–47.

Farid, N.A., Bergström, R.F., Lemberger, L., Ziege, E.A., et al. (1986). "Studies on the disposition of fluoxetine and radioactive isotopes." Poster presented at 15th CINP Congress, Puerto Rico.

Fingl, E., and Woodbury, D.M. (1964). "General principles." In L.S. Goodman, and A.Gilman (Eds.), *The Pharmacological Basis of Therapeutics*. (3rd ed.) (p. 1). New York: MacMillan.

Freeman, H.L., O'Hanlon, J.F. (1995). "Acute and sub–acute effects of antidepressants on performance." *Journal of Drug Development and Clinical Practice*, 7, 7–20.

Frewer, L.J., and Lader, M . (1993). "The effects of nefazodone, imipramine and placebo and combined with alcohol, in normal subjects." *International Clinical Psychopharmacology*, 8, 13–20.

Froley, R., Mrvos, R., and Krenzelok, E.P. (2000). "A profile of methylphenidate exposures." *J Toxicology Clinical Toxicology*, 38, 625–630.

Gillham, R.A., Williams, N., Wiedmann, K., Butler, E., Larkin, J.G., and Brodie, M.J. (1988). "Concentration–effect relationships with carbamazepine and its epoxide on psychomotor and cognitive function in epileptic patients." *Journal Neurology Neurosurgery Psychiatry*, 51, 29–33.

Gleiter, C.H., and Deckert, J. (1996). "Adverse effects of beta-adrenoceptor blockers." *Pharmacopsychiatry*, 29, 201–211.

Gorenstein, C., Bernik, M.A., and Pompeia, S. (1994). "Differential acute psychomotor and cognitive effects on diazepam on long-term benzodiazepine users." *International Clinical Psychopharmacology*, 9, 145–153.

Green, M.F., Marshall, B.D., Wirshing, W.C., Ames D, Marder, S.R., McGurk, S., et al. (1997). "Does risperidone improve verbal working memory in treatment-resistant schizophrenia?" *American Journal of Psychiatry*, 154, 799–804.

Grounds, D., Stocky, A., Evens, P., Scott, C., et al. (1995). "Antidepressants and side effects." *Australian and New Zealand Journal of Psychiatry*, 29, 156–157.

Haenel, T., Stockli, H.R., and Truog, P. (1995). "A case of rare side effects of certain antidepressant drugs." *Nervenartz*, 66, 70–72.

Hale, A.S., and Pinninti, N.R. (1995). "Critical flicker fusion threshold and anticholinergic effects of chronic antidepressant treatment in remitted depressives." *Journal of Psychopharmacology*, 9, 258266.

Hamilton, M.J., Cohen, A.F., Yuen, A.W., Harkin, N., Land G., Weatherley, B.C., et al. (1993). "Carbamazepine and lamotrigine in healthy volunteers: Relevance to early tolerance and clinical trial dosage." *Epilepsia*, 34, 166–73.

Heller, A.J., Chesterman, P., Elwes, R.D.C., et al. (1995). "Phenobarbital, phenytoin, carbamazapine, or sodium valproate for newly diagnosed adult epilepsy." *Journal of Neurology, Neurosurgery and Psychiatry*, 58, 44–50.

Herberg, K.W., and Menke, H. (1981). *Study of the Effects of the Antidepresant Fluvoxamine on Driving Skills and Its Interaction with Alcohol*. Technical Report. Cologne: TÜV Rheinland.

Hindmarch, I. (1992). "A review of the psychomotor effects of paroxetine." *International Clinical Psychopharmacology*, 6, S65–S67.

Hindmarch, I. (1994). "Instrumental assessment of psychomotor functions and the effects of psychotropic drugs." *Acta Psychiatrica Scandinavia*, 89, S49–S52.

Hindmarch, I., Harrison, C. (1988). "The effects of paroxetine and other antidepressants in combination with alcohol in psychomotor activity related to car driving." *Human Psychopharmacology*, 8, 417–422.

Hindmarch, I., and Kerr, J.S. (1992). "Behavioral toxicity of antidepressants with particular reference to moclobemide." *Psychopharmacology*, 106, s49–s55.

Hindmarch, I., Shamsi, Z., Stanley, N., and Fairweather, D.B. (1999). "A double–blind, placebocontrolled investigation of the effects of fexofenadine, loratadine and promethazine on cognitive and psychomotor function." *British Journal of Clinical Pharmacology*, 48, 200–206.

Hindmarch, I., Shilingford, J., and Shillingford, C. (1990). "The effects of sertraline on psychomotor performance in elderly volunteers." *Journal of Clinical Psychiatry*, 12, S34–S36.

Hobi, V., Gastpar, M., Gatstpar, G., Gilsdorf, U., Kielholz, P., et al. (1982). "Driving ability of depressed patients under antidepressants." *Journal of International Medical Research*, 10, 65–81.

Hoehn–Saric, R., Lipsey, J.R., and McLeod, D.R. (1990). "Apathy and indifference in patients on fluvoxamine and fluoxetine." *Journal of Clinical Psychopharmacology*, 10, 343–345.

Hommer, D., Weingarter, H., and Breier, A. (1993). "Dissociation of benzodiazepine–induced amnesia from sedation by flumazenil pretreatment." *Psychopharmacology*, 112, 455–460.

Hughes, A.M., Lynch, P., Rhodes, J., Ervine, C.M., and Yates, R.A. (1999). "Electroencephalographic and psychomotor effects of chlorpromazine and risperidone relative to placebo in normal healthy volunteers." *British Journal of Clinical Pharmacology*, 48, 323–330.

Jackson, D.M., Ryan, C., Evenden, J., and Mohell, N. (1994). "Preclinical findings with new antipsychotic agents: What makes them atypical?" *Acta Psychiatrica Scandinavia*, 89, S41–S48.

Jones, B.A. (1997). "Decreasing polypharmacy in clients most at risk." *AACN Clinical Issues*, 8, 627–634.

Kerr, J.S., Fairweather, D.B., Mahendran, R., and Hindmarch, I. (1992). "The effects of paroxetine alone and in combination with alcohol on psychomotor performance and cognitive function in the elderly." *International Clinical Pharmacology*, 7, 101–108.

King, D.J. (1993). "Measures of neuroleptic effects on cognition and psychomotor performance in healthy volunteers." In I. Hindmarch, P.D. Stonier (Eds.), *Human Psychopharmacology Vol 4* (pp.195–209). West Sussex: John Wiley and Sons Ltd.

King, D.J. (1994). "Psychomotor disturbances induced by neuroleptics." *Acta Psychiatrica Scandinavia*, 889, S53–S59.

King, D.J. (1997). "BAP Consensus Statement. Guidelines for the use of antispychotic drug studies in healthy volunteers." J*ournal of Psychopharmacology*, 11, 201–210.

King, D.J., Best, P., Lynch, D., Mannion, M.F., Montgomery, R.C., Tiplady, B., et al. (1995). "The effects of remoxipride and chlorpheniramine on eye movements and psychomotor performance in healthy volunteers." *Journal of Psychopharmacology*, 9, 143–150.

Kinon, B.J., and Lieberman, J.A. (1996). "Mechanisms of action of atypical anti–psychotics: A critical analysis." *Psychopharmacology*, 124, 2–34.

Kirk, T., Roache, J.D., and Griffiths, R.R. (1990). "Dose response evaluations of the amnestic effects of triazolam and pentobarbital in normal subjects." *Journal of Clinical Psychopharmacology*, 10, 160–167.

Koelega, H.S. (1989) "Benzodiazepines and vigilance performance: A review." *Psychopharmacology*, 98, 145–156.

Koepsell, T.D., Wolf, M.E., McClosky, L., Buchner, D.M., Louie, D., et al. (1994). "Medical conditions and motor vehicle collision injuries in older adults." *Journal of American Geriatrics Society*, 42, 695–700.

Koryagin, A. (1981). "Unwilling patients." *The Lancet*, April 11, 821–824.

Kroboth, P.D., Folan, M.M., Lusch, R.M., Chaikin, P.C., Shukla, U.A., et al. (1995). "Coadministration of nefazodone and benzodiazepines: I pharmacodynamic assessment." *Journal of Clinical Pharmacology,* 15, 306–319.

Kuitunen, T., Mattila, M.J., Seppälä, T., Aranko, K., and Mattila, M.E. (1990). "Actions of zopiclone and carbamazepine, alone and in combination, on human skilled performance in laboratory and clinical tests." *Br J Clin Pharmacol*, 30, 453–61.

Lader, M. (1994). "Historical introduction. Proceedings of the first international meeting on the neuroleptic induced deficit syndrome." *Acta Psychiatrica Scandinavia*, 89, S6–S7.

Lader, M., Melhuish, A., Freka, G., Fredricson Overo, K., and Christensen, V. (1986) "The effects of citalopram in single and repeated doses and with alcohol on physiological and psychological measures in healthy subjects." *European Journal of Clinical Pharmacology*, 31, 183–190.

Lamy, P.P., Salzman, C., and Nevis–Olesen, J. (1992). "Drug prescribing patterns, risks, and compliance guidelines." In C. Salzman (Ed.), *Clinical Geriatric Psychopharmacology* (2nd ed.). (pp. 15–37). Baltimore: Williams and Wilkins.

Langdorf, M.I., Fox, J.C., Marwah, R.S., Montague, B.J., and Hart, M.M. (2000). "Physician versus computer knowledge of potential drug interactions in the emergency department." *Academic Emergency Medical*, 7, 1321–1329.

Larson, E.B., Kukull, W.A., Buchner, D., Reifler, B.V. (1987). "Adverse drug reactions associated with global cognitive impairment in elderly persons." *Annals of Internal Medicine*, 107, 169–173.

Lasher, T.A., Fleishaker, J.C., Steenwyck, R.C., Antal, E.J. (1991). "Pharmacokinetic, pharmacodynamic evaluation of the combined administration of alprozolam and fluoxetine." *Psychopharmacology*, 104, 323–327.

Leonard, B. (1997). *Fundamentals of Psychopharmacology* (2nd ed.). Chichester, New York, Weinheim: John Wiley and Sons.

Levander, T. (1994). "Neuroleptics and the neuroleptic induced deficit syndrome." *Acta Psychiatrica Scandinavia*, 89, S8–S13.

Leveille, S.G., Buchner, D.M., Koepsell, T.D., McClosky, L.W., Wolf, M.E., et al. (1994). "Psychoactive medications and injurious motor vehicle collisions involving older drivers." *Epidemiology*, 5, 591–598.

Leysen, J.E., Gommeren, W., and Schotte, A. (1996). "Serotonin receptor subtypes: Possible roles and implications in anti–psychotic drug action." In J.M. Kane, H.J. Moller, and F.A. Wouters (Eds.), *Serotonin in Antipsychotic Treatment* (pp. 51–75). New York: Marcel Dekker.

Liljequist, R., Linnoila, M., Mattila, M.J., Saario, I., and Seppälä, T. (1975). "Effects of two weeks' treatment with thioridazine, chlorpromazine, sulpiride, and bromazepam, alone or in combination with alcohol, on learning and memory in man." *Psychopharmacologia*, 44, 205–208.

Linnoila, M., Guthrie, S., and Lister, R. (1986). "Mechanisms of drug–induced impairment of driving." In J.F. O'Hanlon, and H. De Gier (Eds.), *Drugs and Driving* (pp. 29–50). London, Philadelphia: Taylor and Francis .

MacPhee, G.J.A., Goldie, C., Roulston, D., Potter, L., Agnew, E., Laidlaw, J., et al. (1986). "Effects of carbamazepine on psychomotor performance in naïve subjects." *European Journal of Clinical Pharmacology*, 30, 37–42.

MacPhee, G.J.A., McPhail, E.M.M., Butler, E., and Brodie, M.J. (1986). "Controlled evaluation of a supplementary dose of carbamazepine on psychomotor functions in epileptic patients." *European Journal of Clinical Pharmacology*, 31, 195–199.

Mandalos, G.E., and Szarek, B.L. (1990). "Dose–related paranoid reaction associated with fluoxetine." *Journal of Nervous and Mental Disorders*, 178, 57–58.

Mander, A., McCausland, M., Workman, B., Flamer, H., and Christophidis, N. (1994). "Fluoxetine induced dyskinesia." *Australian and New Zealand Journal of Psychiatry*, 28, 328–330.

Mann, R.D., Pearce, G.L., Dunn, N., and Shakir, S. (2000). Sedation with non-sedating antihistamines: Four prescription event monitoring studies in general practice." *British Medical Journal*, 320, 1184–1187.

Manni, R., Ratti, M.T., Perucca, E., Galimberti, C.A., and Tartara, A. (1993). "A multi–parametric investigation of daytime sleepiness and psychomotor functions in epileptic patients treated with phenobarbital and sodium valproate: A comparative controlled study." *Electroencephalography Clinical Neurophysiology*, 86, 322–328.

Mattson, R.H. (1989). "Selection of anti–epileptic drug therapy." In R. Levy, R.H. Mattson, B. Meldrum, and J.K. Penry (Eds.) *Anti-Epileptic Drugs* (3rd ed.) (pp. 103–115). New York: Raven Press.

Mattson, R.H., Cramer, J.A., and Collins, J.F. (1992). "Valproate for treatment of partial and secondarily generalized tonic-clonic seizures in adults: A comparison with carbamazapine." *New England Journal of Medicine*, 327, 765–771.

Mattila, M.J., Mattila, M.E., Konno, K., and Saarialho–Kere, U. (1988). "Objective and subjective effects of remoxipride, alone and in combination with ethanol or diazepam, on performance in healthy subjects." *Journal of Psychopharmacology*, 2, 138–149.

Mattila, M.J., and Paakkari, I. (1999). "Variations among non-sedating antihistamines are there real differences?" *European Journal of Clinical Pharmacology*, 55, 85–93.

Mattila, M.J., Patat, A., Seppälä, T., Kalska, H., Jalava, M.L., Vanakoski, J., et al. (1996). "Single oral doses of amisulpride do not enhance the effects of alcohol on the performance and memory of healthy subjects." *European Journal of Clinical Pharmacology,* 51, 161–166.

McClelland, G.R., Ciooper, S.M., and Pilgrim, A.J. (1990). "A comparison of the central nervous system effects of haloperidol, chlorpromazine and sulpiride in normal volunteers." *British Journal of Clinical Pharmacology*, 30, 795–803.

Meador, K.J., Loring, D.W., Abney, O.L., Allen, M.E., Moore, E.E., Zamrini, E.Y., et al. (1993). "Effects of carbamazepine and phenytoin on EEG and memory in healthy adults." *Epilepsia*, 34, 153–157.

Meador, K.J., Loring, D.W., Allen, M.E., Zamrini, E.Y., Moore, E.E., Abney, O.L., et al. (1991). "Comparative cognitive effects of carbamazepine and phenytoin in healthy adults." *Neurology*, 41, 1537–1540.

Meador, K.J., Loring, D.W., Huh, K., Gallagher, B.B., and King, D.W. (1990). "Comparative cognitive effects of anticonvulsants." *Neurology*, 40, 391–394.

Meador, K.J., Loring, D.W., Moore, E.E., Thompson, W.O., et al. (1995). "Comparative effects of phenobarbital, phenytoin, and valproate in healthy adults." *Neurology*, 45, 1494–1499.

Meghji, C. (1994). "Acquired stuttering [letter]." Journal of Family Practice, 39, 325–326.

Meltzer, H.Y., and McGurk, S.R. (1999). "The effects of clozapine, risperidone and olanzapine on cognitive function in schizophrenia." S*chizophrenia Bulletin*, 25, 233–255.

Mirow, S. (1991). "Cognitive dysfunction associated with fluoxtine [letter]." *American Journal of Psychiatry,* 148, 948–949.

Moon, C.A.L., and Davey, A. (1988). "The efficacy and residual effects of trazodone (150 mg nocte) and mianserin in the treatment of depressed general practice patients." *Psychopharmacology*, 95, S7–S13.

Moon, C.A.L., and Jesinger, D.K. (1991). "The effects of psychomotor performance of fluvoxamine versus mianserin in depressed patients in general practice." *British Journal of Clinical Pharmacology,* 45, 259–262.

Neutel, C.I. (1995). "Risk of traffic accident injury after a prescription for a benzodiazepine." *Annals of Epidemiology*, 5, 239–244.

Newhouse, P.A., and Richter, E.M. (1996). "Comparison of sertraline and fluoxetine in depressed geriatric outpatients: Plasma levels and efficacy." Poster presented at the 20th CINP congress, Melbourne.

Nicholson, A.N., Stone, B.M., Turner, C., and Mills, S.L. (2000). "Antihistamines and aircrew: Usefulness of fexofenadine." *Aviation, Space, and Environmental Medicine*, 71, 2–6.

Nolen, T.M. (1997). "Sedative effects of antihistamines: Safety, performance, learning and quality of life." *Clinical Therapeutic*s, 19, 39–55.

O'Hanlon, J.F. (1984). "Driving performance under the influence of drugs. Rationale for, and application of a new test." *British Journal of Clinical Pharmacology*, 18, 121S–129S.

O'Hanlon, J.F. (1991). "Review of buspirone's effects on human performance and related variables." European neuropsycholopharmacology, 1, 489–501.

O'Hanlon, J.F. (1995). "Zopiclone's residual effects on psychomotor and information processing skills involved in complex tasks such as car driving: A critical review." *European Psychiatry*, 10, 137S–144S.

O'Hanlon, J.F. (1996). "Antidepressant therapy and behavioral competence." *British Journal of Clinical Prac*tice, 50, 381–385.

O'Hanlon, J.F., Brookhuis, K.A., Louwerens, J.W., and Volkerts, E.R. (1986). "Performance testing as part of drug registration." In J.F. O'Hanlon, J.J. De Gier (Eds.), *Drugs and Driving*, (pp. 311–330). London: Taylor and Francis.

O'Hanlon, J.F., and Freeman, H. (1995). "Categorizing the behavioral toxicities of antidepressants." *British Journal of Psychiatry,* 166, 421–423.

O'Hanlon, J.F., Haak, T.W., Blaauw, G.J., and Riemersma, J.B.J. (1982). "Diazepam impairs lateral position control in highway driving." *Science*, 217, 79–81.

O'Hanlon, J.F., and Ramaekers, J.G. (1995). "Antihistamine effects on actual driving performance in a standard test: A summary of Dutch experience, 1989–1994." *Allergy*, 50, 234–242.

O'Hanlon, J.F., Robbe, H.W.J., Vermeeren, A., Van Leeuwen, C., and Danjou, P. (1998). Venlafaxine's effects on healthy volunteers' driving, psychomotor, and vigilance performance during 15-day fixed (75mg/d) and incremental (75–150mg/d) dosing regimens." *Journal of Clinical Psychopharmacology*, 18, 212–221.

O'Hanlon, J.F., Vermeeren, A., Uiterwijk, M.M.C., Veggel, van L.M.A., and Swijgman, H.F. (1995). "Anxiolytics' effects on the actual driving performance of patients and healthy volunteers in a standardized test." *Neuropsychobiology*, 31, 81–88.

O'Hanlon, J.F., Volkerts, E.R. (1986). "Hypnotics and actual driving performance." *Acta Psychiatrica Scandinavia,* 332, S95–S104.

O'Hanlon, J.F., Volkerts, E.R., Louwerens, J.W., Gloerich, A.B.M., and Brookhuis, K.A. (1984). "Zopiclone's residual effects on actual driving performance versus those of nitrazepam and flunitrazepam." *Clinical Neuropharmacology*, 7, 620S–621S.

Palmer, B.W., Heaton, R.K., Paulsen, J.S., et al. (1997). "Is it possible to be schizophrenic yet neuropsychologically normal?" *Neuropsychology*, 11, 435–443.

Parrot, A.C. (1987). "Assessment of psychological performance in applied situations." In I. Hindmarch, and P. Stonier (Eds.), *Human Psychopharmacology: Measures and Methods*. Vol 1 (pp. 93–111). Chichester, New York, Brisbane: John Wiley and Sons.

Patat, A., Gandon, J.M., Durrieu, G., Le Coz, F., Curet, O., et al. (1995b). "Effects of single and multiple doses of a new reversible MAO–A inhibitor, befloxatone, on psychomotor performance and memory in healthy subjects." *Human Psychopharmacology*, 19, 111–125.

Patat, A., Paty, I., and Hindmarch, I. (2001). "Pharmacodynamic profile of zaleplon, a new nonbenzodiazepine hypnotic agent." *Human Psychopharmacology Clin Exp*, 16, 369–392.

Patat, A., Perault, M.C., Vandel, B., Danjou, P., Brohier, S., et al. (1995a). "Assessment of the interaction between a partial agonist and a full agonist of benzodiazepine receptors, based on psychomotor performance and memory, in healthy volunteers." *Journal of Psychopharmacology*, 9, 91–101.

Patten, S.B., and Love, E.J. (1994). "Drug-induced depression. Incidence, avoidance and management." *Drug Safety*, 10, 203–219.

Peet, M., and Peters, S. (1995). "Drug-induced mania." *Drug Safety*, 12, 146–153.

Perrault, G.H., Depoortere, R., Morel, E., Sanger, D.J., and Scatton, B. (1997). "Amisulpride: An atypical antipsychotic with D2/D3 dopamine receptor antagonistic activity and limbic selectivity: II behavioral profile." *Journal of Pharmacology and Experimental Therapeutics*, 280, 73–82.

Peselow, E.D., Corwin, J., Fieve, R.R., Rotrosen, J., and Cooper, T.B. (1991). "Disappearance of memory deficits in outpatient depressives responding to imipramine." *Journal of Affective Disorders,* 21, 173–183.

Peuskens, J. (1995). "Risperidone in the treatment of patients with chronic schizophrenia: a multinational, multi-center, double blind, parallel-group study versus haloperidol." *British Journal of Psychiatry*, 166, 712–726.

Polster, M.R., McCarthy, R.A., O'Sullivan, G., Gray, P.A., and Park, G.R. (1989). "Midazolam induced amnesia: implications for the implicit/explicit memory distinction." *Brain Cognition*, 22, 244–265.

Pomara, N., Deptula, D., Medel, M., Block, R.I., and Greenblatt, D.J. (1989). "Effects of diazepam on recall memory: relationship to aging, dose, and duration of treatment." *Psychopharmacological Bulletin*, 25, 144–148.

Prevey, M.L., Delaney, R.C., Cramer, J.A. et al. (1996). "Effect of valproate on cognitive functioning. Comparison with carbamazapine." *Archives of Neurology*, 53, 1008–1016.

Purdon, S.E., Jones, B.D., Stip, E., Labelle, A., Addington, D., David, S.R., et al. (2000). "Neuropsychological change in early phase schizophrenia during twelve months of treatment with olanzapine, risperidone, or haloperidol. The Canadian Collaborative Group for research in schizophrenia." *Archives of General Psychiatry*, 57, 249–58.

Quigley, N., Morgan, D., Idzikowski, C., King, D.J. (1996). "The effect of chlorpromazine and benzhexol on memory and psychomotor function in healthy volunteers." *Journal of Psychopharmacology*, 10, 146–152.

Ramaekers, J.G. (1998). "Behavioral toxicity of medicinal drugs: Practical consequences, incidence, management and avoidance." *Drug Safety*, 18, 189–208.

Ramaekers, J.G., Ansseau, M., Muntjewerff, N.D., Sweens, P., O'Hanlon, J.F. (1997). "Considering the P450 cytochrome system as determining the effects of antidepressants and benzodiazepines on the actual driving performance of outpatients suffering from major depression." *International Clinical Psychopharmacology*, 12, 159–169.

Ramaekers, J.G., Lamers, C.T.J., Muntjewerff, N.D., Verhey, F., Sanders, N., Mobbs, E., et al. (2002). "A comparative study of the effects of carbamazepine and the NMDA antagonist remacemide on road tracking and car following performance in actual traffic." *Psychopharmacology*, 159, 203–210.

Ramaekers, J.G., Louwerens, J.W., Muntjewerff, N.D., Milius, H., de Bie, A., et al. (1999). "Psychomotor, cognitive, extrapyramidal and affective functions of healthy volunteers during treatment with an atypical (amisulpride) and a classic (haloperidol) antipsychotic." J*ournal of Clinical Psychopharmacology*, 19, 209–221.

Ramaekers, J.G., Muntjewerff, N.D., O'Hanlon, J.F. (1995). "A comparative study of acute and sub–chronic effects of dothiepin, fluoxetine and placebo on psychomotor and actual driving performance." *British Journal of Clinical Psychopharmacology,* 39, 397–404.

Ramaekers, J.G., Muntjewerff, N.D., Uiterwijk, M.M.C., Van Veggel, L.M.A., Patat, A. et al. (1996). "A study of the pharmacodynamic interaction between befloxatone and ethanol on performance and mood in healthy volunteers." *Journal of Psychopharmacology*, 10, 288–194.

Ramaekers, J.G., Muntjewerff, N.D., van Veggel, L.M.A., Uiterwijk, M.M.C., O'Hanlon, J.F. (1998). "Effects of nocturnal doses of mirtazapine and mianserin on sleep and on daytime psychomotor and driving performance in young, healthy volunteers." *Human Psychopharmacology Clin Exp* ,13, Suppl 2, S87–97.

Ramaekers, J.G., Swijgman, H.F., and O'Hanlon, J.F. (1992). "Effects of moclobemide and mianserin on highway driving, psychometric performance and subjective parameters, relative to placebo." *Psychopharmacology*, 106, s62–s67.

Ramaekers, J.G., Van Veggel, L.M.A., O'Hanlon, J.F. (1994). "A cross-study comparison of the effects of moclobemide and brofaromine on actual driving performance and estimated sleep." *Clinical Neuropsychopharmacology,* 17, S9–S18.

Ramaekers, J.G., and Vermeeren, A. (2000). "All antihistamines cross blood brain barrier [letter]." *British Medical Journal*, 321, 573.

Rammsayer, T., and Gallhofer, B. (1995). "Remoxepride versus haloperidol in healthy volunteers: Psychometric performance and subjective tolerance profiles." *International Clinical Psychopharmcology*, 10, 31–37.

Ray, W.A., Fought, R.L., and Decker, M.D. (1992). "Psychoactive drugs and the risk of injurious motor vehicle crashes in elderly drivers." *American Journal of Epidemiology*, 136, 873–883.

Ray, W.A., Griffin, M.R., Schaffner, W., Baugh, D.K., and Melton, L.F. (1987). "Psychotropic drug use and the risk of hip fracture." *New England Journal of Medicine*, 316, 363–369.

Richelson, E. (1996). "Synaptic effects of antidepressants." *Journal of Clinical Psychopharmacology*, 16, S1–S9.

Riedel, W.J., Quasten, H., and O'Hanlon, J.F. (1988). *A Study Comparing the Hypnotic Efficacies on Actual Driving Performance of Midazolam 15 mg, Triazolam 0.5 mg, Temazepam 20 mg, and Placebo in Shiftworkers on Night Duty*. Technical report IGVG 88–01. Maastricht: Institute for Drugs, Safety and Behavior, University of Limburg.

Riedel, W.J., and Van Praag, H.M. (1995). "Avoiding and managing anticholinergic effects of antidepressants." *CNS Drugs*, 3, 245–259.

Rikken, G., Scharf, M.B., Danzig, M.R., and Staudinger, H. (2000). "Desloratadine and alcohol coadministration: No increase in impairment of performance over that induced by alcohol alone [abstract]." *Allergy*, 63, 277.

Robbe, H.W.J., and O'Hanlon, J.F. (1995). "Acute and sub–chronic effects of paroxetine 20 and 40 mg on actual driving, psychomotor performance and subjective assessments in healthy volunteers." *European Neuropsychopharmacology*, 5, 35–42.

Roehrs, T., Merlotti, L., Zorick, F., and Roth, T. (1994). Sedative, memory, and performance effects of hynotics." *Psychopharmacology*, 116, 130–134.

Rombaut, N.E.I., and Hindmarch, I. (1994). "Psychometric aspects of antihistamines: A review." *Human Psychopharmacology*, 9, 157–169.

Ruthazer, R., and Lewis, A.L. (1993). "Antidepressants and falls among elderly people in long-term care." *American Journal of Public Health*, 83, 746–749.

Ruiz, F. (1994). "Fluoxetine and the serotonin syndrome." *Annals of Emergency Medicine*, 24, 983–985.

Sakulsripong, M., Curan, H.V., and Lader, M. (1991). "Does tolerance develop to the sedative and amnesiac effects of antidepressants?" *European Journal of Clinical Pharmacology*, 40, 43–48.

Saletu, B., Grünberger, J., Linzmayer, L. and Anderer, P. (1987). "Comparative placebo–controlled pharmacodynamic studies with zotepine and clozapine utilizing pharmaco-EEG and psychometry." *Pharmacopsychiatry*, 20, 12–27.

Saletu, B., and Pekesch, G, (1987a). "Recent advances in clinical pharmacology of benzodiazepines Part II: Pharmacodynamics." *Human Psychopharmacology*, 2, 61–84.

Salinsky, M.C., Oken, B.S., and Binder, L.M. (1996). "Assessment of drowsiness in epilepsy patients receiving chronic anti-epileptic drug therapy." *Epilepsia*, 37, 181–187.

Schmitt, J.A.J., Kruizinga, M.J., and Riedel, W.J. (2001). "Non-serotonergic pharmacological profiles and associated cognitive effects of serotonin reuptake inhibitors." *Journal of Psychopharmacology*, 15, 173–179.

Schmitt, J.A.J., Ramaekers, J.G., Kruizinga, M., Teunisse, S., Van Boxtel, M.P.J., and Vuurman, E.F.P.M., et al. (2002). "Additional dopamine reuptake inhibition prevents vigilance decrement induced by serotonergic reuptake inhibition in man." (Submitted)

Schoemaker, H., Claustre, Y., Fage, D., Rouquier, L., Chergui, K. et al. (1997). "Neurochemical characteristics of amisulpride, an atypical D2/D3 receptor antagonist with both presynaptic and limbic selectivity." *Journal of Pharmacology and Experimental Therapeutics*, 280, 83–97.

Schwartz, J.C., Arrang, J.M., Garbarg, M., and Traiffort, E. (1994). "Histamine." In F.E. Bloom, and D.J. Kupfer (Eds.), *Psychopharmacology: The Fourth Generation of Progress* (pp. 397–405). New York: Raven Press.

Seppälä, T., Linnoila, M., Elonen, E., Mattila, M.J., and Maki, M. (1975) "Effects of tricyclic antidepressants and alcohol on psychomotor skills related to driving." *Clinical Pharmacology and Therapeutics*, 17, 515–221.

Seppälä, T., Linnoila, M., and Mattila, M.J. (1978). "Psychomotor skills in depressed out–patients treated with L–tryptophan, doxepin, or chlorimipramine." *Annals of Clinical Research*, 10, 214–221.

Seppälä, T., Stromberg, C., and Bergman, I. (1984). "Effects of zimeldine, mianserin and amitriptyline on psychomotor skills and their interaction with ethanol: A placebo controlled crossover study." *European Journal of Clinical Pharmacology*, 27, 181–189.

Sharma, T. (1999). "Cognitive effects of conventional and atypical antipsychotics in schizophrenia." *British Journal of Psychiatry,* 174, S44–S51.

Siegfried, K., and O'Connolly, M. (1986). "Cognitive and psychomotor effects of different antidepressants in the treatment of old age depression." *International Clinical Psychopharmacology*, 1, 231–243.

Simons, F.E.R. (1994). "H1 receptor antagonists. Comparative tolerability and safety." *Drug Safety*, 10, 350–380.

Singh, R.K., Gupta, A.K., and Singh, B. (1995). "Acute organic brain syndrome after fluoxetine treatment." *American Journal of Psychiatry*, 152, 295–296.

Spohn, H.E., and Strauss, M.E. (1989). "Relation of neuroleptic and anticholinergic medication to cognitive functions in schizophrenia." *Journal of Abnormal Psychology*, 98, 249–271.

Spring, B., Gelenberg, A.J., Garvin, R., and Thompson, S. (1992). Amitriptyline, clovoxamine and cognitive function: A placebo controlled comparison in depressed outpatients." *Psychopharmacology*, 108, 327–332.

Sproule, B.A., Naranjo, C.A., Bremner, K.E., and Hassan, P.C. (1997). "Selective serotonin reuptake inhibitors and CNS drug interactions." *Clinical Pharmacokinetics*, 33, 454–471.

Stanley, N., Alfort, C.A., Rombaut, N.E.I., and Hindmarch, I. (1996). "Comparison of the effects of astemizole/pseudoephedrine and triprolidine/pseudoephedrine on CNS activity and psychomotor function." *International Clinical Psychopharmacology,* 11, 31–36.

Starr, J.M., and Whalley, L.J. (1994). "Drug–induced dementia. Incidence, management and prevention." *Drug Safety*, 11, 310–317.

Stille, G., and Herberg, K.W. (1989). "Traffic safety in treatment with dosulepin." *Fortschritte der Medizin*, 107, 75–78.

Stone, B., Turner, C., Mills, S.L., Patat, A., and Paty, I. (2000). "Sleep in a noise environment: Hypnotic and residual effects of zaleplon." *Journal of Sleep Research*, 9, S366.

Stuck, A.E., Beers, M.H., Steiner, A., Aronow, H.U., Rubenstein, L.Z., and Beck, J.C. (1994). "Inappropriate medication use in community residing older persons." *Archives of Internal Medicine*, 154, 2195–2200.

Streufert, S., and Gengo, F.M. (1993). "Drugs and behavior: An introduction." In S. Streufert, and F.M. Gengo (Eds.), *Effects of Drugs on Human Functioning* (pp. 1–12). Paris, Basel, Freiburg: Karger.

Stromberg, C., Seppälä, T., and Mattila, M.J. (1988). "Acute effects of maprotiline, doxepin and zimeldine with alcohol in healthy volunteers." *Archives of Pharmacodynamics and Therapeutics*, 291, 217–228.

Theunisssen, E., Vermeeren, A., and Ramaekers, J.G. (2002). "Mequitazine effects on psychomotor and driving performance as a function of dose." Data on file, Maastricht University.

Tompson, P.J. (1991). "Antidepressants and memory: A review." *Human Pychopharmacology*, 6, 79–90.

Townsend, T.N., Lane, J., Dewa, C.S., and Brittingham, A.M. (1998). *Driving after Drug or Alcohol Use: Findings from the 1996 National Household Survey on Drug Abuse*. Washington, D.C.: U.S. National Highway Traffic Safety Administration.

Van Laar, M.W., Van Willigenburg, A.P.P., and Volkerts, E.R. (1995). "Acute and sub–chronic effects of nefazodone and imipramine on highway driving, cognitive functions, and daytime sleepiness in healthy adult and elderly subjects." *Journal of Clinical Psychopharmacology*, 15, 3040.

Van Laar, M.W. and Volkerts, E.R. (1998). "Driving and benzodiazepine use: Evidence that they don't mix." *CNS Drugs*, 10, 383–396.

Van Laar, M.W., Volkerts, E.R., and Van Willigenburg, A.P.P. (1992). "Therapeutic effects and effects on actual driving performance of chronically administered buspirone and diazepam in anxious outpatients." *Journal of Clinical Psychopharmacology*, 12, 86–95.

Van Laar, M.W., Volkerts, E.R., and Verbaten, M. (2001). "Sub–chronic effects of GABA–agonist lorazepam and the 5HT2a/2c antagonist ritanserin on driving performance, slow wave sleep, and daytime sleepiness in healthy volunteers." *Psychopharmacology*, 154, 189–197.

Vermeeren, A., Danjou, P.E., and O'Hanlon, J.F. (1998). "Residual effects of evening and middle–inthe–night administration of zaleplon 10 and 20mg on memory and actual driving performance." *Human Psychopharmacology Clin Exp*, 13, S98–S107.

Vermeeren, A., O'Hanlon, J.F., Declerck, A.C., and Kho, L., (1995). "Acute effects of zolpidem and flunitrazepam on sleep, memory and driving performance, compared to those of partial sleep deprivation and placebo." *Acta Therapeutica*, 21, 47–64.

Vermeeren, A., O'Hanlon, J.F., and Fidler, C. (1996). *A Single-Center, Double-Blind, Placebo-Controlled, Cross-Over Study to Compare the Effects of Four Dosage Regimens of Fexofenadine Hydrochloride on Car Driving and Psychomotor Performance*. Technical Report. Institute for Human Psychopharmacology, Maastricht, The Netherlands.

Vermeeren, A., Ramaekers, J.G., O'Hanlon, J.F. (1998a). "Residual effects on actual car driving of evening doses of chlorpheniramine 8 and 12 mg when used with terfenadine 60 mg in the morning." *Human Psychopharmacology Clin Exp*, 13, S79–S86.

Vermeeren, A., Ramaekers, J.G., O'Hanlon, J.F. (2002). "Effects of emedastine and cetirizine, alone and with alcohol, on actual driving performance of males and females." *Journal of Psychopharmacology*, 15, 57–64.

Vermeeren, A., Riedel W.J. , Van Boxtel, M.P.J., et al. (2002). "Differential residual effects of zaleplon and zopiclone on actual driving: A comparison with a low dose of alcohol." *Sleep*, 25, 224–231.

Volkerts, E.R., Abbink, F., van Laar, M.W., Plomp, T.A., and Maes, R.A.A. (1991). *Comparison of the Effects of Ritanserin 5 mg Bid and Lorazepam 1 mg Tid upon Actual Driving Performance*. Technical report. The Netherlands Institute for Drugs and Doping Research, University of Utrecht.

Volkerts, E.R., and O'Hanlon, J.F. (1986). "Hypnotics residual effects on driving performance as determined by drug, dosage, time after administration and nights of continual use." In J.F. O'Hanlon, and J.J. De Gier (Eds.), *Drugs and Driving*, (pp. 123–136). London: Taylor and Francis.

Volkerts, E.R., Van Laar, M.W., Van Willigenburg, A.P.P., Plomp, P.A., and Maes, R.A.A. (1992). "A comparative study of on the road and simulated driving performance after nocturnal treatment with lormetazepam 1 mg and oxazepam 50 mg." *Human Psychopharmacology*, 7, 297–310

Volkerts, E.R., Verster, S.C., Van Houckelun, S.H.G., et al. (2000). "The impact on car driving ability of zaleplon or zolpidem after middle of the night administration." *Eur Neuropsychopharmacology*, 10, S395.

Von Moltke, L.L., Greenblatt, D.J., Harmatz, J.S., and Shader, R.I. (1994). "Cytochromes in psychopharmacology." *Journal of Clinical Psychopahrmacology*, 14, 1–4.

Vuurman, E.F.P.M., Ramaekers, J.G., Rikker, G., de Halleux, F. (2000). "Desloratadine does not impair actual driving performance: a three–way crossover comparison with diphenhydramine and placebo [abstract]." *Allergy*, 63, 263–264.

Vuurman, E.F.P.M., Van Veggel, L.M.A., Sanders, R.L., Muntjewerff, N.D., and O'Hanlon, J.F. (1996). "Effects of semprex–D and diphenhydramine on learning in young adults with seasonal allergic rhinitis." *Allergy, Asthma and Immunology*, 76, 247–252.

Vuurman, E.F.P.M., Van Veggel, L.M.A., Uiterwijk, M.M.C., Leutner, D., O'Hanlon, J.F. (1993). "Seasonal allergic rhinitis and antihistamine effects on children's learning." *Annals of Allergy*, 71, 121–126.

Weckowicz, T.E., Tam, C.N., Mason, J., and Bay, K.S. (1978). "Speed in test performance in depressed patients." *Journal of Abnormal Psychology*, 87, 578–582.

Weiler, J.M., Bloomfield, J.R., Woodworth, G.G. et al. (2000). "Effects of fexofenadine, diphenhydramine and alcohol in the Iowa driving simulator." *Annals of Internal Medicine*, 132, 354–363.

Weingartner, H.J., Hommer, D., Lister, R.G., Thompson, K., and Wolkowitz, O. (1992). "Selective effects of triazolam on memory." *Psychopharmacology*, 106, 341–345.

Weinstein, A., Wilson, S., Bailey, S., and Nutt, D. (1996). "Sedative antidepressants impair visual detection mechanisms in humans." *Journal of Psychopharmacology*, 10, 141–145.

Weiser, M., Shneider–Beeri, M., Nakash, N., Brill, N., Bawnik, O., Reiss, S., et al. (2000). "Improvement in cognition associated with novel antipsychotic drugs: A direct drug effect or reduction of EPS?" *Schizophrenia Research*, 46, 81–89.

Wesnes, K., Simpson, P., and Christmas, L. (1987). "The assessment of human informationprocessing abilities in psychopharmacology." In I. Hindmarch, and P. Stonier (Eds.), *Human Psychopharmacology: Measures and Methods.* Vol 1 (pp. 79–92). Chichester, New York, Brisbane: John Wiley and Sons.

Wilkinson, D. (1999). "Loss of anxiety and increased aggression in a fifteen-year-old boy taking fluoxetine." *Journal of Psychopharmacology,* 13, 420.

Wilson, S.J., Bailey, J.E., Alford, C., and Nutt, D. (2000). "Sleep and daytime sleepiness the next day following single night-time dose of fluvoxamine, dothiepin and placebo in normal volunteers." *Journal of Psychopharmacology*, 14, 378–386.

Wittenborn, J.R. (1987). "Psychomotor tests in psychopharmacology." In I. Hindmarch, and P. Stonier (Eds.), *Human Psychopharmacology: Measures and Methods.* Vol 1 (pp. 69–78). Chichester, New York, Brisbane: John Wiley and Sons.

Wong, I.C.K., Tavernor, S.J., and Tavernor, R.M.E. (1997). "Psychiatric adverse effects of anticonvulsant drugs." *CNS Drugs*, 8, 492–509.

Woods, J.H., Katz, J.L., and Winger, G. (1992). "Benzodiazepines: Use, abuse, and consequences." *Pharmacological Reviews,* 44, 151–347.

Wylie, K.R., Thompson, D.J., and Wildgust, H.J. (1993). "Effects of depot neuroleptics on driving performance in chronic schizophrenic patients." *Journal of Neurosurgery and Psychiatry,* 56, 910913.

Chapter 8

Cocaine, Methamphetamine and Driving Impairment

Barry K. Logan and Daniel S. Isenschmid

Synopsis

8.1 Introduction

The two principal stimulants used recreationally in North America are cocaine and methamphetamine. Both can have a profound effect on thought processes, decision-making, and psychomotor skills related to driving. They do this through their effects on state of mind and cognition by producing both elation and depression, and by altering mood, judgment, values, and ultimately risk acceptance. Secondly, through their physiological effects, they produce changes in reaction time and vision, fatigue, somnolence, motor agitation, and, correspondingly, impairments in motor skills and divided attention. These apparently contradictory effects for drugs associated with stimulation, improved alertness, and reaction time are explained by dose and chronicity of use, but the mechanism of impairment is complex and may vary considerably between users. This chapter will consider the evidence for the effects described above for both these drugs, as documented from empirical pharmacological principles, epidemiology, case reports, laboratory studies, and driving and flight simulator studies. As the popularity of cocaine remains high, and that of methamphetamine continues to grow and spread, a broad understanding of these drugs will continue to be important in traffic safety and human performance toxicology for the foreseeable future.

8.2 Stimulant Pharmacology

Both cocaine and methamphetamine act by increasing intersynaptic concentrations of the neurotransmitters norepinephrine (NE), dopamine (DA) and serotonin (5-HT), but in contrast to methamphetamine, which stimulates release of these moieties from the presynaptic dopaminergic neuron, cocaine produces this effect by blocking their reuptake from the synaptic cleft into the neuron. The net effect is similar, with elevated norepinephrine being responsible for the classic adrenergic effects observed with cocaine use. The effects include mydriasis, vasoconstriction, hypertension, tachycardia and tachypnea, bladder contraction, and increased blood glucose contributing to the well recognized alerting, and anorectic effects (Goodman and Gilman, 1996; Ellinwood and Kilbey, 1980). From the user's perspective, the desirable effects of these drugs, also mediated by DA, include intense euphoria, psychic energy, heightened sexual excitement, and self-confidence.

Some of the negative effects of these drugs, such as paranoia, hallucinations, and dysphoria, are more often associated with higher intensity use (either greater doses or longer duration) These negative effects have been linked to dopamine release in the mesolimbic system and enhanced release of 5-hydroxytryptamine (5-HT, serotonin) in tryptaminergic neurons, which may account for effects on perception and the idiosyncratic psychoses frequently reported with use of these drugs (Ellinwood and Kilbey, 1980).

There is evidence following escalating binge dose administration of a sensitization to future low dose exposure (Segal and Kuczenski, 1999) and susceptibility under stress (Yui et al., 1999), resulting in stimulant psychosis in sensitized animals, and reoccurrence of psychotic episodes (flashbacks) in humans.

The central stimulatory effects ("rush") of a stimulant are often followed by depression ("crash") (Dackis and Gold, 1985; Gawin and

Kleber, 1986), which will vary in intensity depending on the duration of use and dosage pattern. The positive reinforcement of the rush versus the negative reinforcement of the crash is the principal reason for the development of chronic stimulant abuse. In this respect, recreational patterns of use of the drugs differ largely due to their different half-lives as discussed below.

8.3 Comparative Pharmacological Properties of Cocaine and Methamphetamine

A. Absorption

Both cocaine and methamphetamine are administered in various ways with nasal insufflation, smoking, and intravenous use all being popular. Salt forms of cocaine require conversion to the base in order for them to be smoked ("crack," "freebase"), but methamphetamine salts ("speed," "ice") can be smoked unchanged. The time to reach peak subjective effects for cocaine is significantly faster for smoking (1.4 minutes) than for intravenous use (3.1 minutes) or intranasal insufflation (14.6 minutes) (Volkow et al., 2000). For methamphetamine, the smoking/intravenous route produces peak subjective effects eighteen minutes after the start of smoking, or seventeen minutes after intravenous injection (Cook et al., 1992). Following oral administration the absorption half-life was 0.67 hours and the time to peak was between 2.6 and 3.6 hours. Absorption of methamphetamine after nasal insufflation may be prolonged by nasal drainage and gastric absorption (Volkow et al., 2000), whereas for cocaine, the first pass metabolic effects result in low bioavailability (about 20 percent) via the oral route (Mayersohn, 1978).

B. Metabolism

Cocaine is extensively metabolized primarily to benzoylecgonine and ecgonine methyl ester, and both are further metabolized to ecgonine. If cocaine is used with ethanol, ethylcocaine (sometimes called coca-ethylene), a metabolite produced by the transesterification of cocaine with ethanol may also be observed. Methylecgonidine (anhydroecgonine methyl ester) and ecgonidine (anhydroecgonine) have been identified as useful markers of cocaine ingestion by the smoked route (Cone et al., 1994; Jacob et al., 1990; Jenkins and Goldberger, 1997; Jufer et al., 1995). The mechanisms of cocaine metabolism are not straightforward, however, and the interpretation of cocaine and metabolite concentrations in blood and other specimens is complicated by complex in vitro and in vivo metabolic reactions (Isenschmid, 2002).

A small proportion (<10 percent) of a methamphetamine dose undergoes metabolism by N-demethylation to amphetamine, which itself is metabolized to a variety of metabolites, including norephedrine and p-hydroxyamphetamine. The majority of methamphetamine is excreted unchanged in the urine.

The over-the-counter product "Vicks Inhaler" contains *l*-desoxyephedrine (*l*-methamphetamine), which has only a fraction of the CNS stimulating effects of its *d*-isomer. Even markedly excessive use of this product is unlikely to produce a positive urine test, let alone a positive blood test result, and anecdotal data from workplace drug testing programs suggest that the incidence of l-methamphetamine positives in workplace specimens is virtually unknown (Cooke, 1994; Shippee and Kippenberger, 2000).

Importantly, several other drugs are metabolized to amphetamines including benzphetamine (Didrex®), selegeline (Deprenyl®), famprofazone (Gewodin®), and clobenzorex (Dinintel®). Of these, only selegeline, used in the treatment of Parkinson's disease, is currently available in the United States. When the origin of detected amphetamines becomes an issue, enantiomeric testing can be useful, since many of these compounds produce specific patterns of *d*- or *l*- amphetamine metabolites. Additionally, identification of intermediate or other metabolites of these therapeutic drugs can be helpful.

C. Elimination

Following IV and smoked routes, the average half-life for cocaine is about sixty minutes (Isenschmidt et al., 1992). After intranasal cocaine administration, the average absorption half-life was twelve minutes and the average elimination half-life was eighty-four minutes (Javaid et al., 1983). The rate of benzoylecgonine elimination is slow compared to its rate of formation, accounting for its accumulation in plasma while cocaine concentrations are decreasing. The elimination half-lives for benzoylecgonine were reported as 347, 324, and 213 minutes, respectively, after IV, SM and IN routes of administration (Cone, 1995). Consequently, benzoylecgonine can persist in the blood long after cocaine has fallen to undetectable levels.

Methamphetamine is much less extensively metabolized than cocaine, with the major route of elimination being excretion of the unchanged drug. Consequently, its elimination is strongly dependent on urinary pH. Following oral dosing, the mean elimination half-life was 10.1 hours, with a range of 6.4–15 hours (Cook et al., 1992). After smoking, the average elimination half-life was 11.1 hours, with a range of 8.3–18.2 hours (Cook et al., 1993). After IV administration, the mean elimination half-life was reported as 12.2 hours.

8.4 Psychological and Physiological Effects of Stimulant Use

The experience of the stimulant user is depeneant on many factors—the drug, the route of administration, the dose, the time since last use, whether this is a long term binge or short term episodic use, together with users' experience with the drug, acute and chronic tolerance, the circumstances and environment of use (set and setting), and users' expectations of effect. For the reasons discussed above in terms of their different pharmacology and pharmacokinetics, users of cocaine and users of methamphetamine will have a different experience both quantitatively and qualitatively, while having some features in common. In laboratory studies, experienced cocaine users have been unable to distinguish between cocaine and methamphetamine administered intravenously, and cross-tolerance between cocaine and *d*-amphetamine with respect to their anorectic effects has been demonstrated.

A. Amphetamines

Since patterns of use differ considerably, it is important to consider both low intensity and high intensity effects, as well as early and late phase effects to allow an appreciation of how the drugs may affect driving, and how the nature of the effect may differ depending on the circumstances of use. Low dose amphetamine administration (up to 30 mg/day in divided doses) promotes release of norepinephrine, generating the associated effects of anorexia, increased vigilance and alertness, and some locomotor stimulation. These effects are experienced by the user as a state of increased mental and physical energy, elevated mood and suppressed appetite, and can be accompanied by an improvement in simple reaction time. Physiologically, heart rate will increase, and pupil size may be constricted. Some of the adverse side effects reported even with these low doses include palpitations, elevated pulse and blood pressure, restlessness, CNS over-stimulation, insomnia and other sleep disturbance, dry mouth, GI disturbance, headaches, light sensitivity, irritability, and in the longer term, weight loss, and urticaria (itching weals). The CNS overstimulation can manifest as motor tremors or tics, and ataxia or unsteadiness of gait. Notably absent in most users at these doses is the overwhelming euphoric, elated, feeling which gives the drug its reinforcing affect and addictive potential.

In cases where a driver is fatigued from loss of sleep (24–36 hours without any sleep), the drug may offset some of the fatigue-induced impairment and thus restore performance to baseline level. Amphetamines have been used by the military to combat the effects of fatigue. However, the doses used are small, typically up to 30 mg in divided doses over twelve to twenty-four hours (Newhouse et al., 1989; Emonson and Vanderbeck, 1995; Caldwell et al., 1995; Caldwell and Caldwell, 1997). These studies have consistently shown that controlled low doses of amphetamines have some beneficial effects on restoring baseline performance in complex task performance in severely fatigued subjects, but do not produce enhanced performance in non-fatigued subjects. Furthermore, these effects have only been demonstrated with low doses at which the euphorogenic side effects associated with recreational use are not observed. There is no evidence that readministration of methamphetamine, such as during a binge, will do anything other than compound the existing drug-caused impairment.

Administration of higher doses (up to 100 mg/day in divided doses) in attention deficit/hyperactivity disorder (ADHD) in adults is not recommended but is common, and generally justified by virtue of a positive control of the medical condition. However, higher doses of the amphetamines result in release of increasing amounts of dopamine, the neurotransmitter responsible for the euphoria and feelings of extreme well-being associated with recreational stimulant use, and responsible for its addictive potential. Typical doses in recreational use start at around 30–50 mg/single dose, but can be higher when snorted. This is sufficient to initiate the sought-after euphoric effects. In tolerant users, administration of 100 mg and more in a single IV dose has been reported during a binge.

The high intensity effects of methamphetamine typically include exhilaration and euphoria, rapid flow of ideas, feelings of great physical strength and mental capacity. These euphorogenic effects are distracting and can be overwhelming, causing difficulty with focus on complex tasks, difficulty in divided attention tasks, loss of fine motor control, changes in judgment, values, and risk taking behavior. Also reported are impatience, loss of temper, and aggressive behavior. This excited condition produces changes in speech with incomplete expression of thoughts or ideas, and rapid, confused, and (sometimes) repetitive speech. With prolonged administration such as during binge use, an overall deterioration in sensorium occurs to a greater or lesser extent, with the development of paranoia, delusions, hallucinations, perceptual distortions, and hyper-vigilance. This can progress into a true drug psychosis, which can also occur at lower doses and with less intense use in some individuals with a predisposition to schizophrenia or psychotic behavior. Since this phase of use is often accompanied by a cessation of drug taking, withdrawal from the drug adds depression, agitation, drug craving, and extreme fatigue and sleepiness to the presentation. This "downside" of the drug arguably is more dangerous than the acute phase, since the induced fatigue is a known direct cause of crashes.

From the above considerations, it can reasonably be argued that effects which might affect driving can be present even with low dose use in inexperienced users, through higher dose therapeutic use even in experienced users, and in all phases of recreational use, beginning during the initial euphoria and extending through withdrawal. As a general principle, therefore, any aberrant behavior exhibited by an individual after taking this drug needs to be scrutinized for consistency with the known effects of amphetamine use and abuse. As discussed later, many of the behaviors reported in amphetamine using drivers such as inattention, sleepiness, and inappropriate decision making can be readily attributed to amphetamines.

B. Cocaine

It should be noted that cocaine has no legitimate therapeutic use for treatment of any of the conditions for which amphetamines are used (narcolepsy, ADHD, appetite control) even though from a neurophysiological perspective they might produce some effect. This is because the short half-life of the drug makes its use for treatment of any chronic condition impractical. Cocaine is used topically for its local anesthetic properties in some ear, nose, and throat surgical procedures.

The desirable effects of cocaine from the recreational user's perspective are mediated by dopamine and include intense euphoria, psychic energy, heightened sexual excitement and self-confidence (elevation of mood). As with the amphetamines, low doses of cocaine have been shown to reverse the performance decrements of depressant drugs. One study reported a reversal of performance decrements in reaction time due to sleep deprivation after 96 mg of inhaled cocaine (Fischman and Schuster, 1980). Although stimulants may acutely enhance performance of simple tasks, this may not be the case as the complexity of the task increases (Ellinwood and Nikaido, 1987). Potential undesirable effects may include paranoia, hallucinations, and dysphoria. For example, cocaine-induced hyperexcitability has resulted in rapid steering or braking reactions due to sudden sounds such as horns or sirens (Davis, 1985). As with the amphetamines, increased self-confidence leading to overconfidence is likely to produce a greater willingness in the user to accept risk.

Cocaine also affects vision (Siegel, 1987). These effects include mydriasis, increased sensitivity to light, halos around bright objects, blurred vision, glare recovery problems, and difficulty focusing (Siegel, 1978; Siegel, 1982). Users report "snow lights," flashes or movements of light in the peripheral field of vision, and moving in their direction or trying to avoid or evade them. These can obviously impact driving skills particularly under extremes of light and dark.

The central stimulatory effects ("rush") of cocaine are followed by withdrawal ("depression" or "crash") (Dackis and Gold, 1985; Gawin and Kleber, 1986). The positive reinforcement of the rush versus the negative reinforcement of the crash is the principal reason for the development of chronic cocaine abuse. A crash phase after heavy, chronic cocaine use has certainly been well documented, and this has been reviewed in detail elsewhere (Isenschmid, 2002).

Cocaine withdrawal produces effects that can appreciably impact motor skills, attention and decision-making. Adult volunteers with a history of heavy IV cocaine use were studied in a protocol that investigated changes in behavior when allowed to self-administer cocaine up to six times (32 mg / 70 kg) per session, twice a day (Foltin and Fischman, 1997). Participants reported being more irritable and depressed following a three day binge, and increased craving was observed when associated with stimulus cues after both two and three day binges. A similar study was performed using subjects with an almost-daily cocaine habit. In this study participants could self-administer smoked cocaine up to six times (50 mg; 25 mg for two participants) per session, twice a day (Foltin and Fischman, 1997). This study was also performed using two and three day binge conditions. Participants reported greater craving and changes in mood (feeling more "anxious," "confused," "a good drug effect," "high," "sedated," and less "friendly"), related to the length of the binge.

Cocaine has effects that inherently impact many of the physiological systems necessary for safe and controlled driving It is reasonable to assume that these effects will contribute to deterioration in driving performance after either acute or chronic recreational use.

8.5 Effects of Stimulants on Driving

Information about the likely impact of any drug on driving can be gleaned from a variety of sources including empirical considerations of its pharmacology, case reports of specific presentations associated with the use of the drug, epidemiological studies that associate a drug's use with a range of behaviors, and specific tests of psychomotor or cognitive skills related to driving, and how they are affected by controlled administration of the drug.

A. Empirical considerations

As discussed in the section above, both stimulants alter normal levels of neurotransmitters, which consequently produce behavioral and psychomotor changes. The powerful euphoria associated with recreational use is distracting from mundane tasks like driving, and the hyperactivity and grandiosity can lead to impatience and riskier driving. Equally important, following repeated administration, withdrawal or coming down from the drug can cause a different constellation of symptoms similar to depressant effects, such as dysphoria, low energy, fatigue and sleepiness. Clearly these drug-induced effects are inconsistent with safe driving also. Our understanding of what the intended and side effects of these drugs are puts us in a good position both to interpret the literature on observed effects (discussed next), and to evaluate the subject in a case under review.

B. Epidemiological studies

Epidemiological reports in the drug-impaired driving literature generally suffer from lack of control groups. Nonetheless, stimulants do show up in the blood and urine of drivers killed or injured in traffic accidents, frequently accompanied by driving behaviors that are consistent with the known effects of the drugs. In an early study, amphetamine-using drivers were shown to be more likely to be involved in an accident than either non-drug using drivers or the users of CNS depressants, including barbiturates (Smart et al., 1969). Another epidemiological study that included a control group was published in 1992 by the National Highway Transportation Safety Administration (NHTSA). Among fatally-injured truck drivers, the most frequent type of accident in amphetamine positive drivers involved the driver driving off the road, (50 percent, compared to 32 percent in the drug free control group). In the same data set, fourteen (8.3 percent) of the drivers tested positive for cocaine and metabolites in blood (Crouch et al., 1993). However, drug impairment was considered the sole cause in only four of these cases, in all of which the blood also had either delta-9-tetrahydrocannabinol (the parent drug in marijuana), ethanol above the legal limit, or phencyclidine (National Transportation Safety Board, 1988). In the cases where drug impairment was thought to be a contributing cause to the crash, only two drivers demonstrated the presence of cocaine and metabolites in the absence of other drugs. Fatigue was considered a contributing factor in both of these cases.

The literature on epidemiological studies has been reviewed in detail elsewhere (Logan, 2002). Stimulant use in the trucking industry has been a long-term problem (Lund, 1988). However, a recent survey (Couper et al., 2002), which included voluntary urine drug tests of drivers, suggests that the extent of both over-the-counter and illicit stimulant use has decreased since the introduction of mandatory drug testing in 1987.

C. Laboratory studies

Most laboratory studies are designed to measure specific aspects of psychomotor or cognitive functioning, some of which are certainly relevant to driving, but relatively few actually study driving itself. Those which have tried to assess effects on driving suffer from the limitation of what dose can be administered. Even after a low dose (10 mg/70 Kg) of amphetamine, however, three of eleven subjects self reported impairment in their driving, versus one in the placebo group (Evans et al., 1977). Mitler et al. (1993), in studying the effects of methamphetamine on narcoleptic patients and controls, included thirty-minute sessions on a simple computer based "driving simulator." Methamphetamine produced a dose dependent improvement in performance in narcoleptics up to 60 mg and in controls up to 10 mg, although the controls were performing near optimal levels without the drug.

Other stimulants have been assessed with respect to their effects on driving. Ritalin " (methylphenidate) is used to treat adults with attention deficit hyperactivity disorder (ADHD). It has been shown to reduce rates of accident involvement in these patients in driving simulators (Cox et al., 2000; Jerome and Segal, 2001), but non-ADHD subjects taking the drug showed a slight trend toward poorer driving.

Studies assessing risk acceptance are of interest also because of their obvious implications for driving behavior. Hurst (1962, 1976) evaluated the effects of amphetamine on judgment, decision-making and risk-taking, and concluded not only that a 10–15 mg oral dose of amphetamine increased risk taking, but that it increased self-appraisals of performance to levels not matched by actual performance. Not all published literature agrees that stimulants adversely affect driving, but those that show minimal effects are usually concentrating on low doses that do not reflect recreational use levels.

The effects of stimulants change not only with dose and blood concentration, as is the case for depressants, but with duration and intensity of use, and also the phase of use. The latter refers to whether the predominant effects are those of acute intoxication or of withdrawal. Ellinwood and Nikaido (1987) described models for the effect profile of stimulants, including these considerations. (see Figure 8.1.)

With a dose dependent model that he developed for stimulant impairment with arousal, hyperarousal and withdrawal phases (Logan, 1996), behaviors documented in a series of drivers arrested for driving under the influence of amphetamines were related to the phases. The hysteresis demonstrated that neither the specific degree of impairment nor the phase of intoxication could be predicted from a single blood methamphetamine

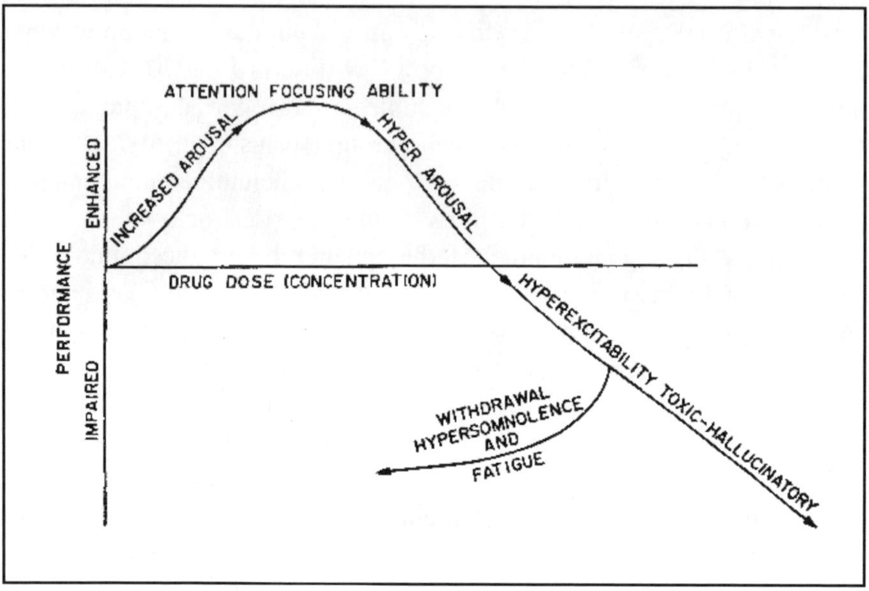

Figure 8.1 *Ellinwood and Nikado model*

concentration. Abuse could be distinguished from therapeutic use when the concentration was greater than 0.20 mg/L. In the cases reviewed in that study, the pattern of the driving (typically one car, drive-off-the-road-type-accidents) was highly suggestive of withdrawal-induced impairment, and several of the drivers reported "falling asleep." Note the similarity with the NHTSA study referenced earlier (National Highway Traffic Safety Administration, 1992).

In ongoing follow-up work, Logan (2001) has reported that in a larger group of drivers (n = 101), who tested positive for amphetamines alone, the predominant driving behaviors that led to their arrest or accident were weaving out of lane (33 percent) and general erratic driving (13 percent). Other reasons for these drivers being stopped included equipment violations, speeding, hit and run, weaving within the lane, and driving stolen vehicles. These drivers displayed a range of behaviors in field sobriety tests from fairly good performance to falling asleep.

There have been relatively few scientific studies on the direct effects of cocaine on driving performance. Laboratory-based studies of the effects of psychomotor stimulants on sensory, motor, attentional and cognitive abilities have been reviewed elsewhere (Heishman, 1998). Of the few studies performed with cocaine, most were limited by the low doses of cocaine that were allowed. At these low doses, most laboratory studies reported performance enhancement in attentional abilities (Higgins et al., 1990; Higgins et al., 1993; Stillman et al., 1993) and no effect on cognitive abilities (Farré et al., 1993; Foltin and Fischman, 1990, 1993, 1988; Higgins et al., 1990).

One study clearly demonstrated how the behavior of subjects arrested for reckless driving varied. Out of 150 subjects, who were determined not to be impaired by alcohol, 13 percent tested positive for prior cocaine use, 33 percent for cannabinoids, and 12 percent for cannabinoids and cocaine (Brookoff et al., 1994). Nearly half of the drivers testing positive for prior cocaine use performed normally on field sobriety tests, including two subjects who were stopped for driving directly into oncoming traffic. Of those testing positive for cocaine, 21 percent were sleepy or slow, 39 percent were happy, carefree and talkative, and 39 percent were combative, argumentative, and paranoid.

Cocaine-induced suspiciousness has been reported as leading to high-speed chases with police (Wetli and Fishbain, 1985). It is not surprising that the use of stimulants has also been associated with road rage (Fong et al., 2001). Several cocaine smokers have reported that driving is impaired during this period and four such users, driving to a cocaine treatment center, were involved in separate collisions resulting in major injuries (Siegel, 1987).

8.6 Stimulants and the DRE Evaluation

Cocaine and methamphetamine fall into the stimulant category in the Drug Recognition Expert (DRE) scheme. The DRE fulfills two important functions: the first is establishing through psychomotor tests (one leg stand, walk and turn, Romberg balance) that the subject is in fact impaired, and the second is to establish, through measurement of physiological signs, which class or classes of drugs are involved. This evaluation forms a critical nexus between the observed driving, which may demonstrate some impairment, and the toxicology test, which confirms which drugs within the drug class are present.

As has been noted, stimulant users may present differently depending on the intensity of their drug use and the phase of their intoxication (i.e., whether acutely excited or in the "tweaking" or withdrawal phase).

Acutely intoxicated stimulant users can show increased pulse and blood pressure, dilated pupils, increased muscle tone, muscle tremors or tics, restlessness, agitation, scratching, and repetitive, rapid speech. During the interview, the subject may appear nervous and paranoid, may have delusions, may hallucinate, and may give confused responses to simple questions. They may also become violent, particularly if startled or frightened, such as may happen when they are taken into the dark room for the pupil exam by the DRE. Officers should be advised to take extreme caution. Because of the dilated pupils, subjects are extremely sensitive to bright lights, such as the penlight or flashlight used during the exam.

Subjects on the "downside" of stimulant use typically display different symptoms. Their vital signs can be depressed, or heart rate and blood pressure may be normal to low. Pupil size has been reported to be in the low end of the normal range (~2–3 mm), and they become drowsy and sleepy, and may "nod off". This symptomatology includes many of the signs associated with narcotic analgesics, or depressant use, such as depressed pulse and blood pressure, so care should be taken with the evaluation. The major distinguishing features are the fact that the subject's pupil, although small, will still react to light, which the narcotic analgesic user's pupil will not. Often the user will appear somewhere along a continuum between these two states displaying a mixture of symptoms.

Studies conducted using elements of the DRE protocol (Heishmann et al., 1996; Heishmann et al., 1998) failed to demonstrate the classical picture of stimulant intoxication or presentation, because the dose used (12.5, or 25 mg of amphetamine, and 48 or 96 mg of cocaine) was too small to produce the effects normally sought by recreational users. These studies are further critiqued elsewhere (Logan, 2002; Isenschmid, 2002). The DRE exam is often criticized for including considerations of statements or admissions the user may make during the process. Irrespective of these limitations, it is still the best tool available to an officer in the field investigating a suspected drug impaired driving case, and it will demonstrate specific impairment which a lab test cannot.

8.7 Conclusions

Methamphetamine and cocaine are potent CNS stimulants as demonstrated by the foregoing analysis. On an empirical level, the effects associated with the recreational use of these drugs are not consistent with safe driving. This includes both the physiological effects on vision and motor control, as well as the psychological effects distorting perception, values, and encouraging risk taking. In any individual case of a stimulant user involved in a traffic accident or arrested for apparent impaired driving, the extent to which these effects are actually present may be difficult to assess. The optimum situation is one in which there is observed driving which is clearly impaired, behavior during contact with witnesses which is characteristic of frank stimulant intoxication, poor performance on field sobriety tests, results of a DRE evaluation consistent with the known indicators for stimulant use, a blood test showing the presence of the drug or drugs, and often admissions by the subject about their drug use and its effects. In practice, rarely do all of these pieces fall into place. This simply places a greater burden on the investigator or toxicologist to carefully and in context assess what information is available and determine to what degree it supports a conclusion of stimulant impairment.

References

Brookoff, D., Cook, C.S., Williams, C., and Mann, C.S. (1994). "Testing reckless drivers for cocaine and marijuana." *N Eng J Med*, 331, 518.

Caldwell, J.A., Caldwell, J.L., Crowley, J.S., and Jones, H.D. (1995). "Sustaining helicopter pilot performance with dexedrine during periods of sleep deprivation." *Aviation, Space, and Enviro Med*, 66, 930.

Caldwell, J.A., and Caldwell, J.L. (1997). "An in-flight investigation of the efficacy of dextroamphetamine for sustaining helicopter pilot performance." *Aviation, Space, and Enviro Med*, 68, 1073.

Cone, E.J. (1995). "Pharmacokinetics and pharmacodynamics of cocaine." *J Anal Toxicol*, 19, 459.

Cone, E.J., Hillsgrove, M., and Darwin, W.D. (1994). "Simultaneous measurement of cocaine, ethylcocaine, their metabolites, and 'crack' pyrolysis products by gas chromatography-mass spectrometry." *Clin Chem*, 40, 1299.

Cook, C.E., Jeffcoat, A.R., Hill, J.M., Pugh, D.E., Patetta, P.K., Sadler, B.M., et al. (1993). "Pharmacokinetics of methamphetamine self administered to human subjects by smoking s-(+)methamphetamine hydrochloride." *Drug Met Disp*, 21, 717.

Cook, C.E., Jeffcoat, A.R., Sadler, B.M., Hill, J.M., Voyksner, R.D., Pugh, D.E., et al. (1992). "Pharmacokinetics of oral methamphetamine and effects of repeated daily dosing in humans." *Drug Met and Disp*, 20, 856.

Cooke, B.J. (1994). "Chirality of methamphetamine and amphetamine from workplace urine samples." *J Anal Toxicol*, 18, 49.

Couper, F.J., Pemberton, M., Jarvis, A., Hughes, M., and Logan, B.K. (2002). "Prevalence of drug use in commercial tractor-trailer drivers." *J Foren Sci*, 47, 562.

Cox, D.J., Merkel, R.L., Kovatchev, B., and Seward, R. (2000). "Effect of stimulant medication on driving performance of young adults with attention-deficit hyperactivity disorder: A preliminary double-blind placebo controlled trial." *J Nerv Ment Dis*, 188, 230.

Crouch, D.J., Birky, M.M., Gust, S.W., Rollins, D.E., Walsh, J.M., and Moulden, J.V. (1993). "The prevalence of drugs and alcohol in fatally injured truck drivers." *J Forensic Sci*, 38,1342.

Dackis, C.A., and Gold, M.A. (1985). "New concepts in cocaine addiction: the dopamine depletion hypothesis." *Neurosci Biobehav Rev*, 9, 469.

Davis, M. (1985). "Cocaine: Excitatory effects on sensorimotor reactivity measured with acoustic startle." *Psychopharmacology*, 86, 31.

Ellinwood, E.H. Jr., and Kilbey, M.M. (1980). "Fundamental mechanisms underlying altered behavior following chronic administration of psychomotor stimulants." *Biological Psychiatry*, 15, 749.

Ellinwood, E.H., and Nikaido, A.M. (1987). "Stimulant induced impairment: a perspective across dose and duration of use." *Alc Drugs and Driv*, 3, 19.

Emonson, D.L., and Vanderbeek, R.D. (1995). "The use of amphetamines in U.S. air force tactical operations during Desert Shield and Storm." *Aviation, Space, and Enviro Med*, 66, 260.

Evans, M.A., Martz, R., Rodda, B.E., Lemberger, L., and Forney, R.B. (1977). "Effects of marihuanadextroamphetamine combination." *Clin Pharm and Ther*, 30, 350.

Farré, M., De La Torre, R., Llorent, M., Lamas, X., Ugena, B., Segura, J., et al. (1993). "Alcohol and cocaine interactions in humans." *J Pharm Exp Ther*, 266, 1364.

Fischman, M.W., and Schuster, C.R. (1980). "Cocaine effects in sleep-deprived humans." *Psychopharmacology*, 72, 1.

Foltin, R.W., and Fischman, M.W. (1990). "The effects of combinations of intranasal cocaine, smoked marihuana, and task performance on heart rate and blood pressure." *Pharmacology Biochem Behav*, 36, 311.

Foltin, R.W., and Fischman, M.W. (1997). "A laboratory model of cocaine withdrawal in humans: Intravenous cocaine." *Exp Clin Psychopharmacol*, 4, 404.

Foltin, R.W., and Fischman, M.W. (1997). "Residual effects or repeated cocaine smoking in humans." *Drug and Alcohol Dep,* 47, 117.

Foltin, R.W., Fischman, M.W., Pippen, P.A., and Kelly, T.H. (1993). "Behavioral effects of cocaine alone and in combination with marihuana in humans." *Drug and Alcohol Dep*, 32, 93.

Foltin, R.W., McEntee, M.A., Capriotti, R.M., Pedrose, J.J., and Fischman, M.A. (1988). "Effects of cocaine, alone and in combination with task performance, on heart rate and blood pressure." *Pharmacology Biochem Behav*, 31, 387.

Fong, G., Frost, D., and Stansfield, S. (2001). "Road rage: A psychiatric phenomenon?" *Soc Psychiatry Psychiatr Epidemiol*, 36, 277.

Gawin, F.H., and Kleber, H.D. (1986). "Abstinence symptomatology and psychiatric diagnoses in cocaine abusers." *Arch Gen Psychiatry*, 43, 107.

Hardman, J.G. and L. E. Limbird (Eds.). (1996). *Goodman and Gilman's The Pharmacological Basis of Therapeutics* (9th ed.). New York: McGraw Hill.

Heishman, S.J. (1998). "Pharmacodynamics," In S. Karch (Ed.) *Drug abuse handbook* (p. 203). Boca Raton, FL: CRC Press.

Heishman, S.J., Singleton, E.G., and Crouch, D.J. (1996). "Laboratory validation study of drug evaluation and classification program: Ethanol, cocaine, and marijuana." *J Anal Toxicol*, 20, 468.

Heishman, S.J., Singleton, E.G., and Crouch, D.J. (1998). "Laboratory validation study of drug evaluation and classification program: Alprazolam, d-amphetamine, codeine, and marijuana." *J Anal Toxicol*, 22, 503.

Higgins, S.T., Bicker, W.K., Hughes, J.R., Lynn, M., Capeless, M.A., and Fenwick, M.A. (1990). "Effects of intranasal cocaine on human learning, performance and physiology." *Psychopharmacology*, 102, 451.

Higgins, S.T., Rush, C.R., Bickel, W.K., Hughes, J.R., Lynn, M., and Capeless, M.A. (1993). "Acute behavioral and cardiac effects of cocaine and alcohol combinations in humans." *Psychopharmacology*, 111, 285.

Hurst, P.M. (1962). "The effects of d-amphetamine on risk taking." *Psychopharmacologia*, 3, 283.

Hurst, P.M., Weidner, M.F., and Radlow, R. (1967). "The effects of amphetamines upon judgment and decisions." *Psychopharmacologia*, 11, 397.

Isenschmid, D.S. (2002). "Forensic toxicology of cocaine." *Forensic Science Review*, 14, 62.

Isenschmid, D.S., Fischman, M.W., Foltin, R.W., and Caplan, Y.H. (1992). "Concentration of cocaine and metabolites in plasma of humans following intravenous administration and smoking of cocaine." *J Anal Toxicol*, 16, 311.

Jacob, P., Lewis, E.R., Elias-Baker, B.A., and Jones, R.T. (1990). "A pyrolysis product, anhydroecgonine methyl ester (methylecgonidine), is in the urine of cocaine smokers." *J Anal Toxicol*, 14, 353.

Javaid, J.I., Musa, M.N., Fischman, M., Schuster, C.R., and Davis, J.M. (1983). "Kinetic of cocaine in humans after intravenous and intranasal administration." *Biopharmaceutics and Drug Disposition*, 4, 9.

Jenkins, A.J., and Goldberger, B.A. (1997). "Identification of unique cocaine metabolites and smoking by-products in postmortem blood and urine specimens." *J Forensic Sci*, 42, 824.

Jerome, L., and Segal, A. (2001). "Benefit of long-term stimulants on driving in adults with ADHD." *J Nerv Ment Dis*, 189, 63.

Jufer, R.A., Oyler, J.M., and Cone, E.J. (1995). "Urinary excretion profile of cocaine, metabolites and pyrolysis product after smoked cocaine." Presented at the Society of Forensic Toxicologists Annual Meeting. Baltimore, MD, October 1995.

Logan, B.K. (1996). "Methamphetamine and driving impairment." *J For Sci*, 41, 457.

Logan, B.K. (2001). "Methamphetamine and driving impairment revisited." Presented at the Society of Forensic Toxicologists Annual Meeting. New Orleans, LA. October 2001.

Logan, B.K. (2002). "Methamphetamine—Effects on human performance and behavior." *Forensic Science Review,* 14, 133.

Lund, A.K., Preusser, D.F., Blomberg, R.D., Williams, A.F. (1988). "Drug use by tractor-trailer drivers." *J For Sci*, 33, 648.

Mayersohn, M., and Perrier, D. (1978). "Kinetics of pharmacologic response to cocaine." *Res Commun Chem Pathol Pharmacol*, 22, 465.

Mitler, M., Hajdukovic, R., and Erman, M.K. (1993). "Treatment of narcolepsy with methamphetamine." *Sleep*, 16, 306.

National Highway Traffic Safety Administration. (October 1992). "The incidence and role of drugs in fatally injured drivers." Report No. DOT HS 808 065.

National Transportation Safety Board Safety Study. (1988). "Fatigue, alcohol, other drugs and medical factors in fatal-to-the-driver heavy truck crashes, Volume 1." Publication No. NTSB/SS90/01. Washington, D.C.: National Transportation Safety Board.

Newhouse, P.A., Belenky, G., Thomas, M., Thorne, D., Sing, H.C., and Fertig, J. (1989). "The effects of d-amphetamine on arousal, cognition, and mood after prolonged total sleep deprivation." *Neuropsychopharmacology*, 2, 153.

Segal, D.S., and Kuczenski, R. (1999). "Escalating dose-binge stimulant exposure: Relationship between emergent behavioral profile and differential caudate-putamen and nucleus accumbens dopamine responses." *Psychopharmacology*, 142, 182.

Shippee, R.L., and Kippenberger, D.J. (2000). "Retrospective study of urinalysis for dl-amphetamine and dl-methamphetamine analysis under current Department of Defense guidelines." *J Anal Toxicol*, 24, 450.

Siegel, R.K. (1978). "Cocaine hallucinations." *Am J Psychiatry*, 135, 309.

Siegel, R.K. (1982). "Cocaine smoking." *J Psychoact Drugs,* 14, 271.

Siegel, R.K. (1987). "Cocaine use and driving behavior." *Alcohol Drugs and Driving*, 3, 1.

Smart, R.G., Schmidt, W., and Bateman, K. (1969). "Psychoactive drugs and traffic accidents." *J Safety Research,* 1, 67.

Stillman, R., Jones, R.T., Moore, D., Walker, J., and Welm, S. (1993). "Improved performance 4 hours after cocaine." *Psychopharmacology*, 110, 415.

Volkow, N.D., Wang, G.J., Fischman, M.W., Foltin, R., Fowler, J.S., Franceschi D., et al. (2000). "Effects of route of administration on cocaine induced dopamine transporter blockade in the human brain." *Life Sci*, 67, 1507.

Wetli, C.V., and Fishbain, D.A. (1985). "Cocaine-induced psychosis and sudden death in recreational cocaine users." *J Forensic Sci*, 30, 873.

Yui, K., Goto, K., Ikemoto, S., Ishiguro, T., and Kamada, Y. (1999). "Increased sensitivity to stress and episode recurrence in spontaneous recurrence of methamphetamine psychosis." *Psychopharmacology* (Berl), 145, 267.

Chapter 9

Marijuana:
A Review, 1990–2002

Marcelline Burns

Synopsis

9.1 Introduction

Marijuana is a very old drug about which there are both old and new controversies. Evidence of its longevity as a therapeutic agent comes from Chinese medical documents of 2736 B.C. Now, almost 5,000 years later, a continuing debate about medical marijuana attests to its currency as a controversial issue.

Although the terms cannabis, marijuana, and THC are used interchangeably in this chapter and elsewhere, the three words actually have distinct meanings. *Cannabis* refers to the botanical genus. It is sometimes classified as *cannabis sativa*, a single genus containing several plants with common attributes. It also is sometimes classified as three distinct botanical groups, *cannabis sativa*, *cannabis indica*, and *cannabis ruderalis*. The term "marijuana" refers to the leaves and flowers (buds) of *cannabis sativa*, which contain an estimated 60–70 cannabinoids. "THC" refers to delta-9-tetrahydrocannabinol, the most potent of the cannabinoids.

Marijuana extracts were listed in 19th century American pharmacopoeia, and the medical literature of that era published papers about using marijuana as a medicine to stimulate appetite and ease muscle spasms as well as to treat migraine, sleep disorders, and convulsions. Its use within the United States solely for intoxicant purposes began when immigrant farm workers and soldiers returning from the Panama Canal Zone brought it with them into this country. Legal and broad social acceptance of personal use of marijuana was not forthcoming, however, and the Federal Bureau of Narcotics under the direction of Harry J. Ansinger launched a vigorous campaign against the "devil weed" and the "reefer madness" it allegedly caused. As a result of that anti-marijuana activity during the 1930s, its use as an intoxicant, although never entirely extinguished, declined sharply for a period of time. Passage of the Marijuana Tax Act in 1937 also essentially ended its legal availability as a medicine.

Marijuana use rebounded dramatically during the 1960s in that decade's climate of youthful, political, and social unrest. It became the drug of choice for a diverse user base. "Potheads" could no longer be identified by economic and occupational characteristics. The "pot problem" no longer resided solely in poor neighborhoods or among a bohemian element of society. Whether affluent or middle class, urban or rural, blue collar or white collar, it sometimes seemed as though all of America's sons and daughters were smoking weed. Getting drunk was "out" and getting stoned was "in", and young people scorned the cocktail parties of their parents' generation in favor of "toking" up. Predictably, the enthusiasm for marijuana sparked controversy, generating antipodal points of view with the division for the most part falling along age and generation lines.

Eventually, a somewhat draconian response came down from the federal level. The 1970 Uniform Controlled Substances Act listed marijuana as a Schedule I drug. That was an action that defined it as a substance that has high abuse potential, lacks accepted medical indications, and is unsafe even under medical supervision. Attempts were promptly launched to change its status to Schedule II and, thereby, to allow legal prescription. Hearings were conducted during the 1980s, but the re-scheduling effort ultimately failed. At the present time, only Dronabinol (Marinol), a commercial THC preparation, is available in the United States. It can be prescribed as an antiemetic or as an appetite stimulant. The debate over medical marijuana policies continues at the state and local level.

Marijuana is the most used illicit drug. The Drug Enforcement Agency's (DEA) web site currently estimates that 33 percent of Americans have used marijuana at least once in their lifetime, and that approximately 11.5 million Americans are users in 2002. The web site of the Australian Drug Foundation places 39 percent of that nation's population in the "had ever used" category and estimates that 18 percent used within the last twelve months. Worldwide, the number of users almost certainly exceeds two hundred million. A recent discussion via an Internet forum (the DRE Listserv) compared the current use levels in the U.S. of marijuana and MDMA ("ecstasy"). The latter is a popular "rave" drug, and its use soared in recent years, but consensus among the discussants (police officers and other professionals whose jobs enable them to monitor the drug scene) was that, excluding alcohol, marijuana unquestionably remains the number one drug of choice at the present time.

Recognizing that these numbers are estimates, and that they vary somewhat by source and over time, they are nonetheless large numbers. By any reckoning, it appears that a great many people choose to use marijuana. Not surprisingly, given that it is an illegal substance that is believed to have various harmful effects, the concern aroused by the estimates of incidence and prevalence has, in turn, generated a substantial body of research. Over the past three decades, investigators from a number of different disciplines conducted many studies to examine wide-ranging marijuana related issues. A large scientific literature reports the findings from that study and is readily accessible. This chapter takes only a limited view of the literature, looking at post-1990 data, reports, papers, and in some cases beliefs and opinions, to revisit some unanswered questions and controversial answers.

9.2 Data Limits

A sizable body of scientific data, as well as a large number of traffic arrests, supports the view that marijuana impairs skilled performance, including motor vehicle operation. Nonetheless, the drug's role in traffic mishaps continues to be challenged in the courtroom. That the challenges occur and are heard by the courts can be attributed at least in part to the limits of marijuana research data. Those limits arise out of both the methodology and the ethics involved in acquiring the kind of data needed.

A comprehensive explication of an impairing substance's contribution to motor vehicle crashes requires both laboratory data, which are available, and epidemiological data, which for the most part are not. The former demonstrate the nature and extent of the performance deficits. The latter are necessary to calculate the crash probabilities associated with those deficits. In the case of marijuana, how many drivers are *on the roadway* under its influence? How many *crash-involved drivers* are under the influence of marijuana? The data needed to answer these questions are sparse at best, and it is a lack in the information base that will not be readily filled.

9.3 Study Methods

Epidemiological data collection is costly, but funding is not the single, or even the major, impediment to undertaking such study. Obtaining appropriate body fluid specimens poses an additional and difficult challenge. Although a non-invasive breath specimen is an acceptable measurement of blood alcohol concentration, there is no equivalent, easily obtained specimen for other drugs. At this point in time, blood specimens are required.

Obtaining blood specimens in an experiment, even in a laboratory with all necessary equipment and personnel, may pose problems. The most obvious one is that potential subjects often decline to participate in an experiment when they learn that it involves multiple blood draws. This self-selection out of the pool of potential subjects creates the possibility that the study sample may be significantly biased. In comparison to the laboratory setting, however, the field environments of roadside surveys and crash investigations present more difficult hurdles for blood sampling. Apart from the logistical and procedural issues involved in drawing blood under less than optimal conditions, there again is a serious question about the sample. It is not clear that drivers who voluntarily agree to a needle stick at roadside are a representative sample of roadway users.

Even if blood specimens can be obtained in the field environment, additional problems remain. For many drugs, including marijuana, the relationship of blood drug level and impairment level is poorly defined or unpredictable. The interpretation of blood drug levels in relation to traffic events and identification of a causal link (if one exists) is not likely to be a simple task.

The pharmacokinetics and pharmacodynamics of drugs are such that often it is not possible to describe their causative roles in crashes. THC blood levels in particular tend not be instructive as to impairment, a fact attributable to the way the drug is absorbed and metabolized. THC is lipophilic, meaning that it binds with fat, with the result that it disappears from the blood rapidly. Peak blood levels occur within about ten minutes of beginning to smoke and then begin to decline while the user is experiencing the most intense subjective effects. Thus, an individual can be impaired when his or her THC blood level is low or non-detectable.

Urine, which frequently is the specimen of convenience in connection with traffic events, provides no direct evidence of impairment by marijuana. The detection of carboxy-delta-9-THC, a non-psychoactive metabolite, in urine indisputably demonstrates that the individual used the drug. The presence of the metabolite may serve to corroborate other evidence of impairment, but it provides no information about the level or influence of the drug at the time of a crash or an offense.

9.4 Experiment Dosing Issues

An additional factor that limits the data available for marijuana, as well as other drugs, is that ethical issues and subject safety impose rigid limits on the amount of drug that can be administered to human subjects. Investigators are neither allowed nor willing to administer doses that might place subjects at risk of injury or death. Doses of marijuana given to subjects in controlled laboratory investigations, therefore, may be smaller amounts than users routinely ingest in their personal use. Since it cannot be assumed that the rate of change in effects as a function of dose is linear, the extrapolation of findings from the lower doses that have been studied to larger amounts is not a straightforward calculation.

The risk of harm from moderate amounts of marijuana smoked by experienced users in a laboratory setting seems to be minimal. Fatalities attributable solely to marijuana have not been reported, and the lethal dose has not been established, although it has been estimated to be several pounds. Marijuana is not known to have major adverse effects on the heart, liver, or gastrointestinal tract, which makes it less pharmacologically damaging than alcohol. Although the smoke contains carcinogens, it is believed that only very heavy users are at significantly increased risk of lung cancer. On the other hand, it is possible that subjects, on occasion, smoke more and smoke differently in a laboratory setting than they would during personal use. Experiments must control the amount of drug intake by administering a fixed amount via paced smoking. Data interpretation would become essentially impossible if subjects were allowed to ingest varying amounts of drug by titrating (adjusting) their intake over an extended time period.

9.5 THC Content

The potency of marijuana (i.e., the percent THC) increased many fold during recent decades. In the 1960s when use began to surge upward dramatically, the THC content of domestic marijuana ranged from .25 percent to 1 percent. During the 1970s, Mexican, Colombian, and Jamaican marijuana with 2 percent to 5 percent THC content dominated the market. That potency now has been outstripped by sinsemilla, which has become a sizable cash crop in California. Its average THC content is 7 percent to 8 percent, but there have been reports of sinsemilla with 20 percent to 30 percent THC.

Increased potency is the outcome of innovative marijuana horticulture. The tops of female plants contain the most THC. They have resinous, oily hairs or stigma that serve the purpose of capturing pollen. Growers discovered that by removing all male plants, thereby insuring that the female plants would not be pollinated, the stigma elongate and produce unusually large amounts of the THC containing resin.

British Columbia growers are an additional source of very high potency (15–25 percent THC) marijuana. They cultivate the plants indoors under controlled, ideal growing conditions and export the high quality product, known as "B.C. bud" principally to the U.S.

Hashish, which is resin from female plants, is another high THC product. When hashish is distilled into hashish oil, the THC content potentially can be as high as 70 percent.

- How does highly potent marijuana affect the user?
- Do users smoke only enough to achieve a specific desired high?
- If high THC potency leads to high intake, what are the physiological and performance consequences?

There appears to be no way for such questions to be answered by investigators who are conducting research in the United States at the present time. To be administered to human subjects in the U.S., cigarettes or loose material must be obtained from NIDA, and that agency to date has not provided high potency marijuana for research purposes.

An article in *High Times* (Gettman, 1995) claims that, "Like responsible alcohol drinkers, most marijuana users adjust the amount of marijuana they consume–they 'titrate' it–according to its potency." It is not evident, however, what the support for that claim might be, other than observation of personal users. Data reported in the scientific literature have been obtained without exception with relatively low potency marijuana.

These various factors affect the study of drugs other than alcohol. Specifically, the limits they impose contribute to the uncertainties and controversies concerning the effects of marijuana.

9.6 Effects on Driving

A broad consensus concerning marijuana effects on driving skills remains somewhat elusive. In a review published a quarter century ago, Moskowitz (1976) reported that ". . . there is a large body of experimental evidence indicating that marijuana impairs the performance of skills important for driving." In a second review in 1985, he again concluded that marijuana is a major safety hazard.

The data available for the Moskowitz reviews in 1976 and 1985 came largely from laboratory studies with driving simulators and other tests of driving-related skills. Since that time, the data source has been extended to studies of actual driving. The National Highway Traffic Safety Administration (NHTSA), U.S. Department of Transportation sponsored a series of studies during the 1990s by investigators in The Netherlands where on-the-road experiments with dosed subjects were permitted. Robbe and O'Hanlon (1993) reported experiments with marijuana on a closed course and in traffic, and with marijuana and alcohol together on city driving. The same investigators later undertook examination of the separate and combined effects of marijuana and alcohol on a road-tracking test and a car-following test (Robbe and O'Hanlon, 1999). More recently, Lamers and Ramaekers (2000) studied the separate and combined effects of marijuana and alcohol on visual search and city driving.

These important studies were carried out under several closed course and actual traffic conditions with different apparatus, low alcohol doses, and low to moderate marijuana doses. The primary measures were subjects' ability to control speed (headway) and lane position (tracking), although various other performance measures and ratings were obtained. The following highlights summarize the reported findings reported in the above-referenced documents.

- Marijuana doses of 100 and 200 mg THC/kg body weight impair road tracking ability with impairment being a function of dose.
- A combination of alcohol at 0.04 percent BAC and THC severely impairs tracking.
- The impairment of tracking by a THC dose of 300 mg/kg is equivalent to the impairment by 0.08 percent BAC.
- A low THC dose of 100 mg/kg does not impair driving in urban traffic to the same extent as 0.04 percent BAC.
- THC doses of 100–200 mg/kg impair the ability to maintain a constant headway.
- A THC dose of 200 mg/kg seriously retards reaction time to the deceleration of preceding vehicle.
- The combined effects of THC and alcohol on headway and reaction time appear to be additive, and the sum can be large and potentially dangerous.
- Neither a THC dose of 100 mg/kg alone nor 0.04 percent BAC alone impairs city driving or decreases visual search frequency at intersections.
- A THC dose of 100 mg/kg in combination with 0.04 percent BAC impairs visual search and is potentially dangerous.

Although the investigators reiterated that alcohol is a more impairing substance than marijuana, they concluded that the moderate impairment measured with marijuana alone could become severe impairment under exceptional circumstances. Importantly, too, they concluded that the combination of THC and alcohol is exceedingly dangerous, representing a serious threat to the driving public. These studies extend and confirm conclusions previously drawn from laboratory studies.

Studies of marijuana effects on driving, whether carried out in a driving simulator in a laboratory or on the road are, by definition, controlled studies. Independent variables and major interacting variables are known and controlled by the experimenter. These include drug dose, time of drug intake relative to driving, smoking method, subject age, gender, health status, experience with marijuana, and test demands and duration. In contrast, when drivers are charged with the traffic offense of driving under the influence of marijuana, those variables are not controlled and generally are unknown and unknowable. The following sections assess the state-of-knowledge for some of those variables that often are the subject of debate.

9.7 Tolerance

The term, tolerance, refers to the changes in the physiological and behavioral responses that occur as a result of regular exposure to a psychoactive substance over an extended time period. As tolerance develops, an increased amount of drug is needed to achieve equivalent effects. Observable behavioral responses and the drug's effect on vital signs decrease.

During the 1970s, investigators reported the development of a "reverse tolerance" with repeated exposure to marijuana. This notion may have originated with the observation that first time smokers often do not experience pleasurable subjective effects. They may engage in several smoking sessions before they experience a "high." Learning in the short term to experience a drug's effects, however, would appear to be a different phenomenon than becoming sensitized to the drug in the long term.

There is evidence that tolerance, as usually defined, develops for some of marijuana's physical effects. Mendelson et al. (1984) found that the increase in heart rate that accompanies intake ceased to occur when subjects consumed marijuana daily over a three-week period. They also noted that clinical signs of intoxication decreased over the period of continual use.

Given regular use of marijuana in sufficient amount over an extended period of time, some degree of tolerance to it, as to any other drug, will develop. There has been relatively sparse study, however, of the time course and the extent of tolerance to other than physical effects. It is an area that merits further study.

9.8 Dependency, Withdrawal and Addiction

The overall conclusion that can be drawn from the scientific literature and clinical reports is that dependence, withdrawal, and addiction may be associated with marijuana use. It is believed these adverse consequences occur only with extremely high doses that are atypical of most use. Nevertheless, some further discussion is merited, because the three terms assume slightly different meanings in different contexts and for different drugs. Furthermore, they are related to set and setting, as well as substance and user, and must be understood in relation to all of these influences.

Drug dependency can have either a psychological or a physical basis, or both. Psychological dependency often has a strong set and setting component with the good feelings and gratification of drug use being closely tied to lifestyle, peer groups, and social interactions. Physical dependency involves a physiological adaptation to the presence of the drug in the body with the result that abstinence from it produces adverse symptoms.

Addiction carries the connotation of a highly negative state. The term, drug addict, evokes images of compulsive craving, drug seeking, furtive behaviors, and criminal activities. Most citizens have had no contact with individuals with these characteristics, but these frightening images are drawn from portrayals in movies, books, and music. In reality, drug addicts are not just the denizens of opium dens, shooting galleries, and alleyway needle-sharing sessions. They are also people who go to work every day, fulfill family responsibilities, and avoid contact with the criminal justice system. In fact, a neighbor, friend or relative may be a prescription drug addict. Individuals who opt to "kick the habit" from some of the more powerfully addicting substances face a severely unpleasant and in some cases life-threatening process that is best undertaken with the support of treatment professionals.

THC is a psychoactive substance and, therefore, the potential for dependency, withdrawal, and addiction must be considered. Schuckit reviewed this topic in 1995. Noting that there is only a limited literature, he found evidence that withdrawal symptoms may occur at the onset of abstinence following a period of exceptionally high doses. Studies of monkeys and rats, and human studies (there actually are individual case reports) are the source of the data. After chronic exposure to marijuana, the animals exhibited increased motor activity, aggression, and tremor, as well as various other signs. The evidence for withdrawal in humans comes from anecdotal accounts that reported symptoms of restlessness, irritability, nervousness, tremor, sweating, salivation, decreased appetite, nausea, and abdominal discomfort. It is noteworthy that Schuckit (1995) characterizes the withdrawal syndrome as rare. If it occurs, the symptoms appear within twelve hours to two days of cessation of use, peak on day three or four, and improve by day four or five.

Given the sparse scientific study, it would be ill advised to make highly definitive statements about the addiction potential of marijuana. Although there is no evidence now that suggests a serious problem, except possibly at high doses, the advent of very potent THC adds an unknown dimension to the issue. Also, essentially nothing is known about consequences for addiction when marijuana is used with or in close proximity to Rave drugs (MDMA, Ketamine, LSD, GHB).

9.9 Passive Exposure

For at least two decades, questions of culpability in marijuana-involved crashes have given rise to claims of passive inhalation of marijuana smoke. That is, a defendant alleges a positive blood or urine test resulted from being exposed to marijuana smoke, but that he or she did not purposefully, perhaps did not knowingly ingest marijuana. Beginning during the 1980s, a number of investigators examined this issue.

The most recent findings are from rigorously controlled experiments by Cone et al. (1990). In one experiment, smoke was so dense in the room that subjects wore goggles to protect their eyes. After this intense exposure the marijuana metabolite carboxy-delta-9-THC was found in subjects' urine at a maximum concentration of 12 ng/ml.

Studies conducted by other investigators during the 1980s reported concentrations in the range 7–27 ng/ml. Since the federally mandated cutoff is 50 ng/ml, none of the levels obtained from passive inhalation under extreme conditions would have triggered the report of a positive urine drug test. The 50 ng/ml cutoff for the immunoassays that are used to screen specimens effectively eliminates passive inhalation as the source a positive test result.

9.10 Immunity

Although the effect of marijuana on the immune system may only rarely become a legal issue, it is of interest nonetheless. Is marijuana immunosuppressive? That question, which has been controversial for several decades, assumes special relevance for individuals with the HIV virus. If they have not developed AIDS, they are told to avoid marijuana, advice that is somewhat misleading in its suggestion of certainty that the drug damages the immune system.

This topic has generated a sizable literature, most of it reported during the 1970s–1980s. There has been less research activity recently, but Hollister undertook a review in 1992. In a telling introductory comment, he notes, "The effects of marijuana on health in general have been marked by polarities of belief or interpretation of evidence often due to the prejudices of investigators." He also points out that immunosuppression data often were obtained from in vitro tests, and the marijuana doses greatly exceeded what is typically used in social settings.

Knowing whether THC acts on the immune system is potentially important information for individuals infected with the HIV virus. It also could be relevant to questions of tolerance. Despite a substantial amount of research, however, it remains unclear whether marijuana suppresses the immune system. The in vitro studies, which indicate some degree of immunosuppression, have been flawed by their use of very high drug concentrations. The evidence from clinical studies has not been compelling. Assuming that Hollister's (1995) belief that research interest in the topic has waned, the question may remain unanswered.

9.11 Summary

After several decades of marijuana study, the following can be concluded about the consequences of smoking marijuana or otherwise ingesting Δ-9 THC:

- Marijuana impairs driving skills.
- The combination of marijuana and alcohol severely impairs driving skills.
- Passive inhalation of marijuana smoke does not produce urine screen results above 50 ng/mL.
- Dependency, addiction and withdrawal symptoms are possible with chronic use of high doses of marijuana.

- There is no scientific evidence that marijuana damages the immune system.
- There is no scientific evidence that serious or long-term health effects are the consequence of moderate use of marijuana.

At the present time, the scientific literature lacks:

- Epidemiological data to fully define the contribution of marijuana effects to motor vehicle crashes
- Study of the effects of high-potency marijuana
- Study of the effects of marijuana in combination with "rave" drugs, such as MDMA, GHB, LSD and Ketamine

In conclusion, the overall picture that emerges from scientific study and informal accounts of marijuana is that the drug has mostly moderate effects. Does it follow that alarmists' views of the "devil weed" can be dismissed? Consider that the drug, the users, and the setting for much of the research differed from those elements in real world use at the present time. Consider, too, that a negative consequence is multiplied many times over by the very large number of users. As a cautionary observation, it would be premature to dismiss all concerns about marijuana.

References

Andrews, J.A., and Duncan, S.C. (1997). "Examining the reciprocal relation between academic motivation and substance use: Effects of family relationships, self-esteem, and general deviance." *Journal Behavioral Medicine*, 20, 6, 523–49.

Augsburger, M., and Rivier, L. (1997). "Drugs and alcohol among suspected impaired drivers in Canton de Vaud (Switzerland)." *Forensic Science International*, 85, 2, 95–104.

Baselt, R.C. (Ed.) (1999). *Disposition of Toxic Drugs and Chemicals in Man* (5th ed.). Foster City: Chemical Toxicology Institute.

Berghaus, G., Scheer, N., and Schmidt, P. (1995). "Effects of cannabis on psychomotor skills and driving performance: A meta-analysis of experimental studies." *Proceedings*, 13th International Conference on Alcohol, Drugs and Traffic Safety, 1, 403–409.

Block, Robert, and Ghoneim, M.M. (1993). "Effects of chronic marijuana use on human cognition." *Psychopharmacology*, 110, 219–228.

Brookoff, D., Cook, C.S., Williams, C., and Mann, C.S. (1994). "Testing reckless drivers for cocaine and marijuana." *The New England Journal of Medicine*, 331, 518–522.

Castle, D.J., and Ames, F.R. (1996). "Cannabis and the brain." *Australia and New Zealand Journal of Psychiatry*, 30, 2, 179–83.

Chait, I.D. (1990). "Subjective and behavioral effects of marijuana the morning after smoking." *Psychopharmacology (Berl)*, 100, 3, 328–33.

Cone, E.J. (1990). "Marijuana effects and urinalysis after passive inhalation and oral ingestion." In C.N. Chiang, and R.L. Hawks (Eds.) (pp. 88–96). *Research Finding on Smoking of Abused Substances*. Natl. Inst. Drug Abuse Rs. Monogr. Ser 99.

Devane, W.A., Hanu, L., Breuer, A., Pertwee, R.G., Stevenson, L.A., Griffin, G., et al. (1992). "Isolation and structure of a brain constituent that binds to the cannabinoid receptor." *Science, 25,* 1882–1884 (comment), 1946–1949.

Doblin, R.E., and Kleiman, M.A.R. (1991). "Marijuana as antiemetic medicine." *Journal of Clinical Oncology*, 9, 1314–1319.

Drummer, O.H. (1995) "Drugs and accident risk in fatally-injured drivers." *Proceedings*, 13th International Conference on Alcohol, Drugs and Traffic Safety, 1, 426–429.

Fortner, N., Fogerson, R., Lindman, D., Iversen, T., and Armbruster, D. (1997). "Marijuana-positive urine test results from consumption of hemp seeds in food products." *Journal Analytic Toxicology*, 21, 6, 476–81.

Good, P.J. (1996). "Sinsemilla." *The DRE*, 8, 1, 7.

Grinspoon, L., and Bakalar, J.B. (1995). "Marijuana as medicine." *JAMA*, 273, 1875–1876.

Heishman, S. J., Arasteh, K. and Stitzer, M.L. (1997). "Comparative effects of alcohol and marijuana on mood, memory, and performance." *Pharmacology, Biochemistry and Behavior*, 58, 1, 93–101.

Hollister, L.E. (1992). "Marijuana and immunity." *Journal of Psychoactive Drugs, April-June*, 24, 159–163.

Huestis, M.A., Sampson, A., Holicky, B., Henningfield, J.E., and Cone, E.J. (1992) "Characterization of the absorption phase of marijuana smoking." *Clinical Pharmacology and Therapeutics*, 52, 31.

Huestis, M.A., Henningfield, J.E., and Cone, E.J. (1992). "Blood cannabinoids: I. Absorption of THC and formation of 11-OH-THC and THCCOOH during and after marijuana smoking." *Journal of Analytical Toxicology*, 16, 276.

Huestis, M.A., Henningfield, J.E., and Cone, E.J. (1992). "Blood cannabinoids: II: Models for the prediction of time of marijuana exposure from plasma concentrations of D-9-tetrahydrocannabinol (THC) and 11-nor-9-carboxy-D-9-tetrahydrocannabinol (THCCOOH)." *Journal of Analytical Toxicology*, 16, 283.

Huestis, M.A., and Cone, E. (1998). "Urinary excretion half-life of 11-nor-9-carboxy-D-9-tetrahydrocannabinol in humans." *Therapeutic Drug Monitoring*, 20, 570–576.

Kirk, J.M., Doty, P., and De Wit, H. (1998). "Effects of expectancies on subjective responses to oral delta-9-tetrahydrcannabinol." *Pharmacol Biochem Behav*, 59, 2, 287–93.

Lamers, C.T.J., and Ramaekers, J.G. (2000). "Visual search and urban city driving under the influence of marijuana and alcohol." DOT HS 809 020, National Highway Traffic Safety Administration, U.S. Dept. of Transportation.

Leirer, V.O., Yesavage, J.A., and Morrow, D.G. (1991). "Marijuana carry-over effects on aircraft pilot performance." *Aviation, Space and Environment Medicine*, March, 221–227.

Marquez, P., Delpla, P., Keerguelen, S., Bremond, J., Facy, F., Garnier, M., et al. (1998). "Prevalence of drugs of abuse in urine of drivers involved in road accidents in France: A collaborative study." *Journal of Forensic Sciences*, 43, 4, 806–811.

Mason, A.P., and McBay, A.J. (1984). "Ethanol, marijuana and other drug use in 600 drivers killed in single vehicle crashes in North Carolina 1978–1981." *Journal of Forensic Sciences*, 29, 987–1826.

Moskowitz, H. (1976). "Marijuana and driving." *Accident Analysis and Prevention*, 8, 21–26.

Moskowitz, H. (1985). "Marijuana and driving." *Accident Analysis and Prevention*, 17, 323–46.

O'Brien, C.P. (1996). "Recent developments in the pharmacotherapy of substance abuse." *Journal Consulting and Clinical Psychology*, 64, 4, 677–86.

Page, T.E. (1992). "Cannabis: From reefer madness to nature's way of saying high and beyond, Part 1." *The DRE*, 4, 1, 11–14.

Page, T.E. (1992). "Cannabis: From reefer madness to nature's way of staying high and beyond, Part 2." *The DRE*, 4, 3, 3–5.

Perl, J., Mascord, D., et al. (1995). "Drug usage by persons suspected of driving under the influence of drugs." *Proceedings, 13th International Conference on Alcohol, Drugs and Traffic Safety*, 1, 81–86.

Pope, H.G. Jr., and Yurgelun-Todd, D. (1996). "The residual cognitive effects of heavy marijuana use in college students." *JAMA*, 275, 7, 521–7.

Risser, D., Stichenwirth, M., Klupp, N., Schneider, B., Stimpfl, T., Vycudilik, W., et al. (1998). "Drugs and driving in Vienna, Austria." *Journal of Forensic Sciences*, 43, 4, 817–820.

Robbe, H.W.J. (1994). *Influence of Marijuana on Driving* (pp. 232). University of Limburg, Maastricht, The Netherlands: Institute for Human Psychopharmacology.

Robbe, H.W.J., and O'Hanlon, J. F. (1999). *Marijuana, Alcohol and Actual Driving Performance.* DOT HS 808 939, National Highway Traffic Safety Administration, U.S. Dept. of Transportation.

Robbe, H.W.J., and O'Hanlon, J. F. (1993). *Marijuana and Actual Driving Performance.* DOT HS 808 078, National Highway Traffic Safety Administration, U.S. Dept. of Transportation.

Rouse, B.A. (1996). "Epidemiology of illicit and abused drugs in the general population, emergency department drug-related episodes, and arrestees." *Clin.Chem*, 42, 8, Pt. 2, 1330–6.

Schuckit, M.A. (1996). "Does marijuana have any medicinal value?" *Drug Abuse and Alcoholism Newsletter*, 25, No. 2.

Schuckit, M.A. (1995). "Is there a clinically significant marijuana withdrawal syndrome?" *Drug Abuse and Alcoholism Newsletter*, 24, No. 2.

Schuckit, M. A. (1994). "Can marijuana cause a long-lasting psychosis?" *Drug Abuse and Alcoholism Newsletter*, 23, No. 5.

Solowij, N., Michie, P.T., and Fox, A.M. (1995). "Differential impairments of selective attention due to frequency and duration of cannabis use." *Biological Psychiatry*, 37, 10, 731–9.

Walsh, J., Buchanan, B., and Leaverton, P. (1997). "Detection of illicit drugs in drivers." *Proceedings, 14th International Conference on Alcohol, Drugs and Traffic Safety*, 2, 485–491.

—— (1997) Marijuana's hidden dangers. *The Drug Influence Examiner*. Vol. 1, No. 2, 1–9.

Chapter 10

The Rave and Club Drug Phenomenon: Dancing with Darkness and Danger

Trinka Porrata

Synopsis

10.1 Introduction

Although there are no new drugs, just new uses and users, the newest drug scene is a world of Xtremes, from the XFL to energy drinks and trendy herbal water to a drug called X[1]. It is a world of ever-younger drug users who want fun without responsibility, pleasure now without regard for the future, and drugs even at the risk of death.

Who thinks about death? Heroes and villains on TV and in computer games die, but they pop back to life. What about friends who died? They took too much GHB. They didn't drink enough water; you need to cool off when you are dancing and using Ecstasy. Maybe they drank too much water. Pass the responsibility to the dead.

This is an era of prescription drug abuse and inconsistent enforcement against illicit drug users and dealers. Candy and toy manufacturers appear to be blind to the source of their sudden good fortune as America's kids inhale and suck on their products to deal with the side effects of Ecstasy. Casual sexual encounters leave in their wake fragile young girls depressed by self-denigration. Not surprisingly, recent research reports that the use of Ecstasy has more negative effects for females than for males

This isn't a drug scene populated by junkies and derelicts. The users aren't men and women using pills to cope with the stress of the business world. They aren't neurotic housewives, quietly intoxicated in suburbia behind lace curtains. This is a new behavior, unlike anything seen before. The kids are tuning in, speeding up and racing ahead with scarcely a thought about the darkness that lies in their paths.

10.2 A "Rave" Defined

Raves in the United States in the 2000s can be defined as any site, licensed or unlicensed, with rave music, atmosphere, and drugs. The music, which is rhythmic and loud, is called techno, trance, jungle, acid, deep house, deep trance, or Zen. The essential elements of a rave are the loud music in a dark environment with laser lighting, drugs, and drug paraphernalia. The drugs are MDMA, LSD, GHB, ketamine, mushrooms, other hallucinogens, marijuana, conventional drugs, and over-the-counter (OTC) drugs.

Raves first emerged during the 1980s in England where they were attended by multi-thousands. Although English law enforcement quickly recognized them as drug festivals and took vigorous police action against them, they remain a problem today. By the late 1980s, rave entertainers had begun to appear at clubs in major U.S. cities. The music of Depeche Mode and Soft Cell is believed to have brought Ecstasy into clubs in America. Raves began as events attended mostly by white, middle class young people, but they have been deliberately and successfully expanded into other groups. X in the 'hood now refers to Ecstasy, not Malcolm, and Asian youth are prominent among attendees.

Ravers, those who attend raves as part of their lifestyle, range in age from twelve to thirty-five years. They often dress in bizarre or baby-like clothing. They drive long distances to remote locations and spend entire nights at raves. They dance to nonstop music, use drugs, and stimulate each other with glow sticks and with touch. At the raves, massage stations help them cope with muscle spasms, a side effect of MDMA. Misting facilities help them deal with overheating, and there is bottled water for sale at inflated prices.

Alcohol is not a significant part of the rave culture. Its depressant effects are avoided in favor of stimulation and altered states. Body-conscious youths believe that alcohol will damage their livers, and that it is easily recognized by law enforcement. They correctly believe that the rave drugs will not lead to cirrhosis of the liver. They incorrectly believe that the drugs are harmless. They ignore or perhaps do not know that if their bodies severely overheat, their livers and kidneys will cease to function and violent seizures, possibly death, will follow.

There are three kinds of raves: underground, semi-underground, and above-ground. Each operation is distinct, but drugs are the common denominator for all of them.

A. Underground rave

The sites for these events, which are promoted as alcohol-free dance parties, are warehouses, open fields, desert land, and other inconspicuous locations where there are no licenses or controls. Tickets often are sold in advance without purchasers knowing the location of the rave. They will have to make multiple phone calls or go to several different places to find where the event will be held. In many cities there is at least one parking lot, usually adjacent to a record store or fast-food restaurant, where young people know they can find the location of any given night's rave or pick up flyers about future parties; MDMA and other drugs may be available at this location as well. With no closing times, participants at underground raves may remain on site to "sleep off" their drugs.

B. Semi-underground rave

The sites for the semi-underground events are public facilities such as fairgrounds, baseball fields, skating rinks, and similar venues. Promoters' negotiations for use of such public facilities include their assurances that the event will be a dance party for kids where alcohol will be banned. The individuals responsible for renting the facilities sometimes naively believe the claims, or if they realize that there will be drugs at the event, they may accept the risk of potential problems, because the facility needs the revenue. Five California teenagers died when their car went over a cliff as they were returning from a rave in a mountain location. Shortly thereafter, a city councilman in another community was asked why, since he knew about that tragedy, he was willing for his city to issue a permit for a rave. He replied that his city was bankrupt and needed the money.

C. Above-ground rave

In a quest for more conventional status, rave promoters began during 1996–97 to edge into licensed clubs, bars, and restaurants. Nightclubs that were then struggling with low attendance were willing to promote Rave Nights as a special theme event. Some clubs were opened for the purpose of catering solely to the rave scene. City officials acquiesced to the raves, telling the promoters, "There will be no problem as long as you abide by the zoning, security, and occupancy requirements, and there are no drugs" Apparently they believed that those requirements would be met.

Music in the clubs is of all types, techno to country western, and the drugs include those commonly found at raves, standard drugs of abuse, and alcohol. Energy drinks, such as Red Bull, which contain caffeine, ephedrine, taurine or other chemicals, are also popular. They extend the duration of MDMA effects and, mixed with shots of liquor, provide a buzz without sleepiness. The unique risk of the combination is that stimulation by the energy drinks may blunt the drinker's awareness of intoxication with the result that an excessive quantity of alcohol will be consumed. Because semi-underground and above -ground events have closing times and attendees must leave the premises, there is a risk that some of them will drive while under the influence of drugs.

Some existing clubs began to hold rave nights, because they needed revenue. Predictably, they soon experienced increased problems with overcrowding, disorderly waiting lines, and drugs. The Hollywood Athletic Club, for example, in 1997 opened a rave venue called Saturday Night Large. During the first five events, they experienced seventeen medical emergencies that were attributed to GHB overdoses.

As cities and counties began to recognize the problems associated with these events, they passed local ordinances designed to regulate them. Unfortunately, that approach simply moved the problem from county to county as promoters sought to evade the patchwork of laws. The state of Florida then addressed the issue more broadly. As part of a statewide enforcement effort, coroners throughout the state were directed to review death cases for the period 1997–99 and to report those related to rave drugs. The coroners reported 175 such deaths for the three-year period, with the largest number related to MDMA, according to the Florida drug czar's office. In 2000, California created a statewide Rave Task Force through the Bureau of Narcotics Enforcement, and several other states now have task forces in place.

10.3 Raves and Law Enforcement

The rave problem exceeds the capabilities of law enforcement. A limited number of officers cannot respond adequately when thousands of young people appear unexpectedly in the desert or in an abandoned warehouse. If officers respond to the scene because of a medical emergency or complaints about traffic, they focus on the medical situation and they try to control traffic, and they may fail to see drug-related activity.

Knowledge of the drugs, terminology, and paraphernalia is essential for law enforcement. To recognize the problem, officers must know what they are looking for and how it will be packaged. Otherwise, they will not understand the mode of dress, the candy, and the odd assortment of containers. Ravers wear baby-like clothing to look innocent and harmless. They wear soft fabrics and interesting textures for tactile sensation, because MDMA enhances the sense of touch. They use lollipops, pacifiers, mouth guards and teething rings to reduce the bruxism caused by MDMA. They use face masks filled with Vicks or similar products with menthol and eucalyptus vapors to enhance breathing. They use candies to hide the drugs, mixing them into a bag of Skittles and concealing them in Tootsie Rolls, or they drill holes and string them onto necklaces and bracelets. Breath freshener at a rave is likely to be liquid LSD. Any bottle is a possible drug container, including beverages, mouthwash, bubble solution, Visine, nasal spray, and purse-size hair spray.

10.4 3, 4 Methylenedioxymethamphetamine (MDMA)

The use of MDMA, which is better known as Ecstasy, has spread like a virus, quietly taking hold beneath the radar screen of law enforcement and the medical world. Most parents and teachers have been blind to it, and police officers are only beginning to learn about it. The raves, which took hold almost invisibly, now have exploded onto the scene with lights and loud music and drugs.

MDMA or Ecstasy is the drug that fuels raves, but it is not an intoxicant in the usual sense. It is not an extremely potent stimulant, although it provides sufficient energy to sustain users through a long session of dancing. It does not produce true hallucinations except in very high doses or with other drugs. Users call it a mind-expander and claim that if everyone in a room of total strangers takes an Ecstasy tablet, they all soon will be best friends. Because it doesn't produce obvious intoxication, it is a drug that is very easy to not notice. In *Buzzed: The Straight Facts about the Most Used and Abused Drugs from Alcohol to Ecstasy*, (Kuhn, et al., 1998) a user wrote:

> You feel open, clear, loving. I can't imagine being angry under its influence, or feeling selfish or mean or even defensive. You have a lot of insights into yourself, real insights that stay with you after the experience is over. It doesn't give you anything that isn't already there. It is not a trip. You don't lose touch with the world. You could pick up the phone, call your mother, and she'd never know.

During a special about Ecstasy on the television show *20/20*, a user said, "I could give you [the interviewer] one, and you'd like it. I could give one to the high school principal, and he'd like it. I don't know anyone who wouldn't like it."

Although MDMA is called the "love drug," a more fitting term for it is the "hug drug". It promotes loving feelings and sexual play, but it inhibits erection and climax. It produces good feelings at the risk of negative effects.

The imprints on MDMA tablets/pills, which look as innocent as Flintstones vitamins or sugar pills, give rise to the names: Ecstasy, XTC, X, Versace, the hug drug, the love pill. The current availability of Ecstasy in large volume reflects both the closed communities in which the drug

Table 10.1
Effects of MDMA

Physiological	Psychological	
	Positive	Negative
Acute renal failure	Closeness in relationships	Agitation
Blurred vision/nystagmus	Entactogenesis	Anxiety
Bruxism (grinding teeth)	Empathogenesis	Delusions
Cerebral edema	Increased self-esteem	Depression
Convulsions/seizures/stroke	Increased self-awareness	Disorientation
Dehydration	Openness	Memory lapses
Headache	Sensory enhancement	Mood swings
Hypothermia		Panic attacks
Increased heart rate		
Increased blood pressure		
Insomnia		
Nausea		
Peripheral vasoconstriction		
Pupil dilation		
Tachycardia		
Trismus (jaw spasm)		
Other muscle spasms		

first flourished and the lack of focus by law enforcement. National and international agencies only recently began to recognize the dimensions of the problem. INTERPOL called an MDMA conference in 1999. The U.S. Drug Enforcement Agency (DEA) sponsored another conference in 2000, and that was followed by a 2001 conference sponsored by the National Institute on Drug Abuse (NIDA).

California agencies and U.S. Customs seized MDMA worth $2.1 million in December 1999. At that time, it was the largest drug seizure in Customs history. They had seized only 1,000 MDMA tablets in 1995. In 1998 the number grew to 400,000, and in 2000 the number exploded to 9.3 million.

It is widely believed, albeit incorrectly, that MDMA is a mixture of mescaline and amphetamine. Actually, it is not a mixture of anything. Though often called a designer drug, meaning a drug created as a variant of a controlled substance to circumvent the controls, MDMA was not created in that fashion. It was synthesized in 1912 as a precursor agent, an intermediate structural compound containing primary constituents for therapeutically active compounds. It is an analog of MDA, and it is related to MDMB and MDEA. It has no approved medical use and has been a

Schedule I drug since 1986. U.S. Army studies that were conducted during the early 1950s and declassified in 1969 reported that it was the most toxic of the investigated substances (Cohen, 1998).

Distribution and sales of MDMA are profitable enterprises. Selling for $15 to $20 per tablet in California, $20 to $35 in other cities, and for even higher prices in remote areas, it is an expensive drug for users. The source price, however, is only $.50 to $2 in Belgium and the Netherlands, and the wholesale price in the U.S. is $8 to $10 per tablet. The DEA Special Testing Lab recently reported that tablets contain an average of 80 to 90 mg MDMA. Thus, one kilogram of pure MDMA yields approximately 10,000 tablets, and there is a very large profit margin at each level of sale.

MDMA tablets in quantities of 10,000 or more are smuggled into the U.S. by couriers aboard commercial flights, via express mail and by airfreight shipments. Most of the tablets from Europe actually are MDMA whereas those made in America are likely to contain less expensive substances. To extend a quantity of MDMA or to substitute for it and thus increase the profit, it is mixed with amphetamine or methamphetamine plus LSD, ketamine, GHB, or another less expensive substance that will give it the hallucinogenic edge. In some cases, the mixtures contain mostly filler or caffeine and ephedrine. Although there are more than 400 recognized logos, the butterfly is the universal symbol for MDMA. Because Remifeminin (black cohosh) also has a butterfly logo, dealers have been able to sell it as Ecstasy.

A. Pills and paraphernalia

Ecstasy looks like candy. The paraphernalia appears innocent and unrelated to drug use. Consider the following ordinary objects that are used to conceal the drug, enhance the experience, or relieve side effects: pacifiers and lollipops, Tootsie Rolls, Skittles, Pez, M&Ms, mouth guards, gel capsules, Vicks inhalers, Vicks with face masks, Tiger Balm, other lotions, glow sticks, lights wands, and palm size vibrators.

Ravers engage in flipping, which is the practice of using multiple substances with a sequence and timing that is intended to produce the best effects. The information presented in Table 10.2 about the order and intervals for taking drugs is posted on various web sites.

MDMA use typically begins with one pill, but tolerance develops rapidly, and the number of pills must be increased to produce the desired ef-

Table 10.2
Rave and Club Drug Polydrug "Flips"

Drug Combination	Term	Instruction (to maximize effects)
LSD and MDMA	Candy flipping	LSD 3 hrs <MDMA
'Shrooms and MDMA	Hippy flipping	MDMA 4 hrs <mushrooms
Mescaline and MDMA	Love flipping	Take at the same time
Ketamine and MDMA	Kitty flipping	MDMA 10 mins <ketamine
PCP and MDMA	Elephant flipping	Take at the same time
DXM and MDMA	Robo flipping	MDMA 20 mins <DXM
2-CB (Nexus) and MDMA	Nexus flipping	Nxus 3–5 hrs >MDMA
2-CT-7 (Lucky 7) and MDMA	Lucky flipping	MDMA first, Lucky 7 later
DMT and MDMA	Time flipping	MDMA first DMT later
MDMA, MDEA and MBDB	Adam and Eve in the Garden of Eden	Take all at the same time

fect. Eventually, the user may take as many as nine or ten pills at one time and then take additional pills later. To offset the cost of their own usage, enterprising individuals purchase the drug in quantity to get a good price and then resell some of the supply. On-site user-dealers likely will not possess a really large quantity. They may be under the influence and oblivious to what is going on around them while selling the drug. Professional dealers, on the other hand, probably will not be taking drugs during sales activity and will be alert to enforcement activities.

MDMA proponents believe the drug has a beneficial role in psychotherapy, that it lowers defenses and allows the release of feelings, acceptance of others, and openness. Given the vulnerability of many youthful users, however, these potentially positive experiences may actually pose serious risk if they occur in an environment where there are no therapeutic professionals.

There are other serious problems associated with MDMA use, three of which have received little attention. First, its effects appear to be inconsistent with safe motor vehicle operation. Research concerning its association with motor vehicle crashes was not begun until 2002, and data are not yet available, but its stimulant effects are consistent with fast driving. The associated visual disturbances (dilated pupils, blurring, light trails) can cause misperceptions, possibly resulting in off-the-road crashes. Subjective effects last about five hours, but impairment is measurable for up to twelve hours, and post-high, post-partying fatigue is an additional risk factor. A sample of serious MDMA-related traffic crashes suggests that traffic safety concerns are merited (Table 10.3).

Table 10.3
Selected MDMA-Related Motor Vehicle Crashes

Location	Crash	Drug(s)
Nevada	Las Vegas dancer veered off road, striking roadway work crew, resulting in six fatalities.	MDMA, marijuana
Nevada	Woman drove onto a sidewalk and into a group of Las Vegas tourists. One man died.	MDMA, marijuana, methamphetamine
California	Camp Pendleton marine crashed his vehicle. A passenger died.	MDMA
California	Female, age 18, drove away from a rave and minutes later struck a police car head on.	MDMA
California	Five young people, returning from a rave, died when their car plunged off a cliff.	MDMA (driver) All passengers drug-positive.
California	Four young Asian females were involved in a traffic accident that left two dead, two with permanent injuries.	MDMA (driver and fatally injured passenger)

A second consequence of MDMA use is tooth damage. Dentists, who may or may not recognize the cause of the problems, are noting an increase in the number of young people with cracked enamel, worn teeth and jaw problems. A 1999 study in Liverpool, England (Spicuzza, 2000) found that individuals using 1.5 MDMA tablets on average four times per month had almost five times more tooth decay than the average person. The study noted that 93 percent of users added to the damage by consuming acidic, carbonated beverages. Those who vomited as a consequence of drug use had additional risk of tooth erosion due to the stomach acids. Dr. Hal Crossley, University of Maryland Dental School, (Spicuzza, 2000) described the damage this way: "I've seen users who have ground their teeth down to nubs. Their molars become flat, polished stubs. The back teeth go and then the front teeth are just ground right down. The enamel in front just dissolves away."

The practice of sucking on lollipops and pacifiers to reduce bruxism adds to dental problems. Dentists also note that the intense drug-inspired sucking can cause orthodontic problems, much like a toddler's excessive thumb sucking. Consistent with their belief that MDMA use is not a problem, users seem unconcerned about damage to their teeth.

The third area of concern is a potential problem that has not been investigated, namely whether the light shows, which are popular at raves, may be causing long-term damage. "Eye candy" refers to light stimulation with lights of varying brightness. Since the lights are held very close, damage may occur as a result of their intensity and proximity to the users' dilated pupils.

B. MDMA and death—or, "Don't hug this drug!"

MDMA-related deaths can result from the drug effects per se, and they can be the consequence of altered perception and judgment. The deaths occur as motor vehicle crashes, sudden collapses, suicide, and risky or bizarre activities. Cohen (1998) notes that autopsies reveal striking changes in the liver, brain and heart. He cites several deaths that occurred during 1994 and 1995. One was a young, first-time user who had told his mother he hated drugs, and that he considered drug addicts and pushers to be the scum of the earth. Another was a teenage water-skiing champion. Still another was a sophomore at the University of California at Santa Cruz who took two MDMA tablets half an hour apart at a San Francisco area rave. As can be seen in Table 10.4, the deaths continue apace.

Table 10.4
A Sample of Recently Reported MDMA-Related Fatalities

Date	Location	Circumstances
1999	Santa Barbara, CA	College student died after taking one MDMA tablet. Friends did not call 911.
1999	Lake Nacimiento, CA	Female, age 18 under the influence of MDMA and alcohol was hanging onto a boat when she disappeared underwater. She was found two days later. Cause of death was cardiac arrhythmia.
1999	Plano, Texas	Former Dallas Cowboys offensive tackle Mark Tuinei had taken MDMA heavily during the weeks prior to his death. Coroner attributed death to MDMA and heroin.
1999	Old Orchard Beach, ME	Female, age 20, died after taking MDMA. It was the third time she had used the drug.
2000	Vacaville, CA	Young man died after taking several MDMA tablets, more than his usual amount. Friends did not call 911. His body temperature was reported as 106° hours after refrigeration at the morgue.
2001	Boulder, CO	Friends gave a female an Ecstasy pill for her 16th birthday. She drank excessive water and died from water poisoning.
2001	Los Angeles, CA	San Diego dentist was charged in the death of a young woman who fell from the 12th floor of a hotel after he gave her Ecstasy. When she became ill from Ecstasy and alcohol, he put her out of the hotel room. Unable to care for herself, she fell to her death.

C. MDMA and the brain

Dr. George Ricaurte and colleagues (2000) reported that MDMA causes permanent changes in the brain. The damage results from a decrease in serotonin, an important chemical messenger that is associated with mood and personality traits. These investigators believe that the damage may decrease over a period of several years, but that some of it is permanent.

Given the large number of users, it appears that the risk of death is not dramatically high, and the greater danger may be damage to long-term mental health. It has been estimated that as many as one in ten users experience such effects. As reported in June, 1997 in the *New Scientist Planet Science,* Dr. Michael Morgan of Sussex University studied serotonin levels in the brains of MDMA users and in an unpublished paper stated:

> In the early nineties, it was thought of as a soft drug, analogous to cannabis, but we now know that Ecstasy is one of the worst drugs in terms of its long-term harm potential. It is more neurotoxic to the serotonin system than any other drug we know, and this kind of permanent brain damage is something you don't see with other drugs. Ecstasy is one of the most pernicious and damaging drugs available—and at the same time the second most popular drug in use. It's a major issue.

Another British study, by Drs. Stephany Biello and Richard Dafters, psychologists at Glasgow University found that MDMA damages users' body clocks, causing a kind of permanent jet lag. They suggest that it disrupts the sensitive clock mechanism in the brain by damaging cells that contain serotonin. The data further indicate that a disrupted serotonin pathway cannot repair itself. Research from the Academic Medical Center, Amsterdam (Reneman et al., 2001) indicates that the drug may cause more loss of brain cells in women than in men.

10.5 Gamma Hydroxy Butyrate (GHB)

GHB is also called G, liquid X, liquid ecstasy, grievous bodily harm, Georgia home boy, scoop, great hormones at bedtime, salty water, everclear, aminos, GH buddy, and blue monster. Since 1990 it has been a federal violation under the U.S. Food and Drug Administration (FDA) rules to manufacture GHB and transport it across state lines for purposes of sales. It became a Schedule I drug on March 13, 2000.

GHB is available in Europe as an anesthetic, but it is not widely used in any medical community. It presently is legally available in the United States solely as an orphan drug for experimental treatment of narcolepsy, and it is under FDA review as a prescription drug for that purpose. It is possible that it will become a Schedule III pharmaceutical product although it will remain a Schedule I drug for illicit use.

GHB is a behavioral depressant and a sedative hypnotic with a steep dosage curve. A very small increase in dose makes a dramatic difference in effects. It is often difficult, however, to specify the effects of GHB, because it is typically taken with other drugs or alcohol. Blood specimens are rarely analyzed for GHB unless a patient's history indicates its use, or circumstances dictate more than routine drug testing. Presently, there is no urine drug screen for it, but progress is being made in quality and availability of both blood and urine testing. Also, a field test for use by law enforcement is being developed.

GHB occurs naturally in minute quantities in the brain and some other tissues in the human body. It induces sleep, lacks analgesic properties, and has no nutritional value. It causes intense intoxication, nausea, coma (sometimes abrupt and profound), uncontrollable seizures, and respiratory depression. Although the objective symptoms mimic a CNS depressant, it may actually be a CNS excitant. Dr. Wallace Winters, who studied GHB when he was a medical officer with the FDA, reports that the brain wave pattern of animals given GHB is that of epileptic seizure. This pattern has not been confirmed in humans.

GHB is rapidly absorbed, and peak plasma concentrations occur twenty to sixty minutes after oral administration. It is almost completely oxidized to carbon dioxide with only about 5 percent eliminated in urine. The half-life of a 12.5 mg/kg dose is twenty minutes.

The subjective effects of GHB are similar to alcohol intoxication. It reduces inhibitions, and may cause aggressive and violent behavior. It reputedly is an aphrodisiac, and users say, "It makes you want to have sex." It also causes nausea, although strangely users have no sense of being ill and no recall of the nausea. Film shot by news crews with hidden cameras shows users becoming wildly giddy and then vomiting as casually as one might spit tobacco into a spittoon. One individual, who was actually having seizures, described an overdose experience as follows:

> I just felt so safe and secure. I just wanted to go to sleep. I thought I was just nodding off. I couldn't understand why the fifty people around me were screaming and hysterical. It was like I was outside, watching myself and them. I could hear them but couldn't understand their reaction. I couldn't seem to communicate my feelings of security to them. Finally, I did become a little anxious, realizing that they must know something I didn't know.

Effects typically resolve very abruptly about four hours after ingestion. There is a rapid transition from severe intoxication to a fully awake state with the user having total amnesia for the preceding hours. Because there is little or no memory of the intoxication episode, the belief that it is less disorienting than alcohol is sustained.

GHB is easily made, and kits can be purchased via the Internet. Its two basic ingredients are available at any chemical supply house. One ingredient is Gamma butyl lactone, which is a solvent that is used for degreasing engines or stripping floors. Another ingredient is sodium hydroxide (lye). Muriatic acid or vinegar is also used, its purpose being to back down the PH level in a manner similar to controlling the PH level of a swimming pool.

GHB is a clear liquid only slightly thicker than water that usually has only a mild nondistinctive odor, though some batches have a horrible odor. It is often packaged to look like ordinary products such as CD cleaner, ink jet cartridge cleaner, plant food, or soap. The container labels, however, reveal unmistakably that it is intended for human consumption. "No aftertaste," "In case of accidental ingestion . . ." and "Mint flavoring added . . ." for example, are not appropriate for cleaning products

Illicitly produced liquid GHB first became popular with bodybuilders. Their initial use stemmed from the belief that it would stimulate the body's production of growth hormones. Because they continue to take it regularly as a sleep or workout aid, they are particularly vulnerable to addiction. Their daily usage gradually increases until they are taking it every one to three hours around the clock. Pleasure from its effects is lost, and they take it as maintenance to avoid withdrawal. The symptoms of withdrawal, which can be life endangering, are sometimes mistaken for symptoms of overdose. Addiction treatment centers do not always understand that three-to-five day detoxification that is effective for other drugs will fail with GHB. Long-term addiction counseling is needed.

This is a party drug with extremely severe consequences. More than 15,600 overdoses have been documented (DEA Office of Diversion Control, 2001). It is associated with the sexual assault of victims who may be invited to try an "energy drink" or an unusual cocktail. Although its salty taste is noticeable, victims apparently do not sense danger.

Table 10.5
Selected GHB-Related Motor Vehicle Crashes

Location	Crash	Drug(s)
Florida	Young woman, on bail only twelve hours from one GHB DUI, kills a woman in a head-on collision. Police failed to recognize GHB intoxication in a prior traffic accident she had.	GHB
Ohio	Wrong-way freeway driver kills mother and two young children in high-speed crash	GHB, MDMA,
New York	College student killed an innocent party in a head-on collision	GHB, alcohol, marijuana
Virginia	Female on GHB dies in traffic accident	GHB
California	In his third known DUI incident (low blood alcohol and GHB not recognized initially), driver plows into vehicle stopped at light, killing innocent driver instantly.	GHB, alcohol
South Carolina	Day-time head on collision in company truck kills toddler	GHB

In Toms River, New Jersey during the Memorial Day weekend of 1999, at least twenty-four people were treated for GHB overdoses. A GHB death followed on June 1, and thirteen more overdoses occurred on the July 4th weekend. Other recent incidents include overdoses by five adolescents in a Michigan community and three thirteen-year-olds at a party in Louisiana. The latter were found frothing blood through their noses, evidence of pulmonary edema. Dr. Jo Ellen Dyer, associate clinical professor of pharmacy, UCSF, California Poison Control System, San Francisco General Hospital has published extensively about this drug. In 2001 she initiated a review of fatalities attributed to GHB, and in a preliminary report of that research estimates that 80 percent of the fatalities involve pulmonary edema, and that 35 percent have enlarged hearts. The latter finding requires further evaluation.

The DEA has attributed seventy-two fatalities to GHB, and review is pending for an additional 145 fatalities. Since the drug is not part of a standard toxicology screen, it is possible that other GHB fatalities have not been recognized. Those who have died generally have been under age thirty, though the range is thirteen to seventy-seven years.

Table 10.6
A Sample of Representative GHB-Related Fatalities

Date	Location	Circumstances
1990	California	A 77-year-old man died after being told by a health food store clerk GHB would restore "good muscle tone."
1996	La Porte, Texas	Teenager died in her sleep after GHB was slipped into her soda.
1996	Landers, California	Going away rave party for 15-year-old turned fatal. He drank on GHB and was left to "sleep it off" by partygoers.
1998	Syracuse, New York	A 26-year-old female on a business trip found dead in her hotel room after having drinks in the hotel bar with a person she knew. GHB had been slipped into her drink.
1999	Toms River, New Jersey	A 27-year-old man was found dead at his home from GHB during holiday weekend when 24 GHB-related overdoses were identified in one area hospital alone.
1999	Austin, Texas	Husband and wife take GHB as "sexual enhancer;" both pass out and wife awakens to find 32-year-old husband dead.
2000	Valdosta, Georgia	Young man took GHB and went into convulsions, frothing at the mouth. Left by friends to "sleep it off" and found dead in the morning.
2000	Beebee, Arkansas	No history of drug abuse; took GHB as a health aid. Tried to stop without medical supervision. After just 36 hours, committed suicide struggling with intense withdrawal symptoms.
2001	Lake Worth, Florida	Read book on GHB, saying it is a safe sleep aid. Died in his sleep from GHB.
2001	Tampa, Florida	Fatal drink served to young man. Supplier (a GHB addict) convicted on murder charges.
2002	San Luis Obispo, California	College freshman found dead in his bed after a fraternity party. He was seen drinking beer; unknown if his consumption of GHB was voluntary or his drink spiked.

One-time use of GHB, especially when mixed with alcohol or other drugs, creates a stunning risk of death. A young woman in Georgia, whose story was featured on a CNN documentary, boldly took a big gulp of GHB while her companions were taking only small sips. As she frothed blood, the supplier of the drug commented that she had killed herself by drinking so much, and another companion complained about her getting blood on the carpet. She was taken to a hospital where she remained comatose until her death three years later.

Several analogs of GHB also are of concern, including gamma butyrolactone (GBL, the precursor to GHB) and 1,4 Butanediol BD, which is converted into GHB within the body by the addition of an oxygen molecule. A third analog, valeric acid (GHV) is marketed as Midnight Blue, Tranquili G, Sublimiss, and 4Sleep. Although Federal legislation covers these chemicals that convert to GHB in the body, many states do not have or have not effectively implemented analog laws. Since analogs involve no manufacturing process, there can be no criminal charges related to manufacturing.

10.6 Ketamine

Ketamine, which is related to phencyclidine (PCP), is found at the same places and events where GHB and Ecstasy are found. Because it is less potent than PCP, it is an attractive option for users who are seeking a more manageable high. It is known as Ketalar, Ketajet, Ketaset, Special K, Ket, Vitamin K, and Green. The latter name refers to the green label on the Ketajet box. Other names include 1980 Acid, Super C, Super Acid, Special L.A. Coke, Honey Oil, Blast, and Gas. Because users sometimes sink into blissful, infantile inertia, they also call it Baby Food. Some users even call it God, apparently believing they have had a spiritual experience under the influence of the drug

Ketamine is a psychedelic drug, which is classified medically as a dissociative anesthetic. Dr. Cal Stevens of Wayne State University discovered it in 1961. Unlike other anesthetics, it does not depress critical vital signs. That attribute accounts for it having been the most commonly used anesthetic on Vietnam battlefields and for its frequent use as an anesthetic with burn patients, for pediatric surgery, and with sexual assault patients. It produces a dissociative state in the central nervous system, and amnesia and profound analgesia are induced, although the patient does not appear to be asleep. Physicians and veterinarians use it only when resuscitation equipment is available, and it never is prescribed as a take-home drug for either humans or animals.

Ketamine first became popular as an abused drug during the 1970s. Abuse levels wavered during the 1980s but rose steadily throughout the 1990s. Because it involves a complicated, multistep synthesis with chemicals that are not readily available, it is not produced clandestinely. Therefore, its route from legal to illegal use is via burglaries of pharmacies, hospitals, and veterinary clinics, or it is smuggled into the U.S. via Mexico. It is a Schedule III drug, and medical facilities are not required to meet stringent storage requirements to prevent theft and diversion.

For licit use, it is produced as a liquid for injection. In illicit use, the liquid is injected, consumed in drinks, or applied to materials that can be smoked. It also may be oven-dried into a crusty residue that then is ground into a fine powder to be inhaled. One 10-ml vial liquid of 100 mg/ml Ketamine yields about one gram of saleable powder. The white, crystalline powder is duller and more powdery than cocaine, and it generally is not cut with any other substance. Powdered K is found in amounts of 0.07 to 0.2 grams in one-inch Ziploc Baggies, paper folds, and capsules

Ketamine can produce pleasant dreamlike states, vivid imagery, hallucinations and extreme delirium. The duration of these effects is only a few hours, but excitement and visual disturbances can recur days or weeks after exposure. Flashbacks are believed to occur more frequently with ketamine than with other hallucinogens.

Signs of being under the influence vary greatly. It may produce bursts of energy, disorientation, and mild-to-severe hallucinations. It also can produce ataxia, slurred speech, dizziness, confusion, blurred vision, anxiety, and insomnia. In larger doses or mixed with alcohol, it may cause vomiting.

The amount ingested by a user, who is known as a K-head, is called a bump. Users typically insufflate 20 mg per nostril, which is about a level coke spoon, and repeat that amount three or four times until the desired effect is achieved. A full-blown psychedelic experience requires about 100 mg. A dose of 0.07 g powder will produce symptoms of intoxication and a mechanical buzzing in the ears. With 0.2 gram, the user enters the mellow, colorful state that is known as K-land. With 0.5 gram, the experience is more likely to be what is known as the K-hole with hallucinations, delirium, and out-of-body experiences. On average, these extreme effects last an hour or less, but judgment, coordination, and the senses may be affected for eighteen to twenty-four hours.

With 1 to 2 mg/Kg administered intravenously or 6 to 13 mg/Kg administered intramuscularly over a period of about a minute, the user experiences dissociation (depersonalization, distortion, fragmented thought) within fifteen seconds and becomes unconscious within thirty seconds. The unconscious state persists for ten to fifteen minutes, analgesia for fifty minutes, and amnesia for one to two hours. Tolerance and psychological dependence develop with frequent exposure. Chronic users report short-term memory loss, impaired vision, and limited attention span. Overdoses can be fatal.

10.7 Phencyclidine (PCP) and Embalming Fluid

PCP was developed by Parke-Davis as an anesthetic. Because it did not depress vital signs, as most anesthetics do, it was viewed as a promising pharmaceutical product. In early trials, however, patients developed severe postoperative problems. As a result, it was discontinued as an investigational drug for human use in 1965. It was reintroduced in 1967 as a large-animal tranquilizer. It surfaced that same year at a San Francisco music festival where it was called PeaCePill. It is alleged that a veterinarian in Hayward, California produced it in the liquid form now known as PCP.

PCP is a dissociative anesthetic like Ketamine and GHB. It results in generalized loss of pain perception with little or no depression of airway reflexes or ventilation. It doesn't directly affect muscular strength, but because users become impervious to pain, they sometimes perform seemingly superhuman feats. Effects last for a few hours up to four days. Death can be a direct effect of ingestion, but it also results from the complications of hyperthermia and violent behavior.

During the early 1980s, Los Angeles was reputed to be the source of 90 percent of the PCP distributed nationwide. In the mid-1990s, the Los Angeles Police Department, Narcotics Division, Clandestine Lab Squad arrested sixteen members of the Bounty Hunters, a South Central gang that was the primary source of PCP. Unfortunately, the gang's manufacturing equipment was never located. It is possible that the 2000s resurgence of PCP is the consequence of old equipment and new gang members, or of the original gang members now being released from jail.

As cocaine and methamphetamine became preferred drugs, PCP use waned. Currently, however, it is being used in combination with embalming fluid. Street talk about this combination, which began in 2001, refers to wets, illy, and fry. Names also include amp, water, sherm, dank or whack. When used alone, PCP was sometimes referred to as embalming fluid, but young people now are ingesting embalming fluid alone as well as in combination with PCP. The pro-drug website Erowid.org believes this reflects a confusion of terms that has turned into a dangerous reality. Embalming fluid is a mixture of formaldehyde, methanol, ethanol, and other solvents, and it is not safe for human consumption. It is a carcinogen that is linked to nasal and lung cancer and possibly is linked to brain cancer and leukemia.

Users dip marijuana or tobacco cigarettes in formaldehyde, or they hollow out Swisher Sweets and Philly Blunts and fill them with formaldehyde-laced marijuana. Formaldehyde can be found in drug stores, beauty supply stores, school science laboratories, and funeral homes.

A candyblunt is a hollow cigar filled with marijuana plus codeine cough syrup. The cough syrup is poured onto the marijuana and oven-dried. With the blunt, a combination of cough syrup, Alize (a bottled passion fruit and cognac drink), or other alcohol may be consumed in an effort to achieve deeper relaxation and euphoria.

In interviews with members of the Texas Commission on Alcoholism and Drug Abuse (Elwood, 1998), users said formaldehyde gives them visual and auditory hallucinations, euphoria, a feeling of invincibility, increased pain tolerance, anger, forgetfulness and paranoia. They also said they believe it does long-term or permanent brain damage, and they told stories about youngsters who used it and now are in custodial care. They reported bizarre effects such as an overwhelming desire to disrobe and a strong distaste for meat. Some warned specifically that it is a bad drug for girls, because it renders them unconscious and makes them vulnerable to sexual assault. Other side effects include headaches, impaired vision, diminished attention, disorganized speech and thoughts, violence, coma, seizures, kidney failure and stroke. The effects last six hours to three days.

10.8 Lysergic Acid Diethylamide (LSD)

LSD, a Schedule I drug, is also known as acid, blotter, stamps, dots, trips, paper, A-bombs, and pyramids. Although it was discovered in 1938, its hallucinogenic properties weren't known until 1945 when a Swiss chemist experienced its effects. It was a popular drug of abuse during the 1970s, but use waned for a number of years. Now it is available again, and it is a staple drug at raves. Sometimes it is mixed with methamphetamine, and the mixture is then substituted for MDMA.

On the party circuit, LSD is available as a liquid, but its most common form is on blotter paper or other paper soaked with the drug. It also is put onto sugar cubes or sticks of chewing gum. It can be dripped or sprayed into the eye or mixed with beverages, a method favored at concerts. In yet another method, it is dried in the indentations of small pieces of the plastic diffuser material used for fluorescent light covers. The user sucks on the bits of plastic that are called gel tabs or pyramids.

Because all LSD is produced illegally, there are no standards for packaging the final product. In liquid form, it often is in small medicine bottles such as Visine or other eye medicines, in Crystal Ice, Binaca Blast and other breath mint bottles, or in small liquid candy bottles. LSD is very potent, and because it is tasteless, colorless, and odorless, it is detectable only by chemical analysis. At $2 to $20, it is less expensive than other rave drugs.

LSD effects are unpredictable, because they vary by dosage and purity as well as by personality and environment. Physical effects include extremely dilated pupils, elevated body temperature, increased heart rate and blood pressure, speech difficulty, loss of coordination, sleeplessness, tremors, profuse sweating, goose bumps, muscle rigidity, loss of appetite, dry mouth, and acute visual sensitivity to light. Sensations and emotions may be dramatically affected, and delusions and hallucinations occur. Users sometimes experience a crossover of senses (synesthesia), hearing colors and seeing sounds.

LSD effects can be highly negative with so-called bad trips during which users are conscious, coherent and oriented but also anxious, fearful, and paranoid. They may become combative or self-destructive. Acute effects wane after two to four hours and are followed by fatigue, headache or possibly a contemplative state. The complete drug experience lasts six to twelve hours. Although tolerance develops rapidly, a week's abstinence restores sensitivity. Psychological dependence develops only after prolonged usage.

Two major arrests in late 2000 and early 2001 are expected to affect the availability, purity and price of LSD for some time. A paper dealer, who was arrested in the San Francisco area in 2000, is believed to have been the source of approximately half of all blotter paper for the past twenty years. Another arrest occurred in early 2001 in Kansas. A chemist had converted an old missile silo into a laboratory, where there was enough LSD to supply the entire country for two and a half years, more than 250 million doses

10.9 Nitrous Oxide

Nitrous oxide (N_2O) is also known as NOZ, whippets (referring to the small cartridges that resemble CO_2 cartridges), and laughing gas. It is an anesthetic, and members of the medical and dental professions sometimes abuse it. It also is used as a propellant in commercial products such as whipped cream and cooking oil spray. Symptoms of inhalation include headache, dizziness, confusion, seizures, and cardiac arrhythmias. If adequate oxygen is not supplied with the gas, there is a high risk of asphyxiation during use. This poses a real danger for young abusers who often make no effort to maintain oxygen levels. Thus, nitrous oxide contributes to the drug-related death toll among young people.

There are a number of sources for nitrous oxide. Large canisters can be stolen from medical and dental offices or supply houses. Medium size canisters can be purchased legally from high performance vehicle shops where it is used as adrenaline for performance cars. Small cartridges or whippets can be purchased for use in homemade whipped cream makers. They can be purchased in kitchen stores and via the Internet. Nitrous oxide is also readily available at the supermarket through the purchase of cans of whipped cream and other products.

Users typically fill balloons from the large sizes containers and then inhale the drug from the balloon, or they rig the container with tubes and soda bottles to form masks. With masks, two or more people can inhale directly from the container. Whippets are opened with a device called a cracker, which then fills a balloon. The crackers were designed solely for this purpose and can be purchased in head shops, sex shops, or over the Internet. Also, instructions for making them from common PVC fittings are posted on the Internet.

10.10 Mushrooms

Mushrooms are known as shrooms or magic mushrooms, and they are popular at raves. The most commonly used species in the U.S., *psilocybe mexicana* and *psilocybe cyanescen*, contain two related compounds, psilocin (4-hydroxy-N, N-dimethyltryptamine) and psilocybin (4phosphoryloxy-N, N-dimethyltryptamine). A book from Duke University Medical Center (Kuhn, et al., 1998) states that psilocybin is not the active ingredient. Apparently, the liver must first remove an extra chemical group, a phosphate group, before the remainder of the molecule (psilocin) can enter the brain.

Mushrooms are dried and ground into a brown or white powder that is put into capsules. A typical dose is four to ten milligrams, the equivalent of two to four mushrooms. Shrooms produce a shorter, milder LSD-type experience. Low doses cause feelings of relaxation, physical heaviness or lightness, and some perceptual distortions. Larger doses cause light-headedness, numbness of facial parts, shivering or sweating, nausea, and anxiety.

10.11 Other Drugs of Interest

The world of drug abuse includes look-alikes and "wannabes." For example, dimethyltryptamine (DMT) is a LSD-like hallucinogen that is sometimes referred to as the businessman's special, because the entire DMT experience develops and ends within an hour. Although the effects are similar, it causes more anxiety attacks than LSD.

There seems to be a growing fascination with Foxy (also known as Foxy Methoxy or 5-MeODIPT) and Lucky 7 (also known as T-7, 7-Up or Tripstasy or 2-C-T-7). In fact, 2-C-T-7 was featured in a *Rolling Stone* magazine article, January 31, 2002, "This much of this drug killed this boy. And it was perfectly legal." Though featuring the deaths of three young men, the major focus of the article was the fact that T-7 has not been controlled. That focus may spawn increased abuse of the substance.

Bufotenine and 5-methoxy dimethyltryptamine (5-MeeO-DMT), which are excreted by the glands of specific frogs, produce brief, hallucinogenic highs and dangerous side effects. Peyote cactus (mescaline) buttons are smoked, chewed, powdered or consumed in tea, and the physical effects are similar to amphetamines, but the subjective experience is similar to LSD. Designer mescaline-like drugs include DOM (2,5 dimethoxy-4-methylphenylisopropylamine (also known as STP), MDA, DMA, MDMA, and NEXUS (2-CB or 4-Bromo-2, 5-dimethoxyphenethylamine). These drugs have amphetamine-type effects with hallucinogenic properties. Some are not controlled substances, but some are analogs of other controlled substances and thus are illegal federally and in states with adequate analog coverage.

10.12 Marijuana and Other Plants

The plant *cannabis sativa*, or marijuana, is also a rave drug, usually smoked after the effects of MDMA have waned. Other plants also interest drug users. For example, *salvia divinorium* currently is being touted as legal marijuana. Kava is a central nervous system depressant that is widely available as a dietary supplement. In late 2001 the FDA issued an alert stating that kava has been banned in Germany due to concerns about liver damage.

Khat (*Catha edulis F*) is a native plant in East Africa and the Middle East. It contains cathinone, an amphetamine that is illegal in the U.S. According to U.S. Customs, seizures increased from 48,000 pounds in 1999 to 70,000 pounds in 2000. Cathinone is a Schedule I drug. It is present in fresh Khat leaves but deteriorates to cathine, a Schedule IV drug, within days of harvest. The effects include migraine headaches, cerebral hemorrhage, myocardial infarction, pulmonary edema, hepatic cirrhosis and decreased sex drive.

Exotic plants used in cultural or religious rituals as stimulants, depressants or other healing properties are a problem for law enforcement. Although they are traditional and legal in other countries, they violate U.S. drug laws. Controversy surrounds the prosecution of immigrants for possession of Khat. One argument is that immigrants should be educated rather than jailed, but the counter-argument is that they must abide by American laws as a condition of living here.

10.13 Over-the-Counter (OTC) Products

Coricidin Cough & Cold tablets are known as Triple C, Skittles or Daze Maker among young people who abuse them. The tablets contain 30 mg of dextromethorphan (DXM), a synthetic drug related to morphine that acts on the central nervous system to suppress the cough reflex. Therapeutic use is limited to four tablets (120 mg total) in a twenty-four-hour period, but abusers take much more, calling it "robo-dosing." They experience effects similar to alcohol, marijuana and PCP with loss of motor control and sometimes with loss of reality. Hallucinations begin with 300–900 mg. At such high doses, it acts as a dissociative anesthetic in the class with ketamine, PCP and GHB. If it is mixed with alcohol or other drugs, the effects and the risks increase. Abusers seek mood elevation, dissociation, and a dreamlike state, but they also get upset stomach, vomiting, body itching, diarrhea, red/blotchy skin, fever and abnormally fast heartbeat.

DXM often is found in pills or powder being sold as Ecstasy, either as an additive or cutting agent or as a deliberate fake. Ingesting large amounts of cough and cold medicines carries an additional risk from other ingredients in the medicines that can be harmful in such excessive quantities.

Cough syrup containing codeine is the subject of a rap song about sipping syrup, and it is a favorite substance of abuse. Over the counter products containing ephedrine are also popular. Even ordinary nutmeg and morning glory seeds can be drugs of abuse. Five tablespoons of nutmeg, which contains myristicin, will cause hallucinations, but the very unpleasant taste limits its use. A handful of morning glory seeds provides a dose of lysergic acid amide (LSA), a precursor to LSD, and produces a mild LSD-type trip.

10.14 Old Drugs, New Issues

Many aspects of raves and rave drugs are unique. The youth and vulnerability of ravers, together with their convictions that their drugs of choice are harmless, create health and social problems. They are problems worthy of attention now. Later may be too late for the many young people who are caught up in the rave scene.

Endnote

1. "X" and Ecstasy refer to 3,4 methylenedioxymethamphetamine.

References

Boal, M. (January 31, 2002). "This much of this drug killed this boy. And it was perfectly legal." *Rolling Stone*. New York. Retrieved June 30, 2002 from http://pqasb.pqarchiver.com/rollingstone/abstract/

Cohen, R.S. (1998). *The Love Drug: Marching to the Beat of Ecstasy*. Haworth Medical Press.

Concar, D. (June 21, 1977). "After the rave, the ecstasy hangover." *New Scientist Planet Science*. Retrieved June 30 from http://www.bassdove.demon.co.uk/rave.htm

Drug Enforcement Agency (DEA). Diversion Control Program. (August, 2001). "Drugs and chemicals of concern: Gamma hydroxybutyric acid (GHB, liquid X, Goop, Georgia Home Boy)." Retrieved June 30, 2002 from http://www.deadiversion.usdoj.gov/drugs_concern/ghb/summary.htm

Elwood, W. (1998). "Fry: A study of adolescent use of embalming fluid with marijuana and tobacco." Texas Commission on Alcoholism and Drug Abuse (TCADA) Research Brief. Retrieved from http://www.tcada.state.tx.us/research/fry.html

Kuhn, C., Swartzwelder, S., Wilson, W. (1998). *Buzzed: The Straight Facts about the Most Used and Abused Drugs from Alcohol to Ecstas*y. New York: W.W. Norton.

Reneman, L., Booij, J., de Bruin, K., Reitsma, J.B., de Wolff, F.A., Gunning, W.B. et al. (2001). "Effects of dose, sex, and long-term abstention from use on toxic effects of MDMA (ecstasy) on brain serotonin neurons." *Lancet*, 358, 9296, 1864–1869.

Ricaurte, G.A., Yuan, J., McCann, U.D. (2000). "(+/-)3,4-methylenedioxymethamphetamine ("Ecstasy")-induced serotonin neurotoxicity: Studies in animals." *Neuropsychobiology*, 42, 1, 5–10.

Spicuzza, M. (March 23, 2000). "Nightly Grind." *San Jose Metro*. Retrieved June 30, 2002 from http://www.alternet.org/story.html?StoryID=128

Swann, N. (1996). "Response to escalating methamphetamine abuse builds on NIDA-funded research." *NIDA Notes*, 5, 11. Retrieved June 30, 2002 from http://www.drugabuse.gov/NIDA_Notes/NNVol11N5/Escalating.html

Chapter 11

Medicinal Drugs: Labels and Warnings

Johan J. de Gier

Synopsis

11.1 Introduction

A. Problem background

Traffic crashes in the fifteen member states of the European Union (EU) lead to 50,000 fatalities and more than 1.5 million injured people each year. Based on current statistics, one out of three Europeans will one day be hospitalized as a result of a traffic crash (Cornelissen, 1997). These figures conceal immeasurable loss and human suffering, as well as considerable loss in economic terms, annually costing our society over 70 billion ECU (*White Paper on Transport Policy*, COM 92/494, European Commission).

It is widely recognized that alcohol use is a causal factor in 20 to 40 percent of fatal road crashes. Medicinal drugs are also known to impair driving ability. Available data allow one to conclude, for example, that use of the most frequently prescribed benzodiazepine tranquilizers more than doubles the risk of injurious accidents (Ray et al., 1992). Neutel (1995) reports extremely high relative risk ratios during the first two weeks of treatment with these drugs. Specifically, there is a five to six fold increase in crash risk, which is comparable to the increased risk with 0.10 percent blood alcohol concentration (BAC).

Impairing medicines are used by an average of ten percent of the adult driver population in the EU. If these users are driving with even twice the risk of being involved in a traffic crash, it can be estimated that the drugs are causing 4,500 deaths, 135,000 injuries and 6.3 billion ECU damage to society each year (De Gier, 1995). This kind of information is critically relevant to traffic safety and needs to be available to physicians and patients. From a public standpoint, the increased relative risk clearly is unacceptable, and policy measures are needed in this area.

B. Labeling to communicate risk

It is widely acknowledged that patients require counseling about the effects of medicinal drugs on driving skills, but it is unrealistic to rely upon the advice of drug manufacturers for the information for that purpose. This problem is well known to prescribing physicians and dispensing pharmacists. Too often the warnings provided in package inserts are vague or illogical, and they sometimes are actually misleading.

To illustrate these kinds of problems, a typical general warning for physicians, pharmacists and patients of a drug's adverse effects on the central nervous system lists "anxiety, confusion, dizziness, euphoria, floating feeling, insomnia, nervousness, paresthesia, somnolence and tremor." An additional warning notes that the "drowsiness and dizziness related to use of the drug may impair mental and/or physical abilities required for the performance of potentially hazardous tasks such as driving or operating machines." In addition to this very general caution, a more specific warning alerts patients to "use caution in such activities until their individual responses to that drug have been well stabilized."

A question arises as to whether the physician's instruction to patients really should be limited to a warning to "allow time to stabilize your responses to the drug before driving." The answer is, "Certainly not." A more effective instruction to the patient, and the most reasonable interpretation of the expected drug effects, would be to advise the patient to avoid driving for a specific time period after each dose of the drug. A major impediment to appropriate warnings, however, is that the drug regulatory authorities approve manufacturers' inadequate statements. Thus, it becomes the physician's responsibility to properly advise the patient. In this chapter opportunities for improving this situation will be discussed. After the description of current labelling systems, primarily based on European experiences, the roles of health care providers and patients will be highlighted.

11.2. Current Labeling Systems

A. Warning systems for drugs and driving

Information about increased crash risk as a consequence of using hazardous therapeutic drugs must be meaningfully communicated to patients. The simplest way to achieve this would be by means of clear warning labels on the packages. Most EU member states, however, do not require exterior warnings on packaging, and patients are informed about impairing effects only by the package insert. Since 1992, European legislation has required warnings regarding the ability to drive or use machines, written in lay language, to be part of the content of the patient drug information leaflet (Council Directive 92/27/EEC).

Exterior warning labels on packaging were introduced in the Netherlands and the Nordic countries in the early seventies and eighties, respectively. A warning system was introduced in 1973 as a practice guideline by the Dutch professional organizations of physicians and pharmacists. It consists of a list of drugs that can adversely affect driving. The listing is based on each drug's pharmacodynamic profile or its therapeutic class. A committee of the Royal Dutch Society for the Advancement of Pharmacy (KNMP) made the label assignments for all drugs licensed in the Netherlands.

Pharmacists are advised to attach a yellow label with black letters for drugs that can adversely affect driving performance. In addition, two other possibilities exist under the practice guideline. One option is that if the physician does not want his patient to be warned of driving impairment, he may tell the pharmacy not to attach the yellow label. Also, if the physician does not want his patient to drive at all, he may ask the pharmacist to attach a red label with text stating that driving is forbidden while using the drug. This prohibition is possible, because Dutch traffic law prohibits driving a vehicle while under the influence of a drug that the driver knows, or should reasonably know, can impair driving performance to a degree that makes him or her unable to drive safely.

In practice, only the use of the yellow label has been accepted and implemented. With the computerization of pharmacy practices, that warning is nowadays routinely printed on the dispensing label, together with other directions for use of the medicine. At the present time, yellow labels are used as extra warnings by approximately two-thirds of Dutch community pharmacists. Physicians never request that the warning should not be affixed, nor do they request the red label, which is presently unknown to many pharmacists.

A package label warning was introduced in Norway in 1981, and it was adopted by Denmark, Finland, Iceland, and Sweden in 1983. A committee of experts created the label, and the Nordic Committee on Medicines oversees the warning system. A label showing a red triangle is printed by the manufacturer on all packages of drugs in the category "especially dangerous," which includes sedative-hypnotics, opioid analgesics and antitussives, antihistamines, some anti-epileptics, centrally acting muscle relaxants and psychostimulants. At the request of the prescribing physician, the label may be affixed to drugs within another category entitled "potentially dangerous," which includes nonnarcotic analgesics, anti-diabetics, anorexants, anti-Parkinson's drugs, hypotensives, neuroleptics, antidepressants, anticholinergics and opthalmologicals. Initially, in dispensing medication labelled this way, pharmacists were also required to provide the patient with a special leaflet containing additional information. This requirement, however, was dropped after three years, because the additional information was judged redundant.

Other systems have been proposed in Belgium, Spain and France. Detailed information is available, however, only for the system proposed in France where it was decided two years ago to have all packages of psychotropic medication show a warning symbol (red triangle with a black care in the centre).

B. Deficiencies of the present systems

The dichotomous systems introduced in the Netherlands and the Nordic countries fail to distinguish either between drugs in the same therapeutic class that could have markedly different effects on driving ability or between different doses of the same drugs. These and other deficiencies are probably responsible for the fact that most patients do not alter their driving behaviors in any significant way as a direct result of the labels. A small-scale questionnaire survey of Dutch patients who were receiving psychotropic medications revealed that 75 percent of them did not respond appropriately (Stout and De Gier, 1982). Patients reported that they used less of their medications, interrupted the dosing regimens, or simply ignored the warning because they did not realize it applied to them.

A second study was carried out subsequent to a general public campaign concerning the influence of drugs on driving (De Rooij and Leufkens, 1988). A questionnaire was distributed to 1,043 patients who were receiving a drug with a yellow label. This study revealed that only 30 percent of the respondents had changed their behavior towards driving. The changes included not driving, driving less, and driving more carefully.

Faced with a difficult decision regarding labelling for the new antihistamine, cetirizine, the KNMP has decided to defer making the decision. It awaits categorization of the drug according to a somewhat more informative Pan-European warning system of the EU's Medicines Evaluation Agency (EMEA).

The Swedish national pharmacy company Apoteksbolaget AB published an evaluation of the Nordic red triangle system in 1987 (Lisper, 1987). A survey of a sample of the general public was conducted by questionnaire to investigate understanding of the meaning of the red triangle. The question was asked, "If you see a red triangle on an medicine box, what does that mean to you?" About half of the respondents said they understood it to mean that one should not drive a car when taking such a medicine. The other half thought it was similar to other warnings, such as "keep out of reach of children," "dangerous" or "poison".

C. Initiative toward a new system

In 1987 the need for an improved warning system for drugs and driving was strongly expressed by a Dutch National Task Force of experts in medicine, pharmacy, law and traffic safety (Van Gruting and de Gier, 1990). The task force emphasized that new scientific knowledge should be applied in compiling drug lists and in improving prescribing and dispensing practices. Consequently, the implementation of a three-tier warning system for identifying the driving hazard potential of every new drug has been proposed by an international group of experts. In consensus, the expert panel proposed that the system be a single European drug label warning system (Wolschrijn et al., 1991). Implementation of such a system would increase the awareness of the general public, healthcare providers and policy makers. To the extent that it might result in healthcare providers regularly prescribing and dispensing the least impairing of several equally efficacious medicines, a major contribution to preventing driving while impaired by medicinal drugs would be expected.

11.3 Opportunities for Improving Label Warnings

A. European Union's *Note for Guidance . . .*

The new warning system based on consensus among scientists and introduced in 1991 (Wolschrijn et al., 1991) was meant to replace the dichotomous systems. The major improvement of the system was its scheme for categorizing drugs according to their potential for impairing driving skills. The European drug regulatory authorities adopted a *Note for Guidance for the Summary of Product Characteristics*, SPC (III/9163/90-EN, final approval by the Committee for Proprietary Medicinal Products 16 October 1991).

In 1998 a survey was conducted to determine how responsible regulatory authorities in the different European countries have reacted to this *Note for Guidance* (De Gier, 1998). The report of survey findings highlights the European ministers of transport resolve that EU member states should encourage the systematic printing of a warning symbol on the packaging of medicines likely to impair driving (ECMT/CM 93/5/Final). The *Note for Guidance* provides the framework needed to categorize drugs in order to provide three different warning symbols reflecting the following categories of Article 4.7 of the SPC ("Effects on ability to drive and use machines"):

On the basis of:

- the pharmacodynamic profile, reported ADR and/or
- impairment of driving performance or performance related to driving, the medicine is:
  1. presumed to be safe or unlikely to produce an effect;
  2. likely to produce minor or moderate adverse effects;
  3. likely to produce severe effects or presumed to be potentially dangerous.

For situations 2 and 3, special precautions for use/warnings relevant to the categorization should be mentioned.

The original *Note for Guidance* (III/9163/ 90-EN) has been included in the rules governing medicinal products in the European Union (Notice to Applicants, Volume 2A, Procedures for marketing authorization, July 1997). Comparing the latest version to the original, the phrase "relevant to the categorization" in the last sentence now is lacking. Also, the notation "1, 2 and 3" for the different categorizations in the original text has been replaced by "a, b and c" in the most recent version. It is likely that these changes were made to avoid emphasis on a 'categorization system', since the application of such a system for drugs and pregnancy was somewhat controversial at that time.

The objective of the 1998 survey of drug regulatory authorities was to provide an overview of opinions and descriptions of the procedures for assessing the warnings about effects on ability to drive and use machines. The following summary was given in the report (De Gier, 1998).

B. Opinions concerning the categorizations mentioned in *Note for Guidance . . .*

Regulatory authorities made two important comments in giving their opinions on the proposed categorization system. First, the relevant descriptions in the *Note for Guidance* were not understood to be a categorization system for the purpose of improving warnings. Consequently, the present procedures for assigning warnings, based on descriptions of the drug's known side effects as provided by the drug manufacturers, were considered sufficient for the purpose of applying the *Note for Guidance*. Second, some regulatory authorities suggested that the categorizations be used for practical reference in addition to the statements on side effects. They believed a category would give the "right weight" to the descriptions, but they also indicated that for that purpose, the terminology such as minor, moderate and severe needed to be defined. Hence, the recommendation is first of all to discuss with the EU's regulatory authorities how a three-tier categorization system can be used as practical reference in order to improve warnings for patients.

C. Procedures for assessing warnings and guidelines for allowing categorization

Generally speaking, the drug regulatory authorities review the data provided by the drug manufacturers and assess whether these data support statements in the *Summary of Product Characteristics*. There are no criteria stipulating the number of reports or the kinds of tests that are needed as a basis for their assessments. It is a case-by-case assessment. Furthermore, the methodology of experimental research on drug effects is still poorly described, although adequate descriptive information exists based on the consensus of scientific opinion.

Some harmonization has been achieved, however. For example, in the provision of a specific *Note for Guidance on the Summary of Product Characteristics* of benzodiazepines as anxiolytics, the recommendation for information to be contained in the warning about the effects of these drugs on the ability to drive and use machines has been standardized. It offers no opportunity, however, for distinguishing between various benzodiazepines when data from experimental or pharmacoepidemiological research demonstrates different behavioral toxicities. Unfortunately, this situation has not been recognized by the drug regulatory authorities as an obstacle to accurate categorization. Hence, it is recommended that better guidelines be established to assist drug manufacturers to select appropriate drug-testing methodologies and to reconsider the use of standard information for the warning section in the *Summary of Product Characteristics*.

D. Failure to categorize

A major problem in the categorization of drugs will be the lack of support from the drug manufacturers who have to submit the relevant data. Even if a standardized methodology is applied to test a drug's impairing properties, there will always be discussion with drug companies. If their drug has been found to be impairing, the issue will be whether it will be assigned to a different category than non-impairing drugs belonging to the same therapeutic class. Drug manufacturers can be expected to fully approve categorization only when their drug can be distinguished as being safer than competitors' drugs.

Some drug regulatory authorities indicated that experimental research alone is not sufficiently convincing evidence to support the formulation of different warnings. They suggested that revision of the warning system should be based on results obtained from studies of large populations who have used the drugs. They propose that the study investigators should assess the risk potential of accident involvement for each individual drug. It is unclear whether there will be a need for the European Medicines Evaluation Agency (EMEA) to provide specific expertise in this area. EMEA is responsible for international harmonization in the approval of pharmaceutical products and also for coordination of national activities in the area of post-marketing surveillance. It is an EMEA responsibility to ensure the safety of medicinal products circulating within the Community. Although most regulatory authorities feel much more comfortable selecting their own experts, some of them would welcome specific expertise provided by EMEA. It is recommended that EMEA initiate an investigation to decide whether or not it should coordinate large-scale, case controlled pharmacoepidemiological surveys. These would use existing databases in different Member States to determine the relative risks of traffic crashes for users of all drugs identified as potentially dangerous.

E. Examples of warnings in the summary of product characteristics

It is an exception, rather than the general practice, whenever the statement in the driving warning is explicit. An example of such an exception is the clear statement in Finland for buspirone (an anxiolytic): "Does not affect driving . . ." (See Table 11.1). The survey found that most driving warnings provided by the different regulatory authorities were vague, illogical and sometimes misleading. In general, the pattern of the warming is the following. The information starts with a list of the drug's effects on the central nervous system. It then states that these effects may impair mental and physical abilities required for the performance of potentially hazardous tasks. The warning ends with the advice that patients should be told to use caution in such activities until their individual responses to the drug have been well established. There is no advice about how to assess or recognize the individual patient's susceptibility to drug impairment.

Table 11.1
Examples of Discrepancies in the Driving Warnings in Different Member States

Drug	EU Member State	Driving Warning in the SPC
Citalopram (anti-depressant)	Spain	Does not impair . . . However, patients should be cautioned . . .
	United Kingdom	Does not impair . . . However, some impairment expected . . .
	Belgium	Does not impair . . . Does not potentiate alcohol effects . . .
	France	Does not show impairment but may affect skills . . .
	Netherlands	May impair . . . Patients should be cautioned . . .
Piracetam (nootropic)	Finland	Some patients may experience drowsiness . . . Caution advised for…
	Belgium	(No data provided in the SPC)
	United Kingdom	No experience on driving . . . Caution should be exercised . . .
Topiramate (anti-epileptic)	France	(Long list of side effects) . . . Patients should be warned . . .
	Finland	May impede motor skills . . .
	United Kingdom	Drowsiness is likely to occur . . . More sedating than other anti-epileptic drugs . . . Could be potentially dangerous . . .
	Belgium	Drowsiness and dizziness are minor side effects . . . But patients should be warned . . .
Lamotrigine (anti-epileptic)	Netherlands	Due to CNS effects patients should be cautious . . .
	Finland	Because of individual response patient has to consult his doctor
Nefazodone (anti-depressant)	United Kingdom	Modest to no impairment . . . However, patients should be cautioned . . .
	Finland	Take into account that the ability to react will slow down . . .
Reboxetine (anti-depressant)	Germany	Does not impair . . . However, patients should be cautioned . . .
	Finland	Patients must be warned about effects on driving . . .
Buspirone (anxiolytic)	Spain	Patients should be warned about effects and advised not to drive . . .
	Finland	Does not affect driving . . .

It would be advisable to investigate in the different Member States what impact present package insert warnings have on physicians' attitudes towards instructing their patients about driving or operating machines, and on patients' intentions and attitudes about changing their customary behaviors while taking the drug. The results will constitute much needed feedback to drug regulatory authorities and drug companies who are responsible for providing the warnings.

F. Opportunities to improve warnings

A slight majority of survey respondents believe that a categorization system could improve the effectiveness of warnings, compared to the long lists of side effects that are currently provided as warnings. The new European *Guideline* on this subject (III/5218/97, final approval September 1998) provides an opportunity to improve the readability of the label and package inserts with specific guidelines for certain categories of medicinal drugs. Clear statements are prescribed, and pictograms may be used as an additional measure if they make the message clearer to the patient.

There are current movements towards categorization systems for the purpose of improving warnings in at least five member states: Belgium, Germany, the Netherlands, France and Spain.

In 2001 Spain became the second country in Europe to officially introduce a categorization system for drugs having a potentially dangerous effect on driving (Del Rio Garcia, 2001). Belgium was the first country that officially introduced the categorization system in April 1999, at the time that the traffic law was changed into a "zero tolerance" law for illicit drugs (Charlier et al., 1999). Medicinal drugs were not included in this new law, but the Belgian minister of transport considered these to be dealt with by preventive measures, such as prescribing and dispensing guidelines and a clear patient information leaflet. Furthermore, professional organizations in these countries have applied the same system in their efforts to support physicians and pharmacists in selecting relatively safer drugs for patients who drive.

The categorization system was originally proposed in 1991 by a group of international experts who wanted a system allowing health care providers and patients to understand more easily the severity of impairment by medicinal psychotropic medicines (Wolschrijn et al., 1991).

Table 11.2

Category	Impairment description for medicinal drugs	Comparison with Blood Alcohol Concentration (BAC)
I	Presumed to be safe or unlikely to produce an effect	Equivalent to BAC < 0.5 g/l (<0.05%)
II	Likely to produce minor or moderate adverse effects	Equivalent to BAC 0.5–0.8 g/l (0.05–0.08%)
III	Likely to produce severe or presumed to be potentially dangerous	Equivalent to BAC > 0.8 g/l (>0.08%)

In order to make the users of the categorization system aware of the meaning of each category, a comparison to the effects of alcohol, which are well known, was suggested by researchers in experimental psychopharmacology in the Netherlands, based on the views on test validation expressed several years ago (O'Hanlon, 1986). Data collected in experimental research, in which over-the-road driving tests have been applied with most frequently used medicinal drugs and alcohol (as "calibration"), have allowed researchers to interpret weaving effects by any drug as equivalent to that produced by a particular blood alcohol concentration (see Table 11.2).

The most important advantage of the three-tier system over "older" dichotomous drug class-based systems or systems based on quotations of long lists of side effects is the focus on the least impairing medications in each therapeutic class.

Since these initiatives will have an effect on the views of patients, physicians and pharmacists, it would be advisable for them to be in accordance with present European Directives and Guidelines aimed at improving the readability of labels and package inserts. Categorization and warning symbols, based on scientific consensus, have been shown to be feasible. By investigating the acceptance of a new warning symbol among patients, health care providers and drug manufacturers, drug regulatory authorities could become more proactive in response to the actual needs of those who use the information presented in the package inserts.

11.4 The Role of Healthcare Professionals

Standard protocols are followed in medical care for diagnosing and treating various diseases and conditions. In those cases where medication is selected as the preferred treatment option, medicines with known side effects that could harm the patient or diminish the drug's action should be avoided. It now is becoming standard pharmaceutical practice to follow up patients who report drug related problems that caused either treatment failure or harm to the patient (Cipolle et al., 1998; Van Mil, 2000).

Special attention is normally given to patients receiving a drug for the first time. In cases in which pharmacists have built trusting relationships with patients, it is feasible to extend their services to include a duty of care for the safe use of medication. Such pharmaceutical care is being well received not only by pharmacists but also by health care authorities in many European countries, the USA, and Australia. These authorities are aware that valuable pharmaceutical knowledge has been under-utilized for many years.

A. Guidelines for prescribing physicians and dispensing pharmacists

Guidelines for prescribing and dispensing practices must ensure that patients receive the maximum benefit of extant knowledge about drugs. Ideally, all advice given to patients will have the approval of the respective professional organizations of physicians and pharmacists. Educators and trainers should be involved in teaching about this process, so that health care providers enter their professions with an understanding of their responsibilities and the advice they should give. In addition, present knowledge of drug categorization should be used to adjust the existing guidelines for all major complaints and illnesses for which psychotropic drugs are prescribed. In other words, if a psychotropic medication is the selected treatment option, the guidelines must document the benefits of using the least impairing drug within that therapeutic class.

B. Consumer and patient education

Patient education has to be a substantial part of the prescribing and dispensing guidelines. Patients require clear instruction about how to recognize undesirable side effects of a drug. They need to understand how their skills may be affected at the initiation of treatment, as well as at all follow-up visits if medications are prescribed repeatedly. The information should be presented both orally and in writing for maximum effectiveness. In rational prescribing and dispensing the following key messages can be de-

Table 11.3
Guidelines for Prescribing and Dispensing Potentially Impairing Medicines

	Prescribing Guidelines	Dispensing Guidelines
1.	Realize that the use of some psychoactive drugs has been associated with an increased risk of causing an injurious accident and that patients should receive this information.	Discuss with prescribing physician what patient information (written and oral) should be provided at the first delivery of a particular impairing drug.
2.	Consider an alternative in the light of experimental research showing large differences between the effects on driving performance of various drugs within the same therapeutic class.	Inform the prescribing physician that alternative drugs exist in case a drug in class II or III has been prescribed, and inform the patient.
3.	Start with the lowest doses of psychoactive medical drugs and whenever possible avoid multiple dosing over the day.	Advise the physician to prescribe the lowest effective dose of a particular psychoactive medicinal drug and to avoid multiple dosing over the day. Inform the patient.
4.	Do not reflexively "double the dose" if patients fail to respond to psychoactive medication.	Advise the physician to try another drug if the patient reports a lack of efficacy after beginning treatment and inform the patient. If higher doses are needed advise the patient to use the largest part before sleep.
5.	Avoid prescribing different psychoactive drugs in combination.	Explain to the patient that poly-therapy with psychoactive drugs is always an experiment with the patient's safety and to avoid driving if treatment cannot be adjusted.
6.	Do not rely upon the manufacturers' advice for counselling patients about the effects of drug upon driving	Explain to the patient why warnings provided by the manufacturer about their drug's effects on driving are vague, illogical and sometime misleading.
7.	Advise patients concerning the ways they can minimize the risk of causing a traffic accident if it is impossible to avoid prescribing an obviously impairing drug or one with unknown impairing potential (See Table 11.4).	Advise the patient the ways they can minimize the risk of causing a traffic accident if they have to use a drug with an impairing potential (See Table 11.4).
8.	Monitor the patient's driving experience with the drug.	Monitor the patient's driving experience with the drug (e.g., at the first refill) and report back to the physician or ask the patient to inform the physician

Table 11.4
Prescribing and Dispensing Information: Guidelines by Drug Class

Drug Class (Little/no impairment)	Risk Factors	Prescribing Information	Dispensing Information
Hypnotics			
Take at night. Temazebpam 10 mg Lormetazepam 1 mg Zolpidem 10 mg	Combination with other psychoactive drugs Liver and/or renal dysfunction Elderly patients: 1/2 the normal dose	Avoid prescribing for longer than 2–4 weeks	Avoid alcohol while taking this drug. Recognize signs[1] of impaired driving. Stop driving if any occur. Avoid taking longer than 2–4 weeks and do not take more than one at night.
Tranquilizers			
No impairment Buspirone 10 mg	No specific risk factors known	Avoid combination with selective serotonin reuptake inhibitors (SSRIs) because of reduced therapeutic effect. Can combine for one week with oxazepam 10 mg t.d.s. if therapeutic response is inadequate (forbid driving).	Avoid alcohol while taking this drug. Recognize signs[1] of impaired driving. Stop driving if any occur.

fined as essential parts (general and drug specific) of the guidelines to be developed for some frequently used therapeutic drug classes (O'Hanlon, 1995; ICADTS Working Group Report on Prescribing and Dispensing Guidelines for Medicinal Drugs Affecting Driving Performance, 2001).

The prescribing and dispensing information needs to include drug class-specific guidelines. Table 11.3 presents examples of specific guidelines. They should include identification of the least impairing drugs within the class, risk factors with each, together with standard prescribing and dispensing information. Although it will be impossible to recommend an alternate drug if the class does not include any really safe drugs (e.g. the hypnotics), there clearly are safer alternatives for anxiolytics and antidepressants that can be recommended. For example, selective serotonin reuptake inhibitors are safer antidepressants that produce little or no impairment of driving performance, as shown in experimental and epidemiological studies (Ramaekers, 1998; Barbone et al., 1998). These drugs may also be effective in the treatment of anxiety disorders (Ballenger, 1999). Another safer alternative in treating generalized anxiety disorders is venlafaxine, an antidepressant that acts by selectively inhibiting serotonin and norepinephrine reuptake (O'Hanlon et al., 1998).

11.5 Conclusions

A scenario that will improve the present situation of inefficient warning systems in most countries will be a joint action program decided by the authorities responsible for drug regulation, public and environmental health, and transport safety and consumer affairs together. This action program is required to implement, maintain, and evaluate a new warning system for drugs that affect driving ability based on drug categorization. New partners, in particular the pharmaceutical industry, organizations of physicians, pharmacists and patients, as well as insurance companies, should be invited to take part. These new partners have a greater awareness of health issues as a result of health education campaigns and public information provided through new media, such as the worldwide web. They realize that the health care industry is changing. Prevention and health-related quality of life issues are becoming determining factors for both policy makers and payers of health care costs.

Drug regulatory authorities are key players in the process of restructuring drug testing programs to assess a drug's potential for impairing psychomotor and driving performance. Experts in the field of human psychopharmacology who have assessed the effects of drugs on driving have provided the relevant information needed to perform this task. The impact of these efforts on drug regulation has been noticed, but it has not had a significant effect on improving warning systems for patients who drive. Experts should be more effective in disseminating their research data to the public, health care providers, and policy makers. Physicians and pharmacists can contribute to the use of safer drugs by monitoring patient outcomes with respect to behavioral impairment. By selecting the least impairing drug in their prescribing and dispensing practices, they play a significant role in enhancing public safety. In order to be able to do this, they have to know how to assess the level of impairment caused by each individual drug. This information is already available for many frequently used "old" and many new medicines. The time has come for patient and consumer organizations to ask who is responsible for not applying this knowledge. It is no option to carry on with the current registration procedures that prevent health care providers and patients from receiving information that would allow them to select and to use the least impairing drug for treatment.

References

Ballenger, J.C. (1999). "Current treatments of anxiety disorders in adults." *Biol Psychiatry*, 46, 1579–1594.

Barbone, F., McMahon, A.D., Davey, P.G., Morris, A.D., Reid, I.C., McDevitt, D.G., et al. (1998). "Association of road-traffic accidents with benzodiazepine use." *Lancet*, 352, 331–1336.

Charlier, C.J., Grenez, O.E., Maes, V.A., Smet, H.C., Verstraete, A.G., Wennig, R.M. (1999). *Invloed van Geneesmiddelen op de Rijvaardigheid* [Impairing effects of medicinal drugs on driving performance]. Brussels, Belgian Institutue for Traffic Safety (BIVV).

Cipolle, R.J., Strand, L.M., and Morley, P.C. (1998). *Pharmaceutical care practice*. New York: McGraw-Hill.

Cornelissen, P.A.M. (1997). "A shared responsibility." Welcome address at the Symposium on Road Safety in Europe. European Parliament, 14 October 1997, Brussels.

De Gier, J.J. (1995). *Drugs Other than Alcohol and Driving in the European Union*. Tech Report HP 95-54. Institute for Human Psychopharmacology, University of Limburg, Maastricht, The Netherlands.

De Gier, J.J. (1998). "Drugs and driving research: Application of results by drug regulatory authorities." *Hum Psychopharmacol Clin Exp*, 13, S133–136.

De Gier, J.J. (1998). *Survey on Warning Systems for Medicinal Drugs Affecting Driving Performance*. Tech Report DGC: 98-02. Institute for Human Psychopharmacology, University of Maastricht, The Netherlands.

De Rooij, F.A., and Leufkens, H.G.M. (1988). *Evaluatie-onderzoek van de Voorlichtings-campagne "Geneesmiddelen en Reactie-vermogen* [Evaluation of the public campaign on drugs and driving]." Tech Report. Utrecht University, Utrecht, The Netherlands.

Del Rio Gracia, M.C., Alvarez Gonzalez, F.J., Gonzalez Luque, J.C. *Guía de prescripción farmacológica y seguridad via*l. Dirrección General de Tráfico, Madrid, 2001.

International Council on Alcohol, Drugs and Traffic Safety (ICADTS). (2001). Working group on prescribing and dispensing guidelines for medicinal drugs affecting driving performance. Oosterhout, The Netherlands.

Lisper B. (1987). Personal communication.

Neutel, C.I. (1995). "Risk of traffic accident injury after a prescription for a benzodiazepine." *Ann Epidemiol*, 5, 239–244.

O'Hanlon, J.F. (1995). "Ten ways for physicians to minimize the risk of patients causing traffic accidents while under the influence of prescribed medication." *Primary Care Psychiatry*, 1, 77–85.

O'Hanlon, J.F., Brookhuis, K.A., Louwerens, J.W., Volkerts, E.R. "Performance testing as part of drug registration," In J.F. O'Hanlon and De Gier, J.J. (Eds.), *Drugs and Driving* (pp. 311–330). London: Taylor and Francis.

O'Hanlon, J.F., Robbe, H.W.J., Vermeeren, A., Van Leeuwen, C., and Danjou, P.E. (1998). "Venlafaxine's effects on healthy volunteers' driving, psychomotor, and vigilance performance during fifteen-day fixed and incremental dosing regimens." *J Clin Psycho-pharmacol*, 18, 212–221.

Ramaekers, J.G. (1998). *Behavioural Toxicity of Medicinal Drugs*. Thesis, Maastricht University, The Netherlands.

Ray, W.A., Fought, R.L., and Decker, M.D. (1992). "Psychoactive drugs and the risk of injurious motor vehicle crashes in elderly drivers." *Am J Epidemiol*, 136, 873–883.

Stout, Q.F. and De Gier, J.J. (1982). "Effect van de geel-zwarte rijvaardigheidssticker op geneesmiddelen [Effect of the yellow-black driving ability sticker on medicines]." *Pharm Wkbld*, 117, 449–455.

Van Gruting, C.W.D., and De Gier, J.J. (1990). *Rapport van de Overleggroep Genees-middelen en Reactievermogen* [Report of the Task Force on Drugs and Driving]. STYX Publications, Groningen, The Netherlands.

Van Mil, J.W.F. (2000). *Pharmaceutical Care: The Future of Pharmacy*. Dissertation, University of Groningen, The Netherlands.

Wolschrijn, H., De Gier, J.J. and De Smet, P.A.G.M. (1991). *Drugs and Driving: A New Categorization System for Drugs Affecting Psychomotor Performance*. Tech Report. Institute for Drugs, Safety and Behavior. University of Limburg. The Netherlands.

Chapter 12

Workplace Drug Testing

Anne D. ImObersteg

Synopsis

12.1 Introduction

During the period 1955 to 1980 the United States experienced a twenty-fold increase in the use of illegal drugs (Nicoli, 1986). The highest illicit drug use rates are among persons aged eighteen to twenty years, the emerging work force in America. In 2000, about 14 million Americans used illegal drugs within one month of a federal survey (DHHS, 2000). This figure represents approximately 6.3 percent of the total population. The abused drugs varied according to age and geographical region with the most popular drug being marijuana and hashish, followed by pain relievers (nonmedical use), cocaine, and other drugs.

In 1993, the societal cost of alcohol and drug abuse reached $400 billion dollars, making it one of the most costly activities in American society (Columbia, 1993). Drug abuse has been correlated with a decline in corporate profitability and an increase in the occurrence of work-related accidents. Workplace drug use is costly to the business owner and industry, and it poses a substantial safety risk to the drug users, coworkers, and the general public. Increased absenteeism, workplace accidents, workers' compensation claims, medical costs and decreased productivity all negatively affect the economy (DHHS, 1998). A United States Postal Service study found that employees who tested positive on their pre-employment drug screen were absent more than twice as often as their drug-free colleagues and had 85 percent more injuries (Normand et al., 1990). Lost productivity and untimely death or illness associated with drug abuse cost American businesses almost $81.6 billion dollars a year (DHHS, 1995).

No occupation is totally free from workers who suffer the destructive effects of drug abuse, but some have been identified as being more at risk than others: construction workers (15.6 percent), sales personnel (11.4 percent), food or drink servers (11.2 percent), laborers (10.6 percent), and machine operators and inspectors (10.5 percent) (DHHS, 1997). Most alarming, a survey determined that more than 60 percent of adult Americans know people who have gone to their place of employment under the influence of either alcohol or other drugs (Hazelden, 1996). In fact, it is estimated that 77 percent of illegal drug users are currently working and affecting the efficiency of the workplace (DHHS, 1991).

12.2 Development of Drug Testing Programs

The interest of an employer in the productivity and welfare of his employees is not a new concept. As early as 1914, a Ford Motor Company profit sharing plan was supplemented by sociological department visits to workers' homes to evaluate their lives in terms of thrift, virtue and sobriety (SAMHSA, 2001). Those employees who did not meet Ford standards had their profit sharing suspended, and if amends were not made within six months, they lost their jobs as well. In the 1940s accidents and absenteeism in the Kaiser shipyards were so prevalent that Kaiser created an in-house healthcare system financed by payroll deductions. These early attempts by industry leaders to identify drug use risk factors were fundamentally flawed, because the plans were unregulated, lacked clear policy statements, and had no standards of performance.

Interest in widespread drug screening developed during the 1960s and 1970s when the military began to screen soldiers returning from duty in Vietnam to identify heroin users. In 1980, the United States Department of Defense published a survey of substance abuse among military personnel and reported 26 percent overall drug use in the military services (Burt et al., 1980). The highest use was among men ages 18–25 years with rates of almost 47 percent in the Navy and Marine Corps. This renewed interest in drug screening raised the issue of establishing clear and comprehensive guidelines.

A. Regulated testing

In 1983, the first regulated program began to take shape. The U.S. Department of Transportation (DOT) in conjunction with the National Institute on Drug Abuse (NIDA) drafted a program of regulated testing. It was initiated in response to the National Transportation Safety Board's (NTSB) concern about the increase in drug and alcohol-related crashes in the transportation industry (Walsh, 1998). It was not until 1986, however, when President Reagan's Commission on Organized Crime released a report connecting drug use with trafficking and organized crime that regulated testing got into full swing (USGPO, 1986). In the report, the commission called upon the president to issue a policy statement expressing the unacceptability of drug use among federal employees and outlining the measures that must be taken to achieve the commission's goals.

The federal government's interest in establishing conditions for employment was not entirely altruistic; a drug testing policy would help governmental agencies accomplish their mission, promote the well being of employees and increase productivity. On September 15, 1986, President Reagan signed the executive order that was the first step toward the ultimate goal of a drug-free federal workplace (EO12564, 1986). The order recognized the impact of drug use in the workplace and established the unprecedented rule of prohibiting federal employees from using illegal drugs on or off duty. The order states in part:

> The Federal Government, as the largest employer in the Nation, can and should show the way towards achieving drug-free workplaces through a program designed to offer drug users a helping hand and, at the same time, demonstrating to drug users and potential drug users that drugs will not be tolerated in the Federal workplace . . . (EO12564, 1986)

On July 11, 1987, Congress passed legislation for implementation of the Order. The goals were to establish uniformity among the drug testing plans of the various agencies, ensure reliable and accurate drug testing, allow employee access to drug testing records, provide confidentiality of drug testing results, and centralize oversight of the drug testing program (DHHS, 1990). This legislation was enacted under Section 503 of the Supplemental Appropriations Act of 1987. The Act placed the burden of providing mandatory guidelines on the Department of Health and Human Services (DHHS), directing that agency to establish "comprehensive standards for all aspects of laboratory drug testing and procedures to be applied in carrying out EO 12564, including standards which require the use of the best available technology for ensuring the full reliability and accuracy of drug tests and strict procedures governing the chain of custody of specimens collected for drug testing" (Supplemental Appropriations Act, 1987). The Secretary of DHHS set mandatory standards for all aspects of laboratory drug testing: who will be tested, when tests will be conducted, what drugs will be covered, and how the tests will be conducted. Testing was authorized for (1) applicant testing, (2) random testing of those employees in sensitive positions that have been designated as testing positions, (3) reasonable suspicion testing, (4) accident or unsafe practice testing, (5) voluntary testing, and (6) testing as part of or as follow-up to counseling or rehabilitation.

In 1988 the first guidelines were published by DHHS in the document *Guidelines for Federal Workplace Drug-Testing Programs*. In 1994, revised *Guidelines* were published (*Federal Register*, 1994). The *Guidelines* establish the testing criteria, specimen matrix allowed, and the limited number of drugs that may be tested in the specimen (DHHS, 1994). The following entities are mandated to follow the *Guidelines*:

- Executive agencies as defined in 5 U.S.C. 105
- Uniformed services, as defined in 5 U.S.C. 2101(3), except for the armed forces as defined in 5 U.S.C. 2101(2)
- Any other employing unit of the federal government, except for the United States Postal Service, Postal Rate Commission, and employing units of the judicial and legislative branches
- Laboratories that have or seek certification to perform urine drug testing for federal agencies under a drug testing program conducted under executive order 12564
- The intelligence community, as defined by executive order 12333, to the extent agreed to by the head of the affected agency

DHHS established the National Laboratory Certification Program (NLCP) to certify laboratories before they are permitted to test specimens that are collected for federal agency drug testing programs. The DOT, Department of Energy (DOE), and the Nuclear Regulatory Commission (NRC) also require the industries they regulate to use these certified laboratories for their workplace drug testing programs. The DOT, in particular, has followed the *Guidelines* very closely. That program was codified in the *Federal Register* (49 CFR Part 40) and became applicable nationwide in the passage of the Omnibus Transportation Employee Drug Testing Act of 1991 (Omnibus, 1991).

Other regulated testing programs included a voluntary program, the Forensic Urine Drug-Testing Program (FUDT), administered by the College of American Pathologists. The FUDT establishes the minimum criteria for reliable urine drug testing procedures, which parallel the general consensus of the scientific community. Although participation in the FUDT is voluntary, many laboratories have an interest in being accredited by the program, because it is one of the few non-governmental programs available to forensic laboratories.

B. Non-regulated testing

Although many private companies perform functions that do not require mandatory adherence to the Federal guidelines and are consequently not involved in regulated testing, it is estimated that over 80 percent of American companies do conduct some type of workplace testing (AMA, 1996). Lack of formal regulation has some benefits and some drawbacks. The most notable drawback is the possible development of a workplace program that lacks procedural oversight and does not mandate adherence to basic forensic testing standards. Lack of adherence to scientifically accepted standards in a company's polices and procedures will increase employee-based legal challenges to any sanctions incurred through administration of the program. Non-regulated testing, however, allows employers to conduct more extensive testing of an employee's biological sample. For example, regulated testing focuses on five major drugs of abuse: cocaine, phencyclidine, opiates, amphetamines, and cannabinoids. Regulated testing often limits the sample matrix to urine and dictates the methods of testing. Non-regulated testing, on the other hand, may allow testing for a multitude of drugs, including prescription drugs, in a variety of testing matrices such as blood hair, sweat, urine, or saliva.

12.3 Establishment of a Drug-Free Workplace Program

The decision to develop and implement a drug-free workplace program begins with the establishment of policies related to the ultimate goal of increased safety and productivity in the workplace. Guidance for the components of a complete program can be found in Section 503 of the Supplemental Appropriations Act of 1987. It requires five major components: a written policy statement, provision for supervisor training, provision for employee education, provision for employee assistance, and the guidelines for drug testing (DOL, 2001). Although these steps are not mandated for non-regulated testing, their inclusion makes a policy clear and may minimize legal ramifications following an employer-based action when a violation by an employee occurs.

A. Written policy

A written policy explicitly states the basis for a program. Thus, the starting point for an effective program is documentation of the employer's requirements, program adherence expectations, and the ramifications of noncompliance. For federal programs, the Act requires the agency to state why the drug-free program is being implemented, to provide a clear description of prohibited behaviors, and to provide a thorough explanation of the consequences of policy violations. Whether the employer must follow the steps established by the Act or is free to develop separate guidelines, the following program components must be included:

- A clear description of prohibited substances and behaviors
- The type of drug testing that will be required and the circumstances (random, post accident, reasonable cause, etc.) that will prompt drug testing
- Procedures for the determination of policy violation
- Consequences of policy violation and the available appeals process
- A statement of when the policy will be enforced
- Documentation of the types of employees to be covered by the policy (e.g., safety-sensitive employees, contractors, pre-employment, or all employees)
- Treatment and rehabilitation services that will be available to employees
- Issues of employee confidentiality

B. Employee assistance programs

Employee assistance programs (EAPs) provide drug abuse education to company managers and drug abuse counseling for employees. An EAP is a benefit to the employer, because it educates managers about drug abuse issues, yet allows them to be separated from the counseling services. It also is an excellent benefit for the employees since it often will become an alternative to dismissal, providing resources for treatment and counseling.

An EAP is a necessary component of any effective program and is a requirement in DHHS-regulated testing. The Act states that the agency shall provide an EAP to help resolve poor work performance due to alcohol, drugs, or other personal problems. A successful EAP must provide treatment and rehabilitation to employees who have tested positive on a drug test or have referred themselves for assistance. In addition, it should disseminate information about drug effects and reinforce knowledge of the impact of drug use in the workplace. Above all, an effective EAP must assure employees that all its functions, including test results and treatment, will be conducted with confidentiality.

C. Employee awareness training

Policies established and enforced in a draconian manner often are not financially beneficial to the employer. Legal consequences and the cost of hiring and training new employees make an employee education program beneficial. Aside from educating the employee about the company policy and program components, it should provide basic information about alcohol and drug abuse in the workplace. The Act requires the EAP administrator to provide employee education to all Federal employees. A model program under the Act includes education about types of drugs, symptoms of drug use, effects of drugs on performance, the role of the EAP, available treatment, and confidentiality issues. EAPs should also include information about the recognition of substance abuse in family members or co-workers, the safety hazards of drug abuse in the workplace, and the available resources for addiction assistance in the company or the community.

D. Supervisor training

Because supervisors provide the first line of drug detection in the workplace, the Act requires federal agencies to develop a training course covering the follows issues (DHHS, 1990):

- Overall policy
- Employee problems with drugs and alcohol
- The supervisor's role and the EAP's role
- Recognition of employees with drug or alcohol problems
- Documentation of performance or behavior problems
- Skills in confronting employees
- Agency procedures regarding referral to the EAP

- Disciplinary action, and removal from safety-sensitive positions (Section 5 of the executive order)
- Reintegration of the employee into the work force
- Written materials for the supervisor

Supervisors should be trained to understand drug abuse issues and to recognize job-performance issues. The monitoring of job performance, rather than the diagnosis of drug abuse, is the main responsibility of a supervisor. Documentation of performance problems will prompt the employee's referral for appropriate assistance. The Act requires supervisor training to include the organization's policy, the supervisor's specific responsibilities, and how to deal with employees who have performance problems. In addition, the supervisor should be trained to monitor job performance, document performance issues, enforce the policy, and make referrals for testing based on reasonable suspicion.

E. Drug testing

A standard drug-free workplace program must allow for drug testing since any sanctions against an employee based on mere suspicion of drug use or influence may not withstand legal review. Executive Order No. 12564 defines illegal drug as any drug on Schedule I or II of the Controlled Substance Act. Since it is impractical to test for all drugs listed in these schedules, the *Guidelines* require than random drug testing programs test urine for marijuana and cocaine, at a minimum. The Agency may add to the minimum list by also testing for opiates, amphetamines and phencyclidine, or request a waiver from DHHS to routinely test for drugs other than the five listed. Note, however, tests for reasonable suspicion or accident, or unsafe practice testing can include other drugs from Schedules I and II (DHHS, 1994). DHHS restricts the test matrix to urine. In non-regulated testing, the employer and the testing laboratory have wide discretion in the choice of methods and drugs.

12.4 The Drug-Testing Process

Vital parts of any drug-free workplace program are the collection of the chosen biological specimen, its analysis for a series of illegal drugs, and the accurate reporting of the results. Non-regulated testing laboratories may use any method for testing; their only oversight is opinion in the relevant scientific community. Regulated testing, on the other hand must take the form of the private CAP-FUDT program or the DHHS *Guidelines*.

Federal agencies of the executive branch must comply with EO12564 (1986), which establishes on and off-duty abstinence from illegal drugs as a condition for employment. Federal grantees and contractors with funding of $100,000 or more must comply with the Drug-Free Workplace Act of 1988. In addition, laboratories involved in testing of federal employees must be certified by the NLCP under the DHHS. In the transportation industry, employers must comply with the Omnibus Transportation Employee Testing Act of 1991. The NRC has established standards for nuclear power producers, and employers with Department of Defense (DOD) contracts must also establish a drug-free program for employees in sensitive jobs.

Private and federal programs are similar in that both are dedicated to maintenance of a high analytical standard. All require the laboratory to have in place a standard operating procedure (SOP) manual that includes a description of the laboratory's chain-of-custody procedures, analytical testing procedures, quality control and quality assurance programs, equipment and maintenance, accessioning and security, personnel qualifications and training, and reporting procedures. The laboratory must also be subject to inspections by the administering program and must require that proficiency samples be tested on a regular basis.

The complete guidelines for CAP-FUDT, the federal program as outlined in the *Federal Mandatory Guidelines,* and the DOT program are not provided here. For the reader's convenience, however, basic scientific concepts in the testing process and examples of the basic requirements of different programs are provided in the following. Note that drug testing is subject to changing needs and technology. The latest revision of the original documents should be consulted for a more thorough list of requirements, clarification of each activity, and recent changes.

A. Collection

Specimen collection is the foundation of the testing process and can affect the reliability and effectiveness of the entire program. Throughout the process, the integrity and identify of the specimen must be maintained, beginning with the collection of the specimen and continuing through the analysis and reporting of the results. The manner of specimen collection, the safeguards against specimen tampering during collection, the correct identification of the specimen, and the accompanying documentation of the chain of custody all are factors which impact the identity and integrity of the specimen.

The chain of custody must document the location of the specimen at all times. It must remain intact and not be broken at any time. The common acceptable chain of custody formation is generally a "Z" formation, representing a Z when the documentation form has two entries per line and takes the following form: A to B, B to C, C to D, and so forth. A to B, C to D would not be acceptable since there would be no documentation of where B placed the specimen or from where C received it, and thus the chain would be broken. DHHS requires use of a standardized custody control form (CCF) and control and accountability of specimens at all times. Every individual in the chain must be identified, and documentation of the individual handling the specimen, as well as the date and the purpose for access to the specimen, must appear on the CCF document (DHHS, 1994).

Since the integrity of a urine drug test hinges on the proper collection of the specimen, DOT has established strict requirements for collection, requiring all procedures to be performed as per 49 CFR Part 40 (DOT, 2000). The correct collection procedures must be followed, and the CCF form must be used. The identity and integrity of the specimen must be maintained, and the collector must fulfill the training requirements of Section 40.33 of Part 40. The training requirements are extensive. As of August 1, 2001, the collector must demonstrate knowledge and compliance in the following areas:

1. Knowledgeable about the current DOT *Urine Specimen Collection Guidelines*, published by DOT
2. Qualification training in the proper collection procedures, completion of the CCF, procedures in solving collection problems (e.g., shy bladder), correction of correctable flaws and identification of fatal flaws (e.g., the specimen ID on the donor's bottle does not match the CCF, or the seal is broken) during collection
3. Demonstration of collection proficiency by completing five consecutive error-free mock collections

4. Attendance of a refresher training course at least every five years
5. Attendance at refresher training course within thirty days if an error in a collection results in the cancellation of a test (fatal or uncorrected flaws)
6. Maintenance of documentation showing the compliance with the requirements in Section 40.33 of Part 40

Each agency or company must have designated collection sites, which are secure and accessible only to authorized personnel, and have the proper procedures in place to ensure the integrity and identity of urine specimens. Such procedures include: the deterrence of dilution of the sample by the donor, requirement for the presentation of a photo identification card by the donor upon arrival, the removal of any donor clothing that may conceal adulteration materials, the washing of the donor's hands prior to urination, the elimination of access by the donor to water during voiding of the bladder, and the collector's observation of the donor prior to urination. All collections must be performed in accordance with applicable regulations and must use a donor number rather than name to ensure the donor's privacy.

Many programs require or allow the collection of split specimens, which permit a portion of the collected sample to be poured into an additional container for independent testing or for use if the original container is destroyed or contaminated. An example of a split collection procedure can be found in the DOT drug testing requirements. In that program, all specimens must be split. At least 45 mL of urine must be collected with 30 mL poured by the collector into bottle A, the primary bottle, and at least 15 mL poured into bottle B. The donor may urinate into a specimen container or into a designated bottle A. The collector then either pours the urine into two specimen bottles that are labeled bottle A and bottle B or, if bottle A was used to collect the specimen, pours an appropriate amount into bottle B.

During the physical collection of the specimen, the donor is given a clean specimen bottle and allowed privacy to void the bladder. Upon receiving the specimen from the donor, the collector must ascertain that a sufficient amount of urine has been voided and also immediately check the temperature of the specimen. A temperature that is less than 90–100° indicates that dilution or substitution may have occurred. If insufficient urine has been voided but the temperature is within range, most programs allow the donor to drink fluids and attempt another collection in the same manner described above.

After collection, the specimen is checked for color and signs of contaminants. Any signs inconsistent with a valid sample must be noted on the chain of custody collection form. The specimen bottle is sealed with tamper-evident tape placed over the cap and down the sides of the bottle. An identification label containing the date, donor's specimen number, and other identifying information (other than the donor's name) is placed on the bottle. The donor then signs the chain of custody form, verifying the collection process. All specimens, even those suspected of being adulterated or diluted, are considered evidence and are sent to the laboratory for testing.

The privacy of the donor during collection is maintained unless certain criteria are met. Under specific circumstances, direct observation of the actual collection may be allowed. For example, employers may specify a direct observation when the donor's test is a follow-up test, and it has been determined that there is no medical reason for a prior specimen to have been invalid. The collector must conduct a direct observation if the temperature of an initial specimen was not within normal range or there was evidence of tampering or adulteration.

B. Accessioning

The accessioning procedure is the gateway to the laboratory testing process. The biological specimen must arrive at the laboratory with the shipping package intact, documentation of a proper chain of custody, and correct identification of the specimen. Broken specimen containers or seals and gaps in the chain of custody all call the specimen integrity into question.

When the specimen is received, laboratory personnel must inspect the package for evidence of possible tampering and compare information on the specimen bottles to information on the accompanying CFF. Most programs have criteria in place for the acceptance or rejection of specimens during the accessioning process. Some flaws are not considered fatal and may be corrected easily by affidavit from the collector. At present, DHHS is reviewing their policies and has proposed a list of minor issues that may appear on the CFF that do not need to be corrected by affidavit. DOT requires that certified laboratory personnel follow the requirements in Section 40.83 of 49 CFR Part 40 in receiving and processing the sample for testing. The laboratory must inspect the CFF and the specimen and note if there are fatal or correctable flaws. Some identified fatal flaws are:

1. The specimen identification numbers of the specimen bottle and CFF do not match.
2. The specimen bottle A seal is broken or shows evidence of tampering. Exceptions are when bottle B of a split specimen can be redesignated as bottle A.
3. The collector's printed name and signature is omitted from the CCF.
4. Specimen bottle A has insufficient urine. Exceptions are when bottle B of a split specimen can be redesignated as bottle A.

Fatal flaws are not correctable, and the specimen must be rejected for testing. Nonfatal flaws can be corrected within five days by affidavit.

Since the accessioning area receives and maintains the urine specimens, the area must be secure and limited to authorized personnel. Entry and exit from the area must be documented. Authorized visitors are allowed in the accessioning area, but they must be escorted at all times.

C. Drugs to be tested

Non-regulated testing has no restriction on the drugs or drug classes that a laboratory may test for in a specimen. In regulated testing, only five classes of drugs are covered: amphetamines, cannabinoids, cocaine, opiates, and phencyclidine. DHHS requires that an "Agency requesting the authorization to include other drugs shall submit to the Secretary in writing the agency's proposed confirmatory test methods, testing levels, and proposed performance test program."

When analyzing for a particular drug or drug class, a laboratory must clearly establish the criteria for the determination of a positive or negative results, identifying a cutoff below which the specimen result will be reported as negative. In non-regulated testing, the laboratory has broad discretion in determining the cutoff level and how the result will be reported. A non-regulated laboratory may allow the cutoff to be determined by the lower limit of detection of the instruments used, or may allow the reported result to be worded in vague terminology such as "possible presence" or "indicated." In regulated testing, however, cutoff levels for screening and

Table 12.1
Cutoff Levels for Screening and Confirmation Tests in Regulated Laboratories

Drug or Metabolite	Screening Test (ng/mL)	Confirmation Test (ng/mL)
Marijuana Metabolite Delta^9-tetrahydrocannabinol-9-carboxylic acid	50	15
Cocaine Metabolite Benzoylecgonine	300	150
Phencyclidine	25	25
Amphetamines Amphetamine Methamphetamine	 1000 1000	 500 500[1]
Opiates Codeine Morphine 6acetylmorphine	 2000 2000 2000	 2000 2000 10[2]

[1]With amphetamine present at a concentration greater than or equal to 200 ng/mL
[2] Only tested if morphine is greater than or equal to 2000 ng/mL

confirmation are mandatory (Table 12.1).

D. Initial test/immunoassay testing

Laboratory analysis of a donor's urine sample is performed in two separate stages. The first analysis is generally called an initial test, a screening test, or a presumptive test. Non-regulated programs may allow a laboratory to use thin layer chromatography or similar technology to screen the urine specimen. DHHS and DOT guidelines mandate that immunoassay techniques be employed. The requirements do not specify which initial immunoassay product to utilize, as long as the product meets U.S. Food and Drug Administration (FDA) requirements for commercial distribution.

Most commercially available immunoassay kits test for the drugs covered by the regulated programs. Immunoassays separate the negative specimens from those that may be positive for a particular drug or drug class. The technology does not yet rise to the standard of certainty that is required for a confirmation test, mainly because there is considerable cross-reactivity with drugs other than the target drug (ImObersteg, 2000).

Lack of specificity is a common problem with immunoassay tests. For example, an immunoassay test for opiates will flag positive for codeine, naloxone, morphine, heroin, hydrocodone, and hydromorphone. Thus, a presumptive positive for opiates can mean that an individual has taken Tylenol® with codeine, Vicodin® for pain relief, or heroin. In addition, depending on the kit, drugs that are not considered an opiate may also cross-react. On occasion, a random false positive will occur, flagging a sample positive when no drug is present.

There are different types of immunoassay techniques on the market. Some common technologies are radioimmunoassay (RIA), enzyme immunoassay (EIA), kinetic interaction of microparticles in a solution (KIMS), and fluorescence polarization immunoassay (FPIA). Some immunoassay techniques utilize an antibody-antigen relationship to identify a drug class in a specimen.

β-lymphocytes and plasma cells create an antibody protein in an immune response to an introduced antigen. This antibody will identify and bind to any similar antigen that is introduced into the host. Commercial immunoassay kits contain a substrate with antibody to a specific class of drugs and also the target drug that is labeled with a tracer. In radioimmunoassay kits, the label is radioactive iodine or carbon, in fluorescence immunoassays the label is a fluorchrome, and in enzyme immunoassays the label is a lysozyme or other enzyme. One of the most popular enzyme immunoassay kits utilized by many NLCP laboratories is the enzyme multiplied immunoassay test, EMIT™, developed by Syva Corporation.

The EMIT™ utilizes a technique known as competitive binding. The drug (antigen) labeled with the enzyme competes with any drug found in the sample for a limited supply of antibodies. When the labeled drug from the kit is bound with the antibody, the enzyme activity is inhibited. The more drug in the sample, the less antibodies available to bind with the kit's enzyme-labeled antigen. By measuring the magnitude of enzymatic change on a substrate, the amount of drug in the donor's sample can be determined. For example, a donor's sample with no target drug will enable most of the kit's enzyme-labeled drug to be bound to the antibodies resulting in an inhibition of the enzyme's activity. When the enzyme activity is inhibited, the substrate in the kit, NAD, cannot be oxidized into NADH. The result is a small absorbance change of 340 mm, measured spectrophotometrically. Conversely, a large amount of drug in a sample will leave few antibodies for the kit's enzyme-label drug, and the enzymes will convert NAD to NADH, resulting in a large absorbance change.

Using the initial cutoffs (Table 12.1), specimens that test below the cutoff level on all initial tests are signed out as negative, and no further testing of the specimen is permitted. For positive test results, multiple rescreening may be an option as long as quality control and guideline cutoffs are used. Some laboratories use a second initial test that is more specific for the drug in question, thereby eliminating a possible false alarm from the broader, first initial test. For example, if a particular assay tends to flag positive for structural amphetamine analogues, a more specific second immunoassay test may be performed.

When conducting an initial test of donor specimens, every batch must contain an appropriate number of calibrators, negative urine samples, controls, and blind samples to ensure the accuracy of test results. Results for donor specimens that are less than the cutoff are considered negative and are not tested further. Positive results are sent on for confirmation.

E. Confirmation tests

If an initial screen indicates that a specimen may be positive for a particular drug or drug class, a confirmation test is performed. Only those specimens that are confirmed positive by a test utilizing an analytical technology different from the screening test may be reported as positive. Nonregulated testing has the option of using a variety of confirmation methods, some of which may not be considered acceptable by the scientific community majority. Under regulated testing, laboratories must use gas chromatography/mass spectromometry (GC/MS) as the confirmation method.

The GC/MS is, in effect, the combination of two instruments. The Gas Chromatograph (GC) separates the components (drugs) by injecting the mixture into a column inside the instrument. The column contains chemicals that slow the migration of some of the compounds and allows other compounds to travel relatively unhindered. The chemical makeup of each compound within the mixture and its interaction with the chemicals in the column determines how long the component will take to travel the entire length of the column. As each compound or drug exits the column, it enters the mass spectrotrometer (MS).

The MS bombards the drug with electrons and shatters the structure into pieces, depending on the weak points in the drug's structure. Theoretically, since each drug structure is different, each will break at different points on the molecule and thus shatter into predictable pieces. The size and quantity of the pieces form a fingerprint of the drug. A proficient scientist can reconstruct the structure of the molecule by evaluating the totality of the ions produced by the electron bombardment. For quantification, the laboratory does not look at the entire scope of ions but rather chooses several unique ions for the identification process. The abundance of one ion (target or quantifying ion) is measured to determine the amount of drug in the specimen. The measured relative abundance of two other ions (qualifier ions) helps assure the proper identification of the drug. Together, the retention time as recorded by the gas chromatograph and the target ion and qualifier ions serve to identify a drug to a fairly high level of certainty.

As with any instrument, the quality and worth of the data achieved through the GC/MS is a function of how the instrument is maintained and operated. Confirmation methods must be validated to ensure the reliable analysis of specimens. Validation includes the determination of carry-over, linearity, precision, specificity, accuracy, limits of quantification, and limits of detection. Confirmations must be by quantitative analysis and must fall within the linear region of the standard curves. Tests that exceed the linear range must be so documented in the laboratory record. Periodic procedure re-validations should be performed.

The calibrators that establish the quantification of the result, and the controls that check the proper results of the calibrators must be used in the analytical run and fall within acceptable ranges of accuracy. The appropriate number of calibrators, negative urine samples, and controls must be used. Some laboratories establish a three-point calibration curve with each batch analysis. Other laboratories use a single point calibration and check a stored, historical calibration curve with the appropriate quality control samples. Quality control requirements for a confirmation test include certified negative urine samples, positive calibrator(s), and controls containing the specific drug to be tested with at least one control at or near the cutoff.

F. Reporting and storage of samples

A person authorized to review the data for accuracy must approve the final test results. In regulated programs, this duty is assigned to a certifying scientist, who reviews all the data from the initial and confirmatory tests and the chain of custody to determine whether the result is justified. The result is then sent to the medical review officer (MRO) on average within five working days after receipt of the specimen by the laboratory. The completed CCF is sent by fax, mail, courier, or electronically to an MRO, not the employer. If the laboratory transmits results to the MRO by facsimile or computer, it must be done in a manner designed to ensure confidentiality of the information.

Confidentiality of records is protected under the Privacy Act, 5 U.S.C., Section 552a et. Seq, and section 503 (e) of the Act. Results may not be disclosed without written permission of the employee unless the disclosure is to the MRO, the EAP administrator who is providing counseling to the employee, a supervisory or management official in the agency, or pursuant to a court order. An applicant for employment is not entitled to the results of the drug test, but an employee may obtain the information by written request.

Results may not be provided verbally by telephone. Quantitative results are not routinely sent, except when the sample is positive for morphine or codeine at a level of 15,000 ng/L or above. All other reports of quantification require a letter request from the MRO. All confirmed positive specimens must be maintained in long-term frozen storage for a minimum of one year. All records must be maintained for two years.

12.5 Additional Program Aspects and Recommendations

A. The medical review officer (MRO)

The DOT and *Federal Mandatory Guidelines* require that an MRO review positive results. An MRO is a licensed physician, responsible for receiving laboratory results generated by an agency's drug testing program. An MRO is knowledgeable about substance abuse disorders and has appropriate medical training to evaluate an individual's positive test result. He or she typically has been trained to review and evaluate the laboratory's implementation of the program's testing of urine samples. The MRO must not have a conflict of interest with the laboratory.

The DOT program requires that when a positive result is reported, the MRO must use due diligence to contact the employee directly and confidentially to determine whether the employee wishes to discuss the result. After three unsuccessful attempts to contact the employee, the MRO requests the designated employer representative (DER) to contact the employee and have the employee call the MRO. Positive results can be verified without interviewing the employee if more than ten days have passed since the reported result, and there has been no success in contacting the employee. Interviews are also not required when more than seventy-two hours have elapsed since the employee was told to contact the MRO, or if the employee refuses to speak with the MRO. The MRO verifies a confirmed positive test for amphetamines, cocaine, marijuana, and PCP unless a legitimate medical explanation for the positive finding exists. If the employee present proofs of a legitimate reason for the presence of the drug in the urine specimen, the test will be deemed negative. However, the MRO may still raise fitness-for-duty issues with the employer. If the sample contained 6-acetylmorphine (6-AM), the test is verified positive. If the test is negative for 6-AM, the result will still be verified positive if the morphine or codeine level is 15,000 ng/mL or more. All other positive opiates tests must be accompanied by clinical evidence of unauthorized use of opiate or opium derivatives. Adulterated or substituted samples are treated as a verified positive if the MRO interviews the employee and finds no medical reason for the result.

B. Public interest exclusions (PIE)

To protect the public against service agents who fail to meet the DOT regulations, the Federal Government has instituted a PIE proceeding policy. A proceeding may be initiated against an MRO, a laboratory, a SAP, a collector, or any service agent who is non-compliant with the program's provisions. The issuing party has the burden of proving by a preponderance of the evidence that the agent was in serious noncompliance with the regulations. The duration of a PIE is one to five years.

C. Blind performance testing

Blind quality control specimens are used as a test of the entire testing process. The current *Guidelines* require each federal agency to ensure that a minimum of three percent blind quality control samples are submitted with the donor specimens. An employer may provide blind samples to the collector, who submits the quality control sample for analysis as if it were a donor specimen. The collector will generate a fictitious social security number or employee identification number, complete a CCF, and properly label a specimen bottle. Only the MRO's copy (copy 4) of the CCF will have the designation "quality control sample" in the donor's identification section. The MRO must determine whether the laboratory reported the correct result when copy 2 of the CCF is received from the laboratory. If the laboratory reports a result different from the one expected, the MRO must contact the laboratory to determine the reason an incorrect result was reported. The MRO may request the laboratory to retest the specimen or to have an aliquot sent to another certified laboratory for confirmatory testing. If the retest result does not confirm the original result, the laboratory likely made an error.

A false negative result is not considered as serious as a false positive. If the retest result confirms that a false positive was reported on a blind quality control sample, the employer and the regulatory office will be contacted, so that an investigation can be conducted. If a specific cause for the false positive is identified, the laboratory will be required to take corrective action to prevent recurrence of the error.

D. Alcohol testing

Not all drug testing programs allow testing for ethyl alcohol. By a 1994 amendment to 49 CFR Part 40, alcohol testing for DOT now is mandated. The regulations are separate from the drug testing requirements, and an MRO review is not required. Alcohol testing may be done in four situations: post-accident, reasonable suspicion, random testing, and return to duty and follow up. At the present time, pre-employment testing is not required. Alcohol screening tests may be performed with breath or saliva specimens. If the alcohol concentration is greater than 0.02 percent (g/100 mL), a confirmation test must be performed on a specified breath alcohol-testing device within thirty minutes of the screening test. Specially trained screening test technicians (SSTs) or breath alcohol technicians (BATs) may perform breath alcohol testing. Only a qualified BAT may conduct a confirmation test, and the test instrument must be on the National Highway Traffic Safety Administration (NHTSA) conforming products list (CPL) for evidential instruments. The screening test may be on the CPL for evidential or non-evidential devices.

All confirmation results must be printed in triplicate and include the date and time, a sequential test number, and the name and serial number of the evidential breath test (EBT) instrument. Confirmation tests must allow a fifteen-minute observation period to insure that alcohol in the oral cavity does not contaminate the test. Before beginning the test, an air blank must be run on the EBT.

A positive result is a confirmation test that is 0.04 percent or higher. Employees who have a positive test must be removed from safety sensitive duty and referred to a substance abuse professional (SAP). A test result between 0.02 percent and 0.039 percent is considered neither positive nor negative, but an employee who tests within this range must be removed from safety sensitive functions until below 0.02 percent or until the next duty period (at least eight hours). Below 0.019 percent, the test is considered negative, and the employee may return to work.

12.6 Special Drug Testing Issues

A. Type of matrix

The best matrix for detecting the presence of drugs depends on the concentration of drug, route of administration, distribution in tissues, and metabolism and excretion pattern of the drug (Anderson et al., 2000). Drug distribution in interstitial and cellular fluids is dependent on physiological and physicochemical properties of the drug. For example, lipid-insoluble drugs cannot permeate cell membranes easily and thus are restricted in their distribution and sites of action. Some drugs bind to plasma proteins, such as the binding of acidic drugs to plasma albumin or the binding of basic drugs to α-1 acid glycoprotein. Lipid-soluble drugs, such as the cannabinoids, accumulate in tissues and fat cells, act a reservoir that prolongs drug action and subsequent elimination from the body, These factors, as well as many more, affect the concentration and detection levels of various drugs in different matrices.

Generally, the purpose for the testing and the information desired dictate the preferred specimen. If an employee is to be tested for cause or post-accident and is available for testing close to the time of the accident or event, a blood specimen may be superior to hair or urine. On the other hand, if the employer wants to determine whether an employee or candidate for employment has a long-term history of drug use, a hair sample will be the best option. An overview of advantages and drawbacks of different sample matrices follows.

1. Hair

Hair serves as a repository for drugs, drug metabolites, vitamins and minerals and other substances that are delivered to the hair root via the blood supply. Most of the drug is deposited in the central part of the hair, the cortex (Kintz, 1996). It takes approximately three to five days for the hair to extrude sufficiently from the scalp to be cut for testing. The amount required for testing varies, but generally sixty to 360 hairs are needed, depending on the length of the hair and the testing technology. The whole shaft of hair can be tested, or it can be segmented to determine the dates of drug ingestion. Segmentation has limited utility, however, since the rate of growth is not identical for all individuals, and not all of one person's hair is in the same growth cycle.

A major advantage of hair as a sample is the ability to determine long-term drug use. Unlike urine or blood, it represents a lengthy record of drug exposure. The rate of hair growth depends on the individual's health and gender and the anatomical location of the hair. In general, the average growth rate for head hair is about 1 centimeter (0.4 inch) per month (Montagna, 1999). A two-inch length of hair thus may represent drug use over the past five months. Although it may be possible for a drug-using employee to maintain sobriety for a short period in order to test negative on an anticipated urine test, it would be more difficult for that employee to abstain for several months.

Drugs are incorporated into hair from three sources: blood supply, sweat and sebum, and passive exposure to the smoke or solid form of a drug (Montagna, 1999). Hair samples are less susceptible to intentional adulteration or substitution, since the donor is always in sight of the collector. Hair contamination from external sources has been shown in children who had been exposed to methamphetamine or cocaine smoke in the home environment (Lewis et al., 1997).

Despite a washing procedure prior to testing, environmental contamination of the hair may still cause a false positive test result (Kidwell, 1988; Kidwell, 1990). Smith and Kidwell (1997) performed a study in which cocaine-using adults and their non-using children were tested. Hair from 92 percent of the adult subjects and 88 percent of the children was positive for cocaine. In addition, hair is continuously in contact with body sweat, and sweat also contains drugs, which may be incorporated into the hair. One study found deuterated cocaine in previously drug-free hair when volunteers, who were administered cocaine, held the hair in their hands for thirty minutes (Henderson et al., 1993). This positive result persisted even after the standard pretest washing procedure.

Another issue arises due to differences in drug uptake by hair depending on ethnicity and hair color (Henderson et al., 1993; Kidwell et al., 1994). Studies by Henderson et al. (1993) showed a bias by ethnicity in the incorporation of cocaine vapor. It was largest for Asian hair, followed by African hair, and finally by Caucasian hair. Reid et al. (1994) demonstrated a difference between black, brown, and blond hair in binding of benzoylecgonine.

Hair testing has enjoyed some popularity in a variety of arenas including family law, insurance cases, custody cases, pre-employment, law enforcement, and the military. In workplace testing, a hair sample is likely to be the best matrix for pre-employment testing only, since it represents drug use over a long time period.

2. Saliva

Saliva is an oral liquid composed of water (90 percent) and various other substances such as mucins and enzymes. Saliva testing is simple to perform, and it is the easiest of available noninvasive methods. It correlates reliably with blood concentrations for certain drugs (Cone et al., 1988). In addition, it differs from urine in that it contains higher concentrations of the parent drug rather than metabolites.

There are, however, a number of factors that affect the concentration of drugs in saliva. It is well known that an increase in saliva pH can alter the partitioning of certain drugs from the blood into the saliva (Kato et al., 1994). Many drugs are weak acids or bases. The distribution of a weak electrolyte is determined by the pK_a and the pH gradient across the membrane. For drugs with a pK_a less than 5.5, saliva concentrations are not pH dependent, and the concentration will correlate with the plasma portion of the blood. However, drugs with a pK_a greater than 5.5 are highly pH dependent. For example, cocaine (pK_a 8.6) concentration is saliva may change by a factor of twelve if the saliva pH changes from 6.5 to 7.6 (Thompson et al., 1987).

Saliva is a good matrix for the determination of drug use during a twelve-to-twenty-four-hour time period (Huestis and Cone, 1998). It is not a useful test for historical drug use, but it may be useful testing prior to employees' engagement in safety-sensitive functions.

3. Sweat

Sweat is a body fluid that has not been fully utilized for drug testing until fairly recently. It is produced mainly by eccrine in the transdermal layer of the skin surface or appocrine glands in specific regions of the body. It is about 99 percent water and 1 percent sodium chloride and other trace materials.

Researchers have known since 1911 that drugs are excreted in sweat (Schramm et al., 1992), and over the years several devices have been used to collect sweat. Many consisted of a pad covered by an occlusive membrane, which trapped both water and solute. This type of patch could not always prevent bacterial growth under the patch, nor did it allow skin under the patch to remain healthy for long-term application. An absorbent pad covered by a non-occlusive membrane, which allows oxygen, water and carbon dioxide to pass through the patch, now is available (Kintz, 1996). A sweat patch collection device developed by Sudormed™ and marketed by Pharm-Chem™ under the trade name Pharm-Chek™ takes advantage of this technological advance. After approval by the FDA, the patch was introduced in the drug detection and testing arena.

The Pharm-Chek™ patch remains on the subject for about a week. It then is removed and placed in a vial with elution buffer to extract the drug. Testing is performed with conventional screening and confirmation procedures. A major benefit of sweat testing is that it is non-invasive and can detect use for a longer period of time than urine (Burns and Baselt, 1995). Other benefits include the detection of parent compounds rather than the more polar metabolites. The membrane will tear if there is an attempt to tamper with the patch after it is applied. These facts have made the device popular in the drug treatment field, custody cases, probation, parole, and social services.

The use of sweat as a testing matrix may be suitable for pre-employment testing, but its use would be unsuitable in for-cause or post-accident testing. Concentrations of drug in the sweat patch are expressed as ng/mL of buffer eluate. This reporting convention makes it difficult to interpret, correlate with the concentration of blood levels, or determine the degree of being under the influence. In addition, certain drugs tend to deposit in adipose tissue, making the issue of recent use more difficult to interpret (Levisky et al., 2000).

The manufacturer claims that the "patch is carefully designed so that contaminants from the environment cannot penetrate the adhesive barrier from the outside, and therefore the patch can be worn during most normal activities (bathing and swimming, for example) without affecting the integrity of the test." (Fortner, 1998). Several scientific articles mirror that opinion with statements that the molecular pore structure of the plastic membrane will exclude substances greater in molecular size than vapor-phase isopropanol (Spiehler et al., 1996). There have been questions, however, of contamination of the patch during application and removal. Early studies indicate that the cleaning solution (70 percent isopropanol) used on the skim prior to the application of the patch does not adequately clean external contaminants from the skin (Kidwell et al., 1997). A 1999 study by the Naval Research Laboratory concluded "the potential for external contamination of the skin (CFWI) as well as contamination of the patch membrane (CFWO) can occur and generate false results." (Kidwell and Smith, 1999).

4. Blood

Blood is a valuable matrix, especially for post-accident determinations of drug use. A 1985 study evaluated existing data on the concentrations of a variety of drugs in drivers to assess the ability of different matrices to detect drug impairment. The study concluded that urine testing is suitable for establishing the need to obtain and analyze blood specimens for THC, the active ingredient in marijuana, and that blood is the only body fluid that may serve in a limited manner to relate drug levels to impairment (DOT, 1985). A blood sample that shows the presence of a significant concentration of an impairing drug can aid in the determination of impairment at the time of an incident. Factors that can affect the determination are whether the blood is drawn from the employee during the expected time frame of drug activity, and whether the employee exhibits signs consistent with the expected effects. Another benefit is the plethora of studies and literature delineating therapeutic versus toxic concentrations of drugs in whole blood or plasma. The major disadvantage to blood testing is the invasiveness of the collection process, the increased hazardous exposure of the collector to possible virulent blood, and the lower concentrations of drugs found in blood as compared to urine.

5. Urine

DHHS currently mandates urine as the specimen for workplace tests. Even in non-regulated testing, urine appears to be the most widely used specimen. Since most workplace testing is either random or pre-employment, recent use is the information sought, not drug impairment. Urine is suitable for the determination of recent use, especially during the past seventy-two hours. The time period during which a drug may be detected in urine depends on several factors including the amount of drug initially consumed, the frequency of drug use, the lipid-solubility of the drug, and the half-life (T1/2) of the drug. For example, the cannabinoids can be detected for more than a month if the donor is a chronic, heavy user. Another advantage is that drugs are ten to 100 times more concentrated in urine than in blood, making detection easier with conventional drug testing instruments.

B. Specimen tampering

During urine collection, the substitution of another substance for the urine sample and adulteration of the sample (by adding chemicals or diluting the sample with water) are common methods of tampering. Masking drugs in urine or causing a false negative result can be achieved in vivo or in vitro. In vivo adulteration is accomplished by consumption of some substance to dilute the urine or change the amount of drug excreted in the urine. Large amounts of water or diuretics will increase the production of urine and lower the drug concentration. Evidence of a dilute specimen allows the employer to instruct the employee to take another test immediately. A positive specimen that is determined to be dilute is treated as a valid positive test.

Consumption of a substance that makes the pH more alkaline will slow the excretion of amphetamines and result in less urine per unit time, effectively lowering drug concentration possibly to a level below the cutoff value. The direct addition of chemicals (e.g., detergents, vinegar, or bleach) into a specimen may create a false negative result by interfering with the screening kit's reagents. Another method of tampering is to substitute urine obtained from a person known to be drug free.

When choosing a program or laboratory, the employer must evaluate the safeguards in place at the collection site and at the testing laboratory. During the voiding of the specimen, the donor must not have access to water to dilute the specimen. This requirement can be met by turning the water line to the sink off during the collection procedure, or by having the employee void where no sink is available. Placing a bluing agent in the toilet will reveal whether the donor diluted the sample with water from the toilet. A temperature indicator on the specimen cup allows a check of the urine temperature to ascertain whether it is consistent with body temperature. DHHS guidelines call for the collector to check the temperature within four minutes of collection, and it must be within 90–100° F. Despite these precautions, a negative urine specimen heated to body temperature by concealment on the donor may be substituted for the donor's urine at the time of collection. The collector's evaluation of temperature and color or smell may not detect adulteration. The laboratory then has the task of determining whether a specimen has been adulterated.

To ascertain whether a specimen was tampered with during collection, the laboratory should test the urine for creatinine levels, specific gravity, nitrites and pH. If the specimen falls outside normal ranges for urine, it is possible that specimen integrity was compromised. Unregulated laboratories often have not established criteria for determination of adulteration or dilution, but regulated programs have addressed this issue. DOT requires specimen validity testing, and the DHHS program strongly encourages the practice. Under their guidelines, a specimen is considered substituted if the urine creatinine concentration is < 5 mg/dL and the specific gravity is < 1.001 or > 1.020. A specimen is considered dilute if the creatinine is < 20 ng/dL and the specific gravity is < 1.003. A sample is considered adulterated if the pH is ≤ 3 or $\geq$, or contains exogenous substances such as nitrites. To report a specimen as substituted, creatinine must be quantitatively measured with two different aliquots, and specific gravity must be determined by refractometry on at least one of these aliquots.

C. "Shy" bladder

Occasionally, a donor may have trouble urinating because of what is termed shy bladder, or merely be unable to provide a sufficient amount of urine for the test. A specimen that is insufficient in volume but meets the temperature requirements must be discarded and an attempt to collect a sufficient amount must be made. Consumption of copious amounts of water sometimes encourages the production of sufficient urine. DOT guidelines direct the donor to consume approximately forty ounces of fluid during a three-hour period, but a donor's decision not to drink fluids in a shy bladder situation is not considered a refusal to test. If the employee still cannot provide a specimen, the collector halts the procedure, makes a notation on the CCF, and notifies the DER and MRO within twenty-four hours. The DER must then direct the employee to obtain a medical evaluation from a licensed physician within five days to explain the medical condition that precluded the employee from providing an adequate specimen. If a medical condition does exist, the MRO must determine if there is clinical evidence that the employee is an illicit drug user.

D. Alternate sources of drug exposure

The purpose of drug testing programs is the detection of illegal drug use by the employee. Some positive drug tests, however, may have their origins in the use of a legal substance or in the unintentional exposure to substances. Passive inhalation of smoked drugs, dermal absorption, foodstuff ingestion, and a laboratory's technical limitations are just a few of the reasons, other than illicit drug use, for a positive urine test (elSohly and Jones, 1995). Thus, it is imperative that the MRO and the employer consider the alternative sources of a positive drug test, prior to the imposition of sanctions.

1. Ingestion of foodstuffs

Use of food products, health oils, and certain beauty products are routes of drug exposure. The use of hempseed oil or tea has been shown to cause a positive urine test for cannabinoids (Steinagle and Upfal, 1999). In one study, a forty-nine-year old man consumed a total of 30 mL of cold pressed hempseed oil per day for four days. Urine samples were collected periodically from the first ingestion to 177 hours. The specimens collected between forty-five and 142 hours contained 12 to 68 ng/mL THCCOOH (Struempler et al., 1997).

During the 1980s, health food stores sold a tea under the trade name, Health Inca Tea. It contained about 1.87 mg cocaine per cup of brewed tea and produced screening results positive for benzoylecgonine twenty-one and twenty-six hours after ingestion (Jackson et al., 1991). The FDA subsequently banned the importation of tea containing residual cocaine, and Health Inca Tea currently does not contain cocaine.

The ingestion of poppy seeds can cause a positive urine test for opiates. The type of poppy seeds, the concentration of drug per gram of seeds, and the amount of seeds ingested play important roles in the amount of morphine ultimately found in the urine. In one study, ingestion of three poppy seed bagels resulted in 214 ng/mL codeine and 29 ng/mL morphine at three hours (Struempler, 987). In another study, the ingestion of 25 grams of poppy seeds from four brands containing 17–294 mcg of morphine per gram seed, resulted in serum levels of up to 13 ng/mL and urine detectability over forty-eight hours (Hayes et al., 1987). The searched literature indicates that, depending on the cutoff level utilized by the laboratory, detection of morphine in urine does not necessarily indicate illegal drug use.

DHHS also recognizes that a positive for codeine or morphine may be a result of dietary poppy seed intake. The MRO is directed to report the result as negative unless there is clinical evidence of illegal opiate use. The *Guidelines* state the MRO "shall determine that there is clinical evidence—in addition to the urine test—of illegal use of any opium, opiate, or opium derivative . . ." Note, however, that 6-acetylmorphine comes only from heroin, and its presence confirms the use of heroin. In addition, the Guidelines permit an MRO to have a written request on file with the laboratory to routinely receive the quantitative values associated with a positive codeine and morphine result, or to request quantitative information about the presence of codeine below the cutoff for specimens reported positive for morphine only.

2. Passive inhalation/absorption

Secondary smoke contains active ingredients and pyrolysis products of a burning substance. The lungs have a large surface area and abundant flood flow enabling a drug to pass readily into the blood stream. Passive inhalation can occur with any smoked substance: marijuana, PCP, cocaine, amphetamine. The level of drug found in a bystander depends on his/her proximity to the smoke, the ventilation of the confined area, the amount of smoke, the concentration of drug in the smoked substance, and the chemical nature of the substance.

The combustion of cannabis results in the conversion of various chemical precursors to form the active constituent of marijuana, THC. Most of the dose enters the smoker's lungs during inhalation, but some amount is released into the air. The THC concentration in the air is directly related to the percent THC in the cigarette, the size of the room in which the smoke is released, the number of "joints" smoked, and the duration of exposure to the smoke. It has been shown that contact with marijuana smoke from four cigarettes may result in a passive inhaler testing positive on a urine screen. In a study by Cone et al. (1987), volunteers were subjected to two concentrations of THC smoke over six days with exposure of one hour per day. Individuals exposed to the smoke from sixteen cigarettes reached RIA levels of up to 100 ng/mL and up to 87 ng/mL on the GC/MS. In another study, a subject confined to a medical ward tested positive for marijuana metabolites due to passive inhalation with concentrations up to 260 ng/mL (Zeidenberg et al., 1977). Morland et al (1985) also detected cannabinoids in blood and urine, and concluded that the, "demonstration of cannabinoids in blood or urine is not unequivocal proof of active cannabis smoking."

DHHS recognizes that passive inhalation does occur and can result in detectable levels of THC and its metabolites in urine. DHHS takes the position, however, that it is unlikely that a nonsmoking individual could unknowingly passively inhale smoke resulting in a drug concentration in urine at or over the cutoff levels used in the federal program.

Passive exposure is not limited to the cannabinoids. There are numerous articles citing incidents of passive exposure by infants and children to crack cocaine vapor resulting in positive urine tests for benzoylecgonine (Heidemann and Gietting, 1990). A study conducted at NIDA's Addiction Research Center, however, demonstrated that individuals passively exposed to crack smoke did not produce a urine positive for cocaine using the Guideline's established cutoff levels (Cone, 1995). In an unrelated study, a 73 Kg man was exposed to vapors produced by the vaporization of 200 mg cocaine free base for thirty minutes; the investigators concluded that "passive exposure to free-base cocaine vapor can produce low positive results . . ." and that it is "probable that a longer exposure period, larger cocaine dose, or a more efficient vaporization temperature would lead to higher urinary benzoylecgonine concentrations" (Baselt, 1991).

Incidents of exposure of police officers to cocaine in work-related situations lead to the conclusions that "passive microingestion of cocaine needs to be considered when examining persons who are in cocaine intensive environments" (Mieczkowski, 1997). Discovery of passive exposure of crime laboratory personnel to cocaine during processing and analysis prompted a recommendation for the use of protective equipment and short exposure times (Le et al., 1992).

Studies of passive exposure to phencyclidine (PCP) have not been reported extensively in the literature, although numerous laboratory studies have examined animal exposure to PCP pyrolysis products. In addition, the literature cites a few instances of accidental exposure to PCP. A woman living above an illegal PCP synthesis laboratory developed psychiatric manifestations of exposure and levels of PCP in her blood (Aniline et al., 1980). Law enforcement personnel who handle PCP have been shown to have it in blood and urine for at least six months after the last know exposure (Pitts et al., 1981).

It is clear that the circumstances surrounding the exposure must be evaluated carefully when evaluating whether a positive result is due to passive exposure. Casual contact in a social setting, or a one-time exposure, can yield a low concentration, but exposure to large amounts of smoke, to smoke with a high concentration of drug, or on a daily basis for a long period of time may yield higher levels. Lipid-soluble drugs pose a special problem in that daily exposure of even low amounts of smoke over a long time period can result in the accumulation of drug in the body and produce a positive test.

E. Amphetamine testing issues

Analysis of the phenethylamines, or amphetamines, has always posed a challenging problem for toxicologists. A positive test result can occur because of medical use of the amphetamines, use of a legal drug that metabolizes to an amphetamine, or the conversion of ephedrine or pseudoephedrine to methamphetamine during the GC/MS testing process.

1. Conversion of ephedrine to methamphetamine during the testing process

In 1990, a false-positive result was reported from the analysis of a proficiency sample by a certified laboratory. Further investigation of the laboratory by DHHS and NLCP revealed that the error was analytical in nature. Specimens reported positive were sent to other laboratories and found not to contain methamphetamine. The origin of the false identification appeared to be the presence of high levels of ephedrine or pseudoephedrine. Other factors included the use of high injection port temperatures in the GC/MS, and the use of derivitizing agents such as 4-carbethoxyhexafluorobuturyl chloride (CB), heptafluorobutyric anhydride (HFBA), N-trifluoro acetcy-l-propyl chloride (TPC) or pentafluoropropionic anhydride (PFPA).

To eliminate further problems, the NLCP now requires that a specimen reported positive for methamphetamine must also contain the metabolite, amphetamine, at a concentration ≥ 200 ng/mL. If this criterion is not met, the specimen must be reported negative. Another way to virtually eliminate the problem is for the laboratory to use periodate in the extraction procedure. Periodate oxidizes primary amines by reaction with -OH and -NH on adjacent carbon atoms. The result is a change in the molecule such that the ion fragments will not be similar to methamphetamine.

2. Enantiomers of methamphetamine

Methamphetaminme and amphetamine exist in two structural forms known as enantiomers, which are non-superimposable mirror images. The two isomers of each substance are designated as *d*- (dextro) and *l*- (levo), indicating the direction in which they rotate a beam of polarized light. The *d*- isomer of each substance has a strong central nervous system stimulant effect, but the *l*- isomer has primarily a peripheral action. A "Vicks Inhaler" contains *l*-amphetamine and affords the possibility that a laboratory positive result could be reported for *l*-methamphetamine or *l*-amphetamine. Selegiline, a monoamine oxidase inhibitor used in the treatment of Parkinson's disease, is metabolized to *l*-methamphetamine and *l*-amphetamine.

DHHS dictates that the MRO should request the laboratory to perform a *d*-, *l*- isomer differentiation. Following "Vicks Inhaler" use, there will be close to 100 percent *l*-methamphetamine with perhaps a small

Table 12.2
Prescription Drugs Containing Opiates and Amphetamines

Product	Drug Present
Marinol Vicks Inhaler®	Cannabinoids
Astramorph PF® Duramorph® MSIR® MS Contin Tablets® Roxanol® Amogel® Diabismul® Donnagel-PG® Infantol Pink® Kaodene with Paregoric® Paregoric Quiagel®	Morphine
Actifed with Codeine Cough Syrup® Codimal PH® SyrupDimetane-DC Cough Syrup® Phenaphen with Codeine® Robitussin A-C® Triaminic Expectorant with Codeine® Tylenol with Codeine (#1, 2, 3, or 4) ® Kaodene with Codeine®	Codeine
Desoxyn® (Gradumet®)	*d*-methamphetamine
Adderall® Benzedrine® Biphetamine® Dexedrine® Durophet® Obetrol®	*d*-amphetamine or racemic *d,l*-amphetamine
Vicks Inhaler®	*l*-methamphetamine

amount of *d*-methamphetamine present as a contaminant. When isomer differentiation is conducted and there is greater than 80 percent *l*-methamphetamine, the results are considered to be consistent with "Vicks Inhaler" use.

12.7 Medical Use of Drugs

Not all drugs found in urine are a product of illegal use. Some of the drugs that can be present as a result of illegal use also are prescribed for therapeutic purposes (Table 12.2), or are present as a metabolite of a prescribed substance (Table 12.3). In certain medical conditions, usage which would otherwise be illegal is permitted. Certain over-the-counter (OTC) preparations contain drugs that can be identified incorrectly as an illegal substance. The MRO has the burden of interpreting test results and should request the donor to submit a copy of his or her medical records as evidence of medications taken near the time of the drug test.

A. Amphetamines

Methamphetamine is a sympathomimetic amine that can be legally prescribed for medical conditions such as obesity, narcolepsy, and attention deficit disorder (PDR, 2001). Both methamphetamine and amphetamine can be produced metabolically by the ingestion of prescribed drugs. Note

Table 12.3
Prescription Drugs—Metabolites

Product	Metabolizes to:
Amphetaminil Clobenzorex (Dinintel®, Finedal®) Ethylamphetamine Fenethylline (Captagon®) Fenproporex (Tegisec®) Mefenorex (Pondinil®) Mesocarb Prenylamine	Amphetamine
Benzphetamine (Didrex®) Dimethylamphetamine Famprofazone Fencamine Furfenorex Selegiline (Deprenyl, Eldepryl®)	Methamphetamine (and amphetamine)

that some of the drugs (dimethylamphetamine, ethylamphetamine, fenethylline) that are listed in Table 12.3 are Schedule I drugs in the United States and have no recognized medical usage (Cody, 1993). They may be found, however, in other countries.

The laboratory's responsibility is accurate identification of methamphetamine or amphetamine in a specimen. It is the responsibility of the MRO to consider the possible origins of the drugs found. The identification of a legal parent drug, when present, then assists in identifying the source of what may be a legal or an illegal substance. Some of the drugs listed in Table 12.3, such as famprofazone and furfenorex, undergo extensive metabolism and little, if any, parent drug is found in urine, but other metabolic products of the drug may be found. For example, deprenyl metabolizes to methamphetamine, amphetamine, and desmethyldeprenyl. Presence of the latter indicates deprenyl as the source. Other considerations include evidence of a valid prescription, and the possible concurrent use of both legal drug and illegal amphetamines.

B. Cannabinoids

Dronabinol is chemically synthesized delta-9-tetrahydrocannabinol (THC). It is sold under the trade name Marinol® in gelatin capsules for oral administration. Marinol® is prescribed for stimulating appetite and preventing weight loss in patients with a confirmed diagnosis of AIDS, for treating nausea and vomiting associated with cancer chemotherapy, and for the management of glaucoma. Again, the MRO should request the donor to submit a copy of his or her medical records or court order authorizing the legal use of Marinol® or marijuana.

C. Opiates

There are a variety of prescription drugs that contain morphine, codeine, or by-products of opium. The use of heroin can be differentiated from these other drugs by the 6-acetylmorphine metabolite that comes only from heroin. Its presence in urine definitively confirms heroin use.

12.8 Legal Aspects of Workplace Drug Testing

The implementation and enforcement of a workplace drug-testing program is always subject to lawsuits by affected employees, as well as state and federal legal guidelines. The legal basis for a workplace program review or criticism may arise from several sources, including constitutional issues (right to privacy, freedom from unreasonable searches, due process), negligence, libel and slander, contract law, and discrimination. Constitutional issues generally arise in the public sector, but they may also apply to private sector employers under specific circumstances. The other three areas are applicable to all employers.

A. Constitutional issues

The Fourth Amendment to the Constitution affords an individual the right to be free from an unreasonable search and seizure by the government. This Amendment, in addition to the Fourteenth Amendment's allowance for due process, are the two major constitutional arguments cited in workplace drug testing issues (Fogel, 1988). Opponents of workplace drug testing often base their arguments on the fundamental right to privacy and the intrusiveness of the collection procedure.

By implication, the Fourth Amendment affords an individual the right to privacy. The concept of an individual's right for a constitutional-based "zone of privacy" was recognized in the 1965 case *Griswold v. Connecticut* (381 U.S.479). The case recognized an individual's right to be "let alone." The United States Supreme Court unanimously held that mandatory drug testing is a search under the Fourth Amendment in the case of *Samuel K. Skinner v. Railway Labor Executives' Associatio*n (489 U.S. 602). However, the Court also held that when drug testing is performed within an employment context, the intrusion is justifiable and does not unnecessarily infringe on privacy interests. To date, it appears that the prevalent view in the work force is that drug testing is not an undue intrusion of privacy when the standards for employment are clearly communicated to the prospective employee, and there is a subsequent contractual basis for reasonable continued performance monitoring.

The due process provision of the Fourteenth Amendment prohibits states from denying federal constitutional rights and does not generally apply to private citizens or entities (*Shelly v. Kramer*, 1948). The authority of Congress to enforce the Fourteenth Amendment, Section 1983 of Title 42 of the United States Code, prohibits interference with federal rights under color of state law. In fact, The Supreme Court in 1966 stated "In cases under Section 1983, 'under color' of law has consistently been treated as the same thing as 'state action' required under the Fourteenth Amendment" (*U.S. v. Price*, 1966).

According to case law, a private employer's action may be considered "state action" and thus regulated under the Fourteenth Amendment if any of the following four are true (Rendell-Baker v. Kohn, 1982):

1. The employer derives his income from the government.
2. The employee is controlled by "extensive and detailed" regulation by the state.
3. The function of the employer is "traditionally the exclusive prerogative" of the state.
4. There is a "symbiotic relationship" between the employer and the government.

Similarly, the Fourth Amendment applies to government actions and is generally not applicable to private sector drug testing. A warrant is generally required for a search to be considered reasonable under the Fourth Amendment (*Payton v. New York*, 1980). However, in regulated industries, an exception to the warrant requirement was developed for searches of premises pursuant to an administrative inspection scheme (*Donovan v. Dewey,* 1981). There are two requirements that will justify the warrantless administrative exception: (1) a strong state interest in conducting an unannounced search and (2) the pervasive regulation of the industry must have reduced the justifiable privacy expectation of the subject of the search.

B. State and federal mandates

An employer must be aware of the state and federal mandates that affect the company's workplace drug testing policy and program implementation. In addition to DOT regulations and the Federal Workplace Act of 1988, which have already been briefly discussed, the following mandates should be considered:

- National Labor Relations Act
- Title VII of the Civil Rights Act of 1964
- American with Disabilities Act of 1990
- The Rehabilitation Act of 1973
- State drug testing laws and city ordinances

Title VII of the Civil Rights Act of 1964, which applies to all private sector employees with fifteen or more employees, prohibits the discrimination against applicants or employees based on race, religion, sex, or national origin. Disparities in sanctions or reasonable cause testing, or a drug testing policy that unfairly impacts a protected class may prompt a Title VII charge. Thus, a workplace drug-testing program that applies policies evenly and without bias is critical to the successful implementation of the program.

State drug-testing laws may restrict an employer's right to implement random drug testing or require specific aspects of a program to be in place. For example, the California Department of Health Services prohibits drug tests not performed by a certified laboratory or licensed physician (California Business and Professional Code, 1999). California also requires that employers with twenty-five or more employees must accommodate those who wish to participate in a substance abuse treatment program, provided the accommodation does not place an undue hardship on the employer (California Labor Code, 2001). On the other hand, Rhode Island only allows drug testing when "the employer has reasonable grounds to believe based on specific aspects of the employee's job performance and on specific contemporaneous observations, capable of being articulated, concerning the employee's appearance, behavior, or speech that the employee's use of controlled substances is impairing his or her ability to perform his or her job." (Rhode Island, 1997)

The confidentiality of medical records and communications in a doctor/patient relationship is generally upheld. A cause of action may be charged and damages may be awarded for the improper disclosure of confidential records or information. Also, state statutes regarding unemployment compensation should be considered. Failing a drug test may be considered misconduct, thereby rendering a discharged employee ineligible for unemployment compensation. For these reasons, it is highly recommended that employers have a legal review of a proposed program and policies to insure compliance with relevant state and local regulations.

The Americans with Disabilities Act of 1990 (ADA) is applicable to employers with fifteen or more employees. Title I of the ADA prohibits employment discrimination against a "qualified individual with a disability." Among other qualified individuals, a person who currently is not using drugs and who is participating or has completed a supervised drug rehabilitation program may qualify (Section 104a). The ADA specifically permits employers to adopt drug testing policies and expressly excludes drug testing as part of the prohibitions against medical inquiries concerning a qualified individual's disability. In fact, a qualified individual expressly does not include an individual who is currently engaged in the use of illegal drugs (Section 104d1).

The Rehabilitation Act of 1973 is similar to the ADA but protects a narrower class of individuals, namely handicapped persons, from certain types of discrimination by the federal government, federal contractors, and federal grantees. In this case, a handicapped person may be an addict who has sought treatment voluntarily (*Nispero v. Buck*, 1989). However, occasional users are not handicapped and thus are not protected. Here, as with the ADA of 1990, employers are not prohibited from testing employees (*Heron v. McGuire*, 1986).

The 1982 National Labor Relations Act (NLRA) was developed to promote, among other things, the flow of commerce and establish legitimate rights of both employers and employees. Drug testing issues were addressed in this updated version of the 1947 Labor Management Relations Act. Case law has established that drug testing of current employees, not applicants, is a mandatory subject of collective bargaining agreements and union contracts (Johnson-Bateman Co., 1989). Employers who hire workers who belong to a union or collective bargaining unit must consult with union representatives or union bylaws. Workplace drug testing policies that are acceptable to collective bargaining agreements is the first step toward the smooth running of the company program.

The Clinical Laboratory Improvement Act and the Clinical Laboratory Amendments (CLIA '88) were created to establish uniform testing standards. Laboratories that are DHHS-certified under the NLCP are specifically exempt from the requirements set forth under CLIA '88. The exemption is limited to the certified laboratories' immunoassay and GC/MS confirmatory testing processes for the five drug classes (DHHS-5) stated in the *Guidelines*. Certified laboratories that perform tests with procedures not in accordance with the *Guidelines* or by methods not certified by DHHS are subject to the technical and regulatory requirements of CLIA '88.

12.9 Conclusions

The effectiveness of a workplace drug-testing program is evident. It is estimated that five to sixteen dollars are saved for every dollar employers invest in an EAP (DOT, 1991). There are scores of statistics that support the benefits of a drug-free workplace program for both the employer and the employee. A contractor firm in Florida saved $100,000 on workers' compensation premiums in 1990, experienced increased productivity, and reduced absenteeism (Delancy, 1994). A small plumbing company in Washington, D.C. saved $385,000 in one year with the implementation of a drug-free workplace program (DOT, 1994).

Employers reap the benefits of a drug-free workplace through increased employee morale, customer satisfaction, and public image. Accidents, production error, absenteeism, employee theft, employee turnover, and legal expenses decrease. The benefits for employees include increased security, productivity, coworker relations, health, and safety. A thorough drug-free workplace program also gives an employee, who may be struggling with substance abuse, the resources to achieve and maintain sobriety and achieve greater career success.

Workplace drug testing programs need continual revisions to keep up with the advances in technology. Drugs outside the DHHS-5 and the inclusion of matrices other than urine are likely to be considered in the near future. New analytical methods will be more specific and sensitive, allowing for more accurate testing. As the concept of workplace drug testing matures, formal policies and the scope of programs will change. Even at this writing, DHHS and DOT are making or considering changes. The following are program issues, which will be addressed or implemented in coming years:

- Alternative matrices (sweat patch and saliva, at minimum)
- Mandatory collection of split specimens
- Mandatory testing of the five major drug classes
- Testing for other drugs, such as MDMA
- "Point of collection" analysis
- Initial testing facilities that perform validity testing and screening only
- Changes in cutoff levels

- Increased validity testing
- Uniform guidelines encompassing all federal agencies
- Increased training and certification requirements for MROs, SAPs, and collectors

Whether an implemented program is voluntary or mandatory, the employer must have in place all the basic aspects of a program: a written policy statement, provision for supervisor training, employee education and employee assistance, and guidelines for drug testing. Inclusion of all these steps will increase the effectiveness of any program and help to achieve the goal for American commerce and the welfare of the work force: a drug-free workplace.

References

American Management Association. (1996)." *AMA Survey Workplace Drug Testing and Drug Abuse Policies Summary of Key Findings*, (pp. 1–8). New York: New York.

Americans with Disabilities Act of 1990, Section 108, 1990, PL 101–336.

Anderson, P., Naik, K., Kinemond, C., and ImObersteg, A. (2000). "Forensic testing for drugs of abuse." *J Pharm Prac*, 3.

Aniline, O., Pitts, F., Allen, R., and Burgoyne, R. (1980). "Incidental intoxication with phencylidine." *J Clin Psychiatry*, 11, 393–394.

Baselt, R., Yoshikawa, D., and Chang, J. (1991). "Passive Inhalation of Cocaine." *Clin Chem*, 37(12), 2160–2161.

Buridi, A., Corman, L., and Redinger, R. (1998). "Hypokalemic nephropathy and nephrogenic diabetes insipidus due to excessive consumption of a soft drink." *S Med J*, 91,1079–1082.

Burns, M., and Baselt, R. (1995). "Monitoring drug use with a sweat patch: An experiment with cocaine." *J Anal Tox*, 17, 41–48.

Burt, M.R. (1980). *Worldwide Highlights from the Worldwide Survey of Non-medical Drug Use and Alcohol Use Among Military Personnel.* Bethesda, Maryland: Burt Associates.

California Business. and Professions. Code, 1999, Section 1206, Supp.

California Labor Code, 2001 §§1025 et seq.

Center on Addiction and Substance Abuse, Columbia University. (1993). *The Cost of Substance Abuse to America's Health Care System*. Report 1; Medical Hospital Costs. New York: Columbia University.

Civil Rights Act of 1964, Title VII of the, 42 U.S.C. §§2000c et seq.

Cody, J.T. (1993). "Metabolic precursors to amphetamine and methamphetamine." *Forensic Sci Rev*, 5, 109.

Cone, E.J., et al. (1987). "Passive inhalation of marijuana smoke: Urinalysis and room air levels of delta-9-tetrahydrocannibinol." *J Anal Tox*, 11, 89–96.

Cone, E.J., Kumor, K., Thompson. L.K., and Sherer, M. (1998). "Correlation of saliva cocaine levels with plasma levels and with pharmacologic effects after intravenous cocaine administration in human subjects." *J Anal Tox*, 12, 200–206.

Cranford, M. (1998). "Drug testing and the right to privacy: Arguing the ethics of workplace drugtesting." *Journal of Business Ethics*, 17, 1805–1815.

Delancy, Marci. (1994). *Does Drug Testing Work?* Washington, D.C.: Institute for a Drug-Free Workplace.

Department of Health and Human Services. (1997). *An Analysis of Worker Drug Use and Workplace Policies and Programs*. Office of Applied Studies, Substance Abuse and Mental Health Services Administration. Rockville, MD: DHHS.

Department of Health and Human Services, National Institute on Drug Abuse. (1991). *National Household Survey on Drug Abuse*. Rockville, MD: DHHS.

Department of Health and Human Services, Substance Abuse and Mental Health Services Administration. (1990). *Model Plan for a Comprehensive Drug-Free Workplace Program*. Publication No. (ADM) 90-1635. Rockville, MD: DHHS.

Department of Health and Human Services, Substance Abuse and Mental Health Services Administration. September 1, 1994. "Mandatory guidelines for federal workplace testing programs." Subpart B, Section 2.1.

Department of Health and Human Services, Substance Abuse and Mental Health Services Administration. (1998). *National Household Survey on Drug Abuse*. Rockville, MD: DHHS.

Department of Health and Human Services, Substance Abuse and Mental Health Services Administration. (1999). *National Household Survey on Drug Abuse*. Rockville, MD: DHHS.

Department of Health and Human Services, SAMHSA CSAP, Workplace Resource Center for Substance Abuse and Treatment, "Drug Free Workplace: Definition, Purpose and History," http://wmcare.samhsa.gov, 11/15/01.

Donovan v. Dewey. 452 U.S. 594, 602–605, 1981.

Department of Labor. (1991). "What works, workplaces without drugs." Washington, D.C.

Department of Labor. "Working partners, small business workplace kit, steps to a drug-free workplace." http://www.dol.gov/asp/programs/drugs/working partners

Department of Labor. (1994). *Working Partners: Substance Abuse in the Workplace*. Washington, D.C.

Department of Transportation. (1985). *Drugs Feasibility Assessment of Chemical Testing for Drug Impairment*. DOT HS 806 920. Washington, D.C.

Department of Transportation *Federal Register* 49 CFR 40, December 19, 2000, Section 40.199.

Donovan v. Dewey. 452 U.S. 594, 602–605, 1981.

ElSohly, M., Jones, A. (1995). "Drug testing in the workplace: Could a positive test for one of the mandated drugs be for reasons other than illicit use of the drug?" *J Anal Tox*, 6, 450–458.

Executive Order 12564 of September 15, 1986, *Federal Register* Vol. 51, No. 180.

Federal Register. (1994)."Mandatory guidelines for federal workplace drug-testing programs." 59(110), 29908–29931.

Fortner, N., Vice President, PharmChem, Inc., Prepared Statement before the House Committee on Government Reform and Oversight Subcommittee on

National Security, International Affairs and Criminal Justice. June 5, 1998. Federal Information Systems Corporation Federal News Service.

Fogel, S.M., Kornblut, G.L., and Power, N.P. (1988). "Survey of the law on employee drug testing." *U Miami L Rev*, 42, 553.

Griswold v. Connecticut, 381 U.S. 479, 1965.

Hayes, L., Krasselt, W., and Mueggler, P. (1987). "Concentration of morphine and codeine in serum and urine after ingestion of poppy seeds." *Clin Chem*, 33(6), 806–808.

Hazelden Foundation. (1996). *Addiction in the Workplace Survey*. Center City, MN.

Heidemann, S., and Gietting, M. (1990). "Passive inhalation of cocaine by infants." *Henry Ford Hosp Med J*, 38(4), 252–254.

Henderson, G.L., Harkey, M.R., and Jones, R. (1993). *Hair Analysis for Drugs of Abuse*. Final Report on Grant Number NIL 90-NIJ-CX-0012 to National Institutes of Justice.

Heron v. McGuire, 803 F. 2d 67, 68(2d Circuit 1986).

Huestis, M., and Cone, E. (1998). "Alternative testing matrices," In S. Karch (Ed.), *Drug Abuse Handbook*, (Chapter 11). CRC Press.

ImObersteg, A. (2000). "Forensic drug testing," In J.T. O'Donnell, and J. Moch, *Drug Injury: Liability, Analysis, and Prevention* (Chapter 26). Tucson, AZ: Lawyers & Judges Publishers.

Jackson, G., Sooday, J., and Poklis, A. (1991). "Urinary excretion of benzoylecgonine following ingestion of health Inca tea," *F Sc. Int*, 49(1), 57–64.

Johnson-Bateman Co., 1989, 295 NLRB No. 26, 1331 L.R.R.M. Cas. (BNA) 1391.

Kato, K., Hillsgrove, M., Weinhold, L., Gorelick, D., Darwin, W., and Cone, E. (1993). "Cocaine and metabolite excretion of saliva under stimulated and nonstimulated conditions," *J Anal Tox*, 17, 6, 338–341.

Kern, K.B., and Meislin, H.W. (1984). "Diabetes insipidus: Occurrence after minor head trauma." *J Trauma*, 24, 69–72.

Kidwell, D.A. (1988). "Analysis of Drugs of Abuse in Hair by Tandem Mass Spectrometry", Proceedings of the 36th American Society of Mass Spectrometry Conference on Mass Spectrometry and Allied Topics, ASMS, San Francisco, CA, June 6–10 (pp. 1364–1365).

Kidwell, D.A., and Blank, D.L. (1990). "Deposition of Drugs of Abuse in Human Hair." Society of Forensic Toxicology Conference on Hair Analysis, May 26, Washington, D.C.

Kidwell, D.A., Blanco, M., and Smith, F. (1997). "Cocaine detection is a university population by hair analysis and skin swab testing." *Forensic Sc. Int*, 84, 65–86.

Kidwell, D.A., and Blank, D.L. (1994). "Mechanisms of incorporation of drugs into hair and the interpretation of hair analysis data," In E.J. Cone, and M. Welch, M. (Eds.), NIDA Research Monograph.

Kidwell, D.A., and Smith, F. (1999). *Susceptibility of PharmChek™ Drugs of Abuse Patch to Environment Contamination.* Publication Number NRL/MR/6170-99-8414, Naval Research Laboratory, Washington, D.C.

Kintz, P. (1996). "Drug testing in addicts: A comparison between urine, sweat, and hair." *Therapeutic Drug Monitoring*, 18, 450–455.

Kintz, P. (Ed.). (1996). *Drug Testing in Hair*. Florida: CRC Press.

Labor Management Relations Act, 1947, 29 U.S.C Section 141.

Le, S., Taylor, R., Vidal, D., Lovas, J., and Ting, E. (1992). "Occupational exposure to cocaine involving crime lab personnel." *J For Sci*, 37(4), 959–968.

Levisky, J.A., Bowerman, D.L., Jenkins, W.W., and Karch, S.B. (2000). "Drug deposition in adipose tissue and skin: Evidence for an alternative source of positive sweat path tests." *Forensic Sci Int*, 110(1), 3–46.

Lewis, D., Moore, C., Morrissy, P., and Leikin, L. (1997). "Determination of drug exposure using hair; Application to child protective cases." *Forensic Sci Int*, 84(1–3),123–128.

Morland, J., Bugge, A., Skuterud, B., Steen, A., Wethe, G., and Kjeldsen, T. (1985). "Cannabinoids in blood and urine after passive inhalation of cannabis smoke." *J For Sci CA*, 30 (4), 997–1002.

Mieczkowski, T. (1997). "Distinguishing passive contamination from active cocaine consumption; assessing the occupational exposure of narcotics officer's to cocaine." *Forensic Sci Int*, 84(1–3), 87111.

Montagna W., and Van Scott, E.J. (1958). "The anatomy of the hair follicle," In W. Montagna, and R.A. Ellis (Eds.), *The Biology of Hair Growth* (p. 39). New York: Academic Press.

Nicholi, A.M. (1983). "The nontherapeutic use of psychoactive drugs: A modern epidemic." *N Eng J Med,* 308, 925–933.

Nispero v. Buck, 720 F. Supp. 1424, 1427 (N.D. Cal 1989).

Normand, J., Salyards, S., and Maloney, J. (1990). "An evaluation of pre-employment drug testing." *J App Psychol*, 75(6), 629–639.

Omnibus Transportation Employee Testing Act of 1991, 1991, Public Law 102–143, Title V.

Payton v. New York, 445 U.S. 573, 1980.

Pitts, F., Allen, R., Aniline, O., and Yago, L. (1981). "Occupational intoxication and long-term persistence of phencyclidine (PCP) in law enforcement personnel." *Clin Toxicol*, 9, 1015–1020.

Physician's Desk Reference, PDR, 55th Edition, 2001, Medical Economics Company, Inc.

Program Document (PD) 35, *Guidance for Reporting Specimen Validity Test Results*. Issued on September 28,1998. Notice to the National Laboratory Certification Program (NLCP) Inspectors and HHS Certified Laboratories.

Program Document (PD) 37, *General Guidance/Criteria for Specimen Balidity testing*. Issued on July 28, 1999. Notice to the National Laboratory Certification Program (NLCP) Inspectors and HHS Certified Laboratories.

Rehabilitation Act of 1973, 29 U.S.C. Sections 701–796 (1982).

Reid, W., O'Connor, F., and Crayton, J. (1994). "The in-vitro binding of benzoylecgonine to pigmented human hair samples." *Clin Toxicol*, 32, 405.

Rendell-Baker v. Kohn, 457 US 830 (1982).

Rhode Island Chapter 136. R.I. Gen. Laws §28-6.5—1 and §28-6.5-2 (Supp. 1997).

Samuel K. Skinner v. Railway Labor Executives' Association, 489 U.S. 602, 1987.

Schramm, W., Smith, R., Craig, P., and Kidwell, D. (1992). "Drugs of abuse in saliva, a review." *J Anal Toxicol*, 16, 1–9.

Shelly v. Kraemer, 334 U.S. 1, 13 (1948).

Smith F.P., Kidwell, D.A. (1997). "Environmental contamination causes positive hair analysis results." XXXV TIAFT Annual Meeting.

Spiehler, V., Fay, J., Forerson, R., Schoendorfer, D., and Niedbala, R. (1996). "Enzyme immunoassay validation for qualitative detection of cocaine in sweat." *Clin Chem*, 42(1), 34–38.

Steinagle, G., and Upfal, M. (1999). "Concentration of marijuana metabolites in the urine after ingestion of hemp seed tea." *J Occup Environ Med*, 41(6), 510–513.

Struempler, R. (1987). "Excretion of codeine and morphine following ingestion of poppy seeds." *J Anal Tox*, 11(3), 97–99.

Struempler, R., Nelson, G., and Urry, F. (1997). "A positive cannabinoids workplace drug test following the ingestion of commercially available hemp seed oil." *J Anal Tox,* 21(4), 283–285.

Substance Abuse and Mental Health Services Administration. (1995). "Substance abuse and mental health statistics sourcebook." Rockville, MD: DHHS.

Substance Abuse and Mental Health Services Administration. (2001). *Summary of Findings from the 2000 National Household Survey on Drug Abuse*. Rockville, MD: DHHS.

Supplemental Appropriations Act of 1987, Section 503, Pub. L. 100-71, 1987, 101 Stat. 391, 468471, codified at 5 U.S.C. Section 7301 note (1987).

Thompson, L.K., Yousefnejad, D., Kumor, K., Sherer, M., and Cone, E. (1987). "Confirmation of cocaine in human saliva after intravenous use." *J Anal Toxicol*, 11, 36–38.

United States of America, President's Commission on Organized Crime, Report to the President and Attorney General: *America's Habit; Drug Abuse, Drug Trafficking, and Organized Crime*. 1986, Washington, D.C.: United States Government Printing Office.

United States v. Price, 383 U.S. 787, 794, n. 7 (1966).

Walsh, Michael J. (1998). "Development and scope of regulated testing," In S. Karch (Ed.), *Drug Abuse Handbook*. CRC Press.

Zeidenberg, P., Bourdon, R., and Nahas, G.G. (1977). "Marijuana intoxication by passive inhalation: Documentation by detection of urinary metabolites." A*m J Psychiatry*, 134, 76–78.

Chapter 13

Law Enforcement's Role in Substance Abuse: Issues Prompting a Reassessment

Stephen J. McAndrew

Synopsis

13.1 Introduction

The preamble of the Anti-Drug Abuse Act of 1988 states, "It is the declared policy of the United States government to create a Drug-Free America by 1995." That deadline has passed. There may have been some rethinking since 1988. The Office of National Drug Control Policy's (ONDCP) 2001–2007 Strategic Plan appears to have reduced its governmental expectations significantly. It states, "Through a balanced array of demand-reduction and supply-reduction actions the ONDCP strives to motivate the drug control community to achieve an overall 50 percent decrease in drug use and availability . . ." (*National Drug Control Policy, Strategic Plan 2001–2007*, p.4, 2001). This change in goals indicates a better understanding of the nature and scope of the drug problem in the United States and calls for more realistic expectations for a substance abuse strategy. The primary tool for this act, as with most efforts toward the eradication of substance abuse in the U.S., is law enforcement. The Anti-Drug Abuse Act of 1988 and its evolved strategic plans are implemented by government leaders with a focus on the direction and deployment of law enforcement assets. The most significant issue facing law enforcement is leadership's need to make better-informed decisions about law enforcement's deployment and training and the nature of drug suppression activities. One way to assist with this process is to examine past and present drug enforcement efforts and, as exemplified in the ongoing evolution of the ONDCP strategic planning process, to adjust accordingly.

The failure of the Anti-Drug Abuse Act of 1988 to reach its goal is an example of law enforcement's general lack of success with substance abuse issues. The reason is not lack of effort. Law enforcement and the criminal justice system have been actively engaged in drug enforcement endeavors (including interdiction, traffic enforcement, street level enforcement, intelligence gathering, and substance abuse education) since the early decades of the twentieth century. In the ONDCP budget, approximately 66 percent of federal dollars spent for the mitigation of substance abuse has been allocated to law enforcement for supply reduction. Approximately 33 percent has been allocated to demand reduction including education and treatment (*National Drug Control February 2000 Strategy Budget Summary*, p. 8). The allocation of funds in the 1999 and 2000 fiscal year budgets is approximately the same.

Substance abuse and the pursuit of intoxication, however, not only remain problematic in the beginning of the new millennium but also present no significant signs of diminishing in the foreseeable future. Based on its lack of success in the main, it may be time to reconsider law enforcement's role in substance abuse abatement, especially the many recurrent and unrealistic demands on it to solve the problem. It would be a disservice to the law enforcement community to evaluate it as the primary entity responsible for eradicating the drug problem. That is, however, an expectation held by many.

The negative effects of the desire for intoxication currently show no signs of abatement. The 2000 Drug Awareness Warning Network (DAWN) report released by the Substance Abuse and Mental Health Services Administration (SAMHSA) notes that emergency room visits increased substantially between 1999 and 2000. Reported emergency room visits involving the Rave Club drug MDMA (Ecstasy) increased 58 percent from 2850 visits in 1999 to 4511 in 2000. The number of heroin/morphine related visits increased 15 percent, from 84, 409 to 97,287 (SAMSHA National Clearinghouse for Alcohol and Drug Information, 2001). Federal spending on the "War on Drugs" increased from 1.65 billion dollars in 1982 to 17.7 billion dollars in 1999 (Office of National Drug Control Policy: Budget Summary, 1992, pp. 212–214; Office of National Drug Control Policy, 2000, p. 94). In 1975, 87 percent of high school seniors surveyed said that they found marijuana, "fairly easy" or "very easy" to obtain. In 1997, 89.6 percent made that statement (National Institute of Drug Abuse, 1997, Table 12).

It is not difficult to find similar statistics regarding the increased or continued use of other currently preferred psychoactive drugs such as ketamine, oxycontin, the benzodiazepines, and gamma hydroxybutrate. Of course, in the maze of naturally occurring and synthetic psychoactive drugs, alcohol remains the most widely used and abused drug. One noted psychopharmacologist and researcher describes the search and use of psychoactive drugs as "The Fourth Drive" (Siegel, 1989). A meaningful discussion of law enforcement's failure to meet expectations regarding substance abuse reduction must begin within the context of impeding issues and influences. Such an examination will yield a better understanding of the reasons why law enforcement has not been able to significantly impact the problem and may point to areas for change. Significant issues include:

- The insidious nature of substance abuse
- The historical pervasiveness of psychoactive substance use
- Historical changes in police administration and management
- Negative influences in drug enforcement deployment and strategy
- Failed drug control strategies: legislative, punitive, and educational

13.2 The Insidious Nature of Substance Abuse

America's approach to substance abuse has been analogous to its approach to the threat of domestic terrorism. For decades, the law enforcement intelligence community, in which the author was a member during the late 1970s and early 1980s, was acutely aware that the United States was ill-prepared to deal with domestic terrorism. Ultimately, a sentinel terrorist event occurred in September of 2001, stunning the nation and redirecting its focus. Prior to that time, domestic terrorism was not a national priority even though it was an insidious activity over time. In the aftermath of the events of September 11, 2001, we learned that the planning process by terrorist organizations had been in process for a number of years and had been inadequately addressed. Overnight, domestic terrorism became a top priority. American political parties demonstrated unusual bipartisanship, and there was a significant effort to immediately form an international coalition to fight terrorism. Law enforcement, legislative, intelligence, and military efforts were directed toward domestic security and the eradication of terrorism. The American people were galvanized into action in a common cause, at least for a time. As with so many aspects of human nature, this level of action occurred after the fact.

The legacy of death, injury, and other costs associated with substance abuse has not yet been associated similarly with a sentinel event. Its impact on the American public also appears to be insidious, and it is not widely perceived as an emergent threat. There were 41,821 deaths on the nation's highways in 2000, 40 percent attributed to alcohol use (National Highway Traffic Safety Administration, 2001). The number and nature of deaths involved in traffic fatalities is certainly no less staggering than those recently attributed to acts of domestic terrorism. In fact, the death count on the nation's highways during each of the past few years has been approximately ten times greater than current estimates of the September 11 toll. The total number of traffic deaths remains somewhat constant each year, but dramatic events capture the lion's share of attention. Finding ways to bring a more subtle issue like substance abuse to the forefront of American consciousness is an ongoing problem fueled by varying degrees of local and national denial. If seriously contemplated, a thoughtful and proactive mindset could be one of the positive lessons learned from the tragic events of September 11, 2001.

13.3 Pervasiveness of Psychoactive Substance Use

Multiple theories attempt to explain why people become addicted to or become physically dependent on psychoactive drugs. Theoretical models place emphasis on factors such as genetics, culture, and neurochemistry. The answer is probably multifactorial incorporating all of the above and other as yet unidentified elements. As a better understanding of the reasons underlying psychoactive drug use develops, it may provide some insight into the scope of the problem.

People, and animals for that matter, develop a strong bond to their psychoactive substances of choice. An accounting of the number of people experiencing problems in relation to alcohol alone attests to the enormity of the problem. In 1993, Ross Deck, a senior policy analyst at the Office of National Drug Control Policy (ONDCP), alluded to the relationship between people and drugs when he stated, "First of all, we are not fighting a drug war anymore. To have a war you must have enemies. In this situation we are our own enemy and we cannot declare victory simply because we killed ourselves." (Deck, 1993). The war on drugs is essentially a war we are fighting with ourselves and with our desire to change our level of consciousness.

The pursuit of psychoactive substances for the purpose of intoxication has been part of human and animal life since the beginning of recorded history. Our love-hate relationship with psychoactive drugs began in the primal forests as a kind of war between plants and animals. The plants adapted to the animals that consumed them for food by producing toxins. When animals ate the plants, they were able to adapt to many of the toxins. It is believed that in some cases the animals experienced an added phenomenon as a result of eating the plants, namely, a change in the level of consciousness. That experience, often pleasant, is now called intoxication (note the word "toxic" as the root). When humans observed animals heal themselves, relieve their pain, or become intoxicated by eating plants, they also tried them, often with similar results (Siegel, 1987).

Studies have shown that many animals, including elephants, bees, birds, and cows, seek and ingest mind-altering substances such as fermented fruit, plants, and seeds. They change their level of consciousness, probably for a number of reasons, including the physiological and psychological rewards. In his book, Intoxication, Dr. Ronald Siegel, researcher and advisor to two presidential administrations, states that, " . . . stupefied bees quickly become victims of predations. The carcasses of 'drunken birds' litter the highways. Cats pay for their addiction to pleasure plants with brain damage. Inebriated elephants destroy property as well as the lives of other animals." (Siegel, 1987).

For many centuries, people and animals have used psychoactive substances with no historically recorded abatement other than seasonal lack of availability of naturally occurring psychoactive plants. Legislative attempts to prohibit their use have been largely ineffective. Seasonal lack of availability of psychoactive substances may be the primary reason that animals are not generally physically dependent and addicted unless they are research animals studied in a laboratory. Humans and animals readily identify and respond to psychoactive substances, because they generally produce similar substances endogenously that act much in the same way. Dr. Siegel (1987) says:

> ethnological and laboratory studies with colonies of rats and islands of primates, and analysis of social and biological history, suggest that the pursuit of intoxication with drugs is a primary motivational force in the behavior of organisms. Our nervous system, like those of rodents and primates, is arranged to respond to chemical intoxicants in much the same way it responds to rewards of food, drink, and sex. Throughout our entire history as a species, intoxication has functioned like the basic drives of hunger, thirst, or sex, sometimes overshadowing all other activities in life. Intoxication is the fourth drive.

Dr. Siegel's "fourth drive," which is described as being biologically and socially pervasive in both man and animal, renders the notion of winning a "war on drugs" questionable. He explains that "we are neither the first nor the most experienced species to develop a passion for drugs, yet, in mimicking the behavior of other animals through millennia, we have become the eager and reckless explorers of intoxication." (Siegel, 1987). As children we spin around in circles to achieve dizziness, not unlike that found in some forms of chemical intoxication. We can hold our breath until similar feelings of dizziness occur, not unlike the oxygen deprivation that occurs with some inhalant use. We run several miles and increase secretions of endorphin, the body's natural pain reliever, thereby achieving a "runner's high." Other ways to change one's level of consciousness include work activities, competitive and noncompetitive sports, meditation, theological pursuits, movies, television, literature, and music. Accomplishing a change of consciousness with the use of psychoactive substances including alcohol is, however, one of the most effective and direct methods available to us.

Our historical romance with psychoactive substances in concert with improved routes of administration, continual increase in potencies, and new knowledge of the acute and long-term effects of psychoactive drugs should cause increased concern about the dangers of many of them. One area of concern should be the recent resurgence in the use of Ecstasy, which is popularly known as "E," and is chemically known as methylenedioxy-n-methylamphetamine or MDMA. Recent research indicates that the physiological and cognitive effects of this drug are uniquely dangerous to the user. As researcher S. Alex Stalcup, M.D. advises, "The major danger of 'E' is a unique pattern of brain injury in which serotonin neurons [nerve cells that produce the chemical serotonin] are destroyed by about two-thirds. This is predicted to have effects not likely to appear for perhaps a decade, of memory impairment, learning impairment, and motor impairment." (Stalcup, 2001) Ecstasy is not a new drug, but it has been recently rediscovered and is being used at levels believed by many to be of epidemic proportion. Users report that Ecstasy brings out emotional responses of loving sensations and emotional bonding with others under the influence. The desire for psychoactive substances such as Ecstasy is so pervasive that it calls for a continued effort to render them as harmless as possible. This concept perhaps foreshadows a pharmacological solution to the problem.

Given the level of psychoactive drug use to achieve various consciousness states, how can law enforcement mitigate this age-old practice or "fourth drive?" As prohibition in the 1920s demonstrated, the complete answer does not lie in the criminal or legislative arenas alone. Legalization of controlled substances risks being interpreted as tacit permission or rationalized support of substance use and abuse. Considered in the context of the desire for intoxication, are expectations for law enforcement regarding the reduction of drug use, inappropriate, misdirected, or unrealistic? Where should law enforcement's efforts be directed? The following section considers areas where efforts have had less than hoped for success.

13.4 Legislation and Substance Abuse

Legislative attempts at mitigating substance abuse with law enforcement as the primary implementation tool have had a relatively short history in the United States. Legislation has attempted to control, limit, eliminate, ensure proper production of, regulate importation and manufacture of, or eliminate the use of psychoactive drugs. The regulations enacted in the twentieth century include, but are not limited to the Pure Food and Drug Act of 1906, which partially focused on accurate content labeling of drugs and patent medicines; the Harrison Narcotics Act and the Jones-Miller Act of 1922 which were intended to eliminate the use of narcotics except for medical use; the Heroin Act of 1924 that made it illegal to manufacture heroin in the United States; and the Boggs Amendment to the Harrison Narcotics Act that called for mandatory sentences for drug violations. In total, there were twenty-nine significant forms of federal legislation enacted between the years 1906 and 1992. In addition, countless laws enacted at the municipal, county, and state levels were directed toward the same issue. What has been the result of these legislative efforts? A Brandeis University study reveals that substance abuse is currently the number one preventable health problem resulting in more deaths, illnesses and disabilities than any other preventable health condition in the United States (United States Department of Labor, 2001).

Legislative efforts in the 1980s were directed toward providing strong penalties for many drug-related crimes. The consideration of capital punishment for drug-related murders is one example. A new cabinet-level position titled "drug czar" was created, naming William Bennett to the post. His approach to substance abuse focused on law enforcement including the construction of more federal corrections facilities and increased hiring of enforcement officers, corrections officers and prosecutors. Although these efforts produced significant numbers of arrests, incarcerations and drug seizures, drug overdose deaths increased 540 percent since 1980 and other drug-related problems worsened (Drucker, 1998). The number of jailed drug offenders increased by a factor of 12 from 1980 to 1995. This is proportional to the number of overdose deaths during the same period. A net result has been the increased incarceration of nonviolent drug offenders. According to the Department of Justice, 85 percent of the increase in the federal prison population from 1985 to 1995 was due to drug convictions.

Rising drug prices would be an indicator of success in drug supply reduction efforts but, in fact, the prices of drugs such as heroin have dropped over time (ONDCP, 1998). Criminal legislation and case law are the primary tools of law enforcement, and the bottom line is that in spite of those tools, there has been no significant mitigation of the substance abuse problem in the United States.

13.5 Productivity-Based Police Management and Its Effects on Drug Enforcement

The 1960s was a time of turbulence and cultural reassessment. There were many contributing elements to the changes that took place in the United States during that period. Some of them were issues of dissent regarding the United States' involvement in Southeast Asia, the resultant clashes between law enforcement and dissenters to the war in Vietnam, the availability and popularity of various psychoactive drugs, and a change in sexual mores coupled with relative economic prosperity. It was a period of cultural introspection and changes that significantly impacted drug enforcement.

Personal rights were enhanced by various decisions of the United States Supreme Court in partial response to a civil rights movement that was moving into full swing. One of the end results was a significant increase in public scrutiny of police operations and management. There was an effort to incorporate the "scientific method" into police management as a way to quantify the return on investment of law enforcement efforts and to increase accountability. Extensive research during the 1960s and 1970s resulted in the incorporation of a statistically based evaluation process into police management. In retrospect, this new methodology was a double-edged sword. On one hand, disciplines such as crime analysis, strategic planning and outcome-based analysis began to be incorporated into law enforcement processes. Properly used, these tools provided guidance for better deployment of law enforcement resources. On the other side of the equation, however, myopic emphasis on the productivity of the individual officer had a deleterious effect on the quality of some activities, including drug enforcement.

In many police agencies, individual officers are still evaluated in large part by "their monthly numbers" as they often refer to them. A police officer's monthly statistics are tracked, and the number of generated "activities" significantly affects his or her performance rating. The tracked numbers include moving citations, misdemeanor citations, parking tickets, contacts with suspicious individuals, and misdemeanor and felony arrests. If an officer's productivity numbers are low in comparison to an established benchmark for the beat, type of assignment, or type of activity, he or she can be given a poor performance evaluation.

One of the ironies of this approach is that if officers are successful in suppressing criminal activity in their beats, they may begin to show a decline in their productivity statistics due to a decrease in criminal activity. If these data are not properly analyzed as a successful suppression of criminal activity, the result is a negative performance review. Another paradox with the productivity-based approach to evaluation arises from the fact that the crimes prevented by police presence or crime prevention efforts generally are not measurable. In the productivity-based paradigm, nonmeasurables are not strongly supported even though such activities suppress criminal activity.

This statistical analysis of productivity was, and often still is, applied in the case of the police investigator. In the area of narcotics investigations, for example, the arrests that produce higher volumes and, therefore, higher numbers are often emphasized in the officer's evaluation. The result is pressure to make many street level criminal arrests for violations such as simple possession of illegal drugs as opposed to more lengthy investigations targeting high-level drug dealers, suppliers, and importers. Productivity-based management focuses on showing high productivity for the dollars spent, and monthly reports emphasize numeric volume.

Long-term, high-level drug investigations are expensive and often do not show significant progress in the short term. The focus on numbers, therefore, results in decreased support by leadership for longer-term investigations. The net result is that quality factors in drug arrests are sacrificed to quantity factors. If one believes that focusing on drug distribution at higher levels of the business hierarchy is an effective method of deterrence, a purely statistical productivity paradigm can be viewed as counterproductive.

The productivity-based management philosophy has persevered and is still in use in many law enforcement agencies throughout the country. Evaluating productivity can be an effective management tool, but there is a need to properly analyze the data with strategically prioritized goals. If the analysis identifies higher-level, long-term efforts as a more effective approach in any given area of enforcement, then clearly a productivity-based "widget" paradigm will be too shortsighted. In time, newer tools such as crime analysis with inclusion of multifactorial contextual data will provide a more legitimate approach to drug enforcement. Until that time, it is important to resist purely short-term productivity-based evaluations and to deploy enforcement toward higher levels of criminal activity.

13.6 Law Enforcement's Educational Approach

Many people believe that educational programs focused on preventing substance abuse are an effective approach to drug problems. There are such programs throughout the United States in rehabilitation centers, schools, youth groups, hospitals and other venues. One significant example is the law enforcement antidrug educational program, Drug Abuse Resistance Education (D.A.R.E.). Developed by the Los Angeles Police Department in 1983, the program places uniformed police officers in schools to provide student training on decision-making and reduction of peer influence. Multiple studies have examined the effectiveness of the D.A.R.E. program. In a summary evaluation, researchers Lynam, Richard Milich, et al. (1999) concluded that, "Although few long-term studies have been conducted, the preponderance of evidence suggests that DARE has no long-term effect on drug use."

One problem with many current educational approaches to substance abuse is that the primary stress is on the negative effects of drugs. That often runs counter to the personal experiences of drug users and erodes the credibility of the program. Further, arbitrarily teaching the "Just Say No" to drugs strategy is overly simplistic. A more truthful and accurate approach to drug education would gain more credibility with young people, many of whom believe (albeit often incorrectly) themselves to be already knowledgeable about psychoactive drugs and their effects. The appropriate content of a comprehensive, honest approach to drug education is extremely age sensitive and must be carefully developed within that context.

The content of drug education programs is ripe for study, especially in the area of law enforcement participation. Will it be effective for young people to receive fact-based information about psychoactive drugs and their effects, or is the "Just Say No" approach going to yield better results? Will young people choose to use or not use psychoactive drugs based on facts, or will they heed law enforcement officers who simply advise them to abstain? Is it possible that the two teaching approaches can be effectively used together? How can they be developed appropriately for multiple age groups?

13.7 Traffic Enforcement and the Drug Recognition Expert Program

Traffic enforcement has been, and continues to be, an appropriate tool for drug enforcement. Officers temporarily remove individually impaired drivers from the roadway. The numbers of people killed or injured on America's highways have remained a relatively stable statistic for a number of years, but this statistic does not identify the involvement of psychoactive drugs other than alcohol. Although it can be argued that without an emphasis on driving-under-the-influence enforcement the number of deaths and injuries would be higher, the current numbers are unacceptable. Traffic enforcement remains a key tool for identifying drug-impaired individuals and temporarily removing them from the control of motor vehicles. There is no question that the work should continue, but it does not influence the substance abuse problem in its entirety. It is a single component of the total scenario.

The Drug Recognition Expert Program (DRE) was initiated by the Los Angeles Police Department in the 1970s. Since the mid-1980s, the National Highway Traffic Safety Administration has promoted it on a nationwide basis, but its expansion and development nationally has been reduced by 1990s budgets.

A DRE follows a standardized and systematic protocol to evaluate a driver's impairment, to determine whether impairment is drug related, and to identify the type of substance(s) causing impairment. A certified DRE has been extensively trained to recognize the signs and symptoms associated with psychoactive drugs and to apply this knowledge in clinical and psychophysical evaluations. The program protocol is based on seven categories of psychoactive drugs each distinguished by a set of observable signs (Golden and McAndrew, 2000). When a DRE completes an examination, he or she opines with a high rate of accuracy whether the individual is impaired, whether impairment is drug-related, and the category of drug or drugs causing impairment.

In many jurisdictions, the DRE program has significantly enhanced a police officer's ability to remove drunk and drugged drivers from the road. The program, which is administered by the International Association of Chiefs of Police, is still evolving in the states and the courts, and many legal issues surrounding the investigation and adjudication of impaired driving cases have been overcome. DREs are valuable resources of information for other traffic and patrol officers who, in many cases, lack the skills to identify alcohol and drug-drivers by virtue of their driving behaviors and psychophysical signs.

The DRE program merits increased support at all levels of government for its continued expansion and development. Numerous jurisdictions across the country currently benefit from the program, and there is a potential for it to become a national clearinghouse for accurate drug information for law enforcement and possibly other communities. The author, for example, uses DRE resource material when teaching psychoactive drug symptomatology in the medical school environment. An examination of drug information available on the Internet, as well as discussions with non-drug trained police officers, reveals that much of the information about psychoactive drugs that is in circulation is anecdotal and incorrect. This is especially true for drug signs and symptoms. Information from the DRE program can significantly improve that situation. Not only will more accurate information about drugs assist officers in the field, but it will greatly enhance the prosecutorial process as well.

13.8 Interdiction and Other Enforcement Efforts

It is commonly known that law enforcement interdiction efforts affect only a small percentage of drugs brought into the United States. This work is nonetheless important. The development of effective coalitions between municipal, county, state, and federal agencies would facilitate coordinated efforts and the exchange of intelligence information. This in turn would minimize redundancy of effort. The effective sharing of information between jurisdictions is a significant problem in effective interdiction and efforts to reduce drug trafficking. It is politically difficult due to jurisdictional and political issues, and resolution will require skilled leadership.

13.9 Treatment as an Integral Part of the Adjudication Process

The incorporation of drug treatment into the adjudication process is a potentially powerful strategy. An examination of the Office of National Drug Control Policy (ONDCP) Drug Control Budget for 1999, reveals that 66 percent of the budget was spent on law enforcement, 22 percent on substance abuse treatment, and 12 percent on youth drug use. Simple incarceration of nonviolent drug offenders has increased the jail population, but there is no evidence that it has affected the substance abuse problem. A 540 percent increase in the drug overdose rate since 1980 does not reflect problem reduction (Drucker, 1998). Since 1992, federal surveys indicate a rise in adolescent drug use despite increased funding in ONDCP budgets and increased arrest and incarceration rates (National Institute of Drug Abuse, 1998). Alcohol and traffic related vehicular accidents have not changed appreciably in several years—40 percent were alcohol-related in 2000, compared to 38 percent in 1999 (National Highway Traffic Safety Administration).

Treatment as an alternative or adjunct to incarceration needs further study. The funds for treatment were increased in the 2001 ONDCP budget, but the largest proportion of expenditures was allocated to law enforcement efforts, not treatment or education. In some jurisdictions, treatment alternatives currently are available in the adjudication process, a strategy that merits application and examination on a wider scale. The qualification criteria for treatment in lieu of, or in conjunction with, incarceration will need to be clearly established.

13.10 Conclusion

The national approach to substance abuse has had few successes, and it appears to need revision. If the problem were given a higher priority than it currently has, what would be the best response by law enforcement? Examination of all aspects of this complex problem is beyond the scope of this chapter, but there are identifiable, fundamental issues that if correctly addressed would enhance law enforcement's efforts. Anti-substance abuse activities can be better integrated into the criminal justice system. The examination of historical successes and failures is a beginning point for efforts to improve practices.

One fact that is pivotal to a realistic planning process is the recognition that the desire to change one's level of consciousness has existed since the beginning of recorded history. Its pervasiveness is indisputable. How then can society, with law enforcement as a subset, reduce such a phenomenon? When discussing the direction for effective action by law enforcement, realistic expectations must be based on the best information available. We start this process by asking questions about current drug enforcement. Would it, for example, be more appropriate for law enforcement to be acknowledged, not as the primary element in the effort to eradicate substance abuse, but rather as an equal partner in a coalition of governmental and non-governmental entities? Other components would appropriately include treatment and rehabilitation, research, private industry, medicine, emergency medical services, the judicial system, corrections, and the academic community. Many may assume incorrectly that this integration of disciplines is already in place, but it is not. The failure to work more cooperatively is attributable to bureaucratic and political processes, as illustrated by failure of the law enforcement community to fully cooperate and share resources within its own ranks. These organizational barriers must be broken down if an effective, efficient approach to the reduction of substance abuse is to occur.

Law enforcement's role must be re-examined. The drug problem is not going to go away, and current efforts are having no significant effect. It is encouraging that there are some indicators of governmental recognition of this fact. For example, the ONDCP 2002 budget includes increased funding for treatment, but the shift is small in relation to other allocations. Additionally, as long as the current model for evaluating police productivity exists, long-term drug investigations will take a subordinate role to street level arrests for minor drug violations. Educational programs such as D.A.R.E. need to provide youth with a decision-making process that is fact-based and can be applied to drugs. Young people need knowledge about both the pros (psychoactive drugs are effective medical treatment) and the cons (consequences of drug abuse are physiological and psychological pathology) of psychoactive drugs. Continued refinement and expansion of the DRE program will benefit law enforcement and other disciplines. The body of knowledge within the program can be used as a resource for consistent and accurate information.

In this country, substance abuse has not been given a high priority as a social problem. The issue is complex, and it does not leave many American families untouched. Its toll is very real and the prognosis is not favorable. Do we await some catastrophic event to bring it to the top of our priorities, or will we begin now to seriously address substance abuse? Until such time that the issues move away from discussion toward action by national leaders, law enforcement's efforts are unlikely to alter the status quo of substance abuse.

References

Anti-Drug Abuse Act of 1988, P.L. 100-690, Section 5251.

Deck, R. (1993). "A new way of looking at the drug war." Proceedings of the 1993 national conference of the bureau of justice statistics and the justice research and statistics association (p. 12). Washington, D.C.: Bureau of Justice Statistics.

Drucker, E. (1998) *Drug Prohibition and Public Health.* Public Health Reports, 114. U.S. Public Health Service.

Golden McAndrew, K., and McAndrew, S. (2000) "Workplace substance abuse impairment." *Journal of the American Association of Occupational Health,* 1, 33.

Lynam, D., Milich, R., Zimmerman, R., et al. (1999). "Project D.A.R.E.: No effects at 10-year follow-up." *Journal of Consulting and Clinical Psychology,* 67(4), 590-593. Retrieved from http://www.apa.org/journals/ccp/ccp674590.html.

National Highway Traffic Safety Administration. (2001). *Child Deaths. Injuries Are Down; Alcohol, Motorcycle Deaths Rise*. Publication NHTSA 49-01. Washington, D.C.: United States Department of Transportation.

National Institute of Drug Abuse. (1998). *Monitoring the Future Survey*. Washington D.C.: Department of Health and Human Services.

National Institute of Drug Abuse. (1997). "Long-term trends in perceived availability of drugs, twelfth graders." *Monitoring the Future Survey*. Washington D.C.: Department of Health and Human Services.

Office of National Drug Control Policy. (2001). *National Drug Control 2001–2007 Strategic Plan*. Retrieved from http://www.whitehousedrugpolicy.gov/publications/pdf/strategic_plan.pdf

Office of National Drug Control Policy, (2000). *The National Drug Control Strategy: 2000 Annual Report*. Washington, D.C.: United States Government Printing Office.

Office of National Drug Control Policy. (2000). National drug control strategy budget summary Feb 2000 executive summary. Retrieved from http://www.whitehousedrugpolicy.gov/publications/policy/budget00/exec_summ.html

Office of National Drug Control Policy. (1998). *National Drug Control Strategy: 1998 Annual Report*. Washington, D.C.: United States Government Printing Office.

Office of National Drug Control Policy. (1992). *National Drug Control Strategy Budget Summary*. Washington, D.C.: United States Government Printing Office.

SAMSA National Clearinghouse for Alcohol and Drug Information. (2001). DAWN emergency department 2000 data. Retrieved from http://www.samhsa.gov/oas /DAWN /2000yrend.pdf.

Siegel, R. (1989). *Intoxication*. New York: E.P. Dutton.

Stalcup, A., M.D. (2001). "Drug Addiction." Proceedings of the 7th annual conference drugs, alcohol, and impaired driving seminar (p. 19). Long Beach: International Association of Chiefs of Police.

The United States Department of Labor. (2001). *Background Information: Workplace Substance Abuse*. Retrieved from http://www.dol.gov/asp/programs/drugs/backgrnd.htm.

Chapter 14

Prosecuting the Drugged Driver

David Sandler

Synopsis

14.1 Introduction

In the early morning hours, a thirty-year-old man and his two companions were driving in a quiet upper middle class suburb of Honolulu when the driver failed to negotiate a curve and instead crossed over the double yellow line. He crashed into a car parked in the driveway of a home in the residential neighborhood and then into the garage. The car went on to crash into the next-door neighbor's carport where it crushed another vehicle. Damages totaled approximately $50,000.

The owner of the vehicle was seen exiting from the driver's side by an off-duty Honolulu Police officer who was a resident of the second house that was struck. The vehicle owner admitted being the driver and also admitted using controlled substances. Other officers who were called to the scene to investigate the crash reported that the driver's impairment was clearly evident.

With obvious impaired driving, an impaired suspect, and admissions of drug use, this appears to be a case that would be easy to prosecute. Nevertheless, it took nearly a year to prosecute, including an extremely lengthy trial. The judge's comments when the guilty verdict was announced a year ago suggested that he thought the case was closed, but it remains in the appellate process.

This chapter will discuss driving-under-the-influence-of-drugs-cases (DUI-drugs or DUID) from the perspective of the prosecutor, and will examine why these cases often are difficult to prosecute. Topics to be covered include the evaluation of cases for prosecution, preparation and presentation of cases for trial, and the countering of challenges that arise in DUI-drug cases. A separate chapter will be devoted to the issue of police officers testifying as drug recognition experts and the case law in this area.

14.2 Case Evaluation—Determining When to Prosecute

DUI-drug cases arise out of a variety of circumstances. For example, suspects are sometimes arrested for drugged driving at roadblocks or as a result of collisions. The most common scenario, however, involves a police officer's observations of what appears to be impaired driving or a stop for a traffic violation. When the officer approaches the motorist, he observes signs of impairment such as bloodshot eyes, a dazed expression, or the inability to comprehend basic questions.

Based upon these observations, the officer asks the driver to perform the standardized field sobriety test (SFST) battery.[1] If the individual cannot perform the SFSTs as instructed, he is placed under arrest. In most cases, the arresting officer will classify this arrest as being for driving under the influence of alcohol (DUI-alcohol). In some jurisdictions, however, the officer need not specify whether he is making the arrest for DUI-alcohol or DUI-drugs. It is enough simply to arrest the suspect for driving under the influence of an intoxicant.[2]

At the police station, the suspect is given a test to determine the concentration of alcohol in his system. This is usually done with a breath-sampling instrument such as the Intoxilyzer 5000. If the results are above the legal blood alcohol concentration (BAC), the suspect is formally arrested and booked. In the past, if the suspect's results were below the legal limit, he was released and no charges were filed.

In the late 1970s, police officers in Los Angeles realized that many impaired individuals with .000-percent BACs were being released, because the agency lacked policies and procedures for further evaluation of the drivers. Some of those officers began to work with researchers, medical personnel, and others to develop evaluation methods. The product of their work is a twelve-step evaluation process that evolved to become the drug influence evaluation.[3]

After the initial development within the Los Angeles Police Department, the National Highway Traffic Safety Administration (NHTSA) undertook laboratory and field studies to assess the validity of the method. The NHTSA studies concluded that the drug influence evaluation (DIE) can be conducted by a properly trained police officer, and that the results of these evaluations meet an acceptable level of accuracy in determining drug impairment.[4]

NHTSA then began curriculum development and a program to teach the twelve-step process to qualified police officers throughout the country. Officers completing this training are certified as drug recognition experts (DRE). Currently, thirty-four states and the District of Columbia have DRE programs. The same program or a similar program has been initiated in foreign countries including Canada and Great Britain.

DREs are able to determine whether or not a suspect is under the influence of drugs, and the type of drug or drugs the suspect has used. This is possible because drugs within a category produce similar effects, and DREs are trained in a systematic and standardized procedure to observe those effects. After conducting a DIE, the DRE consults a symptom matrix, integrates all available information, and reaches a conclusion.[5] If the conclusion is that the suspect is drug impaired, he or she is asked to provide a blood or urine specimen for drug testing. The prosecutor subsequently receives the police report, the DIE report, and the report of the analysis of the blood or urine specimen. Those documents are the basis for the prosecutor's decision as to whether the case is strong enough to initiate formal charges.

The decision to prosecute a DUI-drug case is not an easy one. In DUI-alcohol cases, if the suspect's measured alcohol level is above a certain established level, then that individual is prosecuted. For a number of reasons, including that certain drugs and metabolites of drugs may stay in the user's system for days to weeks, a positive drug test may not be proof beyond a reasonable doubt that an individual was driving impaired.[7] Some defendants are aware of this, and freely testify that indeed they did use a drug, but that they hadn't used it the day of arrest.

To evaluate the strength of the case, the prosecutor considers the report written by the arresting officer, the suspect's performance of the SFSTs, and the information recorded on the DIE record, as well as the results of the drug test. These are the main sources of information for the prosecutor. If drugs were found in the vehicle, or the suspect admitted use, that evidence is also taken into account.

The arresting officer can provide valuable evidence at trial. First, he will be able to testify about his observations of any impaired driving. He also will be able to testify about the suspect's behavior after being stopped, whether he had trouble locating his license and registration, and other observations of his appearance and demeanor. The officer may testify that he smelled an odor on the driver's breath or emanating from the vehicle, or that he initially noticed the driver, because he appear to be smoking marijuana or crystal methamphetamine while operating his vehicle.

The arresting officer usually conducts the SFSTs at roadside, and the tests DRE also conducts them during the DIE. Although this test battery was designed to aid officers in assessing the influence of alcohol, it also reflects impairment by drugs other than alcohol.[8]

Note that horizontal gaze nystagmus, an important component of the SFSTs, does not occur in the presence of all drugs. In drug examinations, therefore, whether it is absent or present is highly significant information. Walking and balance, as displayed in the walk-and-turn test and the one-leg-stand test, may be impaired by any of the commonly abused drugs.

All components of the evaluation play a crucial role. In a systematic examination, the DRE looks for signs and symptoms that are usually present within each of the seven drug categories.[9] Additional signs and symptoms are associated only with specific drugs.[10] There is, however, no criterion number of signs and symptoms that must be reported to support a decision to prosecute the case.

The use of multiple drugs, that is, poly-drug abuse, complicates decisions about prosecution. Individuals may ingest different drugs at different times and in different amounts. Seven different drugs have been found in blood and urine specimens obtained from suspects in Honolulu. The signs and symptoms produced by multiple substances may hamper the ability of the DRE to determine the precise category or categories of drugs a suspect has used.

In almost every state, the DRE can choose which bodily fluid to obtain for analysis. Some substances require a specific fluid (e.g., inhalants are detectable in blood but not in urine). When a suspect refuses or fails to provide a blood or urine specimen, the refusal may result in a lengthy license suspension. In addition, most states will permit trial testimony about the refusal.

If the toxicology report from analysis of the specimen confirms the DRE's opinion, then the prosecutor will most likely agree to charge the suspect. A more difficult situation arises when the DRE has concluded that the defendant was impaired by one category of drugs, and the laboratory test is negative for that category but positive for another. An example of this situation would be a DRE's conclusion that a defendant had been driving under the influence of cannabis, but the drug test was negative for cannabis and positive for a stimulant. In cases such as these, there usually are reasonable explanations for why drug category was incorrectly identified.

Note that cannabis and stimulants both produce the same five of eight signs and symptoms. The suspect may also have used alcohol, over-the-counter drugs, herbs, or medicines, all of which can affect the user and produce signs and symptoms of substance use. Note, too, the suspect actually may have used marijuana recently, but the marijuana metabolite that the laboratory looks for had yet to enter into the suspect's urine.

Consequently, in cases such as these, a prosecutor usually feels comfortable in bringing charges. The fact that the DRE may not have been entirely accurate about the drug the suspect had been using is not necessarily a fatal flaw for a case. Indeed, the drug test can be entirely negative, and the prosecutor can still bring charges and obtain convictions. This occurs when the suspect admits drug use or drugs are found on the person or in the vehicle. The admission or the drugs, along with weaving on the highway, performing poorly on the SFSTs, and strong evidence of impairment from the DIE can be sufficient to obtain a conviction despite a negative drug test. It is important, of course, for the judge and jury to hear testimony about the reasons for a negative drug test when an individual has recently used drugs.

How can a drug test result be negative if the person was using drugs? The main reason is that drug laboratories cannot afford the expense of multiple tests and do not test for every possible drug. Only the most common drugs are searched for in a typical drug screening. Also, individuals use unusual substances, some of which cannot be found by a laboratory. Individuals, for example, lick the backs of frogs that emit a secretion that is a hallucinogen. Some cultures use plant materials, herbs, and teas in the practice of their religion or for other purposes, and some of these materials produce impairment if taken in large quantities.

14.3 Presenting Cases for Trial

In a DUI-alcohol trial, having a BAC reading above the jurisdiction's legal limit with probable cause to stop is usually sufficient evidence. In a DUI-drug case, the lab results alone are not sufficient to convict. In contrast, DUI-drug cases require substantial trial preparation. A number of witnesses may be needed, and the prosecutor may have to educate himself as well as the jury about various toxicological issues.

In a DUI-drug trial, it is unlike that a single fact by itself can prove impairment. The prosecutor must build his case step by step with a series of facts that combine to form a complete picture of impairment. Those facts come from three sources: the arresting officer, the drug recognition expert, and the toxicologist.

The arresting officer obtains clues of impairment through his initial observation of the suspect's driving, the suspect's physical condition, and his performance of the SFSTs. The officer may smell an odor from recently burning drugs or notice drug paraphernalia in the vehicle. An impaired suspect who lacks the odor of alcohol alerts the arresting officer that the suspect may be using drugs. In many jurisdictions, he can use a portable breath-testing instrument at roadside to confirm that the suspect's BAC is zero or low.

In trial, direct examination of the arresting officer must elicit the reasons for the initial stop, the observations of impaired driving, anything the officer saw or smelled, statements made by the suspect, and the suspect's performance of the SFSTs. The first step of the DRE's evaluation is questioning the arresting officer about these aspects of the stop and the arrest. The DRE forms his opinion at the conclusion of his examination of the suspect after considering all information, including everything provided by the arresting officer.

The DRE testimony is crucial in a DUI-drug trial, and the prosecutor needs to prepare him as a witness, especially if it is the first time he has testified in this capacity. Despite their rigorous training, some DREs may feel uncomfortable about testifying and defending their opinions. This is most likely to occur if the DRE conducts evaluations only infrequently, or if the trial date is long after the date of the arrest. It can be very difficult to recall the details of and to defend an examination conducted many months previously. In advance of trial, the prosecutor should provide the DRE with a list of questions and advise him about what to expect on cross-examination.

The questioning of the DRE and issues relating to his status as an expert witness will be discussed in greater detail in Chapter 16. In general, the prosecutor wants the judge or jury to know the officer's credentials. A significant amount of time should be spent detailing his specialized training and his experience, emphasizing the total number of evaluations he has conducted. His opinion and the reasons for his opinion are of the greatest importance..

The third crucial witness is the toxicologist. This part of the trial can be quite lengthy, because everyone who handled the test specimen needs to testify to establish the chain of custody. In addition, there is usually one individual who conducted the general screening test, a second individual who conducted the confirmatory test, and the laboratory toxicologist who certified the results. The toxicologist must be prepared to testify not only about the results of the analysis of the specimen and the drugs that were found but also about the effects of those drugs on the human body and on driving performance.

Although the toxicologist can provide valuable information to support the opinion of the DRE, he cannot conclude, based on the test results alone, that the defendant was impaired. He will not be able to testify about the exact time when the drugs were taken or the amounts that were used. Sometimes, the drug levels found in urine or blood provide clues of recent use, but technology does not make it possible to determine precise details about amount of drug and time factors.

A related toxicological issue involves the accepted definition of a drug within the jurisdiction. Many states define a drug as any substance that impairs an individual's ability to operate a motor vehicle safely. This definition includes inhalants and some exotic herbal substances. Other states limit the definition of drug to Schedule I–IV controlled substances. Although this list includes powerful illicit and prescription drugs, many impairing substances are not included. In these states, an individual who drives under the influence of herbal ecstasy, ephedrine, or kava cannot be prosecuted for DUI-drugs.

The role of the prosecutor at a DUI-drug trial is that of an educator as well as an attorney. Many judges have not handled these cases, and many jurors have not encountered these impairing drugs. Everything must be explained clearly and carefully. An enlarged chart of the twelve steps of the DIE and another of the signs and symptoms matrix should be displayed during the trial. The DRE should bring a pupilometer into court and demonstrate to the jury how it is used to measure pupil sizes. The prosecutor's role is that of an advocate, but in DUI-drug trial he must also be a teacher.

14.4 Common Challenges and Defenses in DUI-Drug Cases

There seems to be an unlimited number of challenges and defenses that arise in DUI-drug trials, and anecdotes abound. In one case, a highly paid defense expert testified that the defendant had put Visine into his eyes, and the effects of a stimulant-like chemical in the Visine caused him to drive impaired. The expert further testified that the marijuana the defendant had used didn't affect him. Rather, the sole source of impairment was the Visine he had used so bloodshot eyes wouldn't alert his parents to his drug use. The defendant was eventually convicted but only after a lengthy trial.

As part of the discovery process, the prosecutor provides the results of the defendant's drug test to the defense attorney, who then will try vigorously to mitigate the results of a positive test. The defendant has to explain the evidence of a drug in his system in some way. The explanation may be, "I was in a room where other people were smoking" or "Sure I used the drugs, but I used them the day before I was arrested."

Since the results of a urine drug test cannot be interpreted as proof that the suspect was driving impaired, the prosecutor must point out that the case is built on the totality of evidence of impairment, and the positive drug test is just one of the items to be considered. In addition, although a positive test alone cannot prove impairment, high levels may enable the toxicologist to testify that the results indicate recent use.

In DUI-drug trials, the defense often includes a statement to the jury that the DRE is "just a cop." His lack of medical training will be emphasized., and if he displays any lack of information about the drug involved in the case, that lack will also be emphasized. In response, the DRE should testify about his extensive training and experience and about his knowledge of the category of drugs at issue. He will, of course, readily acknowledge that he is not a physician, but he can also point out that as a police officer, he comes into contact with individuals under the influence of illegal substances far more often than the average doctor.

Vital signs (blood pressure, heart rate, body temperature) may be elevated or depressed by drugs, and they are checked during a drug evaluation. A common defense argument in response to a DRE's findings is that he did not know the defendant's normal vital signs, and that the defendant's pulse or blood pressure is always higher or lower than normal for some reason unrelated to drug use. It may also be claimed that a medical condition explains poor performance on the walk and turn test and one leg stand test. The DRE should respond that before the tests were given, the suspect was asked if he had any medical conditions that would affect his ability to take the tests. Also, he will be able to testify that the normal ranges for vital signs that DREs rely upon during their evaluations have long been accepted in the medical community.

The symptom matrix lists eight signs and symptoms associated with each drug category. Additional signs and symptoms may be associated with specific drugs within a category. In the individual case, the signs and symptoms reflect dosage levels and other factors, but not all are expected to be present on all occasions with all drug users. Some of the signs and symptoms that are associated with a specific drug will not have been observed in a particular defendant.

The defense can be expected to focus on the missing signs and symptoms. The DRE training manuals and charts will be used to show that a certain sign or symptom of a drug at issues was not observed during the evaluation of the defendant. The DRE, of course, will respond that one individual rarely displays all the signs and symptoms of a drug. Moreover, the usual signs and symptoms may not have appeared, because the defendant had used another substance that masked them.

The DRE's conclusion that the defendant was driving under the influence of drugs will also be challenged by the assertion that the DRE opinion, at best, was a guess. Again, the DRE's lack of medical training and the fact that he did not know the defendant's medical condition may be emphasized. The DRE will respond that his opinion was not a guess but was based upon the observed signs and symptoms that are commonly recognized in the medical community as being associated with specific categories of drugs. The DRE will testify that his opinion was based on the totality of the information available to him, including the observations of the arresting officer and his observations of the defendant during the twelve-step drug influence evaluation.

14.5 Conclusion

Decades ago, convictions for DUI-alcohol were rare. As we enter the 21st century, the status of DUI-drug cases is similar to that early status of alcohol cases. At one time, judges avoided alcohol cases, largely because they lacked sound information on which to base decisions. Defense attorneys raised dozens of legal and evidentiary challenges. Over time, however, convictions for DUI-alcohol became routine as a result of information, training, and experience within the scientific, law enforcement and judicial communities. The enforcement and prosecution of DUI-drug offenses can be expected to follow a similar pattern. At this time, some jurisdictions are well ahead of others in this area. Eventually, however, the legal systems in all fifty states will generate convictions for DUI-drugs in a manner similar to that now obtained for DUI-alcohol.

Endnotes

1. This test battery was developed by the Southern California Research Institute. It consists of three tests: horizontal gaze nystagmus, walk-and-turn, and one-leg stand.

2. Hawaii has amended its law and, as of January 1, 2002, all DUI arrests will fall in the category of driving under the influence of intoxicants

3. See Appendix I—12-Step Drug Influence Evaluation

4. Bigelow, G.E., Bickel, W.E., Roache, J.D., Liebson, I.A., and Nowowieski, P. (1985). *Identifying types of drug intoxication: Laboratory evaluation of a subject-examination procedure.* DOT-HS-806-753, NHTSA, U.S. Department of Transportation, and the National Institute on Drug Abuse.

Compton, R.P. (1986). Field evaluation of the Los Angeles Police Department drug detection program. DOT-HS-807-012, NHTSA, U.S. Department of Transportation.

5. Refer to Appendix IV, Chapter 16.

6. Some states have enacted *per* se laws that result in a finding of guilt if any quantity of an illegal drug is found in the driver's system. These states are Arizona, Georgia, Iowa, Illinois, Minnesota, Rhode Island, Utah, and Indiana.

7. It is important to keep in mind that alcohol is a drug and falls in the category of a central nervous system (CNS) Depressant. It acts similarly to other CNS Depressants. [e.g. , benzodiazepines, barbiturates]

8. Refer to Appendix IV, Chapter 16.

Chapter 15

Defense of Drug Cases

Donald J. Bartell

Synopsis

15.1 Introduction

Anyone engaged in the practice of criminal defense will inevitably be involved in representing people accused of drug offenses. There is a wide reaching labyrinth of drug statutes in the United States. Violations include everything from the manufacture and sales of illegal drugs, to being under the influence of controlled substances. More so perhaps than any other type of offense, the consequences of a drug conviction potentially involves a host of collateral consequences for which the defense practitioner must also be aware. These include forfeiture laws, immigration consequences, and the effect on professional licenses.

Given the pervasive nature of drug cases, the practice in this area is continually evolving. The United States Supreme Court regularly decides cases involving drugs. Individual states are always trying new approaches to address the problem. For example, there are now courts dedicated solely to the handling of drug cases. A wide variety of pretrial diversion programs also exist throughout the country for many offenders. More and more police officers are being trained as drug recognition experts. Even the USA Patriot Act of 2001, passed as an antiterrorism bill after the September 11, 2001 attacks on the United States, will inevitably affect drug cases due to the new money laundering provisions in the bill.

Defending drug cases involves all the traditional aspects of defending a criminal case. This includes conducting a thorough investigation of the case and the filing of appropriate pretrial motions. Defenses of entrapment and pretrial diversion programs are more prevalent in drug cases than in the defense of many other crimes. A defense challenge to the legality of a search by the police is the watershed issue in many drug cases.

15.2 Search and Seizure Issues

The poorest man may, in his cottage, bid defiance to all the force of the Crown. It may be frail; its roof may shake; the wind may blow through it; the storm may enter; the rain may enter; but the King of England may not enter; all his force dare not cross the threshold of the ruined tenement.

—William Pitt, The Elder, in Parliament circa 1763

One of the central issues in representing people charged with drug offenses involves a review of the legality of any search in the case. Did the police lawfully come into possession of the evidence being used against the accused? Drug cases almost always involve search and seizure issues. The lawfulness of the search of a home, automobile, sealed container or even the arrested person, is often at issue in the case. The Fourth Amendment to the United States constitution provides:

> The right of the people to be secure in their persons, houses, papers, and effects, against unreasonable searches and seizures, shall not be violated, and no warrants shall issue but upon probable cause, supported by

> oath or affirmation, and particularly describing the place to be searched, and the persons or things to be seized.

The breadth of this one sentence amendment has resulted in the publication of treatises on the amendment's reach.

A. Standing

The starting point for the defense lawyer in a search and seizure issue is first determining if the client has what has come to be called "standing". In *Jones v. United States*, 362 U.S. 257 (1960), the court pointed out that it is not sufficient for a defendant to claim in a suppression motion that the evidence being challenged would be harmful to his or her cause. Presumably all of the evidence planned on being introduced by the prosecution is intended to have that effect. The court in a series of decisions has required that the unlawful search must in effect be personal to the defendant.

More specifically, the court has ruled that the conduct by the government must have violated the accused person's legitimate expectation of privacy. *Rawlings v. Kentucky*, 448 U.S. 98, 100 S.C. 2556, 65 L.ED.2d 633 (1980), In *Rawlings*, for example, the court held that the defendant did not have standing to object to the search of someone else's purse. The court found that the defendant did not have a legitimate expectation of privacy in the purse of another. See also *United States v. Jacobsen*, 466 U.S. 109 (1984) for the rule applied in a somewhat different context. In *Jacobsen*, private nongovernmental parties conducted the initial search and found a package with white powder in it. DEA agents conducted a subsequent field test for cocaine. The court held that "A chemical test that merely discloses whether or not a particular substance is cocaine does not compromise any legitimate interest in privacy." Id., at page 124.

As might be expected, there is a myriad of cases on the topic of standing. From the defense's perspective, the facts must be developed in the motion in such a way as to show the defendant did have a recognizable privacy interest in the searched area or item. Personalize the issue. Show the steps the defendant took to protect his privacy (The box was taped shut, the curtains were drawn, the apartment was regularly frequented, etc.). Facts make cases and no more so than in cases dealing with standing. Some cases on various standing issues are set forth below.

- *Alderman v. United States*, 394 U.S. 165 (1969) (wiretapping)
- *Brown v. State,* 691 N.E. 2d 438 (Ind. 1998) (live in boyfriend; compare *State v. Westerfield*, 1997 SD 100, N.W.2d 863 (1997)—dating resident)
- *Mancusi v. DeForte*, 392 U.S. 364 (1968) (shared office)
- *Minnesota v. Carter*, 525 U.S. 83 (1998) (brief visitor to premises for the purpose of packaging contraband)
- *Minnesota v. Olson*, 495 U.S. 91 (1990) (overnight guest)
- *Rakas v. Illinois*, 439 U.S. 128 (1978) (passenger's standing re search of car)
- *State v. Araki*, 82 Hawaii 474, 932 P.2d 891 (1996) (store clerk's standing)
- *United States v. Padilla*, 508 U.S. 77 (1993) (conspirator's standing)

B. Searches with warrants

The United States Supreme Court has held that "[t]he task of the issuing magistrate is simply to make a practical, common sense decision whether, given all the circumstances set forth in the affidavit before him, including the 'veracity' and 'basis of knowledge' of persons supplying hearsay information, there is a fair probability that contraband or evidence of a crime will be found in a particular place." *Illinois v. Gates*, 462 U.S. 213, 238 (1983).

A search conducted with a search warrant can be attacked by the defense by making a substantial preliminary showing that the affidavit in support of the warrant contained material false statements. The false averments must have been made knowingly or in reckless disregard of the truth. If the defense makes this preliminary showing, they are entitled to a hearing. "In the event that at that hearing the allegation of perjury or reckless disregard is established by the defendant by a preponderance of the evidence, and with the affidavit's false material set to one side, the affidavit's remaining content is in insufficient to establish probable cause, the search warrant must be voided . . ." *Franks v. Delaware*, 438 U.S. 154, 156 (1978).

Evidence obtained from an invalid search warrant may still be admissible if the police officer that executed the warrant acted in good faith in relying upon the warrant. *United States v. Leon*, 468 U.S. 897 (1984).

Leon indicated that suppression of the evidence is still warranted in at least four instances. They are as follows:

1. "The magistrate or judge issuing a warrant was mislead by information in an affidavit that the affaint officer knew was false or would have known was false except for his reckless disregard of the truth." Id., at 922, citing *Franks*, supra;
2. The magistrate wholly abandoned the judicial role;
3. The affidavit was so lacking in indicia of probable cause that an official belief in it by the officer is unreasonable,
4. The warrant was so facially deficient that the executing officers cannot reasonably presume its validity.

United States v. Leon, 468 U.S. 897, 922 (1984).

The remedy for unlawfully obtained evidence is suppression of the evidence. *Mapp v. Ohio*, 367 U.S. 643 (1961). Evidence directly obtained from the illegal conduct must be suppressed as well as the derivative evidence commonly described as emanating from the "fruit of the poisonous tree." *Wong Sun v. United States*, 371 U.S. 471 (1963).

C. Searches without warrants

In general a warrant is required in order to conduct a search. There are, of course, so many exceptions to the warrant requirement that the rule has been dampened significantly. Permissible warrantless searches include everything from stop and frisk searches, to automobile stop searches, to searches incident to an arrest. Warrantless searches also encompass voluntary consent searches, and searches of items in plain view.

One advantage, from the defense point of view, of challenging a warrantless search is that the burden is on the prosecution to justify the search. The reason for this is that a warrantless search is presumptively unreasonable. *Coolidge v. New Hampshire*, 403 U.S. 443, 454–455 (1971). Thus, all the defense has to do is to show that the defendant has standing to challenge the search, and that the search was conducted without a warrant. The burden is then on the government to justify the search under one of the exceptions to the warrant requirement.

Due to the low threshold for filing a suppression motion in a warrantless search case, many motions may fail, and the seized evidence may not be excluded. Nonetheless, even if the suppression motion is not successful in excluding evidence, there are many tangential benefits in conducting the motion. Chief among these benefits is that the defense gets an opportunity to preview much of the government's case. This preview includes getting to question under oath the officer executing the search. How well the officer conducted the search aspect of the investigation of the case may lead to telling conclusions about the investigation as a whole. How well the officer presents himself or herself in court as a witness will also be seen before the actual trial.

Furthermore, the prosecutor may have problems that do not manifest themselves until the motion is brought. The prosecution may offer better plea bargains before the hearing of a suppression motion. If nothing else, a transcript of any testifying officers can be obtained for possible future impeachment at trial. The benefits of running the motion to suppress should always be examined.

15.3 Investigation in Drug Cases

Defense investigations in drug cases are similar in many respects to investigations in other criminal cases. Some of the unique aspects involve the drugs themselves. Generally an expert will have to be engaged to analyze the substance. Specifically, is the actual substance something that is specifically made illegal by the relevant statutes? It is not unusual for the purveyors of illegal drugs to sell substances that are not exactly what was advertised. Because there are often quantity enhancements in drug cases, the weight of the drugs may also have to be independently verified. For possession cases, an expert can help the defense in determining whether remnants of a drug constitute a usable amount. Also, an expert may be needed to determine whether the quantity and packaging of a drug is sufficient to constitute possession for sales.

In cases involving charges of the defendant being under the influence of a controlled substance, the employment of a toxicologist or physician (who is familiar with the drug in question) is essential. If a drug recognition expert was involved in the evaluation of your client, the defense will generally need help from an expert in addressing the drug recognition expert's conclusions. (See discussion infra.)

Almost always, there is no substitute for visiting the scene. Visiting the scene memorializes the event in the lawyer's mind. If a person is charged with driving under the influence of drugs, the road where the purported weaving took place may be a windy pothole filled street where everyone weaves. If a drug sale took place in a neighborhood, what were the obstructions from the officer's vantage point? During cross-examination, it often behooves the defense attorney to let the arresting officer know, by the nature of the questions, that the attorney has been to the scene. This is a witness control technique that often produces more forthright answers than if the witness believes the lawyer has never been to the scene.

A basic discovery plan should include obtaining the following items:

- All police reports
- All laboratory reports from the prosecution
- In addition to the final laboratory reports that are generally produced, try and obtain the actual chromatograms of the specimen analyzed.
- A portion of the sample for the defense to analyze. Note, based on the right to counsel, the results of a defense analysis of a drug should not be disclosed unless they are going to be used at trial. *Prince v. Superior Court*, 8 Cal.App. 4th 1176 (1992). If the results of defense testing are not favorable, consider using a second expert who did not perform any analysis. This naturally has certain limitations, as the prosecution can note your expert never analyzed the sample in question.
- All audio or videotapes related to the case
- All statements of the defendant and all witnesses.
- Criminal histories of the defendant and all witnesses
- Any reports by any prosecution expert
- Prior transcripts of the testimony of any prosecution experts. If during your cross-examination of a government expert you let it be known that you have a transcript of the expert's prior testimony, the responses to your questions often become surprisingly forthright. This is similar to letting a witness know through your examination that you have been to the scene. Honesty surfaces when the truth is at arms reach. In some instances it may behoove you not to disclose the existence of a transcript to the witness. Holding back is far more effective when you have a devastating piece of prior testimony. Wait until the witness is committed to their new opinion. Then expose them to the jury with their prior inconsistent testimony.

- All photos taken related to the case
- Disclosure of any cooperation agreements made with any person
- Any and all exculpatory evidence pursuant to *Brady v. Maryland*, 373 U.S. 83 (1963).

15.4 Common Trial Issues

Issues in drug cases include all the various issues and defenses afforded in most criminal proceedings. The accused can challenge the veracity of the government's witnesses or argue a case of mistaken identity. The "mule defense," in which the accused person maintains that he or she was unaware that they were transporting drugs, can also be used if the facts so dictate. This defense may be even more enticing if during voir dire, jurors in the particular jurisdiction where the case is being tried, acknowledge that they are aware of the practice by some drug traffickers of using unsuspecting persons to transport narcotics. Reoccurring issues in the defense of drug cases involve the use of the entrapment defense, arguing what constitutes possession of a drug, and the cross-examination of drug recognition experts.

A. Entrapment

The defense of entrapment needs to be explored in the checklist examination of potential drug defenses. It is, however, generally not the best place for the defense to find itself situated, because the defense in effect concedes the commission of a crime by the defendant. A claim must then be asserted that the defendant's conduct is excusable due to the overreaching by the government.

Nonetheless, the entrapment defense may be viable in many instances, or it may perhaps be the only realistic option for the defense. In practice, it is also a defense that readily lends itself to examination with a mock jury panel. The issues are easily defined, and a mock jury trial can provide a preview of the particular appeal this defense will have in a given case. Do not underestimate the average citizen's sense of fair play. If, however, a mock jury summarily rejects the entrapment defense, a different approach may need to be studied.

Depending on the jurisdiction, the defense usually has a subjective or objective test for evaluating law enforcement conduct in the case. For discussion of the subjective test see the United States Supreme Court holding in *Jacobson v. United States* 503 U.S. 540 (1992). Objective tests can be found in *State v. Agrabante,* 830 P.2d 492, 499 (Haw. 1992) and the *California Jury Instructions, Criminal* (sixth edition) 4.61. That instruction reads in pertinent part:

> In deciding whether this defense has been established, guidance will generally be found in the application of one or both of two principles. First, if the actions of the law enforcement agent would generate in a normally law-abiding person a motive for the crime other than ordinary criminal intent, entrapment will be established . . . . Finally, while the inquiry must focus primarily on the conduct of the law enforcement agent, that conduct is not to be viewed in a vacuum; it should also be judged by the effect it would have on a normally law-abiding person situated in the circumstances of the case at hand.

The court should give an entrapment instruction as long as some evidence of the issue is presented at trial. *Mathews v. United States*, 485 U.S. 61, 62 (1988).

B. Possession

Possession of drugs can either be via actual or constructive possession. "Actual possession occurs when the defendant exercises direct physical control over the item, however briefly (e.g., in the hand, clothing, purse, bag, etc.). Constructive possession does not require direct physical control over the item but does require that a person knowingly exercise control or right to control a thing, either directly or through another person or persons." *People v. Austin,* 23 Cal.App. 4th 1596, 1608–1609 (1994). Whether someone has constructive possession is often a debatable proposition. Debatable propositions are, of course, the harbor where reasonable doubt docks.

The Kansas Supreme Court pointed out various factors to consider in determining if a person had possession of drugs in *State v. Bockert*, 893 P.2d 832, 836 (Kan. 1995). The court concluded that factors to consider are the ". . . defendant's previous participation in the sale of drugs, use of narcotics, proximity to the area where drugs are found, and the fact the drugs were found in plain view." The crime of possession of a controlled substance does not require specific intent. Still, it must be proven that the defendant knew the seized substance was a controlled substance. *People v. Amiotte*, 215 Cal.App.2d 176 (1963). It may also be required to show that the amount of the controlled substance was a usable amount. Trace amounts insufficient for use are insufficient for conviction. *People v. Leed*, 64 Cal.2d. 504 (1966).

C. Drug recognition experts

A drug recognition expert (DRE) is a police officer who has received specialized training to determine if a person is under the influence of drugs. Even though it is unlawful to be under the influence of illegal drugs (see for example California Health and Safety Code section 11550) unlike alcohol, there are no statutory per se levels that determine if someone is actually under the influence of a drug.

This is a point that the defense can make in every under the influence of drugs case. In essence, if it is so certain that a person is under the influence of cocaine (given the level of cocaine in his or her blood), why is it that the legislature has not designated a specific quantitative level of the drug as being determinative of someone being under the influence? With alcohol it is illegal to drive with blood alcohol levels of 0.08 percent or 0.10 percent in a given jurisdiction. No such per se levels exist with drugs. The defense attorney should make sure that jurors are aware of this fact.

The DRE attempts to fill this void by evaluating a subject via a twelve-step process. The defense attorney's job is to reopen the void with appropriate cross-examination. The twelve steps are:

1. A breath test for alcohol (typically conducted with a preliminary alcohol screening device)
2. An interview of the arresting officer by the DRE
3. Preliminary examination of the subject (includes an initial pulse rate)
4. Eye exam
5. Field sobriety tests
6. Vital signs—blood pressure, temperature, another pulse rate taken
7. Examination of eyes, nose and mouth in a darkroom
8. Muscle tone
9. Examination for needle marks, and a third pulse rate taken
10. Subject interview

11. Formulation of opinion
12. Taking of a toxicological specimen

Given the advent of the DRE methodology, the first inquiry by the defense is to see if a DRE did an examination of your client. If not, the defense can tout the merits of a DRE examination and claim the investigation is defective as there was no evaluation by a trained DRE. If on the other hand, a DRE did do an examination of your client, (and assuming the results were not favorable) the defense now needs to challenge the DRE's opinion and maybe, even the whole basis of the science.

A starting point is making sure that all of the DRE steps were performed. Most drug recognition experts will concede that the DRE examination must be completely performed as outlined above in order for the evaluation to have any validity. Assuming the steps were properly conducted, the defense can still point out that many symptoms are naturally occurring, and can mimic the symptoms of drug use. For example, just because someone has high blood pressure does not mean they are under the influence of a central nervous system stimulant like methamphetamine. People do have high blood pressure. Similarly, the fight or flight response, which naturally occurs in people under stressful situations (like being arrested), can raise pulse rates and dilate pupils. Also there is a wide variety of legal substances that mimic the effects of illegal drugs. Asthma inhalers, for instance, often contain ephedrine, which is a central nervous system stimulant.

If all else fails, an attack on the DRE science itself may be order. If there is an Achilles' heel in a DRE evaluation, it surely must be that the scientific method is not truly employed. Having the arresting officer tell the DRE officer (see step two above) that marijuana was found on the defendant, and that the there was a pervasive order of marijuana surrounding the defendant, undoubtedly will color the DRE's "independent" conclusion that the defendant was under the influence of marijuana. When the evaluator is told in advance what the subject has taken, this is about as far removed as one can get from a double blind study.

Similarly, the scientific method is lacking in steps three through eight above in that the DRE examiner does not have a prior baseline reading of the subject before conducting the examination. Items three through eight of the DRE exam, commencing with the initial examination of the subject and concluding with a check of the subject's muscle tone, involve an assessment of the subject's physical attributes. The DRE does not know, however, how the subject would normally respond without the use of the alleged illegal substance. Given this, it can be argued that the DRE cannot fairly conclude that poor performance on the field sobriety tests is attributable to being under the influence of drugs. Instead, poor performance may be attributable to the subject being overweight, scared, or simply uncoordinated. It is simply unknown to the DRE how the subject normally performs on these coordination exercises.

Whether a general attack on the science as a whole is undertaken, or whether a specific attack on the DRE evaluation in a particular case is done, the employment of an expert is usually necessary. You may have difficulty finding someone to assist the defense who is a trained DRE as these persons normally are police officers. There are, however, privately trained drug recognition experts. Toxicologists can help, and many physicians are highly suspicious of the claims made by a DRE evaluation. The skepticism of physicians may be due in part to the fact that they were not trained in such evaluations in medical school. This does not diminish the impact their testimony may have on a jury. A board certified emergency room physician's testimony that it would be wonderful if only the DRE's claims were possible puts the prosecution on the defense.

15.5 Diversion

In lieu of trial, a defendant may be eligible to enroll in a drug treatment program. This is typically known as "drug diversion" or simply "diversion." Generally, a defendant foregoes a trial in exchange for the chance to participate in a drug treatment program. Successful completion of the program typically results in the charges being dismissed. Even if diversion is not statutorily an option, some prosecutors may be persuaded to try a non-statutory program developed by the defense. Being creative in this area can pay dividends for the client.

If the defense attorney is going to offer something novel, it is best to have the proposal fully developed before discussing it with the prosecutor. Hopefully, in this way the prosecutor will be less tempted to summarily dismiss the proposal. Claims that the plan is too vague or seemingly unworkable will be harder to advance if the defense has the particulars of a treatment plan already developed. The same is true in making an argument at sentencing. If an alternative sentence is being proffered by the defense, make it as palatable as possible for the court by having a specific plan prepared in advance.

In discussing diversion with a client, counsel must apprise the client of what the required drug treatment program entails. Keep in mind that the client must successfully complete the program in order to gain the legal benefits of diversion. The extent of the program should be discussed with the client before securing the client's consent to opt for the program. For some people, the program requirements may seem too onerous or too difficult to comply with in their particular life situation.

Whether or not the client is eligible for diversion is typically the initial inquiry. The prior history of the defendant or the existence of certain designated charges can preclude eligibility. See for example California Penal Code section 1000, which delineates the requirements for drug diversion in California. Note that a typical eligibility requirement for diversion is that the charges implicate only personal use or possession of drugs. Persons charged with possession for sale, thus, may not be eligible for diversion. If this is the case, the defense's initial campaign may be to try to persuade the prosecutor that the correct offense that should be charged is possession, not sales of controlled substances. Once this is accomplished, an effort to obtain diversion can then be sought.

A decision to offer diversion normally is considered to involve a decision by the executive branch of government. The reason for this is that the government is forfeiting its right to prosecute. Consequently, a grant of diversion often requires the prosecutor's assent. See *Federov v United States*, 600 A.2d 370 (D.C. Ct. App. 1991). There typically is no appeal, or a very narrow right to appeal, if the prosecutor does not agree to a grant of diversion. See *People v. McAlister*, 225 Cal. App.3d 941, 945, 275 Cal. Rptr. 229, 231 (1990).

15.6 Collateral Consequences

A. Immigration implications

The consequences of a drug conviction on the immigration status of a client who is not a United States citizen are enormous. For some clients, the immigration consequences of a conviction may be more paramount than incarceration. Imagine for the moment being uprooted from family, friends, employment, and home and then being deported to a country where you may not have lived for many years. This is the prospect many noncitizens face when they are charged with a drug offense. For the lawyer with such a client, the complexity of immigration law means that you have now fallen into the "briar patch." As a result, it is essential that you consult with an immigration attorney in planning your overall approach to the case. The failure of a defense attorney to properly apprise a client of the immigration consequences involved in a case may constitute ineffective assistance of counsel. *People v. Soriano*, 194 Cal.App.3d 1470, 1482 (1987).

1. Immigration status

The first step is to determine whether the client is a United States citizen. The Fourteenth Amendment to the United States Constitution provides in part: "All persons born or naturalized in the United States, and subject to the jurisdiction thereof, are citizens of the United States and of the State wherein they reside." A United States citizen cannot be deported. The easiest way to determine citizenship status is to make it a consistent practice to specifically ask each and every client if he or she is a U.S. citizen. Every client questionnaire should have a question enquiring as to the citizenship of the client. It may even behoove you to ask if the client has ever been a United States citizen, as in rare instances it may be possible to reacquire lost citizenship.

For those clients who are not citizens, a follow up inquiry should be made as to their immigration status. It should also be determined if they have been the subject of any previous immigration actions. The most dramatic example of the significance of a prior immigration action is if the client has reentered the United States after having been removed for conviction of an aggravated felony. Pursuant to 8 U.S.C. §1326 this conduct can carry up to twenty years in prison.

2. Removal

Being denied admissibility to the United States or being deported from the United States now fall under the rubric of the term "removal". Inadmissibility means that a person cannot enter the United States. Deportation refers to the process of requiring a person who is presently in the country to leave the United States. As it pertains to drug cases, inadmissible aliens are described in 8 U.S.C. §1182 (a)(2)(A)(i)(II). That section reads: "Except as otherwise provided in this chapter, aliens who are inadmissible under the following paragraphs are ineligible to receive visas and ineligible to be admitted to the United States: . . . [if convicted of] a violation of (or conspiracy or attempt to violate) any law or regulation of a State, the United States, or a foreign country relating to a controlled substance (as defined in section 802 of title 21), is inadmissible."

Deportation due to drugs is set forth in 8 U.S.C §1227(a)(2)(B)(i) and (ii). Those sections state:

> Any alien (including an alien crewman) in and admitted to the United States shall, upon the order of the Attorney General, be removed if the alien is within one or more of the following classes of deportable aliens:
>
> (i) Any alien who at any time after admission has been convicted of a violation of (or a conspiracy or attempt to violate) any law or regulation of a State, the United States, or a foreign country relating to a controlled substance (as defined in section 802 of title 21), other than a single offense involving possession for one's own use of 30 grams or less of marijuana, is deportable.
>
> (ii) Any alien who is, or at any time after admission has been, a drug abuser or addict is deportable.

As can be seen, the language in these sections is fairly wide sweeping. A person who is determined to be a drug abuser or drug addict can be deported even without a criminal conviction.

3. Aggravated felony

In drug cases the most serious immigration implications arise from a conviction for trafficking in a controlled substance. Drug trafficking constitutes an aggravated felony for immigration purposes. (8 U.S.C. §1101 (a)(43)(B)) Numerous onerous consequences accompany an aggravated felony. To begin with, an aggravated felon, who is not a permanent resident, is subject to expedited deportation proceedings and is not entitled to bail. Political asylum is not available, and the cancellation of removal proceedings cannot be attempted. Also as mentioned above, reentry after deportation for an aggravated felony can carry a lengthy prison sentence. Therefore, an aggravated felony conviction is the first step in things to be avoided by the defense.

It must be noted that section 8 U.S.C. §1101 (a)(43), which defines the term, aggravated felony, includes a multitude of other offenses besides drug trafficking. Thus, as far as the aggravated felony status is concerned, it is of no use to plea bargain to a racketeering charge (for which a sentence of more than one year may be imposed) in exchange for having a drug trafficking charge dropped. The reason for this is that both constitute an aggravated felony under 8 U.S.C §1101 (a)(43). Still, there are some possible solutions to minimize the immigration consequences of drug cases.

4. Possible solutions

- Try to avoid having the charges brought. The possibility of a cooperation agreement with the government needs to be explored with the client. If the client is interested in cooperating with the government, but the attorney is uncomfortable with this approach, the client may need to be referred to alternate counsel.
- If charges are brought, try to have them dismissed. See, for example, the discussion infra on search and seizure motions.
- Consider a diversion program or any other pretrial program that does not require a conviction. See 8 U.S.C. §1101(a)(48)(A) for the definition of what constitutes a conviction for immigration purposes. A pretrial diversion program that requires a guilty plea, may for example, constitute a conviction even if the conviction will later be set aside. In Re Punu, Int. Dec. 3364 (BIA 1998), WL 546634 (BIA).
- If the charges cannot be dismissed, then win the trial. Recognizing that this is sometimes simpler to utter than execute, be mindful that trying the case may preclude other options if the trial is lost.
- Avoid a conviction for an aggravated felony or a drug offense as they are defined in the code. Try and be sentenced under the federal program for first offenders pursuant to 18 U.S.C. §3607. Similar state programs may be an option in states under the jurisdiction of the Federal Ninth Circuit Court of Appeals. See *Lujan-Armendariz v. INS*, 222 F.3d 728 (9th Cir. 2000).
- Plead to something that is not strictly defined as a triggering offense. Consider, for example, pleading to being an accessory after the fact, as this may not be a conviction relating to illegal drugs. See *Castaneda de Esper v. INS,* 557 F.2d 79 (6th Cir. 1977). Similarly, a

single conviction of simple possession of 30 grams or less of marihuana may also be an option. 8 U.S.C. §1101(f)(3). Also in the case of *Coronado-Durazo v. INS*, 123 F.3d 1322 (9th Cir. 1997), the court ruled that the crime of solicitation, even though it pertains to the solicitation of drugs, is not a controlled substance violation.

- Be mindful in plea-bargaining around a drug charge that you do not admit to one of the myriad of other offenses that have immigration consequences.
- Obtain a pardon.
- Recognize that you are not an immigration lawyer. Immigration law is a complicated field that is constantly changing. Your job is to understand the general strategy and have an immigration attorney on board to consult with you throughout the case.

B. Asset forfeiture

Asset forfeiture proceedings are widespread throughout the United States. Both the federal government and the individual states have mechanisms to forfeit ill obtained property. Virtually any type of property is subject to forfeiture actions. There are criminal forfeiture proceedings (18 U.S.C. §982 and 21 U.S.C. §853), but most proceedings are civil in nature. Probably the reason for is that the burden of proof is lower in civil cases. Also civil cases do not afford the full panoply of constitutional protections that criminal cases do.

A civil action is an in rem proceeding against the property itself. This is why upon review you will see many of the cases entitled the government versus a certain amount of cash, or the state versus the name of a boat. The defendant is actually the property. See for example, *U.S. v. $38,000.00 in U.S. Currency,* 816 F2d 1538 (11th Cir. 1987).

Since the defendant is the property, a claimant must establish standing in order to file a claim to recover the property. The standing issues in forfeiture actions are conceptually similar to the standing issues discussed earlier in this chapter with respect to search and seizure standing. The emphasis in forfeiture actions is that the claimant must establish an ownership interest, a secured creditor interest, or a possessory interest in the subject property. *$38,000.00 in U.S. Currency*, Id.

1. Initial considerations

The initial consideration when faced with a forfeiture action is to discern the immediacy for which a response is due. Thirty days is not atypical. The next decision then is whether or not to file a claim. Nota bene: if your client has been involved in activity that might lead to criminal charges, the risk of self-incrimination in filing a claim must be weighed against the benefit of trying to recover the seized property. As a general rule, when in doubt do not file a claim. As discussed below, because the proceedings are civil in nature, a civil claimant does not have the same constitutional protections a criminal defendant acquires.

Another immediate concern for the defense attorney is how is the attorney going to get paid? Are the attorney fees subject to forfeiture? The United States Supreme Court has ruled that assets designated for attorney's fees are still subject to forfeiture. *U.S. v. Monsanto,* 491 U.S. 617 (1989).

2. Constitutional concerns

As mentioned previously, due to the fact that forfeiture proceedings are generally civil in nature, there are lessened constitutional protections afforded a civil claimant than a criminal defendant. A civil claimant may decline to testify, but the privilege against self-incrimination does not protect the civil claimant from being called to the witness stand. *U.S. v. $250,000.00 in U.S. Currency*, 808 F.2d. 895 (1st Cir. 1987). Once called as a witness, the failure to testify can result in a variety of adverse implications in the civil case.

A seizure done in violation of the fourth amendment does not bar the property from a forfeiture action. Unlawfully obtained evidence is subject to suppression, but the seized property itself is not. *One 1958 Plymouth Sedan v. Pennsylvania*, 380 U.S. 693 (1965). Since a forfeiture action is civil in nature, the Sixth Amendment right to appointed counsel does not apply.

The eighth amendment protection against cruel and unusual punishment does not apply to civil forfeiture actions either. That portion of the eighth amendment prohibiting excessive fines does, however, apply. *Alexander v. U.S.*, 509 U.S. 544 (1993).

C. Professional licenses

Like representing a noncitizen, when representing a client facing drug charges who has a professional license, there are considerations beyond the actual criminal case. The defendant with a professional license may be more concerned about the continued ability to practice his or her profession than the punitive aspects of the criminal case. Unlike cases with immigration consequences, in which the negative consequences are largely alleviated by a successful defense of the case, a professional may still be subject to discipline despite being exonerated in the underlying criminal matter. *Holt v. Department of Food and Agriculture*, 171 Cal.App.3d 427, 433 (1985). Avoiding the conviction, of course, is still paramount as a conviction is usually conclusive proof of the charged conduct in a disciplinary hearing. The conviction can be used as a sword. An acquittal is unavailing as a shield.

In order to be a cause for discipline, a criminal conviction generally needs to be substantially related to the qualifications of the profession, or be a crime of moral turpitude. Therefore, try and avoid having your client being convicted of any of the foregoing. Steps you can take to help alleviate future licensing problems are:

- Try not to get a felony conviction.
- Better yet, try not to get any conviction.
- Investigate the possibility of diversion and its impact on disciplinary proceedings in the relevant jurisdiction.
- As mentioned above, avoid convictions involving moral turpitude and those related to the practice of the profession.
- If the client is convicted, present to the court a sentencing plan that does not involve a sentence prohibiting the practice of the client's profession. For example, regular drug testing may address some of the court's concerns.
- Consult with an attorney who practices before the particular licensing board in question.

15.7 Conclusion

The defense of drug cases requires careful consideration of a variety of issues. It is a changing field with the development of new statutes, cases, and programs almost being the norm. The criminal defense attorney must stay abreast, if not ahead, of any changes to ensure the constitutional rights of the accused are protected.

Chapter 16

Expert and Opinion Testimony of Law Enforcement Officers Regarding Identification of Drug-Impaired Drivers

David Sandler

Synopsis

Prosecutors have attempted to use police officers as expert witnesses in a variety of areas over the decades. Each time prosecutors offer police officers as experts to give their opinions on scientific or technical matters, their qualifications as experts face severe challenges. In recent years, in Hawaii and numerous other jurisdictions, prosecutors have attempted to utilize police officers as expert witnesses for their opinions as to whether or not the defendant was under the influence of drugs. This occurs on a daily basis in cases where the police charge the defendant with driving under the influence of drugs. In addition, police officers have testified as experts regarding drug impairment in cases involving murder, manslaughter, and vehicular homicide.

Mainly due to the growing number of drugged driving arrests nationwide, there is no greater use of police officers as expert witnesses in criminal trials than in this relatively new area of drug recognition. As of August 2000, there were over 5,200 police officers specially trained in the area of drug recognition in the United States.[1] They have the title of "drug recognition experts" (DREs), but whether or not the courts should recognize them as "experts" has been the subject of intense litigation.

In the typical drugged driving case, a police officer observes unusual driving behavior or a traffic violation that leads him to believe the driver may be impaired. The officer pulls the driver over, and asks him for his driver's license and registration. At this time, the officer observes additional signs of impairment such as bloodshot eyes, dilated pupils, incoherent speech, and fumbling with documents. He then asks the suspect to participate in a field sobriety test.[2]

There is no strict pass/fail score for the field sobriety test. Consequently, many believe these "tests" should be referred to as "tasks." Based upon the officer's observations on how well the suspect performed these tasks, observations of the suspect's driving, the odor or presence of alcohol or drugs, statements made by the suspect, or any additional observations made by the officer, the officer determines whether or not to arrest the suspect for driving while impaired.

Where there is any indication that the impairment is due to alcohol, the officer arrests the suspect for driving under the influence of alcohol (DUI-Alcohol). This maybe the result of alcohol being on the person's breath or a container of an alcoholic beverage found in the car. The officer then brings the suspect to the police station where the police administer a chemical test to determine the amount of alcohol in the person's system.[3] If the result of the chemical test shows the suspect was above the legal limit, which is .10 in most states and .08 in Hawaii and a few other states, then the police formally arrest the individual for DUI-Alcohol.[4] In the past, if the individual's alcohol reading was below the legal limit, the police released him. This was done even though all the evidence demonstrated that he was impaired and presented a danger on the highway. Now, in thirty-four states and the District of Columbia, the police do not automatically release these suspects and put them back on the roads.[5] Instead, the arresting officer will call for a police officer specially trained in the area of drug recognition in order to further the investigation.

The issue as to whether or not this specially trained officer should be recognized by the courts as an expert and be able to render an opinion as to whether or not the suspect was impaired by drugs is the subject of this article. The article details the development of the drug recognition expert program in Section II, explains the training received by DREs in Section III, and outlines how drug influence evaluations are conducted in Section IV. Section V of the article discusses all the major cases that have been decided regarding the issue of allowing DREs to testify as expert witnesses, and Section VI gives an overview of DRE expert testimony in Hawaii.

16.1 The Drug Recognition Expert

Driving under the influence of drugs ("DUI-Drugs") has surfaced as a growing problem in America and throughout the world.[6] "Drugged drivers" endanger the lives of everyone on the road, and increase the economic and noneconomic societal costs related to driving.[7] There is little doubt that the increase in collisions caused by drugged drivers, including those caused by drivers under the influence of prescription medication, is a major factor causing higher insurance premiums for everyone.[8]

In the early 1970s, Los Angeles Police Department (LAPD) officers noticed many of the individuals they arrested for DUI-Alcohol registered very low or zero alcohol concentration readings.[9] The officers suspected the individuals were impaired by drugs, but they lacked the necessary skills and training to support their suspicions. In the mid-1970s, two LAPD sergeants, a traffic officer and a narcotics officer, collaborated with various medical professionals to develop a simple, standardized procedure for recognizing drug influence and impairment.[10]

In the early 1980s the LAPD's drug recognition program attracted the attention of the National Highway Traffic Safety Administration (NHTSA).[11] NHTSA worked with the LAPD to standardize the protocol, and their combined efforts led to the development of the Drug Evaluation and Classification (DEC) program.[12] The DEC program was validated by a 1984 controlled laboratory study[13] and a 1985 field validation study.[14] These studies demonstrated that a properly trained DRE could successfully identify drug impairment and accurately determine the category of drugs causing the impairment.[15]

In 1984, NHTSA and the National Institute on Drug Abuse (NIDA) sponsored a controlled laboratory study. The study, conducted by researchers at the Johns Hopkins University, involved subjects who were drug dosed and then individually evaluated by four experienced DREs.[16] Subjects received either a placebo or a single drug.[17] Neither the subjects nor the officers were told what drug, if any, had been administered.[18] This study concluded that DREs correctly identified 95 percent of drug-free subjects as "unimpaired," DREs correctly classified 98.7 percent of high-dose subjects as "impaired," and DREs correctly identified the category of drugs for 97 percent of the high-dose subjects.[19]

In 1985, NHTSA and the LAPD collaborated on a field evaluation study.[20] An independent laboratory analyzed blood samples drawn from persons actually arrested for DUI-Drugs.[21] The results of this 173-subject case study, were very similar to earlier findings and demonstrated that trained DREs were able to "predict" the presence of certain types of drugs in the majority of cases.[22] This study indicated that when DREs said that drugs other than alcohol were present, drugs were detected 94 percent of the time; DREs correctly identified at least one drug other than alcohol in 97 percent of the suspects evaluated; when DREs identified a suspect as impaired by a specific drug category, the category was detected in the suspect's blood 79 percent of the time; and in almost 50 percent of the suspects, the DREs were entirely correct in identifying all of the categories detected in the blood (most of these suspects had used multiple drugs, other than alcohol).[23]

The most comprehensive study of the DEC program completed to date is the Drug Recognition Expert Validation Study.[24] This study examined the drug influence evaluation records for 500 suspects who were evaluated in Arizona over a fifty-three month period, and the corresponding toxicological analyses of the suspects' specimens.[25] Among the major conclusions were: the DRE program is a valid method for identifying and classifying drug-impaired drivers; DREs are able to recognize drug impairment and identify the drug(s), by category, which cause the impairment; and various drug categories produce specific observable signs and symptoms that DREs are able to detect.[26]

Overall, the Arizona study found that at least one of the categories of drugs that the DRE predicted appeared in subsequent drug testing in 83.5 percent of all cases.[27] Other field studies have produced confirmation rates of 88.2 percent in California, 81.3 percent in Texas, 84.5 percent in Minnesota, and 88 percent in Oregon.[28] In 1999, during the second year of drug testing in the DRE Program in Hawaii, toxicological confirmations for at least one category of drugs was 88.2 percent.[29]

It is important to keep in mind that merely because a lab report turns out to be "negative" does not necessarily mean the subject was drug free. Just because the lab was not able to confirm the DRE's findings does not mean that the DRE's analysis and conclusions were incorrect. For some very valid reasons, there are times when the toxicology lab simply is unable to confirm the DRE's findings.[30] There are indeed instances when an individual has drugs in his system although the lab test turns out "negative."[31]

On the other hand, just because a drug test comes up positive, does not necessarily mean the individual is under the influence of a particular drug. Metabolites of certain drugs may appear in low levels in a person's system weeks after the drug was ingested. Unless the drug levels are extremely high, toxicology results standing alone cannot prove impairment. This is why the role of the DRE is crucial. The DRE is trained to identify specific signs of impairment. Some of these signs may be visible, and others are obtained through taking some basic tests such as blood pressure, pulse rate, and body temperature.

The DEC Program, has received endorsements from the NHTSA, [32] the International Association of Chiefs of Police (IACP),[33] the U.S. Department of Justice (DOJ), [34] the American Bar Association (ABA), [35] and the National Commission Against Drunk Driving.[36] Additionally, hundreds of law enforcement agencies at the local, state, and federal levels, as well as private industry, employ the DEC.[37]

In 1987, NHTSA started DEC pilot programs in Arizona, Colorado, New York, and Virginia.[38] In 1988, NHTSA added Utah, California, and Indiana.[39] In 1989, NHTSA greatly expanded the DEC program, and currently thirty-four states and the District of Columbia are participating.[40] The program began in Hawaii in the late 1990s with the Maui County Police Department producing the first certified DREs in the state.

The DRE training program encompasses over 100 hours of intensive classroom instruction and formal training.[41] This includes a basic overview of field sobriety tests, in-depth sessions on each drug category, and education in human physiology and drug pharmacology.[42] Officers are required to pass a written examination in order to complete the classroom portion of their training and before starting the field certification phase of their training.[43] As part of the field certification phase, an officer conducts actual drug evaluations under the supervision of a certified DRE instructor.[44] In order for a trainee to achieve certification as a DRE, his opinions must be confirmed by laboratory analysis of biological specimens collected during the training examinations.[45] After completing the twelve drug influence evaluations, DRE candidates must pass another comprehensive examination followed by a detailed interview with a DRE instructor.[46]

A DRE makes three determinations: (1) whether or not the suspect's impairment is consistent with his breath alcohol level ("BrAC"); (2) whether or not the suspect is under the influence of drugs, as opposed to suffering from some type of medical condition; and (3) if the suspect is under the influence of drugs, what specific category (or categories) of drugs are involved.[47] Since many medical conditions produce effects that mimic drug impairment, the DRE needs to be able to quickly and accurately assess the arrestee for the presence of these conditions.[48] Only after ruling out these medical conditions does a DRE proceed with an evaluation to determine under which category of drugs the person is under the influence.[49] The DRE is not required to identify a specific drug, only the general category of drugs.[50] The DRE's conclusions guide laboratories by narrowing the universe of drugs that need to be tested, thereby decreasing the cost of the analyses and increasing the likelihood of useful results.[51]

16.2 The Drug Evaluation and Classification Process

The drug evaluation process uses a variety of readily observable signs and symptoms that are medically accepted as reliable indicators of drug influence.[52] It is a systematic, standardized method of examining a suspect to determine whether the suspect is impaired by one or more categories of drugs.[53] The process is systematic because it is based on a variety of observable signs and symptoms that are known to be reliable indicators of drug impairment.[54] A DRE does not reach a conclusion based on a single element of the examination, but on the totality of the facts.[55] These facts are obtained from observations of the suspect's appearance, behavior, eyes, oral and nasal cavities, vital signs, the performance of psychomotor tests, and the suspect's statements.[56]

The process is standardized because it is conducted in exactly the same way, by every DRE, for every suspect.[57] A DRE does not omit any steps of the examination, even if a step is not expected to provide a positive indicator of the type of drug(s) that the DRE may suspect.[58] Additionally, the DRE never modifies the examination by including some additional test that he or she thinks may be helpful.[59] Standardization is important because it helps to avoid errors and promotes professionalism.[60] To ensure the drug evaluation is systematic and standardized, each DRE completes a drug influence evaluation form on every suspect evaluated.[61]

The law does not require suspects to participate in a drug influence evaluation.[62] If a suspect refuses to participate in an evaluation, however, the police officer involved will base his decision to arrest on his observations that usually consist of evidence of impaired driving, evidence of physical impairment, and the lack of indicators of alcohol use.[63] In Hawaii, as in most states, however, the failure to submit to a drug test if there is probable cause to believe the suspect was driving under the influence of drugs will result in a license suspension.[64]

16.3 The DRE as an Expert Witness

DREs identify drug impairment and categorize the drug involved based upon general observations and the shared signs and symptoms caused by the different drugs in each of seven drug categories.[65] DREs form their opinions by collecting and recording data in a standardized and systematic way, and render opinions based on the totality of the circumstances.[66] DREs know that not everyone who appears impaired is actually under the influence of alcohol or drugs. They also are well aware that not everyone reacts the same way when taking drugs.

Consequently, prosecutors argue DREs are qualified to testify as experts on drug impairment by virtue of their training, experience, skill, and education. By virtue of this special training and experience, DREs will be able to assist the trier of fact to understand the evidence and reach a conclusion. Meanwhile, defense attorneys contend the DRE protocol is nothing more than "voodoo science," and police officers lack the necessary medical training to accurately reach conclusions regarding drug impairment.

As previously discussed, hundreds of governmental agencies and many private organizations endorse the DRE program.[67] Two states, Maine and Maryland, have enacted statutes recognizing drug recognition experts.[68] Maryland law states that individuals trained as DREs may request drug tests from drivers whom they have reasonable grounds to believe are driving under the influence of drugs.[69] The officers must be trained through a program in conjunction with the National Highway Traffic Safety Administration or through a program with requirements that are the substantial equivalent of the NHTSA program.[70] Maine has a similar law, but refers to these specially trained police officers as drug recognition technicians rather than drug recognition experts.[71]

16.4 Case Law Upholding the Admission of DRE Testimony

An overwhelming majority of courts throughout the country have held DREs are qualified to testify as expert witnesses, and every appellate court in the United States that has ruled on this issue has concluded DREs are qualified to testify as expert witnesses.[72] Each appellate decision found that the DRE is an expert based upon training and experience.[73] In addition, in 1997, a federal district court issued a written decision in support of the right of DREs to testify as experts.[74]

The first case to address the admissibility of DRE testimony was *State v. Johnson.*[75] In *Johnson*, the Honorable Rita Jett determined that the procedures used by DREs met the standard established in *Frye v. United States*.[76] On appeal, the Arizona Supreme Court "recognized that the basic methodology used by DREs is the deduction of drug influence through the observation of generally accepted signs and symptoms and, is neither new [n]or novel."[77] Chief Justice Stanley G. Feldman further observed that "the component examination procedures had been established for fifty years."[78] Accordingly, the justices of the Arizona Supreme Court unanimously rejected the application of *Frye* to the DRE protocol and declined jurisdiction to reconsider Judge Jett's decision.[79]

In 1991, the Suffolk County District Court of New York considered the admissibility of DRE testimony in *People v. Quinn.*[80] The court found that "[t]he protocol is relatively simple" and held that the "HGN test and the DRE protocol meet the standards enunciated by *Frye* . . ."[81]

In *State v. Klawitter*,[82] the Minnesota Supreme Court held that DREs may testify concerning the observations made while following the twelve-step drug evaluation protocol and based on those observations, may give an opinion on the impairment.[83] The *Klawitter* court reasoned that:

> [T]he protocol followed by the [DRE] is not itself a scientific technique but rather a list of the things a prudent, trained and experienced officer should consider before formulating or expressing an opinion whether the subject is under the influence of some controlled substance . . .[O]f the twelve steps of the protocol, few of them seem to call for any particular medical or scientific training or skill on the part of the officer.[84]

Although the defense challenged the officer's capability to draw conclusions on the defendant's impairment based on the twelve-step protocol, the court disagreed.[85] Writing for the majority, Justice Coyne explained that:

> [T]he protocol does not involve any scientific skill or training on the part of the officer. Drug recognition training is not designed to qualify police officers as scientists but to train officers as observers. The training is intended to refine and enhance the skill of acute observation which is the hallmark of any good police officer and to focus that power of observation in a particular situation.[86]

The court justified the use of the twelve-step protocol for recognizing drug impairment with the explanation that a standard procedure used by all officers leads to greater accuracy and consistency.[87] The only problem the court found with the testimony of the officers trained in drug evaluation is their title of "drug recognition expert."[88] Justice Coyne explained that such a title may be misleading and stated that "[p]erhaps the officer can be called a 'drug recognition officer' or some other designation which recognizes that the officer has received special training and is possessed of some experience in recognizing the presence of drugs without suggesting unwarranted scientific expertise."[89]

Justice Wahl dissented. He argued that "a police officer's application of medical or scientific tests and the rendering of an opinion on drug impairment based on those tests is an 'emerging technique' that warrants a *Frye* inquiry."[90] Justice Wahl argued that the DRE protocol does not meet the *Frye* standard and therefore an opinion on impairment based on that protocol should be inadmissible.[91] He concluded by stating that "[p]ersons driving motor vehicles under the influence of a controlled substance should be apprehended and convicted, but they should not be convicted by the force of an opinion of impairment based on and enhanced by a DRE protocol which has not been proved to be valid and reliable."[92]

In *United States v. Everett*,[93] a United States magistrate allowed DRE testimony to be admitted. The magistrate found that *Daubert v. Merrell Dow Pharmaceuticals. Inc*.[94] did not apply to the DRE protocol because the protocol was made up of nothing more than physical observations. The *Everett* court explained, "the testimony of the DRE is based upon observations and tabulations of the results of those observations. He or she is not propounding a scientific principle or theory in testifying about the performance of the various steps of the evaluation and what the findings or observations were."[96] The court stated that multiple physical observations "used in concert, to reach a conclusion, does not necessarily elevate the result from the technical to the scientific. The pertinent components of the DRE protocol have long been established and used in the medical community as part of physical examinations . . . ."[97]

The court held that "upon the appropriate foundation being laid, the drug recognition evaluation protocol conducted by [the DRE], together with his conclusions drawn therefrom, shall be admitted into evidence to the extent that the DRE can testify to the probabilities, based upon his or her observations and clinical findings . . . ."[98] More importantly, the court held that a DRE is a technical expert and not a scientific expert.[99] The DRE is deemed to have specialized knowledge, and to base his opinion on observation, training, skill, and experience.[100] A DRE can testify as to this specialized knowledge since it will assist the trier of fact to understand the evidence.[101] However, the court mentioned a preference for using the title of "drug recognition examiner," rather than "drug recognition expert," explaining that the term "expert" is presumptuous and possibly infringes on the court's discretion to determine who are experts.[102]

In *Mace v. State,*[103] the Arkansas Supreme Court unanimously held that a police officer trained as a DRE qualifies as an expert under Rule 702 of the Arkansas Rules of Evidence.[104] Chief Justice Arnold explained that the lower court qualified the officer "as an expert for a narrow purpose-whether [the defendant] was impaired because of some kind of intoxicant," and agreed with the lower court that the officer's "specialized training and knowledge aided the circuit court in determining this fact in issue."[105]

Although the defendant asserted that the officer should not have been qualified as an expert in drug recognition, the court found the officer possessed specialized knowledge that would assist the jury to decide the fact in issue.[106] Chief Justice Arnold explained, "[I]f some reasonable basis exists from which it can be said that the witness has knowledge of the subject beyond that of ordinary knowledge, the evidence is admissible as expert testimony."[107]

In 1998, the Utah Court of Appeals addressed the issue of officers testifying as drug recognition experts in *State v. Layman.*[108] In *Layman*, the defendant argued that the trial court should not have admitted DRE testimony concerning his intoxication because it was not analyzed under *State v. Rimmasch,*[109] a Supreme Court of Utah decision that outlined the admissibility of scientific evidence.[110] In determining the admissibility of scientific evidence, the *Layman* court concluded that DRE testimony is opinion and not scientific testimony, and therefore does not have to meet the test for scientific evidence.[111] The court explained, "*Rimmasch* analysis applies only to expert testimony based on scientifically derived facts or determinations, and not to an expert's personal observations and opinions based on his or her education, training, and experience."[112]

In 1998, a Florida Appeals Court held in *Williams v. State*[113] that DRE testimony and evidence is admissible because it is reasonably accurate, reliable, and relevant.[114] They also held that although the tests DREs use to determine drug use are "quasi-scientific," they are not new or novel and therefore *Frye* does not apply.[115] The defendant argued that the DRE testimony should not be admitted because the State did not establish the reliability of the DRE protocol.[116]

The Williams court distinguished between the general portion of the DRE protocol and its subsets HGN, VGN, and LOC.[117] Regarding the general portion of the DRE protocol, the court stated:

> [b]ecause the tests, signs and symptoms of the protocol are within the common understanding of the average layman, the general portion of the protocol is not "scientific" within the meaning of *Frye*. The fact that some of the examinations in the protocol are borrowed from the medical profession does not elevate the protocol to scientific status.[118]

The DRE's opinion is not a medical diagnosis, but rather the result of tests "within the common experience and understanding of the average person."[119] The court stated:

> [p]olice officers and lay witnesses have long been permitted to testify as to their observations of a defendant's acts, conduct, and appearance, and also to give an opinion on the defendant's state of impairment based on those observations. Objective observations based on observable signs and conditions are not classified as "scientific" and thus constitute admissible testimony.[120]

The court explained that any conflicting studies or scientific articles may be introduced by the defense to challenge the DRE testimony, yet held that "common sense mandates DRE testimony is relevant in a prosecution for driving under the influence of a controlled substance, because it shows a probability that a person was impaired by alcohol and/or drugs."[121]

The Washington Supreme Court is the most recent state Supreme Court to consider the admissibility of DRE testimony. In *State v. Baity,*[122] the court ruled DRE evidence admissible under *Frye* because it is generally accepted in the relevant scientific communities.[123] In its unanimous decision, the court held the DRE may testify if the conclusions regarding impairment are based on his or her observations and clinical findings, and not by way of scientific standards.[124] Judge Talmadge explained that "[f]or the same reason that the [c]ourt would admit the testimony of an officer testifying about his observations . . . of an alcohol intoxicated driver, even though the officer could be wrong, this [c]ourt finds the same justification for admitting the testimony of the DRE here for the same purposes."[125] The court confined its holding to apply only when all twelve steps of the drug evaluation protocol have been undertaken.[126] The court further explained that "[t]he officer also may not predict the specific level of drugs present in a suspect. The DRE officer, properly qualified, may express an opinion that a suspect's behavior and physical attributes are or are not consistent with the behavioral and physical signs associated with certain categories of drugs."[127]

In May 2000, the Oregon Court of Appeals issued a decision regarding the admissibility of DRE testimony.[128] The trial court ruled DRE testimony was scientific evidence and that it met the admissibility requirements for scientific testimony.[129] The court of appeals agreed, and stated that "the DRE protocol has achieved a significant degree of acceptance within the relevant scientific community that weighs in favor of its admissibility for the purpose of establishing the influence of controlled substances."[130]

In other cases around the country, courts faced with the issue of the admissibility of DRE testimony have reached similar results. In *Harris v. Schmitt,*[131] the Arizona Court of Appeals upheld an administrative order suspending the defendant's license for driving under the influence of drugs and failing to provide a urine sample.[132] The court relied upon a DRE officer's opinion that the defendant was under the influence of a stimulant.[133] The defendant claimed the DRE officer was still in training and not certified to administer the drug influence evaluation.[134] The court, however, held that "under these circumstances, in which Officer Jex [DRE] testified about his prior experience and his supervisor was present and concurred in his assessment, any issue about Jex's testimony could only relate to its weight, not its admissibility."[135] Here, even though the DRE had not yet received his certification, the court determined that it was proper for his opinions to be admitted at the administrative hearing.[136]

The Court of Appeals of Texas addressed the admissibility of drug recognition testimony in *Hooker v. Texas*.[137] The *Hooker* court held that there was sufficient evidence to sustain a prosecution for driving while intoxicated by prescription drugs where the defendant initially refused to submit to a DRE evaluation.[138] The defendant argued that although the arresting officer was a DRE, his expertise in recognizing drug intoxication depended upon the administration of a variety of tests, "only two of which were actually performed."[139] The officer explained that he could only perform two of the tests because the defendant was unable to perform any others.[140] The court recognized the officer's experience and training and held that "[b]ased upon the testimony and exhibits before the jury . . . we find that any rational trier of fact could have found, beyond a reasonable doubt, that appellant had lost the normal use of his mental or physical faculties from ingesting the controlled substance Vicodin on the night in question."[141]

In 1996, a New York appellate court affirmed the admissibility of expert testimony given by a DRE on the subject of drug metabolization and the defendant's metabolization of and impairment by cocaine.[142] The court rejected the defendant's challenge regarding the admissibility of the

DRE's testimony.[143] The court stated that "[t]he attack on [the DRE's] expertise was not supported by any evidence. Defendant's conclusary allegations as to [the DRE's] limitations as an expert fail to make out a ground for exclusion of his testimony."[144]

In *Duffy v. Director of Revenue,*[145] the Missouri Court of Appeals upheld the administrative suspension of the defendant's license for driving under the influence of drugs based in part upon testimony of the DRE officer.[146] The defendant argued the director failed to give a proper *Frye* foundation for the testimony of the DRE.[147] The court rejected the defendant's argument and explained, "where scientific proof of sobriety is offered to establish reasonable grounds that an individual was driving while intoxicated sufficient to revoke an individual's driving privileges . . . it is not necessary to lay a *Frye* foundation."[148]

In *Arizona v. Hammonds,*[149] an officer noticed that a suspect he pulled over displayed signs of intoxication.[150] When the BrAC revealed low concentrations, the officer suspected that the defendant's intoxication resulted from drug use.[151] The DRE administered a series of tests and eventually concluded that the defendant was under the influence of drugs.[152] The trial court admitted this opinion testimony.[153]

16.5 DRE Expert Testimony Held Admissible in Hawaii

In Hawaii scientific and technical evidence is admissible if it comports with the mandates of Hawaii Rules of Evidence, Rule 702. Rule 702 states:

> If scientific, technical, or other specialized knowledge will assist the trier of fact to understand the evidence or to determine a fact in issue, a witness qualified as an expert by knowledge, skill, experience, training, or education may testify thereto in the form of an opinion or otherwise. In determining the issue of assistance to the trier of fact, the court may consider the trustworthiness and validity of the scientific technique or mode of analysis employed by the proffered expert.[154]

The leading Hawaii case in interpreting this rule is *State v. Montalbo*.[155] Here, the Hawaii Supreme Court explained that courts should weigh general acceptance of a theory, along with whether

1. the evidence will assist the trier of fact to understand the evidence or to determine a fact in issue;
2. the evidence will add to the common understanding of the jury;
3. the underlying theory is generally accepted as valid;
4. the procedures used are generally accepted as reliable if performed properly;
5. the procedures were applied and conducted properly in the present instance.[156]

A court should then consider whether the evidence is more probative than prejudicial.[157]

In a hearing on a Motion in Limine to Preclude DRE Testimony, a Honolulu district court evaluated the issue of DREs testifying as experts.[158] The defendants presented two witnesses in support of their Motion to Preclude DRE Testimony: (1) Dr. John P. Morgan, M.D., professor of pharmacology, City University of New York Medical School, and (2) Dr. John Medford Corboy, M.D., board-certified in ophthalmology.[159] In opposition to the motion, the State presented the following witnesses: (1) Sergeant Thomas Page, head of the DRE program, Los Angeles Police Department; (2) Dr. Zenon Zuk, M.D., California; (3) Dr. Clifford Wong, M.D., head of the Clinical Laboratory of Hawaii, Toxicology; (4) Mr. Robert Adler, toxicologist, Arizona; (5) Dr. Karl Citek, doctor of optometry, Oregon; (6) Dr. Marcelline Burns, doctor of psychology, cofounder and director of the Southern California Research Institute; and (7) Officer Shermon Dowkin, drug recognition expert, Honolulu, Hawaii.[160]

The court made seventeen findings of fact in its decision regarding the DRE protocol.[161] Included were the following:

- The twelve-step DRE evaluation process is a systematic assessment of a suspect's vital signs and physical appearance and is not a new or novel scientific procedure.
- The DRE protocol is a technical, not scientific, application of long-established and accepted scientific principles and procedures drawn from medicine and police practices and procedures.
- The DRE protocol produces an accurate and reliable determination as to whether or not a suspect is impaired by drugs, as well as the category of drugs that the suspect has used.

- The extensive, rigorous, in-depth training of police officers as reflected in their training manuals enable DREs to accurately observe the signs and symptoms of drug impairment and to reach trustworthy and valid conclusions.
- DRE testimony represents an area of specialized knowledge based upon observation, education, training, skill, and experience.[162]

The court concluded that *Frye* and *Daubert* do not apply to the DRE protocol because the procedures underlying the twelve steps are not new or novel.[163] The DRE protocol is held to be "a compilation of tried and true procedures utilized by medical science and the law enforcement community in similar contexts for many years."[164] The court also held that *Frye* and *Daubert* were inapplicable because the DRE protocol involves technical knowledge, not scientific knowledge.[165] The court went on to say, however, that even if it applied *Frye* and *Daubert* in this case, DRE testimony, including opinion testimony would still be admissible.[166]

Although some courts have concluded the DRE protocol is "scientific," DREs are generally considered "technical" rather than "scientific" experts.[167] DREs' opinions are based on observation, education, training, skill, and expertise.[168] The DRE is not a doctor, pharmacologist, or toxicologist. Nonetheless, the DRE has specialized knowledge that will assist the trier of fact to understand the evidence. Thus, while there is a scientific explanation for pupil dilation, "the DRE is not testifying about the underlying physiological mechanism that controls pupil dilation, only whether the pupils were dilated."[169] Furthermore, while the DRE may make observations that are scientifically explainable, those observations are not themselves scientific.[170] Testimony from a DRE involves "technical knowledge" and not "scientific knowledge." The difference between these two terms is spelled out in *State v. Fukusaku,*[171] in which the Hawaii Supreme Court stated:

> "Scientific knowledge" must be distinguished from "technical knowledge." Expert testimony deals with 'scientific knowledge' when it involves the validity of the scientific principles and the reliability of the scientific procedure themselves. In contrast, expert testimony deals with 'technical knowledge' when it involves the mere application of well-established scientific principles and procedures. In such a situation, be-

> cause the underlying scientific principles and procedures are of proven validity/reliability, it is unnecessary to subject technical knowledge to the same type of full-scale reliability determination required for scientific knowledge. Thus, although technical knowledge, like all expert testimony, must be both relevant and reliable, its reliability may be presumed.[172]

In *Fukusaku*, the Hawaii Supreme Court stated that "[b]ecause scientific principles and procedures underlying hair and fiber evidence are well established and of proven reliability, the evidence could be treated as 'technical knowledge' . . . [and] an independent reliability determination was not necessary."[173]

Prosecutors contend the scientific principles and procedures underlying the DRE protocol have been proven to be valid and reliable, and the DRE protocol is not an attempt to advance a new scientific theory or technique. They argue that DREs simply report what they are trained to observe and make conclusions based on widely accepted medical principles. DREs are merely technicians applying their observations to principles utilized by the medical community for decades. Consequently, according to the distinction between "scientific" knowledge and "technical" knowledge set forth in *Fukusaku*, DREs testify as "technical" experts.[174]

This distinction between "scientific evidence" and "technical evidence" may not play such a crucial role in the future as it has in the past. The initial standard for the admission of expert testimony was developed in *Frye v. United States*.[175] The *Frye* standard requires a party offering new or novel scientific evidence to demonstrate the evidence is generally accepted to be accurate and reliable in the relevant scientific community.[176]

Daubert v. Merrell Dow Pharmaceuticals, Inc.[177] modified the Frye standard. The *Daubert* test does not require the scientific theory to have been accepted in the scientific community.[178] According to *Daubert*, other factors such as testing, publication, error rate, and reliability should be taken into account when determining the admissibility of expert testimony.[179]

The *Daubert* decision left some confusion as to whether or not non-scientific expert testimony was subject to its standards. Many courts, including those in Hawaii, continued to make the distinction between "scientific experts" and "technical experts" as previously discussed.[180] In

1999, the U.S. Supreme Court attempted to clarify this issue in *Kumho Tire Co., Ltd. v. Carmichael.*[181] Here, the Court held that both "scientific experts" and "technical" experts were subject to the gatekeeping role of the courts.[182] At the same time, however, the Supreme Court stated that the judge acting as the gatekeeper does not have to base his decision on the criteria established it in *Daubert.*[183] *Daubert* criteria could be used as well as any other relevant criteria that would help the court determine the reliability of the proposed expert testimony.[184]

What does the *Kumho* decision mean for the drug recognition expert program? Since most state appellate courts have yet to rule on the issue of DRE testimony, it is anticipated they will look to *Kumho* for guidance. Because of the timing, it may not come as a surprise if some states, Hawaii included, use a case involving DREs as a mechanism to address the issue of qualifications of expert witnesses.

Overall, the *Kumho* decision can be viewed in a positive light by both prosecutors and defense attorneys who work on the DRE expert witness issue. No longer will there be any need to spend time arguing if the DRE should be considered a "scientific expert" or a "technical expert." Moreover, courts will be given the flexibility to develop standards that are relevant to the DRE protocol in order to determine reliability. Courts will not be straightjacketed into any type of set formula. This will allow more creativity for the parties, and give both sides better opportunities to present their arguments.

The only time the Hawaii Supreme Court has looked into the area of drug recognition was back in 1989 before there were any officers trained as DREs in Hawaii.[185] At that time, the Hawaii Supreme Court held that expert testimony regarding the behavioral effects of drugs is relevant and admissible in determining whether or not a suspect was driving under the influence of drugs and in determining the precise drug the defendant was using.[186] In *State v. Engcabo,*[187] the police stopped the defendant because he was driving in an erratic manner.[188] When the police officer observed the defendant, he noticed the defendant's eyes were bloodshot, his pupils were constricted, and that he had three puncture marks on his left arm.[189] The police officer also noticed a syringe with residue on the floor of the vehicle.[190]

The Supreme Court of Hawaii reversed the defendant's conviction because the State failed to provide evidence of the specific drug the defendant was alleged to have been using.[191] In doing so, however, the court held that the State could have proven the specific drug the defendant had been using even without him submitting to a drug test by engaging "an expert to testify as to the behavioral effects of a specific drug."[192] In a few years, the Hawaii Supreme Court will likely answer the question as to whether or not police officers trained in the drug recognition expert program qualify as experts in this context.

Hawaii courts traditionally hold that police officers are qualified to testify regarding their opinions that a person was under the influence of alcohol. Hawaii case law concerning the admissibility of opinion evidence in DUI-Alcohol cases certainly suggests that police officers should be able to testify regarding their opinions that a person was driving under the influence of drugs other than alcohol. In *State v. Nishi,*[193] the Intermediate Court of Appeals of Hawaii, citing, *State v. Murphy,*[194] stated that a lay witness may express an opinion regarding another person's sobriety, provided the witness has had an opportunity to observe the other person.[195]

16.6 Conclusion

The decision in *Kumho* and the extensive litigation around the country regarding police officers specially trained in drug recognition will give many states, including Hawaii, the opportunity to rewrite its standards on the admissibility of expert testimony. Regardless of the precise formula each jurisdiction develops to deal with the admissibility of expert witness testimony, the proponent of an expert witness will always need to prove reliability. Through both laboratory studies and field experience, it has been demonstrated that the DRE protocol is a reliable means for detecting drug impairment. It would seem a police officer, or any individual who is properly trained and follows the protocol, can formulate accurate conclusions. If this foundation is properly established, the drug recognition testimony should be admissible. DRE testimony provides courts with a mechanism to address those who operate vehicles on our roads and highways while intoxicated by drugs rather than alcohol.

Endnotes

1. Telephone interview with Carolyn Cockroft, grant technical management specialist, International Association of Chiefs of Police (Aug. 2000). Over 1000 of these individuals have received additional training and hold the title of instructor. Id.

2. See National District Attorney Association. "The Drug Recognition Expert Program." In *Prosecuting the Drugged Driver* (1999) (on file with author) [hereinafter Drug Recognition Expert Program]. The National Highway Transportation Safety Administration sponsored two studies that directly led to the development of the Standardized Field Sobriety Test battery. Id. at 7 n. 8. The Southern California Research Institute conducted both studies: "Psychological Tests for DWI Arrest" and "Development and Field Test of Psychophysical Tests for DWI Arrest." Id.

   The standardized field sobriety test consists of three parts. First, the suspect's eyes are examined for nystagmus, which is the jerking of the pupils. The presence of nystagmus is a sign of the use of alcohol and certain other types of drugs. The second test is the walk and turn test. The final test is the one-leg stand test. Id. at 7-8.

3. U.S. Dept. of Transp, *The Drug Recognition School, Student Manual* IV-3 (1993) (on file with author) [hereinafter *Student Manual*].

4. Haw. Rev. Stat. §291-4 (2000).

5. International Association of Chiefs of Police (IACP), "IACP DECP State Coordinators," (Sept. II, 2000) (on file with author). The states include: Arizona, Arkansas, California, Colorado, Florida, Georgia, Hawaii, Idaho, lllinois, Indiana, Iowa, Kansas, Louisiana, Maine, Maryland, Massachusetts, Minnesota, Missouri, Nebraska, Nevada, New Hampshire, New Jersey, New Mexico, New York, North Carolina, North Dakota, Oklahoma, Oregon, Rhode Island, Texas, Utah, Virginia, Washington, and Wisconsin. Id. In addition, the program has expanded to Canada, Australia, Norway, and Sweden, and a program is anticipated to begin in South Africa in the near future. Drug Recognition Expert Program, supra note 2, at 15.

6. See Nat'l Dist. Attorneys Ass'n. "Drugs in American Society," in *Prosecuting the Drugged Driver* 4–7 (1999) (on file with author) [hereinafter *Drugs in American Society*]. Comparatively, alcohol-impaired driving has a long and well-established history. While they share similar characteristics, there are important distinctions between DUI-Alcohol and DUI- Drug cases. See Id.

7. DUI-Alcohol and DUI-Drugs combine for over 16,000 deaths, one million injuries, and $45 billion in costs to society each year. See Jim Michie, *First Time Study Highlights Need for Increased Awareness of Substance Use and Driving Behaviors*, at, http://samhsa- extl.samhsa.gov/PRESS/981226s.htm (last visited Nov. 6, 2000).

   Accurate data on DUI-Drugs alone is difficult to obtain. *Student Manual*, supra note 3, at II-5. First, many impaired drivers are not detected. Id. Second, since many drug users also drink alcohol, they are frequently arrested and tabulated in statistics only as alcohol-impaired drivers. Id. Third, those involved in crashes are often chemically tested only for alcohol. Id.

   Despite these difficulties, various studies have reported on the degree of drug-impaired driving. A California study showed that 51 percent of 440 young male drivers killed in crashes had used drugs other than alcohol. *Drugs in American Society*, supra note 6, at 6–7. Similarly, a Tennessee study of injured victims of motor vehicle crashes showed that 40 percent of the drivers tested positive for at least one drug other than alcohol. Id. A national study, *Driving after Alcohol or Drug Use* estimates that within a single year, 46.5 million (28 percent of drivers) have used drugs and/or alcohol within two hours before driving. Of the 46.5 million, approximately nine million Americans (5 percent of drivers) used drugs within two hours before driving. This survey included face-to-face interviews with 11,847 drivers sixteen years and older who reported having driven a motor vehicle on at least one occasion in the twelve months prior to the interview. *Driving after Drug or Alcohol Use Report: Highlights* at http://samhsa- extl.samhsa.gov/OAS / driverrprt/fnldrf11.htm (last visited Nov. 6, 2000).

8. See Jim Michie. *First Time Study Highlights Need for Increased Awareness of Substance Use and Driving Behaviors*, at http://samhsa-extl.samhsa.gov/PRESS/981226s.htm, supra note 7.

9. See Nat'l Dist. Attorneys Ass'n. "The Drug Recognition Expert Process," in *Prosecuting the Drugged Driver* 5 (1999) (on file with author) [hereinafter *Drug Recognition Expert Process*].

10. Id. Los Angeles Police Department Officers Sergeant Richard Studdard (retired) and Detective Len Leeds (deceased) were largely responsible for the early development of ORE procedures. Id.

11. See generally *Student Manual*, supra note 3 (acknowledging the efforts of the LAPD). The NHTSA is a part of the Department of Transportation. Its leadership role in development and implementation of the DEC program produced scientific validation of the program, effective training and certification standards, and rapid expansion and institutionalization of the program. Id. at III-35.

12. Id.

13. George E. Bigelow, Ph.D., et. al. *Identifying Types of Drug Intoxication: Laboratory Evaluation of a Subject Procedure*, 16 (May 1985) (on file with author).

14. Richard P. Compton. *Field Evaluation of the Los Angeles Police Department Drug Detection Procedure*, 24 (Feb. 1986) (on file with author).

15. Bigelow, supra note 13, at 12; Compton, supra note 14, at 22.

16. Bigelow, supra note 13, at 2.

17. Id. at 4.

18. Id. at 1.

19. Id. at 13–16.

20. Compton, supra note 14, at 3.

21. Id. at 1–2.

22. Id. at 22–24. The use of alcohol with other drugs was common, with 50 percent of the suspects who had used drugs having also used alcohol (thus making the detection of other drugs more difficult). Id. at 11. Furthermore, only six of the suspects (3.7 percent) who had used drugs had

Blood Alcohol Contents equal to or greater than 0.10 percent w/v. Id. at 14. It is likely that most, if not all, of the remainder of the suspects would have been released if the drug symptoms had not been recognized by the DREs. Id.

23. Id. at 22.

24. Eugene V. Adler and Marcelline Burns. *Drug Recognition Expert Validation Study: Final Report to Governor's Office of Highway Safety*. State of Ariz. (June 1994) (on file with author).

25. Id. at Abstract.

26. Id. at 55.

27. Id. at 33.

28. Brief of Appellant at 19-20, *State v. Baity*, (Wash. 2000) (Nos. 98115104 and 970186124).

29. Telephone interview with Dr. Clifford Wong, director of toxicology services, Clinical Laboratories of Hawaii (Oct. 2000).

30. The most common reasons given by toxicologists for this are:

Limited testing—Because of the substantial costs involved, a specimen is not tested for all possible drugs.

Cut-off levels—If there are only low-levels of the drug present falling below the laboratory's cutoff levels, then that drug will be reported out as a "negative."

Type of test given—Evidence of drug use may appear in the urine, but not the blood, or vice-versa.

Time the test was given—Drugs metabolize at different rates.

Inability of laboratory equipment to locate evidence of drug use—Evidence of drug use is measured in one one-millionth of a gram. Sometimes laboratory equipment is not sophisticated enough or is otherwise unable to detect such minute particles.

Student Manual. supra note 3, at IV-20–22.

31. Id. at IV-21.

32. Bigelow, supra note 13; Compton supra note 14.

33. *Student Manual*. supra note 3, at 1-1.

34. Id.

35. Id.

36. Id.

37. See discussion infra note 67.

38. Drug Recognition Expert Program, supra note 2, at 14.

39. International Association of Chiefs of Police (IACP). "IACP DECP State Coordinators," (Sept. 11,2000) (on file with author).

40. Id.

41. See Nat'l Dist. Attorneys Ass'n. "Drug Recognition Expert Training Course," in *Prosecuting the Drugged Driver*, 7 (1999) (on file with author) [hereinaf-

ter *Drug Recognition Expert Training Course*]. This figure includes original training in alcohol, drugs, and field sobriety testing at the police academy, specialized field sobriety testing training, horizontal gaze nystagmus training, and DRE "pre-school" and "school." See id. See also infra note 43 (discussing "pre-school" training).

42. *Student Manual*, supra note 3, at 1–3.

43. U.S. Dept. of Transp. "Preliminary Training for Drug Evaluation and Classification: The Pre-School" app. 4 (1993) (on file with author) [hereinafter *Preschool*]. Candidates must receive a score of at least 80 percent. Id.

44. Id. at app. 4–5. The trainee must complete at least twelve drug influence evaluations. Id.

45. Id. at app. 5. Student DREs must submit a minimum of nine physical specimens to a lab for analysis. The lab analysis is compared to the student DRE's opinion as to the type of drug influencing the individual. The student must achieve a 75 percent lab confirmation rate. Id.

46. Id. at app 6. For a complete description of all the requirements a DRE candidate must complete in order to obtain DRE certification. See id. at app.: "Standards for the Drug Evaluation and Classification Program."

47. "Drug Recognition Expert Process," supra note 9, at 2; see infra Appendix IV, "Indicators Consistent with Drug Categories."

48. "Drug Recognition Expert Process," supra note 9, at 2.

49. Id.

50. Id. at 3. Just as the officer does not need to determine the type or brand of alcohol a suspect has consumed in order to offer an opinion that the individual is driving under the influence of alcohol, the DRE is not expected to ascertain the precise drug the suspect is using in order to reach a conclusion regarding drug impairment. *Drug Recognition Expert Program*, supra note 2, at 16-17.

51. *Drug Recognition Expert Program*, supra note 2, at 16.

52. See *United States v. Everett*, 972 F. Supp. 1313, 1320 (D. Nev. 1997). The pertinent components of the DRE protocol have long been established and used in the medical community as part of physical examinations (e.g., blood pressure and heart rate, observations of the eyes, nose and mouth). Other compo-

nents are identical to those used by police officers in evaluations for alcohol impairment (e.g., horizontal gaze nystagmus (HGN) and field sobriety tests). Whether and how the various components of the protocol are impacted by various classes of drugs are sufficiently established to permit the DRE to draw conclusions and reach opinions based upon observations. The validity of those conclusions or accuracy of the observations is certainly subject to cross-examination and other methods of impeachment but any errors in that regard do not make the underlying steps of the DRE protocol junk science, or scientific at all. Id. (citations omitted); see infra Appendix IV, "Indicators Consistent with Drug Categories."

53. *Student Manual*, supra note 3, at IV-I.

54. Id.

55. Id. See also infra, Appendix III, "Twelve-Step DRE Evaluation Matrix."

56. *Student Manual*, supra note 3, at IV-I.

57. Id. One accepted exception deals with differing state requirements regarding *Miranda* warnings. The manner in which officers administer *Miranda* rights may vary from state to state.

58. Id.

59. Id.

60. Id.

61. See Nat'l Dist. Attorneys Ass'n, P*rosecuting The Drugged Driver*, app. C (1999) (on file with author).

62. *Drug Recognition Expert Process*, supra note 9, at 4–9. The Twelve Step Drug Influence Evaluation consists of the followings steps:

(1) Breath alcohol test to determine the suspect's breath alcohol content (BrAC); (2) interview of the arresting officer, in which the DRE discusses the circumstances of the arrest with the arresting officer; (3) preliminary examination and first pulse, in which the DRE asks the suspect questions about his health and observes the suspect's physical condition and behavior. The examination includes a check of pupil size and pulse; (4) eye examination in which the DRE checks for nystagmus and lack of convergence; (5) divided attention psychophysical tests in which the DRE observes whether the suspect can follow various tests of coordination. The tests include the Romberg Balance Test, walk and turn test, one-leg stand, and finger-to-nose test; (6)

vital signs and second pulse, in which the DRE takes the suspect's blood pressure, temperature, and pulse; (7) dark room examination, in which the DRE measures the suspect's pupil sizes under four different lighting condition and examines the suspect's nasal and oral cavities for signs of ingestion; (8) examination for muscle tone; (9) check for injection sites and third pulse; (10) suspect's statements and other observations; (11) opinion of the evaluator; and (12) toxicological examination, in which the DRE requests a urine and/or blood sample from the suspect, which is then sent to the toxicology lab for analysis. Id.

On January I, 1998, a law went into effect in Hawaii requiring those whom the police had probable cause to believe were driving under the influence of drugs to submit to a urine or blood test or lose their licenses for one full year. See Haw. Rev. Stat. §286-157.3 (2000).

63. *Student Manual*, supra note 3, at IV-I.

64. Haw. Rev. Stat. §286-157.3 (2000).

65. *Student Manual*, supra note 3, at 11-2-3. The seven categories of drugs are: central nervous system (CNS) depressants, CNS stimulants, hallucinogens, phencyclidine (PCP) and its analogs, narcotic analgesics, inhalants, and cannabis. Id.; see also infra Appendix IV.

66. See *Student Manual*, supra note 3, at IV-I.

67. See, e.g., letter from T. Edward Corley, M.D., president and Barry R. Weiss, M.D., Emergency Medical Services Committee, Broward County Medical Association, to Stephen K. Talpins, Esq., assistant state attorney 1-2 (March 1, 1994) (on file with author); letter from N. Ralph Frankel, M.D., president, Dade County Medical Association, to Whom It May Concern 1 (Jan. 25, 1994) (on file with author); letter from Richard P. Maulion, M.D., president, Broward County Psychiatric Society, to Whom It May Concern 1 (Jan. 14, 1994) (on file with author); letter from Pat Chinn, M.D. president, Phil Hellreich, M.D., legislative chair, and Gerald McKenna. M.D., physicians' health chair, Hawaii Medical Association to Whom It May Concern 1 (Feb. 12, 1999) (on file with author). In addition, the United States Department of Transportation stated in its 1996 Report to Congress:

> The Drug Evaluation and Classification Program has been remarkably successful in producing meaningful results in the critical areas of developing and implementing the program, saving lives on our nation's roads, strengthening partnerships, gaining court acceptance, as well as achieving self-sufficiency and showing a steady return on investment. NHTSA's leadership role in development and implementation of the DEC program produced scientific validation of the program, effective

training and certification standards, and rapid expansion and institutionalization of the program.

U.S. Dept. of Transp., *A Report to Congress on the Drug Evaluation and Classification Program* 19 (Apr. I, 1996) (on file with author) [hereinafter *Report to Congress*].

68. See ME. Rev. Stat. Ann. tit. 29-A, §§2525,2526 (West 1999); MD. Code Ann., Transp. §16-205.1 (2000).

69. Md. Code Ann., Transp. §16-205.1 (2000).

70. Id.

71. Me. Rev. Stat. Ann. tit. 29-A, §2526 (West 1999).

72. See *Mace v. State*, 944 S.W.2d 830 (Ark. 1997); *State v. Klawitter*, 518 N.W.2d 577 (Minn. 1994); *State v. Baity*, 991 P.2d 1151 (Wash. 2000); *Williams v. State*, 710 So. 2d 24 (Fla. Ct. App. 1998); *State v. Layman*, 953 P.2d 782 (Utah Ct. App. 1998); *State v. Sampson*, 6 P.3d 543 (Or. Ct. App. 2000).

73. Id.

74. *United States v. Everett*. 972 F. Supp. 1313 (D. Nev. 1997).

75. *Report to Congress*, supra note 67, at 14.

76. *Frye v. United States*, 293 F. 1013 (D.C. Cir. 1923) (holding that a party offering new or novel scientific evidence must demonstrate that the evidence is generally accepted to be accurate and reliable in the relevant scientific community).

77. *Report to Congress*, supra note 67, at 14.

78. Id.

79. Id.

80. 580 N.Y.S.2d 818 (N. Y.D.C. 1991).

81. *Quinn*. 580 N. Y.S.2d at 826 (referring to *Frye v. United States*, 293 F. 1013 (D.C. Cir. 1923)).

82. 518 N.W.2d 577 (Minn. 1994).

83. Id. at 586.

84. Id. at 584.

85. Id.

86. Id. at 585.

87. Id. at 586.

88. Id.

89. Id. at 585.

90. Id. at 586.

91. Id. at 587.

92. Id.

93. 972 F. Supp. 1313 (D. Nev. 1997).

94. 509 U.S. 579 (1993).

95. *Everen*, 972 F. Supp. at 1320.

96. Id. at 1319.

97. Id. at 1320.

98. Id. at 1326.

99. Id. at 1321.

100. Id.

101. Id. at 1326.

102. Id. at 1316 n. 2.

103. 944 S.W.2d 830 (Ark. 1997).

104. Id. at 542.

105. Id. at 542.

106. Id. at 834.

107. Id. (citing *Dillon v. State*, 877 S.W.2d 915 (Ark. 1994)).

108. 953 P.2d 782 (Utah Ct. App. 1998).

109. 775 P.2d 388 (Utah 1989).

110. *Layman*, 953 P.2d at 785.

111. Id. at 786 (italics added).

112. Id.

113. 710 So. 2d 24 (Aa. Dist. Ct. App. 1998).

114. Id. at 32–33.

115. Id. at 28–29 (italics added). For example, DREs use the horizontal gaze nystagmus (HGN) test, the vertical gaze nystagmus (VGN) test, and the lack of convergence (LOC) test, each scientifically based, in helping to determine whether a suspect is under the influence of drugs. Id. at 27.

116. Id. at 28.

117. Id.

118. Id. at 28 (italics added).

119. Id.

120. Id. at 28–29.

121. Id. at 33 (citation omitted).

122. 991 P.2d 1151 (Wash. 2000).

123. Id. at 1160–61.

124. Id.

125. Id. at 1159 (citing *United States v. Everett*, 972 F. Supp. 1313, 1324 (D. Nev. 1997)).

126. Id. at 1160; see discussion supra note 62.

127. Baity, 991 P.2d at 1160–61.

128. *State v. Sampson*, 6 P.3d 543 (Or. Ct. App. 2000).

129. Id. at 547.

130. Id. at 553.

131. 885 P.2d 1125 (Ariz. Ct. App. 1994).

132. Id. at 1126.

133. Id.

134. Id.

135. Id. at 1126–27.

136. Id. at 1126.

137. 932 S.W.2d 712 (Tex. Ct. App. 1996).

138. Id. at 714–15.

139. Id. at 713.

140. Id. at 714.

141. Id. at 715.

142. See *State v. Villeneuve*, 232 A.D.2d 892, 895 (N.Y. App. Div. 1996).

143. Id.

144 Id.

145. 966 S.W.2d 372 (Mo. Ct. App. 1998).

146. Id. at 377.

147. Id. at 374.

148. Id. at 377 (citing *Nuyt v. Dir. of Revenue*, 814 S.W.2d 690 (Mo. Ct. App. 1991)).

149. 968 P.2d 601 (Ariz. Ct. App. 1998).

150. Id. at 603.

151. Id.

152. Id.

153. Id. at 603.

154. Haw. R. Evid. 702 (1999).

155. 73 Haw. 130, 828 P.2d 1274 (1992).

156. Id. at 140, 828 P.2d at 1280–81.

157. Id. at 140, 828 P.2d at 1281.

158. *State v. Cheung*, Nos. 098304309, 098304512 (Haw. Dist. Ct. Apr. 21, 1999) (on file with author). Seven additional defendants, also represented by the Office of the Public Defender, were joined for purposes of this motion. Id.

159. Id. at 7.

160. Id.

161. Id. at 8–10.

162. Id.

163. Id. at 12 (citations omitted).

164. Id. (citing *People v. Quinn*. 580 N.Y.S.2d 818.827 (1991)).

165. Id.

166. Id. at 13.

167. Nat'l Dist. Attorneys Ass'n. "The DRE as Expert Witness," in *Prosecuting the Drugged Driver* 7 (1999) (on file with author).

168. Id.

169. Id. Just as an individual does not need to understand how a television operates in order to determine if the set is working properly, the DRE does not

need to know the scientific explanation of how drugs cause impairment in order to see impairment. Id.

170. See *State v. Layman*, 953 P.2d 782 (Utah Ct. App. 1998) (affirming a lower court decision admitting DRE testimony because it is opinion and not scientific testimony); *State v. Klawitter*, 518 N.W.2d 577, 584 (Minn. 1994) (holding that the DRE protocol is not itself a scientific technique).

171. 85 Hawaii 462, 946 P.2d 32 (1997).

172 Id. at 473, 946 P.2d at 43.

173. Id. at 474, 946 P.2d at 44.

174. Id. at 473, 946 P.2d at 43. In *United States v. Everett*, the court held DRE protocol was made up of nothing more than physical observations. The court stated these physical observations did not elevate the DRE protocol from a mere technical procedure to a scientific procedure and recognized the components of the DRE examination have long been practiced and accepted in the medical field. See *United States v. Everett*, 972 F. Supp. 1313, 1320 (D. Nev. 1997).

175. 293 F.1013 (D.C. Cir. 1923).

176. See id. at 1014.

177. 509 U.S. 579 (1993).

178. Id. at 588.

179. Id. at 593–94.

180. Walter G. Amstutz and Bobby Marzine Harges. "Evolution of Controversy: The Daubert Dilemma. The Application of *Daubert v. Merrell Pharmaceuticals Inc*. to Expert Testimony of Law Enforcement Officers in Narcotics Related Cases," 23 U. Haw. L. Rev. ___ (forthcoming 2001).

181. 526 U.S. 137 (1999).

182. Id. at 147.

183. Id. at 152.

184. Id.

185. See *State v. Engcabo*, 71 Haw. 96, 99, 784 P.2d 865, 866–67 (1989).

186. See id.

187. 71 Haw. 96, 784 P.2d 865 (1989).

188. Id. at 97, 784 P.2d at 865.

189. Id. at 97, 784 P.2d at 866.

190. Id.

191. Id. at 99, 784 P.2d at 867.

192. Id. (emphasis added).

193. 9 Haw. Ct. App. 516, 852 P.2d 476 (1993).

194. 451 N.W.2d 154,155 (Iowa 1990).

195. *Nishi*, 9 Haw. Ct. App. at 522, 852 P.2d at 479.

Appendix I
Qualifying a Police Officer as a DRE Expert Witness

In order to qualify a police officer trained in drug recognition as an expert consistent with the decisions reached in *Daubert* and *Kumho Tire*, the prosecutor may utilize the questions set forth below. These questions should be asked after general questions have been asked about the officer's background, education, and law enforcement experience. For each question on the list, prosecutors should ask a series of follow-up questions depending upon the witness's responses. It is important to ask follow-up questions in order to help the witness educate the judge and jury about the DRE program and the method used to evaluate drug-impaired drivers. In some instances, areas for follow-up have been listed. Meanwhile, defense attorneys should note that these are the areas the government is going to emphasize in its attempt to qualify its witness as an expert.

Drug Recognition Training and Experience

1. Did there come a time during your service as a police officer that you became interested in the drug recognition expert program?
2. What is the drug recognition expert program?
3. When and where did this program get started?
4. When did the program begin in this state?
5. How many states currently utilize the drug recognition expert program as a means to identify drug-impaired drivers?
6. Has the program been adopted in any foreign countries?
7. What is the role of the drug recognition expert or DRE?
8. What specialized training have you received in regards to drug recognition?
   A. Address: standard field sobriety test training
   B. Address: DRE pre-school and school
   C. Address: any additional training
9. How were you selected to receive this training?
10. What is the National Highway Traffic Safety Administration or NHTSA?
11. What is its role in regards to the training you received and the DRE program?

12. As part of your training, did you have to take any examinations?
13. Did you pass those examinations?
14. After passing those examinations were you automatically certified as a DRE?
15. What else did you need to do?
    A. Address: certification process
    B. Address: awarding of DRE certificate and enter it into evidence
16. What is a drug influence evaluation?
    A. Have a blowup of a chart listing the twelve steps marked for identification (State's exhibit #1) (Appendix III)
    B. Address: twelve-step systematic approach
    C. Address: uniformity across the country
17. What is the Symptomatology Matrix or, as it is sometimes called, the Signs and Symptoms Matrix?
    A. Have a blowup of the matrix marked for identification (State's exhibit #2) (Appendix IV).
    B. Address: seven categories of drugs
    C. Address: eight signs and symptoms
    D. Address: poly-drug use
18. On (date) did you perform a drug influence evaluation on the defendant?
19. Did you follow all of the steps listed in State's exhibit #1?
20. Did you use the Signs and Symptoms Matrix, State exhibit #2, in reaching your conclusions?
21. Have any studies been conducted in order to determine whether or not the twelve-step DRE protocol used in conjunction with the Signs and Symptoms Matrix result in accurate findings regarding drug impairment?
    A. Address: Johns Hopkins University laboratory study
    B. Address: Los Angeles field study
    C. Address NHTSA' s role in these two studies
22. Admit the two charts into evidence and display them throughout the trial. If the court requires additional foundation information, ask the court to take judicial notice of the seven published appellate decisions listed in the Appendix II. All seven decisions found the DRE methodology as a reliable means to detect drug impairment.
23. Is alcohol a drug?

24. What category of drugs does alcohol fall within?
25. How many arrests have you made for DUI-Alcohol?
26. How many arrests have you made for driving under the influence of drugs other than alcohol?
27. How many drug influence evaluations have you conducted?
28. How are the results of those evaluations recorded?
29. Of all the drug influence evaluations you have conducted, how many times did you conclude the suspect was under the influence of drugs?
30. Of those evaluations where you concluded the suspect was under the influence of drugs, how many times were your conclusions confirmed by subsequent laboratory testing?
31. In those situations where you concluded the suspect was under the influence of drugs, yet the lab report came out negative, did that mean you were incorrect? Explain.
32. Go through the first ten steps of the drug influence evaluation step by step.
33. Ask the court to qualify the witness as an expert in drug recognition on the basis of his specialized training and experience.
34. Ask the witness to give his opinion regarding the defendant's impairment, and to describe in detail what that opinion is based upon.
35. Have the witness describe what, if anything, he did in regards to step 12, the toxicological sample.

Appendix II
Some Important Court Decisions

State Supreme Court published decisions

Arkansas—*Mace v. State*, 944 S.W.2d 830 (Ark. 1997).
Minnesota—*State v. Klawitter*, 518 N.W.2d 577 (Minn. 1994).
Washington—*State v. Baity*, 991 P.2d 1151 (Wash. 2000).

State Appellate Court published decisions

Florida—*Williams v. State*, 710 So. 2d 24 (Fla. Ct. App. 1998).
Utah—*State v. Layman*, 953 P .2d 782 (Utah Ct. App. 1998).
Oregon—*State v. Sampson*, 6 P.3d 543 (Or. Ct. App. 2000).

Federal court published decisions

Nevada—*United States v. Everett*, 732 F. Supp. 1313 (D. Nev. 1997).

Appendix III
The Twelve-Step DRE Evaluation Matrix

1. Breath alcohol test
2. Interview of arresting officer
3. Preliminary examination
   - first pulse
   - initial angle of onset
   - initial estimate of pupil size
4. Eye examination
   - HGN—lack of smooth pursuit
     nystagmus at maximum deviation
     angle of onset
   - vertical nystagmus
   - lack of convergence
5. Divided attention tests
   - Romberg balance
   - walk and turn
   - one-leg stand
   - finger to nose
6. Vital signs
   - pulse: 60–90 bpm (normal range)
     30 seconds × 2 = bpm.
   - blood pressure 120–140 Systolic (normal range)
     70–90 Diastolic
   - body temperature 98.6°F ± 1.0°F (normal range)
7. Dark room checks
   - pupil Size 3.0mm–6.5mm (normal range)
     room light near total darkness
     indirect light direct light
   - ingestion examination
     nasal area oral cavity
8. Check for muscle tone
9. Check for injection sites—third pulse
10. Questioning of subject—observations
11. Opinion of evaluator
12. Toxicological sample

Appendix IV
Indicators Consistent with Drug Categories

Indicators Consistent with Drug Categories

	Depressants	Stimulants	Hallucinogens	PCP	Narcotic Analgesics	Inhalants	Cannabis
HGN	Present	None	Present	None	None	Present	None
Vertical Nystagmus	Present (High dose*)	None	None	Present	None	Present (High dose*)	None
Lack of Convergence	Present	None	None	Present	None	Present	Present
Pupil Size	Normal (1)	Dilated	Dilated	Normal	Constricted	Normal (4)	Dilated (6)
Reaction to Light	Slow	Slow	Normal (3)	Normal	Little or none visible	Slow	Normal
Pulse Rate	Down (2)	Up	Up	Up	Down	Up	Up
Blood Pressure	Down	Up	Up	Up	Down	Up/Down (5)	Up
Body Temperature	Normal	Up	Up	Up	Down	Up/Down/Normal	Normal

*High dose for that particular individual

Footnote: these indicators are those most consistent with the category, keep in mind that there may bevariations due to individual reaction, dose taken and drug interactions.

1. SOMA, Quaaludes usually dilate pupils.
2. Quaaludes and ETOH may elevate.
3. Certain psychedelic amphetamines cause slowing.
4. Normal but may be dilated.
5. Down with anesthetic gases, up with volatile solvents and aerosols.
6. Pupil size possibly normal.

About the Author

Marcelline Burns, Ph.D. is a research psychologist. She was a co-founder of the Southern California Research Institute in Los Angeles where she continues to conduct research. The primary focus of her laboratory experiments over the past three decades has been the effects of alcohol and other drugs on human performance and behavior with an emphasis on the effects on driving skills. She and her colleagues developed the standardized field sobriety tests (SFSTs), and she studies and consults with the drug recognition expert (DRE) program. She has conducted field studies of both the SFSTs and the DRE program. In connection with these topics, she lectures and trains law enforcement and other criminal justice professionals, serves as a forensic consultant, and provides expert trial and deposition testimony. She earned a Bachelor of Arts from San Diego State University, a Masters from California State University, Los Angeles, and a Ph.D. from the University of California, Irvine.

The Contributors

Donald J. Bartell, Attorney at Law
Bartell, Beloian & Hensel
Riverside, CA

Michael R. Corbett, Ph.D.
Scientific Director, The Forensic Toxicology Institute
Mississauga, Ontario, Canada

Johan J. de Gier, Ph.D.
Department of Pharmacoepidemiology and Pharmacotherapy
Faculty of Pharmacy
Utrecht University, The Netherlands

Olaf H. Drummer, Ph.D. (Med), BAppSc(Chem)
Victorian Institute of Forensic Medicine and Department of Forensic Medicine, Monash University
Southbank, Australia

Anne D. ImObersteg, M.S., J.D.
Director, Anne ImObersteg and Associates
San Jose, CA

Daniel S. Isenschmid, Ph.D.
Chief Toxicologist, Wayne County Medical Examiner's Office
Detroit, MI

Wayne Jeffrey
I/C Toxicologist
Vancouver, BC, Canada

Caroline T. J. Lamers, M.Sc.
Universiteit Maastrict, Brain and Behavior Institute, Experimental Psychopharmacology Unit
Maastricht, The Netherlands

Barry K. Logan, Ph.D., DABFT
Director, Forensic Laboratory Services Bureau, Washington State Toxicologist, Washington State Patrol

Stephen J. McAndrew, M.A.
Assistant Director Food and Nutrition Services, Dartmouth-Hitchcock Medical Center
Lebanon, NH

Thomas E. Page, M.A.
Drug Recognition Expert, retired LAPD
Pasadena, CA

Trinka Porrata, B.S.
Drug Consultant, retired LAPD Narcotics Detective
Pasadena, CA

Johannes G. Ramaekers, Ph.D.
Universiteit Maastrict, Brain and Behavior Institute, Experimental Psychopharmacology Unit
Maastricht, The Netherlands

Wim J. Riedel, Ph.D.
Universiteit Maastrict, Brain and Behavior Institute, Experimental Psychopharmacology Unit
Maastricht, The Netherlands

Laurent Rivier, Ph.D.
Scientific consultant in forensic toxicology and doping in sports, Laurent Rivier Scientific Consulting
Lausanne, Switzerland

David Sandler, J.D.
Deputy Prosecutor, City of Honolulu
Adjunct Professor, University of Hawaii, West Oahu, Chaminade University, Troy University

Jeroen A. J. Schmitt, Ph.D.
Universiteit Maastrict, Brain and Behavior Institute, Experimental Psychopharmacology Unit
Maastricht, The Netherlands

Index

B

D

E

G

H

I

J

K

L

M

N

National Institute on Drug Abuse (NIDA), 10, 18, 241, 259, 278, 301, 329, 341, 344, 376, 401

pseudoephedrine, 184, 209, 330–331

Q

R

S

T

U

V

W

X

Z